The Gilded Age

The Gilded Age

REVISED AND ENLARGED EDITION

H. WAYNE MORGAN

EDITOR

SYRACUSE UNIVERSITY PRESS

Contents

Preface

In the early 1960's the Editor organized a symposium designed to examine critically the historical facts and interpretations available on the period in American history generally known as the Gilded Age. *The Gilded Age: A Reappraisal* appeared in 1963 and has served enough readers to warrant a revised and enlarged edition.

The focus remains on the post–Civil War generation. The introductory chapter has been enlarged to cover new material in this edition and establish the theme of nationalization amid industrial change. Essays on genteel reform, the currency question, the Democratic party, populism, the Republican party, and foreign policy were written especially for this edition. The other chapters have been edited, updated, or thoroughly revised.

The authors describe and analyze their subjects in perspective, showing the era's historical contributions and contemporary vitality. With varying degrees of emphasis, each essay illustrates the generation's efforts to unify the nation and create a meaningful body of policy, ideals, and taste. The period illustrations selected for reproduction here serve to emphasize those goals.

No collective work can be inclusive. The contributors deal with the major problems that consciously affected most people at the time, and many more subjects might be included if space and scholarly information permitted. We hope to inform readers of, and above all to stimulate interest in, the varied affairs of an important generation in our nation's history.

H. WAYNE MORGAN

University of Texas at Austin
Fall, 1969

Illustrations

The Gilded Age

H. WAYNE MORGAN

1

Toward National Unity

THE PICTURE IS COMPELLING; one sees it in mirth and muffled pity. There is Colonel Beriah Sellers amid incredulous townfolk, plotting with a magisterial wave an inland empire of the future. It will occupy this unlikely spot, named after a suitably great historical event or person. A gilt cane marks in muddy ruts the broad outline of riches and success. Here will converge the bustling river traffic; a huge canal grant will soon remedy the abscence of waterways. The railroad will run there, despite the hopeless terrain. And the new city will blaze with the lights of glamor and prosperity.

The picture is familiar. It is the stereotype of bloated dreams, foolish optimism, and grandiloquence that allegedly ruled the post–civil War generation. No man caught that side of it better than Mark Twain, who named it "The Gilded Age." His portrait of Colonel Sellers—vain, pompous, and overblown, a pathetic innocent amid corrosive change—influenced nearly everyone who studied the period.

A famous jurist said the Constitution was what the judges said it was. History is often what historians say, and the Gilded Age has fared poorly at their hands. For three scholarly generations, it was either a distasteful result of the war's thwarted expectations, or the prelude to something better in the twentieth century. It was lifeless, or organized in bright stereotypes as a "great transition" or "watershed." Vernon Parrington's widely read *The Beginnings of Critical Realism in America* (1930) dismissed it as "the Great Barbecue," a time of wanton materialism and coarse taste. Charles Beard fortified this view, and wrote more of forces than of individuals. But he condemned "the cash nexus" that supposedly produced the era's vulgarity and inequities. Matthew Josephson wrote two acidulous works, *The Robber Barons* (1934) and *The*

1

Politicos (1938), whose chilly economic determinism appealed to New Deal scholars. Their students dominated college teaching for another generation.

Few if any people chose to see that generation by its own lights. Dramatic change and reform always captivate historians. They accepted the biting criticism of self-styled "reformers" and intellectuals, and preferred the brooding Henry Adams to the popular James G. Blaine. Nor did scholars question these critics' motives or seek progressive patterns in the era's swirling change. And historians, who are usually liberal Democrats, dismissed a supposedly Republican era without examining labels.

This was not surprising. The array of new pressures and demands bewildered the men who met them. The struggle to organize national life in new patterns, and the search for a viable collective identity ran all through the era's dynamic growth. The men who saved the Union did not quite know what to do with it. The war involved a basic desire for stability and release from tension, yet the America of 1865 was caught in permanent and accelerating change. Critics often overlooked the proportions and range of national problems. Geography itself had changed. New states and territories in the Far West formed the bare outline of an almost separate country. States around the Great Lakes and in the Mississippi Valley had yet to fit an integrated economy. The South seemed stagnant, detached from a Union it could not formally leave. Americans accustomed to scope forgot the impact of distance and time on customs, tastes, and attitudes. What economic system could deal equally with a Pacific Coast facing the Orient, an Atlantic Coast competing with Europe, and a Gulf Coast looking toward South America? What did wool producers in Wyoming share with heavily industralized Pennsylvania or New Jersey? Could a New Yorker understand the full meaning of a California orange that crossed a half-empty continent on a new railroad?

The country took pride in youth and vitality, little realizing that it was older than any nation except Great Britain. In orderly government, constitutional practice, and accepted public ideals, it outranked France, Germany, Italy, Russia, or even Japan and China. Its industrial system would shortly outstrip those of all these countries. An invisible gap between old institutions and new problems subtly defined the limits of optimism. What, after all, did Carson City share with Boston? Was Duluth in the same country as New Orleans? Old attitudes and ideals would unify some aspects of this new industrial society, but few knew if the country could accommodate such variety.

A disparate population filled the geographic outline. European farmers took up land. Foreign professionals staffed new colleges, became doctors or dentists, taught school, practiced law, or entered social services. Masons, carpenters, and bricklayers from a dozen countries built industrial cities. Iron-puddlers, brakemen, miners, chemists, and unskilled workers entered the expanding economy. They differed in religion, attitudes toward regulation and customs—the human things that baffled planners and governments. This rapid growth and diversity produced unprecedented social strains. Farmers suspected that cities corrupted the youth and that bankers were evil. Boston sophisticates looked down on western rustics. Chicago competed with New York for art and music, aiming to be more than a railhead or stockyard. "Native Americans" naturally wondered if a democratic society espousing individual freedom could survive the shocks of pluralism.

These abrasions and tensions reflected the central fact that the United States was not yet a *nation* despite its Constitution and ideals. It emerged from the Civil War a collection of regions, varying in age, economics, population, and social attitudes. Much of the West was not even surveyed, and hostile Indians threatened settlers. Industrialism inevitably would create a national economy, sending shock waves into every part of life, but whether this would also form a body of national aspirations and retain enough individualism to prevent social disruption was the central question before an inexperienced generation.

Amid bewildering changes, the rhetoric of "Americanism" was a stabilizing force. Established citizens and newcomers emphasized opportunities but also thought that material well-being fostered the social progress and harmony important to everyone. Few Americans, or men anywhere, believed in actual equality. The country's unifying ideals and rhetoric rested on the concept of equal and expanding opportunity for talent. Immigrants readily accepted "Americanization," provided it did not threaten private beliefs and customs. Few people in any station were willing to go beyond this. State planning and government regulation were alien; most Americans quickly decided that "socialism" leveled downward.

These problems and possible solutions were most obvious in the economy. By the late 1880's, American receptiveness to new ideas and methods built a new industrial plant that sent more goods to more people. But it also moved steadily into "trusts" that threatened the competition which Americans thought was the key to controlling change. People read about the American Dream come true for John D. Rockefeller and Andrew Carnegie, but their very success lessened the chances of emulators. The rise of experts in management, advertising, production, and design, responsible only to directors, enhanced public fears that individual business had melted into a faceless corporate structure unresponsive to social pressure.

Yet the movement against trusts in the 1880's, which produced the Interstate Commerce Commission Act and Sherman Antitrust Law, reflected the desire to regulate a unifying and efficient economy. Few people wanted to change trains a dozen times to avoid an "octopus." Reformers sought to retain a sense of personal identity, while preventing price-fixing, unequal rates, and monopolies. They would reaffirm society's right and responsibility to direct growth and prevent wasteful speculation. Critics also wished to remove business interests from politics and keep both spheres responsive. Americans always distrusted any power detached from a skeptical constituency. They would make business explain its progress to the public.

Genteel critics lamented the decline of a hierarchical America, and developed a body of national beliefs based on laissez-faire economics and small government. But while intellectuals sought ideal standards of conduct, politicians organized the new nation from experience. The Republican party, barely a generation old, elected presidents but lacked a national majority. Democrats controlled eight of ten sessions of Congress during the period. Mired in localism and committed to retrenchment, the Democrats were obstructive and negative, yet they made a formidable comeback from wartime obloquy and still represented the country's dominant political tone. The struggle to endow freedmen with human rights had alienated many who fought to save the Union. The Democrats' rhetorical commitment to Jacksonian rusticity, small government, and a simpler America attracted voters who feared government efforts to make order of chaos. The "solid South" gave them a formidable base in presidential elections and disproportionate power in Congress. Public suspicion of federal power, personally restrictive in the recent war, could help Democrats carry doubtful midwestern states. Republican centralism, promotion, regulation were still new in American life. Far from being secure, the GOP ran for its life, and some commentators thought it would disappear like other third parties.

Such tension was a blessing. Political insecurity kept men like James G. Blaine, William McKinley, and John Sherman in touch with shifting constituencies. This sharpened their skill at fruitful compromise and developed a workable national viewpoint. Democrats criticized the "bloody shirt," while vigorously waving it against Negro voters. But Republicans correctly refused to forget prewar Democratic policies that had hindered national development. A newly triumphant Democratic party might easily enhance states-rights everywhere and adopt a paralyzing combination of laissez-faire economics and the Jacksonian myth of every man his own philosopher.

Only a strong, expert, central government could have avoided unequal economic development, but the United States did not have the tradition, the machinery, or the public desire for central direction. Republican spokesmen had to run the risk of uneven development and poor supervision inherent in indirect methods while enacting the greatest program of economic nationalism since Hamilton. While William Graham Sumner taught the virtues of laissez faire, politicians funded every major sector of a mixed economy, and Herbert Spencer's facile ideas of automatic progress appealed more to intellectuals than to businessmen accustomed to pursuing the main chance.

Tariff protection was the foundation of Republican development. Maintaining effective intraparty unity on the issue, leaders legislated for an urban-industrial constituency that included skilled workers, prosperous farmers, businessmen, and professionals. Protection stabilized a home market and generated profits for reinvestment that lessened dependence on foreign capital while expanding the industrial plant. It appealed strongly to skilled workers and to farmers selling dairy products, poultry, meats, and truck crops in urban markets. Producers of varied raw materials such as wool in California and Vermont, lumber in Michigan and Maine, coal in West Virginia and Alabama, hides in Texas and Ohio, supported the tariff. It especially appealed to underdeveloped western states, and to the growing Midwest which faced immediate competition from Canada. The policy also enhanced the GOP's nationalism.

Democratic leaders understood the emotional and material appeals of protection, but Southerners historically sought low tariffs for agrarians selling in world markets. Interests in shipping, the export-import trade, banking, and fabrication industries desiring cheap raw materials were also Democratic. And low rates fitted the party's dislike of government. But Pennsylvania's Samuel J. Randall brilliantly led congressmen who were Democratic on most issues except protection. "Randall and his forty thieves" thwarted revision and angered those who hoped to refurbish the party's poor image with tariff reform. President Cleveland unsuccessfully headed a crusade against "unjust taxation" in 1888. His victory on the same issue in 1892 was shortlived. Hard times dissolved the party and its warring components seemed parochial and selfish compared with united Republicans.

Republican leaders also successfully managed the volatile currency question. While repudiating "rag money" and free coinage, they adopted limited bimetallism and gold redemption throughout the 1870's and 1880's. After the crash of 1893, they proposed various compromise plans that seemed constructive and moderate beside Cleveland's rigid gold standard policies, and William McKinley triumphed in 1896 while pledging to seek an international silver agreement while sustaining gold redemption.

The GOP always had a whiggish tone. It promoted national economic sectors with the means at hand, often against fierce Democratic opposition. It admitted new states, funded a unifying transportation system, and distributed the public domain. Less spectacularly, Congress promoted basic scientific inquiry through the Coast and Geodetic Survey, special commissions, western and polar exploration, agriculture experiment stations, and land grants for education. Systematic supervision of these developments was impossible in a vast country lacking a regulatory tradition, yet Republicans took the lead in enacting the ICC Act, and the Sherman Antitrust Law when popular demands for regulation came. The federal government was often ill-equipped for many sophisticated problems, but it did respond to voter demands, and national authority moved slowly against state power in a time of strict constitutional construction.

The sumptuous display that permeated politics reflected widespread individual participation and interest. In an era of close national contests, every ballot mattered. The period marked a high point of voting, and no generation absorbed more technical information from the printed and spoken word. Presidents steadily protected their power against both Congress and local leaders. Republican executives like Hayes, Garfield, and Arthur accepted civil service reform both to stabilize the bureaucracy and to weaken the spoilsmanship that sustained rival leaders. In defining new goals, satisfying material interests, and engaging individual voters, party politics helped build a new national spirit. By the century's end, after a generation of intense debate and struggle, there was a national party system. It was a crucial legacy, defining a nationalism that common men could understand, and establishing the means for new governmental functions.

The trend toward national standards was evident in culture and the arts. Major city newspapers printed copious wire service news. Readers could follow world crises, confident that they were someone else's problem. Syndicated columnists offered depth coverage of new subject matter, including fashions, travel, the arts, and high society. Until the century's end, when technology created newspaper syndicates, individualistic editors enlivened most newspapers.

Engraving and photography animated magazines, books, and newspapers by the 1890's. Few generations could boast an audience for such a variety of publications. The *Nation, Harper's Weekly,* and *The Century Magazine* informed an expanding middle class, while *Frank Leslie's Illustrated Magazine* enlightened a larger audience with social, cultural, and political news. Specialized publications like the *Commercial and Financial Chronicle, Wall Street Journal,* and *Banker's Magazine* were influential beyond professional audiences. Engineers, chemists, educators, cattlemen, and doctors exchanged information in special reviews. Academic journals discussed new science and thought.

The novels of sentiment and pluck naturally won the largest reading public, but there was always an audience for William Dean Howells and Mark Twain. Controversial writers like Stephen Crane, Frank Norris, and regional figures left a national imprint. Struggling to outline the American experience, each contributed to a national consciousness. Howells' realism defined middle-class verities but sought a widened social ethic. Local color ironically testified to an emerging national literary attitude, seen as Garland, Jewett, G. W. Cable, Bret Harte, and others feared the new industrial society would submerge individualistic types. Even Henry James delineated an American style by forcing characters to define their experience against older models. As always, the great public read costume romances and sentimental fiction, but these works ironically testified to a growing unity by offering the comfort of an understandable past.

The circus, Wild West show, and minstrelsy gave a similar view of wild animals and exotic places, whether in Boston or Des Moines. Advertising, new communication methods, and good transportation helped the dramatic arts. Joseph Jefferson and Ellen Terry played both Shakespeare and Dumas in a thousand towns. Chautauqua began life as an educational program resembling the prewar lyceum. Affluence let major cities establish opera houses, symphony orchestras, and art galleries. This spread of "culture" inevitably affected national taste, while allowing for individual style. All in all, it slowly outlined both America's unique qualities and her place in the broader stream of world culture. The rules of organization applied to entertainment as it became big business catering to national taste.

Fewer people bought paintings than read books, and the plastic arts usually fitted the "finishing" ideal of a polite but shallow social set. Landscapes, stagnant European academicism, and amateurish local color were dominant, yet Frederic Remington had many admirers. His soldiers, Indians, and scouts were exotic types to nonwesterners. But they also liked his impressionistic technique, use of light, new colors, and space. By the 1890's, Thomas Eakins, Winslow Homer, and the emerging urban-oriented "Ashcan School" had a small but influential audience. French impressionism quickly appealed to American connoisseurs. Interest in realism and contemporary life-styles slowly invaded the academies.

The expanded educational system, while funded in localities, was committed to national skills and ideals. Curriculum reform made some teaching relevant to the new society, though fundamental changes were necessarily uneven in such a large country. Higher education boasted academic entrepreneurs worthy of steel and oil—like William Rainey Harper, who pursued an ideal University of Chicago largely at the expense of John D. Rockefeller. Major state universities, teachers' colleges, and agricultural institutes expanded, though the ideal of cheap college education for nearly everyone was remote. Academic planners hoped to adapt Germanic methods of exact research to American social needs. Experts from these new schools and from European universities entered industry, teaching, and government. In pure science and speculative thought, American figures steadily gained international stature.

These changes and additions did not destroy reigning social beliefs. Schoolchildren imbibed old ideas on thrift, hard work, and material success at home and in McGuffey's readers. Inevitably, much style and taste was derivative as Americans sought a unified standard. Architecture reflected older traditions in public building. Ornamentation covered utility, and the new skyscraper usually wore a dated facade. Its complex interior, however, involving new hydraulics and engineering, was innovative. The streets, lights, and service utilities around it answered new urban-industrial demands. Mass housing was seldom pleasing, but new technology made it possible in any style. Many homes reflected the garbled attitudes of both occupant and designer, but the best houses emphasized light, space, and individualistic decoration. Hesitant innovation and jangling eclecticism, so evident at the Columbian Exposition, testified to the difficulty of creating a distinctive style in a pluralistic society whose components varied greatly in age, climate, and tastes.

As in all eras, the dynamism of life carried individuals, but many businessmen, politicians, artists, and thinkers consciously promoted acceptance of change. They assumed that their vital pluralistic society would tolerate personal styles, free from an oppressive past and the class structure that hampered Europeans. This optimism faltered only twice, significantly in the depressions of the 1870's and 1890's. But pluralism was tougher than the pessimists who predicted class warfare. The cementing ideals held firm.

That sense of national power found a dramatic outlet in overseas expansion. The nation traditionally substituted a reflexive patriotism for foreign policy. But by the 1890's, self-interest coincided with emotional needs to take the United States into world affairs. Individuals sought markets and security and to express their humanitarianism. But expansion captivated the public as a whole as an expression of national power and vitality. Having at last established a unified nation, the people, albeit half-consciously, responded to appeals of "pride," "duty," and "destiny" which seemed to confirm that success. Most Americans still accepted a liberal ideal of popular government that justified the desire to free Cuba. At the same time, statesmen in pursuit of order and stable growth hoped to influence "backward" areas.

And so prosperity, the triumph of a nationalized political view in 1896, and a renewed sense of authority allowed Americans to end the century on an optimistic note. Yet for all the obvious solid achievement and stirring rhetoric, a sense of unease accompanied the new century. Not everyone was prosperous; many were not hopeful. A great deal in the nation's affairs remained undigested. Perhaps it was a time to pause and take stock. The farmers who staged the "Populist revolt" were dormant under prosperity, but their grievances against urban-industrial power remained. The war between Haves and Have-nots which some pessimists predicted did not occur. Labor leaders would accept the unifying economy if business dealt with unions, and only a handful of people embraced socialistic or "radical" doctrine. The great majority of Americans would continue to seek a balance between freedom and material progress, but there was a growing sense that bigness, efficiency, and order somehow threatened liberty. Many diffuse elements were ready to follow articulate critics of corporate impersonality. The antitrust issue, combining emotional tension and apparent self-interest, was ready to revive.

While the national outline was clearer than ever, some elements, like the Negro, were casualties of rapid development and new technology. The Negro's relative isolation in the South made him invisible to most Americans. The Radical Republican ideal of land distribution, education, and federal protection of the Freedmen's civil liberties never won majority support. Most intellectuals and even old abolitionists refused to challenge public indifference after the mid-1870's, as tariff protection, the currency question, and other new issues absorbed the electorate. Most Negroes remained trapped with hostile whites in an antiquated

southern agrarian system that industrialism seemed unable to break.
Few people raised the issues of social equality, voting rights, or civil
liberties.

In national politics, Democratic obstruction and the GOP's lack of a
working majority defeated serious efforts to enforce or increase the
Negro's statutory rights. Republican administrations could only dispense
patronage to leaders. The Blair Education Bill of the 1880's was designed to reduce illiteracy among both whites and blacks in the South,
but fears of federal power and public indifference defeated it. The Harrison administration's effort to guarantee voting rights in the Federal
Elections Bill of 1890 also failed. Economic and sectional interests in
the form of protection and free silver overrode what seemed a dated
issue to the public.

Negro migration northward did not increase dramatically until the
new century. Poverty, isolation, and lack of skills kept most Negroes
from confronting urban life. Those who migrated won only marginal
improvement. They often voted in northern states, but could not develop
an interest bloc to outweigh prejudice. Conservative craft unions remained the preserve of skilled whites, who feared both job competition
and social integration. Poor economic opportunity only enhanced the
Negro's social isolation.

Yet even the emerging ghettoes of Chicago, New York, or Pittsburgh
offered more than back-country Alabama or Mississippi. Some Negro
leaders tried to channel resentment at bigotry into a greater desire to
succeed within the prevailing ethos, but at best they created a few opportunities within a segregated society. White philanthropists and some
public agencies funded special education, but few Negro professionals
served more than their own community. No great champion or new
public demand shaped a recognizable political or economic constituency
which politicians had to heed. Booker T. Washington easily became the
Negro's accepted champion by espousing self-help. He fought the sepa-
rate-but-equal doctrine covertly, with little general effect on his fellows.
Racial inequity and its attendant tensions remained the nation's greatest hidden dimension.

It seemed easier to assimilate the foreign-born than the Negro. In
the 1870's, some 2.2 million people emigrated to the United States.
Another 5 million came in the next decade. Even in the depressed
nineties, some 4 million immigrants entered the country. Cheap transportation, available land, and a high industrial growth rate permitted
their absorption even amid cyclical recessions. But the influx of foreigners and the steady migration from farm to city posed a whole new

set of problems which were often beyond available expertise, and whose optimum solution lay outside the reigning individualistic ethic.

Most newcomers settled in cities in the Northeast and around the Great Lakes. Most naturally had some skill with which to earn a living, and they contributed immensely to the economy. Unskilled men wheeled barrows, dug ditches, sawed trees, and dug coal; many young women became servants. But almost as many others were masons, carpenters, or glass-fitters, or brought critical skills to specialized trades like glass-blowing, pottery, tin- and copper-smithing, and handcrafts. A few were doctors, teachers, chemists, geologists, or even artists. The great majority embraced the American ethic. Whatever the limitations of their housing, income, or social acceptance, they were better off than in Europe.

Despite some crises, the system did not threaten their individual customs or tastes, and it thus worked for stability. America seemed to offer upward mobility for their children, if not for themselves, which naturally blunted appeals to abandon accepted values and hopes. Urbanization in a decentralized governmental system inevitably brought tensions and inequities. Only a tradition of central planning, wholly outside the American experience and distasteful even to newcomers, would have mitigated confusion and imbalance. But the American willingness to tinker with problems produced a surprising amount of innovation.

By the century's end, a slowly clarifying awareness of tensions and half-realized dreams ironically underlined the country's fresh cohesion. Pluralism, economic order, political organization, better communication, and new cultural ideas did not automatically solve daily problems. Laudable progress in most sectors of life seemed to emphasize the men and ideals left behind or only partly absorbed. Many who had worked to unify the nation now feared the system would dominate the people.

But this uneasiness was not pessimism. Few except mordant intellectuals doubted America's basic soundness or adaptability. Rationality and judgment had already regulated much of the fast-paced change. The political system responded to voter pressure—laws might curb men's excesses. Social innovation accompanied the new technology. Professional organizations in economics, sociology, law, the sciences, and education developed plans for national problems. By the 1890's, social workers were compiling statistics and drafting programs to eradicate poor housing, provide children's special needs, and meet public health problems. A body of expertise arose from hard experience to manage streets, provide police and fire protection, plan parks, purify water and treat sewage, and extend welfare services in the sprawling cities which were industrialism's monuments. Americans moved against these problems sooner than their counterparts abroad. Their accomplishments were quite as impressive as their mistakes.

The critical "progressivism" which came was basically an effort to use local pressure to keep public institutions flexible, but the reformers who attacked industrialism's bad symptoms after 1900 did not repudiate nationalism, order, or efficiency. Their desire to regulate and plan drew on ideas already rooted. Their search for impartial agents to manage technical matters testified to expertise created in the Gilded Age. The hope of transferring public action from professional politicians to a broader amateur electorate reaffirmed the belief in partisan activity and individual ability which characterized their fathers' generation. The thrust of reform was not against the system, but against some of its operations and inevitable inequities.

The Gilded Age was transitional, but the velocity and variety of change set it apart from its predecessors. In a broad sense, it was the first "modern" American generation. In view of the complex demands it faced, and a lack of tested solutions, the generation's response to challenge was impressive. Its hesitations and half-measures reflected uncertainty rather than poor intent. Well-being did expand for an astonishing number and variety of people. Pluralism was functional, and innovation, variety, and willingness to adapt within unifying values marked all of American life.

No generation solves all its real problems. The temptation to apply present knowledge to past performance, or to seek refuge in nostalgia, is always strong. The America of 1865–1900 seems compellingly comfortable, but the confident, bearded men, the big houses, the settled pace of life are deceptive. Those who lived through the nationalizing process did not find it easy or romantic. Growth required wit, skill, and tolerance, but they succeeded, and built a nation.

JOHN TIPPLE

$\mathcal{S}$ 2 $\mathcal{Q}$

Big Businessmen and a
New Economy

IT IS MORE THAN COINCIDENCE that the beginning of the Robber Baron legend, the portrayal of the big businessman as a warlike brigand cheating and plundering his way to millions, was contemporaneous with the inauguration of the corporation as the major instrument of business control in the United States. After the Civil War, the large corporation began to dominate the American economic scene. In those same years, Charles Francis Adams, Jr., launched his first assault against the "Erie robbers," and his brother, Henry Adams, warned of the day when great corporations, "swaying power such as has never in the world's history been trusted in the hands of mere private citizens," would be controlled by one man or combinations of men who would use these new leviathans to become masters of the nation.[1]

Such dangerous potentialities were not recognizable prior to the Civil War because the majority of businesses operated as local enterprises, usually as individual proprietorships, partnerships, or as small closed corporations in which ownership and control were almost invariably synonymous.[2] Under most circumstances, the power and influence of the businessman were limited to the immediate environs of operation and seldom extended beyond state boundaries. Equally important, there existed among most businessmen of prewar days a nearly universal desire and a practical necessity for community esteem. This governed their conduct, kept their ventures well within the limits of individual liability, and tended to restrain irresponsible profiteering. Antebellum criticisms of the businessman therefore were few and sporadic. Disapproval usually focused on the speculator or stock gambler, and was often inspired by an agrarian distrust of big-city ways.[3]

13

The bloody struggles of the Civil War helped bring about revolutionary changes in economic and political life. War needs created almost insatiable demands for goods—arms, munitions, clothing—and offered some manufacturers unsurpassed opportunities to make fortunes. More important, the stimulus of massive military demands alerted entrepreneurs to new concepts of the power and possibilities of large-scale enterprise: "The great operations of war, the handling of large masses of men, the influence of discipline, the lavish expenditure of unprecedented sums of money, the immense financial operations, the possibilities of effective cooperation, were lessons not likely to be lost on men quick to receive and apply all new ideas." [4] Though the war prevented general economic expansion, the new ideas were profitably applied to the peacetime economy.

With the rich resources of the trans-Mississippi West open to private exploitation, the businessman had singular opportunities to become wealthy. Before him spread an immense untapped continent whose riches were his virtually for the taking; new means to turn these resources to profitable account were at hand. A host of new inventions and discoveries, the application of science to industry, and improved methods of transportation and communication were ready to assist the businessman. But all these aids would have been valueless without effective means to put them to work. The practical agency to meet these unprecedented entrepreneurial demands on capital and management proved to be the corporation. The stockholding system provided immense capital beyond the reach of any individual, and the corporate hierarchy presented a feasible solution to the greatly augmented problems of management.

The corporation was no novelty. It had served political as well as economic purposes in seventeenth-century America; as an instrumentality of business its use antedated the discovery of this continent. Seldom before in American history, however, had the corporation been used on such a large scale. From a relatively passive creature of legalistic capitalism, it was transformed by fusion with techniques into a dynamic system spearheading economic expansion.

The impact of the newborn corporation on American society was almost cataclysmic. In the first few decades of its existence the modern corporate system enabled the nation to develop more wealth more rapidly than in any period since the discovery. But it also menaced hallowed economic theories and usages, threatening to ride like a great tidal wave over the traditional democratic social and political beliefs. Its size alone was sufficient to change fundamental social and economic relationships. Of the newly formed United States Steel Corporation an awed commentator wrote at the turn of the century: "It receives and expends more money every year than any but the very greatest of the world's national governments; its debt is larger than that of many of the lesser nations of Europe; it absolutely controls the destinies of a population nearly as large as that of Maryland or Nebraska, and indirectly influences twice that number." [5] Moreover, this concentrated economic power normally gravitated into the hands of a few, raising up a corporate ruling class with great economic authority. [6]

Though the meteoric rise of the so-called Robber Baron to unheralded positions of power was inseparably bound to the large corporation, there were other factors behind his sudden emergence into popular view as the outstanding phenomenon of nineteenth-century business life. One of the most important of these was a stable government dedicated to the preservation of private property and devoted to an ambiguous concept of laissez faire. Through political alliances, principally with the Republican party, the big businessman consolidated his economic triumphs. Although in the past the commercial and manufacturing interests of the North had received favors from the federal government in the form of bounties to fisheries and protective tariffs, after the defection of the South they were in the envied position of a pampered only child. With almost incestuous concern, a dotingly partisan Congress bestowed upon them lavish railroad subsidies, new and higher tariffs, and a series of favorable banking acts.

The economic supremacy of the North had been guaranteed by military victory in 1865, but it was doubly insured by the actions of the radical Republicans during the process of southern reconstruction. The Fourteenth Amendment, whether intended for such purposes or not, was used by the courts to protect the corporation and to prevent attempts by the states to undermine its position of power. [7] The election of General Grant to the presidency in 1868 and 1872, backed by the leading representatives of the business community, the great financiers, and speculators, politically secured the issue of northern prosperity. Despite the panic of 1873, there were obvious signs that the business of the country had, as the *Nation* put it, "adapted itself to the situation created for it by Republican legislation." [8]

Within this artificial paradise, private profits were sacred. The inheritance tax had expired in 1870, the income tax was abandoned in 1872, and an attempt to revive it in 1894 was invalidated by the Supreme Court in 1895. [9] Corporate or excess profits taxes did not exist. By 1890, the bulk of government revenue was derived from customs duties and excises on liquor and tobacco, all taxes upon the nation's consumers. [10]

Under such conditions, stock market volume attained the million-share mark in December, 1886, and industrial capital almost doubled itself every ten years.[11]

The dedicated businessman could make money on an unprecedented scale. Though John D. Rockefeller never quite became a billionaire, his fortune in 1892 reportedly amounted to $815,647,796.89.[12] Andrew Carnegie did nearly as well. The profits from his industrial empire in the decade 1889 to 1899 averaged about $7,500,000 a year and, in 1900 alone, amounted to $40,000,000.[13] In the following year he sold out his interest for several hundred million dollars.[14] Such fortunes, exceptional even for those days, emphasized the wealth available to the big business-man. In 1892, two New York newspapers engaged in a heated contest to count the number of American millionaires, the *World* uncovering 3,045 and the *Tribune* raising it to 4,047.[15] Regardless of the exact total, millionaires were becoming fairly common. By 1900, for instance, the Senate alone counted twenty-five millionaires among its members, most of them the well-paid agents of big business— a notorious fact that led some suspicious folk to dub that august body the "Rich Man's Club" and the "House of Dollars." [16]

This sudden leap of big businessmen into new positions of wealth and power caught the public eye. To Americans accustomed to thinking primarily of individuals, the big businessman stood out as the conspic-uous symbol of corporate power—his popular image encompassing not only his personal attributes and failings but combining also the more amorphous and impersonal aspects of the business organization by which he had climbed to fortune. Just as the diminutive Andrew Carnegie came to represent the entire steel-making complex of men and decisions which bore his name, so the lean, ascetic John D. Rockefeller personified Standard Oil, and the prominent nose and rotund figure of J. P. Morgan signified the whole of Wall Street with its thousands of operators, its ethical flaws, and its business virtues.

Big businessmen were usually attacked not for personal failings, though they had them as well as the lion's share of wealth, but as the recognizable heads of large corporations. When Carnegie and Rocke-feller gave up business careers and became private citizens, the rancor against them almost ceased. Instead of being censured for past actions, which had been widely and vehemently criticized, they were praised as benefactors and good citizens. Public castigation of the steel trust was shifted from "Little Andy" to the broader shoulders of Charles Schwab. The odium of monopoly which had surrounded his father was inherited by John D. Rockefeller, Jr. Only as the active and directive heads of great corporations, and not as subordinates or members of a business elite, were big businessmen branded "Robber Barons" and indicted for alleged crimes against society.[17]

If the big businessman was not resented as an individual but as a power symbol wielding the might of the great corporation, the provocative question arises of why there was such resentment against the corporation. The answer is that the large industrial corporation was an anomaly in nineteenth-century America. There was no place for it among existing institutions and no sanction for it in traditional American values.

Institutions and values had been built around the social and political concept of the free individual. Born to the natural rights of life, liberty, and property, he was originally subject only to the law of nature. By being or becoming a member of society, the individual did not renounce his natural rights (because this gift of God could not be alienated) but submitted to certain restraints beyond those imposed by nature for the evident good of the whole community. The basis of this ideology was the presumed constancy of nature in moral as well as physical operations, and the universal efficacy of its laws. By asserting that these inevitable laws of nature constituted truth, and by setting out from the will of God or nature, eighteenth-century Americans sought to erect an inviolable system proceeding from natural causes and therefore not subject to human error. Fanciful as they seemed, these were the generally accepted premises of government and society inherited by Americans of the nineteenth century.

In such a closed system there was no ready place for the large industrial corporation which was neither an individual nor a natural manifestation. As an artificial person created by charter and comprising many individuals and their wealth, the corporation was infinitely greater in size and power than the isolated individual about whom American society had been conceived. Unlike the individual, the corporate body was not ordinarily exposed to natural hazards of decay and death, having in effect been guaranteed immortality by the society which fathered it. Where individual accumulation of wealth and power was limited to a lifetime, corporate possibilities were almost limitless. Freed from death, and incidentally from death dues and inheritance taxes, the corporation waxed strong upon the accumulated lifetimes and earnings of many individuals.

A further complication, the hazard of which increased directly in proportion to corporate size and power, was that the corporation as an unnatural creation was born without natural reason—"the common rule and measure God hath given mankind"—and was therefore not intrinsically subject to the governance of nature. In ideological terms, the corporation, since it could not be counted upon to follow the moral precepts of nature, was an outlaw to the society which spawned it.

What was to be done with such a monster? Either the corporation had to be made to conform to American institutions and principles or those institutions and principles had to be changed to accommodate the corporation. This was the dilemma first seriously confronted by Americans during the Gilded Age, and the issue that set off the great movement of introspection and reform which activated the American people for the next fifty years.

Most flagrantly apparent was the destructive effect of the large corporation upon free competition and equal opportunity. According to the accepted theory, which was a projection of the doctrines of liberal democracy into the economic sphere, the ideal economy—the only one, in fact, sanctioned by nature—was made up of freely competing individuals operating in a market unrestricted by man but fairly ruled by the inexorable forces of natural law. The ideal polity was achieved by bargaining among free and equal individuals under the benevolent eye of nature. It was assumed that, in economic affairs, impartial rivalry between individual entrepreneurs and free competition would automatically serve the best interests of society by preventing anyone from getting more than his fair share of the wealth.

In early nineteenth-century America, this self-regulating mechanism seemed to work. Where businesses and factories were small, prices and output, wages and profits, rose and fell according to supply and demand. Every man appeared to have equal opportunity to compete with every other man. Even after the war, the individual businessman was forced, in the interests of self-preservation, to observe the common rules of competition. Ordinarily his share of the market was too small to permit any attempt at price control unless he joined with others in a pool, a trade association, or another rudimentary price-fixing agreement. The average businessman eschewed trade agreements, not out of theoretical considerations but for the practical reason that such coalitions did not work very well, often suffering from mutual distrust and the pursuit of centrifugal aims.

But what was true in a world of individual proprietors and workers was not necessarily correct for the corporation. It possessed greater unity of control and a larger share of the market and could either dictate prices or combine successfully with other corporations in monopolistic schemes.[18] By bringing to bear superior economic force which to a great extent invalidated the tenets of the free market, the large organization put the big businessman in the favored position of operating in an economy dedicated to the idea of freely competing individuals, yet left him unhampered by the ordinary restrictions. Under such auspicious circumstances, he soon outdistanced unorganized rivals in the race for wealth.

This unfair advantage did not go unchallenged. As the earliest of the large corporations in the United States, the railroads were the first to come under concentrated attack. The immense extension of railways after 1865, and the crucial nature of their operations as common carriers, exposed their activities to public scrutiny and subjected their mistakes or misdeeds to considerable publicity. Popular resentment against the railroads in the early 1870's grew hottest in the farming states of the Midwest, but indignant reports from all over the country accused railroads of using monopoly power against equal opportunity.

A most frequent criticism, common to both East and West, was that railway superintendents and managers showed unreasonable favoritism by discriminating between persons and places, offering rate concessions to large shippers, charging more for short than long hauls, and giving preferential treatment to large corporations in the form of secret rebates and drawbacks. That these preferential rates might sometimes have been forced upon the railroads by pressure from business made little difference. The popular consensus was that this elaborate system of special rates denied the little man equal opportunity with the rich and influential, breaking the connection between individual merit and success. The ultimate effect extended further monopoly by preventing free competition among businesses where railway transportation was an important factor.[19]

The Standard Oil Company seemed to be the outstanding example of a monopoly propagated in this manner, the charge being that the determining factor behind Rockefeller's spectacular conquest of the oil business had been this railway practice of secrecy and favoritism which had aided his company and ruined others. By collecting rebates on their own shipments and drawbacks on those of competitors, Standard had gained virtual control of oil transportation. It then could regulate the prices of crude oil, with the detrimental result, so Henry Demarest Lloyd charged, that by 1881, though the company produced only one-fiftieth of the nation's petroleum, Standard refined nine-tenths of the oil produced in the United States and dictated the price of all of it.[20]

As the whipping boy among trusts, Standard undoubtedly got more than its share of criticism, yet by contemporary standards of competition, the corporation was fairly adjudged a monopoly. Through the testimony of H. H. Rogers, an executive of the company, The Hepburn Committee in 1879 was able to establish that 90 to 95 percent of all the refiners in the country acted in harmony with Standard Oil.[21] In 1886, the monopolistic proclivities of the oil trust were attested to by the Cullom Committee:

> It is well understood in commercial circles that the Standard Oil Company brooks no competition; that its settled policy and firm determination is to crush out all who may be rash enough to enter the field against it; that it hesitates at nothing in the accomplishment of this purpose, in which it has been remarkably successful, and that it fitly represents the acme and perfection of corporate greed in its fullest development.[22]

Similar convictions were expressed by a New York senate committee before which Rockefeller and other executives testified in 1888.[23] Four years later, in 1892, the Supreme Court of Ohio declared that the object of the Standard Oil Company was "to establish a virtual monopoly of the business of producing petroleum, and of manufacturing, refining and dealing in it and all its products, throughout the entire country, and by which it might not merely control the production, but the price, at its pleasure." [24]

These findings were reaffirmed by new investigations. In 1902, the United States Industrial Commission reported that Standard, through its control of pipe lines, practically fixed the price of crude oil. In 1907, the commissioner of corporations supported and amplified this conclusion. The company might fall short of an absolute monopoly, the commissioner pointed out, but its intentions were monopolistic.[25] In 1911, the United States Supreme Court confirmed this allegation, observing that "no disinterested mind" could survey the history of the Standard Oil combination from 1870 onward "without being irresistibly driven to the conclusion that the very genius for commercial development and organization . . . soon begot an intent and purpose . . . to drive others from the field and to exclude them from their right to trade and thus accomplish the mastery which was the end in view." [26]

Far from regarding the intricate system of business combination he had developed as a monster to be curbed or destroyed, a big businessman such as Rockefeller looked proudly upon his creation as a marvel of beneficence, an extraordinary and distinctive expression of American genius. And Carnegie contended "not evil, but good" had come from the phenomenal development of the corporation. He and others pointed out that the world obtained goods and commodities of excellent quality at prices which earlier generations would have considered incredibly cheap. The poor enjoyed what the richest could never before have afforded.[27]

The big businessman supported his actions as being entirely in keeping with the business requisites of the day. Rather than engaging in a conscious conspiracy to undermine equal opportunity, he had sought only the immediate and practical rewards of successful enterprise, rationalizing business conduct on the pragmatic level of profit and loss.

Instead of deliberately blocking free competition, big businessmen maintained that their actions were only natural responses to immutable law. Charles E. Perkins, president of the Chicago, Burlington and Quincy Railroad Company, denied deliberate misuses of power in establishing rates, and claimed that the price of railroad transportation, like all other prices, adjusted itself. Discriminatory practices were viewed as part of an inevitable conflict between buyer and seller, a necessary result of competition.[28] The payment of rebates and drawbacks was simply one method of meeting the market. In answer to the accusation that the railroads had made "important discriminations" in favor of Standard Oil, an executive of that company replied: "It may be frankly stated at the outset that the Standard Oil Company has at all times within the limits of fairness and with due regard for the law sought to secure the most advantageous freight rates and routes possible." [29] Rockefeller went on record as saying that Standard had received rebates from the railroads prior to 1880, because it was simply the railroads' way of doing business. Each shipper made the best bargain he could, hoping to outdo his competitor.

Furthermore, Rockefeller claimed this traffic was more profitable to the railroads than to the Standard Oil Company, stating that whatever advantage the oil company gained was passed on in lower costs to the consumer. Just as his company later justified certain alleged misdemeanors as being typical of the sharp practices prevailing in the oil fields in the early days, so Rockefeller exonerated the whole system of rebates and drawbacks on the grounds that everybody was doing it, concluding cynically that those who objected on principle did so only because they were not benefiting from it.[30]

Yet despite his public rationalizations, the big businessman's attitude toward competition was ambivalent. He lauded it as economic theory, but denied it in practical actions. Theoretically, there was no such thing as an absolute monopoly; there was always the threat of latent competition. Whenever a trust exacted too much, competitors would automatically appear.[31] Competition as a natural law would survive the trusts. "It is here; we cannot evade it," declaimed Carnegie. "And while the law

may be sometimes hard for the individual, it is best for the race, because
it insures the survival of the fittest in every department." [32]

In practical matters, however, the big businessman acted as if the law
had long since become outmoded, if not extinct. Progressive opinion in
the business world heralded the growing monopolistic trend as a sign of
economic maturity. Increased concentration in capital and industry was
defended as necessary and inevitable.[33] Monopolistic practices in general
were upheld in business circles on the grounds that they prevented
disastrous competition. In the long run they benefited, rather than plun-
dered, the public by maintaining reasonable rates and prices.[34] "There
seems to be a great readiness in the public mind to take alarm at these
phenomena of growth, there might rather seem to be reason for public
congratulation," announced Professor William Graham Sumner of Yale.
"We want to be provided with things abundantly and cheaply; that means
that we want increased economic power. All these enterprises are efforts
to satisfy that want, and they promise to do it." [35] Many big businessmen
believed that, practically at least, the trust proved the superiority of combination over competition.

Though the claim was not always true, the business virtues of economy and efficiency were allegedly the trust's chief advantages. The combination was spared the folly and wastefulness of unrestrained competition, and gained huge savings in cross freight, advertising, sales, and
executive expenses. The survival of only the most productive forms of
business resulted in greater efficiency and cheapened production which in
turn meant higher wages and lower prices.[36] In this respect, Standard Oil
was represented as a model trust. According to its supporters, it was
formed to curb speculation, waste, and over-production. As Standard
took pains to inform stockholders, the company owed its success not to
illegal or reprehensible methods but to efficient organization.[37]

In his account of the birth of America's first great trust, Rockefeller
advanced a generalization common to big businessmen, that combination
arose in response to economic necessity. It was accurate up to a point,
but not universally applicable. Rockefeller's description of the founding
of Standard Oil was an interesting description of the genesis of monopoly
from the big businessman's viewpoint. In the beginning, Rockefeller
related, because refining crude petroleum was a simple and easy process
and because at first the profits were very large, all sorts of people went
into it—"the butcher, the baker and the candlestick maker began to refine oil." The market was soon glutted, and the price fell until the trade
was threatened with ruin. At that moment "It seemed absolutely necessary to extend the market for oil . . . and also greatly improve the

processes of refining so that oil could be made and sold cheaply, yet with a profit." So, "We proceeded to buy the largest and best refining concerns and centralize the administration of them with a view of securing greater economy and efficiency." [38] Though the birth pangs of Standard Oil obviously have been softened and somewhat simplified in the telling, it was on essentially this same basis that Carnegie explained the genesis of trusts in manufactured articles.[39]

Clearly, the operative point of view that consolidation of capital and industry was indispensable to the successful execution of the tasks which had developed upon modern business was the one embraced by big businessmen. In principle most of them agreed with the blunt statement of America's leading financier: "I like a little competition," J. P. Morgan was quoted as saying, "but I like combination better." [40] The choice was not between competition and monopoly, but between fighting to secure a monopoly by driving out competition in a bitter, destructive war and trying to obtain price control through industry-wide agreement.

Many, nevertheless, still paid lip service to the abstraction, though most had already rejected competition in practice.[41] This glaring incongruity between behavior and theory ridiculed the notion that such economic generalizations as free competition were natural "laws," timeless and placeless and entitled to sanctity. Rather than a competent expression of fact, the hedonistic theory of a perfect competitive system had turned out to be simply an expedient of abstract reasoning.

What in earlier and more halcyon days had been attributed to the benign operation of the law of competition was, in most instances, an absence of competition. Before the Civil War, competition was virtually dormant in many parts of the United States largely because of intervening geographical factors. Where it did exist, it usually operated on a local rather than a national scale, cushioning a large portion of the economy from the hardships of rigorous competition. The limitation of the nation's transportation system often allowed local businessmen a certain amount of monopoly power, and backward communications, particularly a lack of reliable market information, had a similar effect.[42] The trouble in many localities was that there was not always enough competition. These imperfections of competition in the antebellum period, however, tended to be eliminated by tremendous postwar advances in transportation and communication. Business rivalry also was intensified by the application of new technology to industry and nationalized by the substitution of the big interstate corporation for smaller local, individual, and partnership enterprises. The immediate outcome was competition with a vengeance, and the inauguration of a species of commercial warfare of a magnitude and violence unheard of in economic history. In the long run, the brutal realities of this cutthroat struggle were unpalatable to the public and big businessmen alike. But while the latter sought to shield themselves by erecting monopolistic barriers, the American people extolled the virtues of free competition and looked back fancifully to an earlier, more ideal state of economic affairs which, if anything, had been distinguished by a notable lack of competition.

That faith in the mythical virtues of competition prevailed widely. The majority of the American people took it for granted that competition was the normal way of life in business.[43] Henry Demarest Lloyd, an outstanding critic of big business, found it highly paradoxical that the American people who were so inalterably opposed to anarchy in politics advocated it in business. Worse yet, Americans had accepted industrial anarchy as their ideal of economic conduct.[44] Free competition was the shibboleth of practically all reform movements except that of the Socialists. It spurred the Grange, motivated the Single-Taxers and the Populists, and dominated the economic thought of the Progressives. Most of them desired, or thought they desired, free competition. On this matter there existed no clear partisan line. Members of Congress proclaimed "the norm of a free competition too self-evident to be debated, too obvious to be asserted." [45]

The belief in competition was an assertion of economic egalitarianism midway between the Gospel of Wealth and the Social Gospel, adopting neither the doctrine of stewardship by the chosen few nor the sweeping substitution of cooperation for competition.[46] It was a subtle interweaving of the Anglo-Saxon belief that the common law, as well as natural law, always favored competition over monopoly and native American opposition to privilege.[47] Some of the basic attitudes in this complex were clearly derived from classical economic theory. The economists whose works were most widely read were Adam Smith, John Stuart Mill, and David Ricardo; their laissez-faire attitude toward monopoly dominated the teaching of economics. "All our education and our habit of mind make us believe in competition," said the president of Yale. "We have been taught to regard it as a natural if not a necessary condition of all healthful business life. We look with satisfaction on whatever favors it, and with distrust on whatever hinders it." [48] The Darwinian theory of biological evolution was also generally interpreted as supporting popular notions about competition and individual initiative, although this was more apparent than real.[49] This ingrained habit of economic reasoning retarded public understanding of the new financial and industrial order, but the belief proved more important than its actual relevance. Sentiment, not fact, prompted American action against big business.[50]

On the question whether the corporation had to be made to fit American institutions and principles, or those institutions and principles had to be changed to accommodate the corporation, the American people almost unanimously declared for the first. If economic despotism was the outcome of unchecked corporate growth, then the corporate monster must be brought under control. The way out was the way back. The economy must be restored to a former golden time of competitive capitalism when the older individualistic values held sway, and the common man was free from monopolistic pressures.

The way backward, however, was not to be all the way. Completely breaking the trusts was rejected by the more realistic who wanted regulation. Somewhat paradoxically, they proposed to liberate competition by imposing new restrictions in the name of freedom. They were not too sure that unrestrained competition was the economic panacea they sought. They justified the theoretical incongruity of their stand on the moral grounds that such restrictions were to be imposed only to prevent unfair competition. Apparently it never occurred to them that to acknowledge the defective working of natural law against corporate immorality was an ingenuous admission that the sacrosanct principle of competition was invalid in the long run. Wilfully blind to the logical inconsistencies of this position, the majority clamored for governmental regulation in the interests of equal opportunity: "We must either regulate . . . or destroy." [51]

Responding to popular demand, Congress in 1890 passed the Sherman Act "to protect trade and commerce against unlawful restraints and monopolies," thus converting an economic myth into public policy. According to the ideology behind this law, there existed a direct cause and effect relationship between competition and monopoly. If the monpolistic obstacles in business were removed, the trend would immediately reverse itself; full and free competition would automatically return. Despite the stark realities of the growing trust and combination movement of the late 1880's, the public's confidence in the efficacy of this self-regulating mechanism set the tone of all subsequent federal action, whether for regulation or trust-busting.[52] Facts, however, proved otherwise. The Sherman Act, even when bolstered by later legislation, failed to halt or reverse the combination movement. It made evident the ineptitude of any legislation that regarded competition as a self-perpetuating and natural guarantor of economic justice rather than an intellectual hypothesis without institutional support.

The principal effect of legalizing the myth of competition was to encourage the growth of large combinations by deflecting the attack upon them into purely ideological channels. Since 1890, federal antitrust laws have symbolized the American democratic belief that "the only proper type of society is composed of unorganized competitive individuals." All attempts to curb big business by government action have been a ritual clash between an anachronistic ideal and a modern need, "the answer of a society which unconsciously felt the need of great organizations, and at the same time had to deny them a place in the moral and logical ideology of the social structure." [53]

Though the corporation had seemingly conformed to American institutions and principles under antitrust laws, those institutions and principles had really accommodated the corporation. By declaring the corporation to be an individual, with natural rights of life, liberty, and property, the Supreme Court in 1886 had seriously invalidated that basic concept of American society, the free individual.[54] This doctrine could be applied logically only to the individual as proprietor, partner, or even operating owner of a small company, but the jurists ignored the intrinsic conflict between the individualistic myth and the corporate reality, evoking the strained future efforts of the Supreme Court to dress "huge corporations in the clothes of simple farmers and merchants." [55]

In establishing the legal fiction that the corporation was a person before the law, entitled to the rights and privileges of a citizen, the court undermined the ideal of the morally responsible individual by extending the individualistic ethic to the amoral impersonality of the modern corporation, and in the long run it subordinated the ideal to the right of property. To accord a legal robot equal rights with a living person in the holding and protection of property under the Constitution was to exalt corporate property above the individual person and to pervert the traditional faith in individualism into a juridical sophism. As the course of American legal history from 1886 to the 1930's amply disclosed, such was the ultimate effect of the personification of the corporation.

In condemning trusts as "dangerous to Republican institutions" and in branding corporate leaders as Robber Barons "opposed to free institutions and free commerce between the states as were the feudal barons of the middle ages," aroused Americans of the Gilded Age had clearly seized upon the major issue.[56] They had somehow recognized that American society with its individualistic traditions was engaged in a life-and-death struggle with the organized forces of dissolution.

The once-welcome business and industrial concentration threatened the foundations of the nation. There was more individual power than ever, but those who wielded it were few and formidable. Charles Francis Adams, Jr., denounced these "modern potentates for the autocratic misuse of that power":

The system of corporate life and corporate power, as applied to industrial development, is yet in its infancy. . . . It is a new power, for which our language contains no name. We know what aristocracy, autocracy, democracy are; but we have no word to express government by monied corporations. . . . It remains to be seen what the next phase in this process of gradual development will be. History never quite repeats itself, and . . . the old familiar enemies may even now confront us, though arrayed in such a modern garb that no suspicion is excited. . . . As the Erie ring represents the combination of the corporation and the hired proletariat of a great city; as Vanderbilt embodies the autocratic power of Caesarism introduced into corporate life, and neither alone can obtain complete control of the government of the State, it, perhaps, only remains for the coming man to carry the combination of elements one step in advance, and put Caesarism at once in control of the corporation and of the proletariat, to bring our vaunted institutions within the rule of all historic precedent.[57]

Yet the public already sensed that something had gone wrong with American institutions and values. With less understanding than Adams, they felt that somehow the old rules had been broken. Behind their growing animosity to the big businessman was the feeling that in some way he cheated his countrymen. The belief was becoming fairly common that extreme wealth was incompatible with honesty. "The great cities," Walt Whitman wrote in 1871, "reek with respectable as much as non-respectable robbery and scoundrelism." [58] There were undoubtedly moral men of wealth, but many Americans agreed with Thomas A. Bland, who in *How to Grow Rich* suggested: "In all history, ancient and modern, the examples of men of honest lives and generous hearts who have become rich . . . is so rare as to be exceedingly exceptional, and even these have invariably profited largely . . . by the labor of others." [59]

Very revealing in this regard was the portrayal of the big businessman in contemporary fiction. Socialist writers naturally depicted him as a "criminal of greed" or an "economic monster" who with other "business animals" preyed upon the life of the nation. Oddly enough, however, in an age when the corporation made unprecedented achievements in production and organization to the enrichment of countless people, when material success was widely favored as a legitimate goal, scarcely a single major novelist presented the big businessman as a hero or even in a favorable light. Except at the hands of a few hack writers, the business or industrial leader was consistently portrayed as powerful and capable, but nonetheless an enemy of American society.[60] This may have reflected the bias of the aesthetic or creative temperament against the pragmatic money-maker, but the big businessman was in disfavor with most of American society.

In the popular mind, the vices of lying and stealing were legendarily associated with Wall Street. The big businessmen who dominated "the street" were regarded by some as the ethical counterparts of the pirate and buccaneer. By the simple devices of "stock-watering" or the issuance of fictitious securities not backed by capital assets, speculators were generally believed to have stolen millions of dollars from the American people.[61] In the opinion of the more jaundiced, the men of Wall Street had barely escaped prison bars. "If the details of the great reorganization and trustification deals put through since 1885 could be laid bare," contended Thomas W. Lawson, a financier turned critic, "eight out of ten of our most successful stock-jobbing financiers would be in a fair way to get into State or federal prisons." [62]

The iniquity of Wall Street was not merely legendary, but had firm basis in fact. Though not all speculators were swindlers nor all speculation gambling, only a small number of the stock exchange transactions were unquestionably of an investment character. The vast majority were virtually gambling.[63] Many corporations, although offering huge blocks of stock to the public, issued only the vaguest and most ambiguous summary of assets and liabilities. While this was not iniquitous in itself, secrecy too often cloaked fraud.[64]

The men at the top who had used the corporate device to make millions did not see it this way at all. They justified their millions on the ground that they had fairly earned it.[65] Cornelius Vanderbilt, at the age of eighty-one, boasted that he had made a million dollars for every year of his life, but added that it had been worth "three times that to the people of the United States." [66] Others shared his belief. In *The Railroad and the Farmer*, Edward Atkinson made practically the same statement, asserting that the gigantic fortune of the older Vanderbilt was but a small fraction of what the country gained from the development of the railway system under his genius.[67] The Reverend Julian M. Sturtevant of Illinois College also envisioned the Vanderbilts and Astors of the world as "laborers of gigantic strength, and they must have their reward and compensation for the use of their capital." [68] Carnegie maintained that great riches were no crime. "Under our present conditions the millionaire who toils on is the cheapest article which the community secures at the price it pays for him, namely, his shelter, clothing, and food." [69]

Most Americans, however, did not so readily accept this evaluation.

Some recognized that the big businessman in pursuing private ends had served national prosperity—the majority felt that he had taken extravagant profits entirely out of proportion to the economic services he had rendered. Rockefeller's millions were thought to be typical of the fortunes made by the Robber Barons, representing "the relentless, aggressive, irresistible seizure of a particular opportunity, the magnitude of which . . . was due simply to the magnitude of the country and the immensity of the stream of its prosperous industrial life." [70] The feeling was general that the great fortunes of all the big business magnates—Vanderbilt, Gould, Harriman, Stanford, Carnegie, Morgan, and the rest—represented special privilege which had enabled them to turn the abundant natural resources and multitudinous advantages offered by a growing nation into a private preserve for their own profit.

The public at large was not clearly aware if it, but the chief instrument of special privilege was the corporation. Though public franchises and political favoritism played a large part in the aggrandizement of the Robber Barons, in the money-making world of late nineteenth-century America special privilege invariably meant corporate privilege. The corporation enabled Vanderbilt to unify his railroads while making large speculative profits on the side. The same device made it possible for men like Rockefeller to create and combine private enterprises embodying new technological and financial techniques while diverting enormous profits to themselves. The corporation was the constructive power behind the building of the cross-country railroads, but it was also the destructive instrument used by Jay Gould, Tom Scott, Collis P. Huntington, and others to convert them into quick money-making machines with no regard for their obligations as public carriers.[71]

The problem remained of establishing the relationship of big businessmen to the corporation. Judging by their conduct, they were not fully cognizant of the tremendous power placed in their hands by the corporation with single men controlling "thousands of men, tens of millions of revenue, and hundreds of millions of capital." Or they wilfully exerted this prodigious force for private benefit regardless of consequences to the nation or ideals. Unhappily, most of those labeled Robber Baron by their contemporaries fell into the latter category.[72] Cornelius Vanderbilt held the law in contempt. Except where his own interests were involved, he had little regard for the consequences of his actions, manipulating and watering every corporate property he captured. One year after he took over the New York Central railroad, he increased the capitalization by $23,000,000, almost every cent of which represented inside profits for himself and friends. When admonished that some of his transactions were forbidden by law, he supposedly roared, "Law! What do I care about the law? Hain't I got the power?" [73] He confirmed this attitude in testimony before the committee on railroads of the New York State Assembly in 1869.[74] But Vanderbilt's methods were in no way exceptional. Most of the biggest businessmen made their millions in similar fashion. Twenty-four who because of notoriety and conspicuous power might be regarded as "typical" Robber Barons combined the role of promoter with that of entrepreneur. Stock manipulation along with corporate consolidation was probably the easiest way to wealth that ever existed in the United States. The exuberance with which promoters threw themselves into it proved that they were well aware of its golden possibilities.

As a consequence of these reckless corporate maneuverings, however, public opinion turned against the big businessman. While from a corporate point of view the conduct of the money-makers was often legal, although ethically dubious, the public often felt cheated. Puzzled and disenchanted by the way things had turned out, they questioned the way every millionaire got his money, and were quite ready to believe that a crime was behind every great fortune. While its exact nature escaped them, they felt they had been robbed. The classic statement of this feeling of outrage appeared in the Populist platform of 1892: "The fruits of the toil of millions are boldly stolen to build up colossal fortunes for a few, unprecedented in the history of mankind; and the possessors of these, in turn, despise the Republic and endanger liberty." [75]

The inchoate charges were basically accurate: too much wealth was being selfishly appropriated by a few. By the irresponsible use of the corporation, essentially a supralegal abstraction above the traditional laws of the land, they were undermining individualistic institutions and values. Big businessmen like John D. Rockefeller were attacked as Robber Barons because they were correctly identified as destroyers, the insurgent vanguard of the corporate revolution.

HERBERT G. GUTMAN

🙰 3 🙰

The Workers' Search for Power

UNTIL VERY RECENT TIMES, the worker never seemed as glamorous or
important as the entrepreneur. This is especially true of the Gilded Age,
where attention focuses more readily upon Jim Fisk, Commodore Vanderbilt, or John D. Rockefeller than on the men whose labor built their
fortunes. Most studies have devoted too much attention to too little. Excessive interest in the Haymarket riot, the "Molly Maguires," the great
strikes of 1877, the Homestead lockout, and the Pullman strike, has obscured the more important currents of which these things were only
symptoms. Close attention has also focused on the small craft unions,
the Knights of Labor, and the early Socialists, excluding the great mass
of workers who belonged to none of these groups and creating an uneven
picture of labor in the Gilded Age.[1]

Labor history had little to do with those matters scholars traditionally
and excessively emphasize. Too few workers belonged to trade unions to
make the unions important. There was a fundamental distinction between
wage earners as a social class and the small minority of the working
population that belonged to labor organizations. The full story of the
wage earner is much more than the tale of struggling craft unions and the
exhortations of committed trade unionists and assorted reformers and
radicals. A national perspective often misrepresented those issues important to large segments of the postbellum working population and to other
economic and social groups who had contact with the wage earners.[2]
Most of the available literature about labor in the Gilded Age is thin, and
there are huge gaps in our knowledge of the entire period.[3] Little was
written about the workers themselves, their communities, and the day-
to-day occurrences that shaped their outlook. Excessive concern with
craft workers has meant the serious neglect of the impact of industrial

31

capitalism—a new way of life—upon large segments of the population.

A rather stereotyped conception of labor and of industrial relations in the Gilded Age has gained widespread credence, and final and conclusive generalizations about labor abound:

> During the depression from 1873 to 1879, employers sought to eliminate trade unions by a *systematic* policy of lock outs, blacklists, labor espionage, and legal prosecution. The *widespread* use of blacklists and Pinkerton labor spies caused labor to organize *more or less* secretly and *undoubtedly* helped bring on the violence that *characterized* labor strife during this period.[4]

One historian asserts: "Employers *everywhere* seemed determined to rid themselves of 'restrictions upon free enterprise' by smashing unions."[5] The "*typical* [labor] organization during the seventies," writes another scholar, "was secret for protection against intrusion by outsiders."[6] Such seemingly final judgments are questionable: How *systematic* were lockouts, blacklists, and legal prosecutions? How *widespread* was the use of labor spies and private detectives? Was the secret union the *typical* form of labor organization? Did violence *characterize* industrial relations?

It is widely believed that the industrialist exercised a great deal of power and had almost unlimited freedom of choice when dealing with his workers after the Civil War. Part of this belief reflects the weakness or absence of trade unions. Another justification for this interpretation, however, is more shaky—the assumption that industrialism generated new kinds of economic power which immediately affected the social structure and ideology. The supposition that "interests" rapidly reshaped "ideas" is misleading. "The social pyramid," Joseph Schumpeter pointed out, "is never made of a single substance, is never seamless." The economic interpretation of history "would at once become untenable and unrealistic . . . if its formulation failed to consider that the manner in which production shapes social life is essentially influenced by the fact that human protagonists have always been shaped by past situations."[7]

In postbellum America, the relationship between "interest" and "ideology" was very complex and subtle. Industrial capitalism was a new way of life and was not fully institutionalized. Much of the history of industrialism is the story of the painful process by which an old way of life was discarded for a new one so that a central issue was the rejection or modification of a set of "rules" and "commands" that no longer fitted the new industrial context. Since so much was new, traditional stereotypes about the popular sanctioning of the rules and values of industrial society either demand severe qualification or entirely fall by the wayside. Among questionable commonly held generalizations are those that insist that the worker was isolated from the rest of society; that the employer had an easy time and a relatively free hand in imposing the new disciplines; that the spirit of the times, the ethic of the Gilded Age, worked to the advantage of the owner of industrial property; that workers found little if any sympathy from nonworkers; that the quest for wealth obliterated nonpecuniary values; and that industrialists swept aside countless obstacles with great ease.

The new way of life was more popular and more quickly sanctioned in large cities than in small one- or two-industry towns. Put another way, the social environment in the large American city after the Civil War was more often hostile toward workers than that in smaller industrial towns. Employers in large cities had more freedom of choice than counterparts in small towns, where local conditions often hampered the employer's decision-making power. The ideology of many nonworkers in these small towns was not entirely hospitable toward industrial, as opposed to traditional, business enterprise. Strikes and lockouts in large cities seldom lasted as long as similar disputes outside of urban centers. In the large city, there was almost no sympathy for the city worker among the middle and upper classes. A good deal of pro-labor and anti-industrial sentiment flowed from similar occupational groups in the small towns. Small-town employers of factory labor often reached out of the local environment for aid in solving industrial disputes, but diverse elements in the social structure and ideology shaped such decisions.

The direct economic relationships in large cities and in small towns and outlying industrial regions were similar, but the social structures differed profoundly. Private enterprise was central to the economy of both the small industrial town and the large metropolitan city, but functioned in a different social environment. The social structure and ideology of a given time are not derived only from economic institutions.[8] In a time of rapid economic and social transformation, when industrial capitalism was relatively new, parts of an ideology alien to industrialism retained a powerful hold on many who lived outside large cities.

Men and their thoughts were different in the large cities. "The modern town," John Hobson wrote of the large nineteenth-century cities, "is a result of the desire to produce and distribute most economically the largest aggregate of material goods: economy of work, not convenience of life, is the object." In such an environment, "anti-social feelings" were exhibited "at every point by the competition of workers with one another, the antagonism between employer and employed, between sellers and buyers, factory and factory, shop and shop." [9] Persons dealt with each other less as human beings and more as objects. The *Chicago Times*, for example, argued that "political economy" was "in reality the autocrat of the age" and occupied "the position once held by the Caesars and the Popes." [10] According to the *New York Times*, the "antagonistic . . . position between employers and the employed on the subject of work and wages" was "unavoidable. . . . The object of trade is to get as much as you may and give as little as you can." [11] The *Chicago Tribune* celebrated the coming of the centennial in 1876: "Suddenly acquired wealth, decked in all the colors of the rainbow, flaunts its robe before the eyes of Labor, and laughs with contempt at honest poverty." The country, "great in all the material powers of a vast empire," was entering "upon the second century weak and poor in social morality as compared with one hundred years ago." [12]

Much more than economic considerations shaped the status of the urban working population, for the social structure in large cities unavoidably widened the distance between social and economic classes. Home and job often were far apart. A man's fellow workers were not necessarily his friends and neighbors. Face-to-face relationships became less meaningful as the city grew larger and production became more diverse and specialized. "It has always been difficult for well-to-do people of the upper and middle classes," wrote Samuel Lane Loomis, a Protestant minister, in the 1880s, "to sympathize with and to understand the needs of their poorer neighbors." The large city, both impersonal and confining, made it even harder. Loomis was convinced that "a great and growing gulf" lay "between the working-class and those above them." [13] A Massachusetts clergyman saw a similar void between the social classes and complained: "I once knew a wealthy manufacturer who personally visited and looked after the comforts of his invalid operatives. I know of no such case now." [14] The fabric of human relationships was cloaked in a kind of shadowed anonymity that became more and more characteristic of urban life.[15]

Social contact was more direct in the smaller post–Civil War industrial towns and regions. *Cooper's New Monthly*, a reform trade union journal, insisted that while "money" was the "sole meausre of gentility and respectability" in large cities, "a more democratic feeling" prevailed in small towns.[16] "The most happy and contented workingmen in the country," wrote the *Iron Molder's Journal,* "are those residing in small towns and villages. . . . We want more towns and villages and less cities." [17] Except for certain parts of New England and the mid-Atlantic

states, the post–Civil War industrial towns and regions were relatively
new to that kind of enterprise. Men and women who lived and worked in
these areas usually had known another way of life, and they contrasted
the present with the past.

The nineteenth-century notion of enterprise came quickly to these
regions after the Civil War, but the social distance between the various
economic classes that characterized the large city came much more slowly
and hardly paralleled industrial developments. In the midst of the new
industrial enterprise with its new set of commands, men often clung to
older "agrarian" attitudes, and they judged the economic and social behavior of local industrialists by these values.

The social structure of the large city differed from that of the small
industrial town because of the more direct human relationships among
the residents of the smaller towns. Although many persons were not
personally involved in the industrial process, they felt its presence. Life
was more difficult and less cosmopolitan in small towns, but it was also
less complicated. This life was not romantic, since it frequently meant
company-owned houses and stores and conflicts between workers and
employers over rights taken for granted in agricultural communities and
large cities.[18] Yet the non-urban industrial environment had in it a kind
of compelling simplicity. There the inhabitants lived and worked together, and a certain sense of community threaded their everyday lives.

The first year of the 1873 depression sharply suggested the differences between the large urban center and the small industrial town.
There was no question about the severity of the economic crisis. Its consequences were felt throughout the entire industrial sector, and production, employment, and income fell sharply everywhere.[19] The dollar value
of business failures in 1873 was greater than in any other single year between 1857 and 1893.[20] Deflation in the iron and steel industry was especially severe: 266 of the nation's 666 iron furnaces were out of blast by
January 1, 1874, and more than 50 percent of the rail mills were silent.[21]
A New York philanthropic organization figured that 25 percent of the
city's workers—nearly 100,000 persons—were unemployed in the winter months of 1873–74.[22]

"The simple fact is that a great many laboring men are out of work,"
wrote the *New York Graphic*. "It is not the fault of merchants and manufacturers that they refuse to employ four men when they can pay but one,
and decline to pay four dollars for work which they can buy for two and
a half." [23] Gloom and pessimism settled over the entire country, and the
most optimistic predicted only that the panic would end in the late spring
months of 1873.[24] James Swank, the secretary of the American Iron and

Steel Association, found the country suffering "from a calamity which may be likened to a famine or a flood." [25]

A number of serious labor difficulties occurred in small industrial towns and outlying industrial regions during the first year of the depression, revealing much about the social structure of these areas. Although each had its own unique character, a common set of problems shaped them all. Demand fell away and industrialists cut production and costs to sell off accumulated inventory and retain shrinking markets. This general contraction caused harsh industrial conflict in many parts of the country. "No sooner does a depression in trade set in," observed David A. Harris, the conservative head of the Sons of Vulcan, a national craft union for puddlers and boilermen, "than all expressions of friendship to the toiler are forgotten." [26]

The *New York Times* insisted that the depression would "bring wages down for all time," and advised employers to dismiss workers who struck against wage reductions. This was not the time for the "insane imitations of the miserable class warfare and jealousy of Europe." [27] The *Chicago Times* stated that strikers were "idiots" and "criminals." Its sister newspaper, the *Chicago Evening Journal*, said the crisis was not "an unmixed evil," since labor would finally learn "the folly and danger of trade organizations, strikes, and combinations . . . against capital." [28] *Iron Age* was similarly sanguine. "We are sorry for those who suffer," it explained, "but if the power of the trade unions for mischief is weakened . . . the country will have gained far more than it loses from the partial depression of industry." Perhaps "simple workingmen" would learn they were misled by "demagogues and unprincipled agitators." Trade unions "crippled that productive power of capital" and retarded the operation of "beneficent natural laws of progress and development." [29] James Swank was somewhat more generous. Prices had fallen, and it was "neither right nor practicable for all the loss to be borne by the employers." "Some of it," he explained, "must be shared by the workingmen. . . . We must hereafter be contented with lower wages for our labor and be more thankful for the opportunity to labor at all." [30]

In cutting costs in 1873 and 1874, many employers found that certain aspects of the social structure and ideology in small industrial towns hindered their freedom of action. It was easy to announce a wage cut or refuse to negotiate with a local trade union, but it was difficult to enforce such decisions. In instance after instance, and for reasons that varied from region to region, employers reached outside of their environment to help assert their authority.

Industrialists used various methods to strengthen their local positions with workers. The state militia brought order to a town or region swept by industrial conflict. Troops were used in railroad strikes in Indiana, Ohio, and Pennsylvania; in a dispute involving iron heaters and rollers in Newport, Kentucky; in a strike of Colorado ore diggers; in two strikes of Illinois coal miners; and in a strike of Michigan ore workers.[31]

Other employers aggravated racial and nationality problems among workers by introducing new ethnic groups to end strikes, forcing men to work under new contracts, and destroying local trade unions. Negroes were used in coal disputes.[32] Danish, Norwegian, and Swedish immigrants went into mines in Illinois, and into the Shenango Valley and the northern anthracite region of Pennsylvania. Germans went to coal mines in northern Ohio along with Italian workers. Some Italians also were used in western Pennsylvania as coal miners, and in western and northern New York as railroad workers.[33] A number of employers imposed their authority in other ways. Regional, not local, blacklists were tried in the Illinois coal fields, on certain railroads, in the Ohio Valley iron towns, and in the iron mills of eastern Pennsylvania.[34] Mine operators in Pennsylvania's Shenango Valley and Tioga coal region used state laws to evict discontented workers from company-owned houses in midwinter.[35]

The social structure in these small towns and the ideology of many of their residents, who were neither workers nor employers, shaped the behavior of those employers who reached outside local environments to win industrial disputes. The story was different for every town, but had certain similarities. The strikes and lockouts had little meaning in and of themselves, but the incidents shed light on the distribution of power in these towns on important social and economic relationships which shaped the attitudes and actions of workers and employers.

One neglected aspect of the small industrial town after the Civil War is its political structure. Because workers made up a large proportion of the electorate and often participated actively in local politics, they influenced local and regional affairs more than wage earners in the larger cities. In 1874, few workers held elected or appointed offices in large cities. In that year, however, the postmaster of Whistler, Alabama, was a member of the Iron Molder's International Union.[36] George Kinghorn, a leading trade unionist in the southern Illinois coal fields, was postmaster of West Belleville, Illinois.[37] A local labor party swept an election in Evansville, Indiana.[38] Joliet, Illinois, had three workers on its city council.[39] A prominent official of the local union of iron heaters and rollers sat on the city council in Newport, Kentucky.[40] Coal and ore miners ran for the state legislature in Carthage, Missouri, in Clay County, Indiana, and in Belleville, Illinois.[41] The residents of Virginia City, a town famous in western mythology, sent the president of the local miners' union to Congress.[42] In other instances, town officials and other officeholders who were not wage earners sympathized with the problems and difficulties of local workers or displayed an unusual degree of objectivity during local industrial disputes.

Many local newspapers criticized the industrial entrepreneur, and editorials defended *local* workers and demanded redress for their grievances. Certain of these newspapers were entirely independent; others warmly endorsed local trade union activities.

The small businessmen and shopkeepers, lawyers and professional people, and other nonindustrial members of the middle class were a small but vital element in these industrial towns. Unlike the urban middle class they had direct and everyday contact with the new industrialism and with the problems and outlook of workers and employers. Many had risen from a lower station in life and knew the meaning of hardship and toil, and could judge the troubles of both workers and employers by personal experience. While they invariably accepted the concepts of private property and free entrepreneurship, their judgments about the *social* behavior of industrialists often drew upon noneconomic considerations and values. Some saw no necessary contradiction between private enterprise and gain and decent, humane social relations between workers and employers.

In a number of industrial conflicts, segments of the local middle class sided with workers. A Maryland weekly newspaper complained in 1876: "In the changes of the last thirty years not the least unfortunate is the separation of personal relations between employers and employees." [43] While most metropolitan newspapers sang paeans of joy for the industrial entrepreneur and the new way of life, the *Youngstown Miner and Manufacturer* thought it completely wrong that the "Vanderbilts, Stewarts, and Astors bear, in proportion to their resources, infinitely less of the burden incident to society than the poorest worker." [44] The *Ironton Register* defended dismissed iron strikers as "upright and esteemed . . . citizens" who had been sacrificed "to the cold demands on business." [45] The *Portsmouth Times* boasted: "We have very little of the codfish aristocracy, and industrious laborers are looked upon here with as much respect as any class of people." [46]

In 1873 when the depression called a temporary halt to the expansion of the Illinois mining industry, Braidwood, Illinois, was less than a dozen years old.[47] Coal mining and Braidwood had grown together, and by 1873, 6,000 persons lived in the town. Except for the supervisors and the small businessmen and shopkeepers, most residents were coal miners. Braidwood had no "agricultural neighborhood to give it support" and "without its coal-shafts" it would have had "no reasonable apology for existing." The town had three coal companies, but the Chicago, Wilmington and Vermillion Coal Company was by far the largest, and its president, James Monroe Walker, also headed the Chicago, Burlington and Quincy Railroad. This firm operated five shafts and employed 900 men— more than half the resident miners. Most of the owners did not live in the town. The miners were a mixed lot, and unlike most other small industrial towns in this era Braidwood had an ethnically diverse population. About half the miners came from Ireland. Another 25 percent were English, Welsh, and Scotch. A smaller number were Swedes, Italians, and Germans, and still others came from France and Belgium and even from Poland and Russia. There were also native-born miners. "The town of Braidwood," a contemporary noted, "is . . . nearly akin to Babel as regards the confusion of tongues." Although they came from diverse backgrounds, they were a surprisingly cohesive social community. A trade union started in 1872 was strong enough to extract a reasonable wage agreement from the three coal firms. A hostile observer complained that nearly all the voters were miners and that a majority of the aldermen and justices of the peace "are or have been miners."

The depression cut the demand for coal and created serious problems for the operators. By March, 1874, at least 25 percent of the miners were unemployed, and the town was "dull beyond all precedent." In late May the operators, led by the Chicago, Wilmington and Vermillion firm, cut the rate for digging coal from $1.25 to $1.10 a ton and cut the price for "pushing" coal from the work wall to the shaft nearly in half. They announced that the mines would close on June 1 unless the men accepted the new contract for a full year. The miners' efforts to compromise and suggestions of arbitration were summarily rejected, and the mines closed.

The Chicago, Wilmington and Vermillion company approached private labor contracting agencies in Chicago and recruited a large number of unskilled laborers, most of whom were Scandinavian immigrants and were not miners. Three days after the strike began, sixty-five Chicago workers arrived. More came two weeks later, and a few arrived daily until the end of July when the number increased sharply. At the same time, anticipating trouble in putting the new men to work, the operators brought special armed Chicago Pinkerton police to the town.

Difficulties plagued the operators from the start. The miners realized they had to check the owners' strategy in order to gain a victory. As soon as new workers arrived, committees of miners explained the difficulty to them. "We ask the skilled miners not to work," the leader of the strikers explained. "As to green hands, we are glad to see them go to work for we know they are . . . a positive detriment to the company." All but three of the first sixty-five new workers decided to return to Chicago and, since they lacked funds, the miners and other local residents paid their rail fare and cheered them as they boarded a Chicago-bound train. By mid-July one shaft that usually employed two hundred men had no more than ten workers. At the end of July, only 102 men worked in the mines, and not one of them was a resident miner. The disaffected miners also met the challenge of the Pinkerton men. The miners appointed a seventy-two-man committee to prevent violence and to protect company property. The mayor and the sheriff swore in twelve of these men as special deputies, and, with one exception—when the wives of certain miners chased and struck the son of famed detective Allan Pinkerton—the miners behaved in a quiet and orderly manner.

Braidwood's tiny middle class "all back[ed] the miners." They denied complaints by the owners that the miners were irresponsible and violent. One citizen condemned the coal companies for creating "excitement so as to crush the miners" and declared that "public sympathy" was "entirely" with the workers. The operators wanted Pinkerton and his men appointed "special deputies" and made "merchant police" with power to arrest persons trespassing on company properties, but the mayor and the sheriff turned them down and deputized the strikers. Mayor Goodrich forbade parading in the streets by the Pinkerton men, and the sheriff ordered them to surrender their rifles and muskets. He did not want "a lot of strangers dragooning a quiet town with deadly weapons in their hands," and feared the miners "a good deal less than . . . the Chicago watchmen."

The operators faced other troubles. Local judges and police officials enforced the law more rigorously against them and their men than against the resident miners. Two new workers who got into a fight one Sunday were arrested for violating the Sabbath law and fined fifty dollars and court costs. Unable to pay the fine, they were put to work on the town streets. Another, jailed for hitting an elderly woman with a club, was fined one-hundred dollars and court costs. A company watchman was arrested four times, twice for "insulting townspeople."

Frustrated in these and other ways by the miners and the townspeople, the operators finally turned for help to the state government, and E. L. Higgins, the adjutant general and head of the state militia, went to Braidwood to see if troops were needed. Higgins openly supported the mine owners. He tried to prevent union men from talking with new workers, and although he asked the mayor to meet him in the office of the Chicago, Wilmington and Vermillion firm, he "never went to see the officers of the city . . . to gain an unprejudiced account of the strike." "If this is what the military forces and officers are kept for," one miner observed, "it is high time . . . such men [were] struck off the State Government payroll and placed where they belong." Mayor Goodrich reminded Higgins that neither the Braidwood nor the Will County authorities had asked for state interference. In a bitter letter to the *Chicago Times,* Goodrich wondered whether Higgins had come "in his official capacity or as an agent of the coal company," and firmly insisted that "the citizens of this city were not aware that martial law had been proclaimed or an embargo placed upon their speech."

Unable fully to exercise their authority in the town and worried about the possibility of losing the fall trade, the operators surrendered to the strikers fourteen weeks after the struggle began. The final agreement pleased the miners. They were especially amused when the Chicago, Wilmington and Vermillion company agreed to send all the new workers back to Chicago. A spokesman for the operators, however, bitterly assailed the Braidwood mayor and other public officials for their failure to understand the meaning of "peace, order, and freedom." Surely the operators had further cause for complaint in 1877 when Daniel McLaughlin, the president of the miners' union, was elected mayor of Braidwood, other miners were chosen aldermen, and one became police magistrate.

Manufacturers in the small industrial iron towns of the Ohio Valley such as Ironton and Portsmouth, Ohio, and Newport and Covington, Kentucky, had similar troubles.[48] Several thousand men and fifteen iron mills were involved in a dispute over wages that lasted for several months. The mill owners who belonged to the Ohio Valley Iron Association cut the wages of skilled iron heaters and roller men 20 percent on December 1, 1873. After the workers complained that the manufacturers were taking "undue advantage" of them "owing to the present financial trouble," their wages were cut another 10 percent. The valley mill owners worked out a common policy; they decided to close all the mills for a month or so in December and then reopen them under the new scale. Hard times would bring new workers.

Although the mill owners in large cities such as St. Louis, Indianapolis, and Cincinnati found it easy to bring in new workers from the outside, it was another story in the small towns. They could hire new hands in Pittsburgh, Philadelphia, and other eastern cities, but the social environment in Covington, Portsmouth, Newport, and Ironton made it difficult to keep these men. Fellow townspeople sympathized with the locked-out workers. In such an environment they were a relatively homogeneous group and made up a large part of the total population of the town. When workers agitated in small towns, paraded the streets, or engaged in one or another kind of collective activity, their behavior hardly went unnoticed.

The difficulties small-town iron manufacturers faced especially beset Alexander Swift, owner of the Swift Iron and Steel Works in Newport, Kentucky. Although his workers suffered from almost indescribable poverty after the factory closed, they would not surrender. When Swift reopened the mill, he hired armed "special policemen." Some of the new workers left town after they learned of the conflict, and the "police" accompanied the rest to and from their work. The old workers made Newport uncomfortable for new hands. There was no violence at first, but many strikers and their wives, especially the English and Welsh workers, gathered near the mill and in the streets to howl at the "black sheep" going to and from work. The Newport workers exerted pressure on them in "the hundred ways peculiar to workingmen's demonstrations." Swift was embittered, for by the end of January only a few men worked in his mill.

He was not alone. Mill owners in Covington, Ironton, and Portsmouth faced similar difficulty. Early in February, therefore, the Ohio Valley Iron Association announced that unless the men returned to work on or before February 20 they would lose their jobs and never again be hired in the valley iron mills. When most of the workers refused to return, they were fired. New workers were quickly brought to the towns, and Swift demanded special police protection for them from the Newport City Council, but it assigned only regular police. Crowds jeered the new men, and there were several fights. A large number of new workers again left Newport. "We never went any further with those fellows," a striker explained, "than calling them 'black sheep' and little lambs.' " Swift vainly appealed to the police to ban street demonstrations by the workers and their families, then armed the new men with pistols. When the strikers and their supporters gathered to jeer them, one of the imported laborers shot wildly into the crowd and killed a young butcher's helper. The enraged crowd chased Swift's men out of the city. After blaming the shooting on the failure of the Newport authorities to guard his men properly, Swift closed the mill.

These events did not go unnoticed in the Ohio Valley. The *Portsmouth Times* leveled a barrage of criticism at Swift and the other manufacturers. It asked whether or not they had a "right" to circulate the names of strikers in the same manner as "the name of a thief is sent from one police station to another." Such action was "cowardly . . .

intimidation," and the *Times* asked: "Does not continued and faithful service deserve better treatment at the hands of men whose fortunes have been made by these workmen they would brand with the mark of CAIN? . . . Is this to be the reward for men who have grown gray in the service of these velvet-lined aristocrats? . . . Out on such hypocrisy!" After the shooting in Newport, the *Times* turned on Swift and called him a "blood-letter." Violence was wrong, the *Times* admitted, but "If the gathered up assassins from the slums and alleys of the corrupt cities of the East are brought here to do deeds of lawlessness and violence, the stronger the opposition at the beginning the sooner they will be taught that the city of Portsmouth has no need of them."

Immune to such criticism, Swift continued to try to break down the strength of the Newport workers. In the end he succeeded. He realized that the only way to weaken the strikers was to suppress their power of public demonstration and therefore urged the Newport mayor to enforce local ordinances against dangerous and "riotous" crowds, asked the Kentucky governor to send state militia, and even demanded federal troops. Although the mayor banned "all unusual and unnecessary assemblages" in the streets, Swift still asked for state troops, and on March 5, the Kentucky governor ordered twenty-five members of the Lexington division of the state militia to Newport. Their arrival weakened the strikers and created a favorable environment for Swift. Street demonstrations were banned. The police were ordered to arrest "all persons using threatening or provoking language." When a number of unskilled strikers offered to return at the lower wage, Swift turned them away. He also rejected efforts by a member of the city council to effect a compromise with the old workers. A week after the troops arrived and three and a half months after the start of the lockout, Swift was in full control of the situation. New men worked in his factory, and the strikers admitted defeat.

The use of troops, however, was bitterly condemned in the Ohio Valley. A reporter for the *Cincinnati Enquirer* found that the "general opinion" in Newport was that Swift's maneuver was "little else than a clever piece of acting intended to kindle public sentiment against the strikers and . . . gain the assistance of the law in breaking up a strike." A Newport judge assailed the Kentucky governor, and a local poet sang of the abuse of public power:

> Sing a song of sixpence
> Stomachs full of rye,
> Five-and-twenty volunteers,
> With fingers in one pie;

> When the pie is opened
> For money they will sing,
> Isn't that a pretty dish
> For the City Council Ring?

There was less drama in the other Ohio Valley iron towns than in Newport, but the manufacturers in Portsmouth, Ironton, and Covington faced similar trouble. The old workers persuaded many new hands to leave the region. When fourteen men from Philadelphia arrived in Ironton and learned of the troubles for the first time, they left the city. Strikers paid their return rail fare. The same happened in Portsmouth, and the departing workers declared: "A nobler, truer, better class of men never lived than the Portsmouth boys . . . standing out for their rights." Non-strikers in these towns also acted contrary to the manufacturers' interests. Each week the *Portsmouth Times* attacked the mill owners. "We are not living under a monarchy," the *Times* insisted, and the "arbitrary actions" of the employers were not as "unalterable as the edicts of the Medes and Persians."

A Covington justice of the peace illustrated something of the hostility felt toward the companies. Three strikers were arrested for molesting new hands, but he freed one and fined the others a dollar each and court costs. A new worker, however, was fined twenty dollars for disorderly conduct and for carrying a deadly weapon. He also had to post a five-hundred-dollar bond as a guarantee that he would keep the peace.

In the end, except in Newport where Swift had successfully neutralized the power of the workers, a compromise wage settlement was finally worked out. Certain mills brought in new men, but some manufacturers withdrew the blacklist and rehired striking workers. A friend of the Ohio Valley iron manufacturers bitterly complained: "Things of this sort make one ask whether we are really as free a people as we pretend to be." This devotee of classical laissez-faire doctrine sadly concluded: "If any individual cannot dispose of his labor when and at what price he pleases, he is living under a despotism, no matter what form the government assumes."

Although hardly any Negroes worked in coal mines before 1873, soon after the depression started mine operators in the Ohio Hocking Valley recruited hundreds from border and southern cities. Some had been sparingly employed in certain Indiana and Ohio mines, but attracted little attention. It was different in the Hocking Valley in 1874. A large number of white miners struck and showed an unusual degree of unanimity and staying power. They found support from members of the local middle class, and the operators, unable to wear down the strikers, brought in Negroes. Although the miners were defeated, the problems they raised for their employers indicated much the same social environment as that in Braidwood and the Ohio Valley iron towns.

The railroad opened new markets for bituminous coal, and the years between 1869 and 1873 were a time of great prosperity. In 1870, 105,000 tons left the valley, and in 1873 just over 1,000,000 tons were shipped. Two years later, more than 20 percent of the coal mined in Ohio came from the Hocking Valley. Although entry costs were low, the ten largest firms in 1874 employed nearly two-thirds of the valley's miners.[49]

The miners fell into two social groupings. Those born in and near the valley had spent most of their lives in the mines and often held local positions of public trust and esteem. A Cincinnati reporter found that miners held "a good position in society . . . as a class" and filled "a fair number of municipal, church, and school offices." These men had seen their status depersonalized as they quickly became part of a larger labor force, dependent on a distant and uncontrollable market. They unavailingly complained when operators brought in many more miners than needed for full-time work. A perceptive observer found that many of the older miners "have worked in these mines since they were boys and feel they have an actual property right to their places." Most of the new men who flocked to the valley after 1869 came from distant areas, and a good number were from England, Wales, and Ireland. The rapid growth of the industry made it difficult to support trade unions in the valley.[50]

Economic crisis in 1873 suddenly punctured the region's prosperity. At best, miners found only part-time employment, and cash wages were less common than usual, for working miners were paid mostly in 90-day notes and store credit. The operators complained that labor costs were too high and made the selling price of coal in a competitive but depressed market prohibitive. Talk of wage cuts, however, turned the miners toward trade unionism, and in December, 1873, they founded several branches of the newly established Miners' National Association. The operators in turn formed a region-wide trade association, and each of them posted a $5,000 bond as proof he would follow its directives. They also announced a sharp wage cut effective April 1, 1874, and entirely proscribed the new union.

Prominent union leaders lost their jobs. One operator closed his supply store "for repairs," and another locked his men in a room and insisted that they sign the new wage agreement. But the union thrived. Only nine "regular" miners favored the new contract, and no more than twenty-five or thirty regulars refused to join the union. The union men agreed to the lower wage but refused to abandon their organization. The operators remained adamant and insisted that the "progress or decay" of the region hinged on the destruction of the new union—"a hydra too dangerous to be warmed at our hearth." A strike over the right of labor organization started on April 1.[51]

The strike brought trouble for the operators. Except for the *Logan Republican,* the weekly valley newspapers either supported the strikers or stood between them and the operators.[52] No more than thirty regular miners accepted the new contract on April 1, and only seventy men entered the mines that day. Local public officials declined to do the bidding of prominent operators. The New Straitsville police deputized strikers, and after Governor William Allen sent the state inspector of mines to investigate reported miner violence, country and town officials assured him there was no trouble and a committee of merchants and "other property owners" visited Allen "to give him the facts."

New Straitsville town officials joined the miners to check the effort of operator W. B. McClung to bring in from Columbus "a posse" of nine special police armed with Colt revolvers and Spencer rifles. The miners felt it "unnecessary" for armed police to come to "their quiet town," and men, women, and children paraded the streets in protest. They made it uncomfortable for McClung's police, and he promised to close his mine and return the men to Columbus. But the mayor, on the complaint of a miner, issued a warrant for their arrest for entering the town armed, "disturbing the peace and quiet." Ordered to stand trial, the nine left town after McClung's superintendent posted their bond.

Except for the Nelsonville operators, other owners closed their mines on April 1 for two months and waited out the strikers. Toward the end of May, the operators divided among themselves. A few settled with strikers, but the largest rejected arbitration and rebuked the union.[53] Compromise was out of the question, insisted the more powerful operators, and they attacked the governor for not sending militia. The triumph of the union would soon lead to the "overthrow" of "our Government and bring upon us anarchy and bloodshed that would approach, if not equal, the Communism of Paris." [54]

Unable to exert authority from within, the owners brought in between 400 and 500 Negroes in mid-June. Most came from Memphis, Louisville, and Richmond; few were experienced coal miners. They were offered high wages, told nothing of the dispute, and were generally misinformed about conditions. One employer admitted that "the motive for introducing the Negro was to break down the white miners' strike."

Another boasted of his "great triumph over Trades-Unions" and called the use of Negroes "the greatest revolution ever attempted by operators to take over their own property." Gathered together in Columbus, the Negroes then were sped by rail to one of the mines which was turned into a military camp. The county sheriff, twenty-five deputies, and the governor's private secretary were also there. Apparently with the approval of these officials, the operators armed the Negroes with "Government muskets," bayonets, and revolvers, and placed them on "military duty" around the property. No one could enter the area unless endorsed "by the operators or police." In the meantime, state militia were mobilized in nearby Athens, in Chillicothe, and in Cincinnati.[55]

Anger swept the Hocking Valley when the strikers learned of this. The first day 1,000 miners and their families stood or paraded near the Negro encampment. No violence occurred, but the men called across picket lines of armed Negroes and urged them to desert the operators. The second day even more miners paraded near the encampment and urged the Negroes to leave. The miners succeeded in "raiding" the operators with an "artillery of words," and around 120 Negroes went back on the operators. Two of the defectors admitted they had been "led by misrepresentations to come North" and "wouldn't interfere with white folks' work." They defended unions as "a good thing" and advocated "plenty of good things" for everyone. The strikers housed the Negroes in union lodge rooms, and with the help of local citizens raised about five-hundred dollars to help them return South. But this was only a small victory for the strikers. Enough Negroes remained to strengthen the hand of the operators and to demoralize the union men. Negroes went to other mines, even though strikers begged them not to work and "mothers held their children in their arms pointing out the negroes to them as those who came to rob them of their bread." [56]

Outside the Hocking Valley, the press applauded the operators. The *Cleveland Leader* thought the strikers were "aliens"; the *Cincinnati Commercial* called them drunkards, thieves, and assassins. In the Hocking Valley, however, some residents complained of the "mercenary newspaper men and their hired pimps." The valley newspapers especially criticized the owners for using Negroes. Some merchants and other business folk also attacked the operators. Certain Nelsonville businessmen offered aid to the strikers and unsuccessfully pleaded with the operators to rehire all the miners. The police also were friendly, and the New Straitsville mayor prevented the sending of militia to his town.[57]

Destruction of the union and the introduction of Negro workers did not bring industrial harmony. There were strikes over wage cuts in

1875 and 1877, and conflict between Negro and white miners. In 1875, when the men resisted a wage cut, the employers tacitly admitted that their power in the valley still was inadequate. Two of them, W. F. Brooks and T. Longstreth, visited Governor Allen and pleaded that he "restore order" in the valley towns. The governor was cautious, however, and sent no troops. But their pleas revealed the employers' anxieties and need for outside power.[58]

Nothing better illustrated the differences between the small town and large city than attitudes toward public works for the unemployed. Urban newspapers frowned upon the idea, and relief and welfare agents often felt that the unemployed were "looking for a handout." The jobless, one official insisted, belonged to "the degraded class . . . who have the vague idea that 'the world owes them a living.' " Unemployed workers were lazy, many said, and trifling.[59]

Native-born radicals and reformers, a few welfare officers, ambitious politicians, responsible theorists, socialists, and "relics" from the pre–Civil War era all agitated for public works during the great economic crisis of 1873–74. The earliest advocates urged construction of city streets, parks and playgrounds, rapid transit systems, and other projects to relieve unemployment. These schemes usually depended on borrowed money or fiat currency, or issuance of low-interest rate bonds on both local and national levels. The government had aided wealthy classes in the past; it was time to "legislate for the good of all not the few." Street demonstrations and meetings by the unemployed occurred in November and December of 1873 in Boston, Cincinnati, Chicago, Detroit, Indianapolis, Louisville, Newark, New York, Paterson, Pittsburgh, and Philadelphia. The dominant theme at all these gatherings was the same: unemployment was widespread, countless persons were without means, charity and philanthropy were poor substitutes for work, and public aid and employment were necessary and just.[60]

The reaction to the demand for public works contained elements of surprise, ridicule, contempt, and genuine fear. The Board of Aldermen refused to meet with committees of jobless Philadelphia workers. Irate Paterson taxpayers put an end to a limited program of street repairs the city government had started. Chicago public officials and charity leaders told the unemployed to join them "in God's work" and rescue the poor and suffering" through philanthropy, not public employment.[61]

The urban press rejected the plea for public works and responsibility for the unemployed. Men demanding such aid were "disgusting," "crazy," "loud-mouthed gasometers," "impudent vagabonds," and even "ineffable asses." They were ready "to chop off the heads of every man addicted to clean linen." They wanted to make "Government an institution to pillage the individual for the benefit of the mass." Hopefully, "yellow fever, cholera, or any other blessing" would sweep these persons from the earth. Depressions, after all, were normal and necessary adjustments, and workers should only "quietly bide their time till the natural laws of trade" brought renewed prosperity. Private charity and alms, as well as "free land," were adequate answers to unemployment. "The United States," said the *New York Times,* "is the only 'socialistic,' or more correctly 'agrarian,' government in the world in that it offers good land at nominal prices to every settler" and thereby takes "the sting from Communism." If the unemployed "prefer to cling to the great cities to oversupply labor," added the *Chicago Times,* "the fault is theirs." [62]

None of the proposals of the jobless workers met with favor, but the demand by New York workers that personal wealth be limited to $100,000 was criticized most severely. To restrict the "ambition of building up colossal fortunes" meant an end to all "progress," wrote the *Chicago Times.* The *New York Tribune* insisted that any limitation on personal wealth was really an effort "to have employment without employers," and that was "almost as impossible . . . as to get into the world without ancestors." [63]

Another argument against public responsibility for the unemployed identified this notion with immigrants, socialists, and "alien" doctrine. The agitation by the socialists compounded the anxieties of the more comfortable classes. Remembering that force had put down the Paris Communards, the *Chicago Times* asked: "Are we to be required to face a like alternative?'" New York's police superintendent urged his men to spy on labor meetings and warned that German and French revolutionaries were "doing their utmost to inflame the workingman's mind." The *Chicago Tribune* menacingly concluded, "The coalition of foreign nationalities must be for a foreign, non-American object. The principles of these men are wild and subversive of society itself." [64]

Hemmed in by such ideological blinders, devoted to "natural laws" of economics, and committed to a conspiracy theory of social change so often attributed only to the lower classes, the literate nonindustrial residents of large cities could not identify with the urban poor and the unemployed. Most well-to-do metropolitan residents in 1873 and 1874 believed that whether men rose or fell depended on individual effort. They viewed the worker as little more than a factor of production. They were sufficiently alienated from the urban poor to join the *New York Graphic* in jubilantly celebrating a country in which republican equality, free public schools, and cheap western lands allowed "intelligent working people" to "have anything they all want." [65]

The attitude displayed toward the unemployed reflected a broader and more encompassing view of labor. Unlike similar groups in small towns, the urban middle- and upper-income groups generally frowned upon labor disputes and automatically sided with employers. Contact between these persons and the worker was casual and indirect. Labor unions violated certain immutable "natural and moral laws" and deterred economic development and capital accumulation.[66] The *Chicago Times* put it another way in its discussion of workers who challenged the status quo: "The man who lays up not for the morrow, perishes on the morrow. It is the inexorable law of God, which neither legislatures nor communistic blatherskites can repeal. The fittest alone survive, and those are the fittest, as the result always proves, who provide for their own survival." [67]

Unions and all forms of labor protest, particularly strikes, were condemned. The *New York Times* described the strike as "a combination against long-established laws," especially "the law of supply and demand." The *New York Tribune* wrote of "the general viciousness of the trades-union system," and the *Cleveland Leader* called "the labor union kings . . . the most absolute tyrants of our day." Strikes, insisted the *Chicago Tribune,* "implant in many men habits of indolence that are fatal to their efficiency thereafter." Cleveland sailors who protested conditions on the Great Lakes ships were "a motley throng and a wicked one," and when Cuban cigar makers struck in New York, the *New York Herald* insisted that "madness rules the hour."

City officials joined in attacking and weakening trade unions. The mayor forbade the leader of striking Philadelphia weavers from speaking in the streets. New York police barred striking German cigar workers from gathering in front of a factory whose owners had discharged six trade unionists, including four women. Plain-clothes detectives trailed striking Brooklyn plasterers. When Peter Smith, a nonunion barrel maker, shot and wounded four union men—killing one of them—during a bitter lockout, a New York judge freed him on $1,000 bail supplied by his employers and said his employers did "perfectly right in giving Smith a revolver to defend himself from strikers." [68]

Brief review of three important labor crises in Pittsburgh, Cleveland, and New York points out different aspects of the underlying attitude toward labor in the large cities. The owners of Pittsburgh's five daily newspapers cut printers' wages in November, 1873, and formed an association to break the printers' union. After the printers rejected the wage cut and agreed to strike if nonunion men were taken on, two newspapers fired the union printers. The others quit in protest. The *Pittsburgh Dispatch* said the strikers "owe no allegiance to society," and the other publishers condemned the union as an "unreasoning tyranny." Three publishers started a court suit against more than seventy union members charging them with "conspiracy." The printers were held in $700 bail, and the strike was lost. Pittsburgh was soon "swarming with 'rats' from all parts of the country," and the union went under. Though the cases were not pressed after the union collapsed, the indictments were not dropped. In 1876, the *Pittsburgh National Labor Tribune* charged, "All of these men are kept under bail *to this day* to intimidate them from forming a Union, or asking for just wages." A weekly organ of the anthracite miners' union attacked the indictment and complained that it reiterated "the prejudice against workingmen's unions that seems to exist universally among officeholders." [69]

In May, 1874, Cleveland coal dealers cut the wages of their coal heavers more than 25 percent, and between four- and five-hundred men struck. Some new hands were hired. A foreman drew a pistol on the strikers and was beaten. He and several strikers were arrested, and the coal docks remained quiet as the strikers, who had started a union, paraded up and down and neither spoke nor gestured to the new men. Police guarded the area, and a light artillery battery of the Ohio National Guard was mobilized. Lumber heavers joined the striking workers, and the two groups paraded quietly on May 8. Although the strikers were orderly, the police jailed several leaders. The strikers did not resist and dispersed when so ordered by the law. In their complaint to the public, they captured the flavor of urban-industrial conflict:

> The whole thing is a calumny, based upon the assumption that if a man be poor he must necessarily be a blackguard. Honest poverty can have no merit here, as the rich, together with all their other monopolies, must also monopolize all the virtues. We say now . . . we entertain a much more devout respect and reverence for our public law than the men who are thus seeking to degrade it into a tool of grinding oppression. We ask from the generosity of our fellow citizens . . . to dispute [*sic*] a commission of honest men to come and examine our claims. . . . We feel confident they will be convinced that the authorities of Cleveland, its police force, and particularly the formidable artillery are all made partisans to a very dirty and mean transaction.

The impartial inquiry proved unnecessary; a few days later several firms rescinded the wage cut, and the strikers thanked these employers.[70]

Italian laborers were used on a large scale in the New York building trades for the first time in the spring of 1874. They lived "piled together like sardines in a box" and worked mainly as ragpickers and street cleaners. They were men of "passionate dispositions" and, "as a rule, filthy beyond the power of one to imagine." Irish street laborers and unskilled workers were especially hard on Italians, and numerous scuffles between the two groups occurred in the spring of 1874. In spite of the revulsion toward the Italians as a people, the *New York Tribune* advised employers that their "mode of life" allowed them to work for low wages.[71]

Two non-Italians, civil engineers and contractors, founded the New York Italian Labor Company in April, 1874. It claimed 2,700 members, and its superintendent, an Italian named Frederick Guscetti, announced: "As peaceable and industrious men, we claim the right to put such price upon our labor as may seem to us best." The firm held power of attorney over members, contracted particular jobs, provided transportation, supplied work gangs with "simple food," and retained a commission of a day's wages from each monthly paycheck. The company was started to protect the Italians from Irish "adversaries," and Guscetti said the men were willing to work "at panic prices." The non-Italian managers announced the men would work for 20 percent less in the building trades. Employers were urged to hire them "and do away with strikes."[72]

Protected by the city police and encouraged by the most powerful newspapers, the New York Italian Labor Company first attracted attention when it broke a strike of union hod carriers. Irish workers hooted and stoned the Italians, but the police provided them with ample protection. The *Cooper's New Monthly* complained that "poor strangers, unacquainted with the laws and customs and language of the country," had been made "the dupes of unprincipled money sharks" and were being "used as tools to victimize and oppress other workingmen." This was just the start. The firm advertised its services in *Iron Age*. By the end of July, 1874, it had branched out with work gangs in New York, Massachusetts, and Pennsylvania.[73]

There is much yet to learn about the attitude toward labor that existed in large cities, but over all opinion lay a popular belief that "laws" governed the economy and life itself. He who tampered with them through social experiments or reforms imperiled the whole structure. The *Chicago Times* was honest, if callous, in saying: "Whatever cheapens production, whatever will lessen the cost of growing wheat, digging gold, washing dishes, building steam engines, is of value. . . . The age is not one which enquires when looking at a piece of lace whether the woman who wove it is a saint or a courtesan." It came at last almost to a kind of inhumanity, as one manufacturer who used dogs and men in his operation discovered. The employer liked the dogs. "They never go on strike for higher wages, have no labor unions, never get intoxicated and disorderly, never absent themselves from work without good cause, obey orders without growling, and are very reliable." [74]

The contrast between urban and rural views of labor and its fullest role in society and life is clear.[75] In recent years, many have stressed "entrepreneurship" in nineteenth-century America [76] without distinguishing between entrepreneurs in commerce and trade and those in industrial manufacturing. Reflecting the stresses and strains in the thought and social attitudes of a generation passing from the old pre-industrial way of life to the new industrial America, many men could justify the business ethic in its own sphere without sustaining it in operation in society at large or in human relationships. It was one thing to apply brute force in the marketplace, and quite another to talk blithely of "iron laws" when men's lives and well-being were at stake.

Not all men had such second thoughts about the social fabric which industrial capitalism was weaving, but in the older areas of the country the spirits of free enterprise and free action were neither dead nor mutually exclusive. Many labor elements kept their freedom of action and bargaining even during strikes. And the worker was shrewd in appealing to public opinion. There is a certain irony in realizing that small-town America, supposedly alien and antagonistic toward city ways, remained a stronghold of freedom for the worker seeking economic and social rights.

But perhaps this is not so strange after all, for pre-industrial America, whatever its narrowness and faults, had always preached personal freedom. The city, whose very impersonality would make it a kind of frontier of anonymity, often practiced personal restriction and the law of the economic and social jungle. As industrialism triumphed, the businessman's powers increased, yet he was often hindered—and always suspect—in vast areas of the nation which cheered his efforts toward wealth even while condemning his methods.[77]

Facile generalizations are easy to make and not always sound, but surely the evidence warrants a new view of labor in the Gilded Age. The standard stereotypes and textbook clichés about its impotence and division before the iron hand of oppressive capitalism do not quite fit the facts. Its story is far different when surveyed in depth, carrying in it overtones of great complexity. And even in an age often marked by lust for power, men did not abandon old and honored concepts of human dignity and worth.

GEOFFREY BLODGETT

❧ 4 ❧

Reform Thought and the
Genteel Tradition

THE GILDED AGE was a trying time for gentlemen of reformist persuasion. By background and expectation they were prepared to take an active part in public affairs. They thought their talents were relevant to the task of creating an orderly national environment, yet few generations of reformers had greater trouble establishing a satisfactory connection with the processes of government. They experienced enormous difficulty in communicating with fellow Americans who listened to other voices. By the end of the century their brand of genteel liberalism had lost its meaning, and gave way to a fresh and bolder ideology.

The origins of modern liberalism are commonly located in the massive social turmoil of the 1890's, which called into question the governing assumptions of the older liberal tradition. The intellectual rebellion of the nineties still echoes in the pages of scholarship devoted to the Gilded Age. In the process of identifying and elaborating the terms of the rebels' quarrel with their elders, historians have shattered the claim of the earlier generation on modern sympathies.[1]

The difference between the two sorts of liberals was clear. The nineteenth-century variety clung doggedly to Adam Smith's anti-mercantilist message; the modern liberal came to accept a mixed economy and the welfare state. Nineteenth-century liberals imagined their thoughts were guided by the cosmic verities of natural law. Their successors celebrated instead the ethic of pragmatic calculation. Careful social relativism replaced the sweeping commands of immutable moral authority. Where once the liberal reformer tried to elevate politics beyond the reach of common ignorance, the modern liberal sought to meet the demands of a

55

clamoring swarm of rival interest groups. American pluralism, the nemesis of the liberal reformer of the Gilded Age, became respectable. Earlier liberals responded to the cues of a narrow transatlantic, Anglo-American intellectual community, whereas the modern liberal assumed the lonely task of shaping American autonomy in a global setting. The liberal of the last century was comfortably trapped in an almost fatalistic faith in automatic human progress. Today's reformer appreciates the impact of human decisions on social change, and knows that his choices can foster both progress and disintegration.

From his risky perch in the 1970's the liberal might well regard his cloistered intellectual ancestor of the 1870's with lofty condescension. The well-buttoned reformer of that day, constrained by a fund of social thought which provided few clues to current popular desires, hardly matched the era's mood. Contemporary politicians perceived his marginal grip on public life, regarded him as a nuisance, and in a notable bipartisan effort tried to drive him out of sight with a barrage of ridicule questioning his political virility. In a roistering, muscular age which vaunted rugged manliness, the reformers' insistence on propriety stamped them as the "third sex" of American politics. Party spokesmen dismissed them as "political hermaphrodites," "eunuchs," "man-milliners," and "miss-Nancys." The smirking phrases sustained a vicious insult: the liberal reformers became the gelded men of the Gilded Age.[2]

Alienation from the party system accounted in large measure for these recurring images of sexual oddity in the indictment against them. Their quest for civil service reform, which threatened traditional procedures for rewarding party loyalty, provoked a savage anti-intellectualism among their critics. Diffidence in mixing with professional politicians, a bleak record in contesting for office themselves, the tendency in times of political stress to cluster on the fringe of the party arena in search of group morale—all this gave currency to the hostile epithets employed against them.[3]

This poor reputation was not simply a function of partisan abuse. Men sympathetic to their views, and even some reformers, used a vocabulary of fraternal self-criticism remarkably similar to that of opponents, and only slightly diminished in its intensity of rebuke. John Murray Forbes, the Boston capitalist who befriended many a reformist cause, once chided Harvard Professor Charles Eliot Norton for "criticizing the out of door men who are trying to meet the practical issues as they arise," adding, "I forgive you the *coolness* which grows out of your retirement among the classic groves of Cambridge!" Henry Adams relished Senator Timothy Howe's characterization of him as a begonia, and toyed over the metaphor with loving irony. As a begonia, he had reason to feel conspicuous, useless, thirsty, and fading. Carl Schurz angrily denounced the critics of reform virility as "contemptible triflers," but acknowledged privately that his more skittish colleagues often recoiled "from the actual battle after having made all sorts of strategic movements to bring it on." The liberals were not blind to the limits of their effectiveness.[4]

The charge of political inadequacy revealed a circumstance among them which ran deeper than the fact of party isolation. Their quest for national influence above the play of conventional politics was not unusual. The American party system has repeatedly inspired an ethic of political independence among sensitive and educated men.[5] Yet later reformers achieved much greater success in challenging established political mores, and rarely experienced the vituperation that pelted these patrician reformers. The peculiar difficulties of these gentlemen involved more than the prickly style of reformist righteousness. Their problems sprang from the distinctive structural conditions of the society they tried to influence. They sought a national, cosmopolitan function in a social matrix which remained profoundly local in the roots of its organization. This was the crucial fact behind their isolation.[6]

Henry Adams had spoken for them while the Civil War still raged. "We want a national set of young men like ourselves or better," he wrote home from London, "to start new influences not only in politics, but in literature, in law, in society, and throughout the whole social organism of the country—a national school of our own generation." Adams shared a gathering desire among northern intellectuals for an institutional network of trained intelligence to control the course of postwar national development. His European perspective enabled him to forecast the difficulties involved. The random geographical dispersal of American cultural facilities, in contrast with the highly centralized arrangements of England and France, separated and insulated like-minded intellectuals from one another. Fragmentation of purpose among them was a fact of long standing. Adams doubted whether his native land could support a national elite.[7]

After the war a small band of cosmopolitan Americans, scattered across the continent from Boston to Chicago, tried to accomplish what Adams yearned for. The fate of the effort illuminated the problems of patrician reform. About a dozen men formed the core of this potential elite. They included Adams and his brother Charles; Norton; Schurz; the economists Edward Atkinson and David A. Wells; the lawyer-politician, Jacob D. Cox; the writer and landscape architect, Frederick

Law Olmsted; and journalists Samuel Bowles, George W. Curtis, Edwin L. Godkin, and Horace White. These men ran an interlocking directorate of liberal intelligence. Though no one of them was intimately acquainted with all the rest, the fabric of personal friendship among them was extensive. They sensed a collective identity, and the cross-lacing patterns of their private correspondence knit them together as a group.

Their daily occupations scarcely measured the range of their competence or the broad horizon of their interests and expectations. Averaging thirty-six years of age in 1865 (Olmsted at forty-three was the oldest and Henry Adams at twenty-seven the youngest), they were gentlemen of eclectic professional ability. Many of them (including Bowles, Curtis, Norton, Olmsted, and Schurz) had achieved substantial distinction in the prewar years. The ease with which they moved from one career to another validated their assumption of catholic intellectual prowess sprawling across lines of professional specialization. Law, teaching, writing, publishing, and public service seemed potentially within their grasp. If they radiated an air of political authority which seemed excessive to the practitioners of that craft, they claimed scarcely less for literature, architecture, diplomacy, and warfare. Their expertise was seamless and multi-competent. Their span of public interests matched the dimensions of the national community they wanted to instruct.

Geographical mobility was another common trait. The peripatetic habits of Carl Schurz were extreme, but also symptomatic. Arriving from Europe at the age of twenty-three, Schurz spent three years in Philadelphia and six in Wisconsin before assuming a diplomatic mission to Madrid and then a command in the Union Army. In 1866 he moved to Detroit; a year later he left for St. Louis. From 1869 to 1881 he lived mostly in Washington, as senator and Cabinet officer. Then he moved to New York City, remaining there despite the constant lure of Boston. Throughout his career Schurz spent long months on the lyceum circuit. Trains, hotel rooms, and hired lodgings were the habitat of this homeless man for years on end. Yet alone among his fellow reformers, Schurz enjoyed a national political constituency. The far-flung German-American voting community was the essential base of his influence in the Republican Party.

Olmsted's career as a sculptor of landscape also kept him moving. When he began work on Central Park he lived on Staten Island. He dropped his labors to serve with the U.S. Sanitary Commission in the war; left for California in 1863; returned to Manhattan in 1865; remained there through the 1870's; then moved to suburban Boston. Meanwhile he pursued his craft at sites scattered from Newport to Yosemite.

Henry Adams migrated endlessly to and from Washington. Jacob Cox, originally a New Yorker, grounded himself in Ohio politics in the 1860's and moved from the governorship to a Cabinet post. But after that his residence first in Cincinnati, then in Toledo, and again in Cincinnati, enforced a declining interest in public office. Godkin spent most of his career in and around New York City after his arrival from England in 1856, but his affection for the city was always controllable. Though he never landed the university post he dreamed of, he lived in Cambridge for a while in the 1870's. The transplanted New Englander Horace White spent most of the postwar decade in Chicago editing the *Tribune,* and then moved to New York in 1881 to help Godkin and Schurz run the *Evening Post.*

Others stayed in one place after the war, maintaining varying degrees of contact with local life. Bowles spent a lifetime in Springfield, Massachusetts, trying to make the *Springfield Republican* "a first class paper in a fourth class town." [8] Atkinson remained a Boston man, participating intermittently in the local affairs of suburban Brookline. Norton's life began and closed at Shady Hill in Cambridge, but he shunned the city enclosing his family estate, and escaped each summer to the tiny town of Ashfield in the Berkshire foothills. Curtis settled on Staten Island in the 1850's, serving after 1863 as a somewhat ornamental editor of *Harper's Weekly* and as a decidedly ornamental member of the New York Republican party. He joined Norton in pastoral retreat at Ashfield each summer. Wells moved from Washington to Norwich, Connecticut, in 1870. There he tried repeatedly to gain a political foothold in the local congressional district but never succeeded. Only Charles Francis Adams achieved a sense of continuing control over the politics of his home city. From the Adams family race-place at Quincy, Massachusetts, he worked the antique machinery of the Quincy town meeting with great personal satisfaction until 1887, when a local political upheaval broke his influence and sent him to a quieter Boston suburb.[9]

Their primary professional and political preoccupations organized the lives of these men on a tier transcending the prosaic fact of local isolation. Their roots were shallow and easily snapped; their sense of "place" was non-geographic. Their knowledge of the population around them was largely vicarious—and carefully filtered. They selected friendships with precision and did not mix kindly with strangers. Their neighborhood was national.

One summer shortly after the war, the Godkin and Olmsted families traveled through the White Mountains of New Hampshire. The crowd of ordinary vacationers who thronged the hills irked both men. Godkin par-

ticularly resented being herded about in carriages from vista to vista
within earshot of the "inane conversation" of "pork packers, shoe dealers, stock 'operators,' and gentlemen in the dry goods line"—worthy
folk whose banal talk oppressed him. Norton chided his friend for impa-
tience with American manners, and promised that in another hundred
years the situation would improve. Godkin then jovially suggested that in
another hundred years the problem would be wholly solved: "We shall
fly about through the hills by ourselves, and flap our wings over the
densely packed wagons and stages with disdain." [10]

The cosmopolitan gentry cherished the vision of a good society whose
architecture would support men like themselves in functional roles well
above the crowd. This model social structure would somehow enforce
order, hierarchy, deference, and stability amid accelerating change. Their
faith in the democratic experiment was more contingent on these preferences than they cared to admit. Some were openly nostalgic for a pre-
Jacksonian society of recognized ranks and gradations. Others knew the
past was beyond recapture. "I am apt to think," Curtis once mused,
". . . that the charm of those 'rare old days' is mainly in our imaginations.
The golden age is always a long way behind us." [11]

Most of them believed in the 1860's that American society was still
responsive to the ministry of an active and resourceful elite like themselves. At times the population seemed to shift and sprawl beyond control, and they wondered how well Americans understood the virtues of
graduated change. A social structure which allowed an ordinary man to
fulfill himself by surmounting his origins and denying his "place" was ad-
mittedly precarious for those on top. Nevertheless, they admired the raw,
muscular, self-improving strength of the common American. It was the
genius of the country's porous social arrangements to reward the efforts
of the obscure and unlettered. Mobility at the bottom of society created
problems, but it oriented people at the bottom toward the top, and kept
them accessible to instruction from above. The prewar increase in the
numbers of unassimilated foreign immigrants, floating detached and
beyond reach in the larger cities, was worrisome. But in the 1860's the
immigrant was not a priority concern.

The gentry disliked the rich more than they feared the poor. They
valued demonstrated personal character rather than accumulated wealth
as the correct credential of social authority. They distrusted the narrow
mercenary spirit of the freshly rich class of merchants thrusting up in
New York and western cities. The absence of social grace among the
new rich betrayed their single-minded pursuit of the dollar. Their abrasive
behavior was especially unpleasant because they presumed so much on

recent success, and often claimed an instant power in public affairs. Headstrong, unpolished, and unreflective, they exhibited a bold authority in politics which was profoundly unsettling. Their insistent flaunting of money and showy wastefulness before common folk made them, Olmsted believed, "the one really dangerous class of a republic." [12]

Searching for standards to measure these new men of wealth, the gentry turned to the antebellum Boston merchant prince. "Boston is the only place in America where wealth and the knowledge of how to use it are apt to coincide," Godkin wrote in 1871. The decorum, social restraint, and sober personal responsibility luminous in the character of men like Peter Chardon Brooks provided an awesome model for mixing money and grace. The reform enthusiasms of John Murray Forbes suggested the capacity of well-bred millionaires for judicious exercise of political power. Hopefully, such examples would remain viable in the postwar era.[13]

The gentry faced the new day with guarded optimism. A ramshackle social structure needed regirding; the ethic of responsibility had to be reasserted in business and politics; the masses required constant prompting. These tasks were large but not hopeless. Olmsted, who had earned a solid reputation as a social critic on the strength of his observations on the antebellum South, surveyed the problems of his own society with confidence:

> Improvement has got to come slowly through a general improvement of society. As the rich men become somewhat weaned from excessive business excitements and more general in their interests, more comprehensive in their intelligence and more unselfishly patriotic, and as the poor become more stable, become more frequently house-owners or lease holders and less frequently tenement lodgers, as rents are reduced and they live in a more civilized way, as the schools are improved substantially and the proportion of foreign born population is reduced . . . and a reputable press caters to the real literary wants of the working class, your government will improve.[14]

Faith in the drift of society toward equilibrium was common among his friends. They shared a good opinion of the staying power which Northern democracy demonstrated in the war. They were determined to guide that power with their wisdom.

Events quickly challenged the optimism of these men about the course of American social change. They offered talents to a population which neither desired nor acknowledged the need for their help. Its fluid nature precluded direction by any cosmopolitan group lacking local economic or political authority. They were an elite with neither an organized base nor an organized audience. The conditions of national institutional disarray they hoped to remedy were precisely the conditions which would frustrate their efforts.

The argument over slavery had obscured the full dimensions of their plight. That quarrel in most cases inspired their interest in national politics. Atkinson, Bowles, Cox, Curtis, Olmsted, Schurz, and White had all plunged vigorously into the free-soil, antislavery cause of the 1850's, and instinctively joined the new Republican party. They felt that the purpose of politics, like the purpose of the party, was national, goal-oriented, and moral. The sectional crisis pulled political thoughts away from the mundane social realities of northern society; a consuming animus against southern slavery suspended their interest in critical scrutiny of structural conditions nearer at hand—and while their attention was averted, the velocity of local change at home outstripped any capacity for comprehension. The new political society to which they returned in the mid-1860's had moved beyond the range of their control.

In retrospect, the disorganized and atomistic state of antebellum northern society is manifest. Its political institutions suffered with colleges, churches, banks, and businesses from a common malaise of "excess democracy." [15] The gentry's discovery of these conditions was belated but scarcely imperceptive. During the quarter-century preceding the war, while national leaders grappled helplessly with problems of continental strife, local politicians had transformed community political life throughout the urban North. Street-corner politics generated a new class of local leadership to man the scaffolding of the two-party system. In cities ranging in size from New Haven to New York and Philadelphia, older patrician leadership gave way to local merchants, small manufacturers, and professional politicians. The new breed built their power from the ground up out of strategic friendships, close involvement in local community organizations, business clubs, volunteer fire brigades and militia companies, and election to municipal boards and councils. They cut their teeth on the most urgent preoccupations of their constituents: public schooling, tax rates, water supply, ethnic and religious animosity. They were self-trained, popular specialists in the new craft of urban government. Through caucus control, systematic canvassing of ward voters, and partisan management of local newspapers, they linked their power to statewide party organizations. Access to mayoralties, congressional seats, and governorships was increasingly contingent on the support of local political managers. In the party system's federated structure, density of organization at the bottom tiers far exceeded that of national political life. The process of selecting leaders, communicating critical decisions, and enforcing party discipline remained highly localized.[16]

The wildfire sweep of the Republican party across the North in the late 1850's opened abundant opportunities for bright, adaptable young men skilled in the new politics. The troubled fortunes of the Democratic party often accelerated their rapid rise from community to regional influence. By 1865 the Republican party had achieved most of its ideological goals announced in the 1850's. Meanwhile, its working personnel had established managerial authority in city, state, and congressional politics throughout the North.[17]

The dismal implications of this quiet political revolution unfolded only gradually for the gentry. The war's concussion left them convinced not so much of Republican virtue as of Democratic depravity, and they were not immune to the emotions of the bloody shirt. Wartime memories, and the raucous local character of the Democratic party in the Northeast, enforced an abnormal Republican identity which survived among them into the 1880's.

But the meaning of being a Republican had changed so radically that the label was meager satisfaction. The entrenchment of professional party managers completed the gentry's local isolation. As the wealthy publisher-scholar Henry C. Lea reported to Norton from Philadelphia, the grip of local municipal Republican politicians denied the chance for Republicans of his sort to influence community decisions. The party had "obtained so firm a hold of the city government here that spoliation and corruption are almost as unblushing as in New York." Lea intended to organize a third force, independent of ward managers in both parties, to rout the "cliques" and "wirepullers" promptly: "It seems to me that it ought to be an easy thing for the better elements of society to associate together and rescue politics from the degradation which in our large cities is becoming such an open scandal."

That was in 1866. Fourteen years later Lea was still trying, but his crisp confidence had disappeared. "I do not allow myself to anticipate any very decided measure of success," he told Norton in 1880, "possibly because we here live so completely under the domination of a perfectly organized and vigorously managed machine that one grows hopeless of any permanent change for the better." A fellow patrician confirmed the helplessness of the Philadelphia elite before the local managers: "these men have experience and command all the avenues to power, and every channel of communication with the heads of the government and the party is in their hands. All we want is a hearing." [18]

A pervading pattern of local isolation and ineffectiveness showed through the gentry's rhetoric of moral disapproval of the men who had usurped control. From Ohio, Cox complained of "the combination of loafers and roughs who usually have primary meetings to themselves in cities," and admitted in 1880 that ignorance of ward politics precluded his serving as a campaign organizer for Cincinnati. "I have been so much out of the city," he confessed, "that I know very few of the active men in the local circles." From Boston, reformers complained that the proliferation of city officeholders had deadened hopes for effective intervention by outsiders. "All real interest in municipal voting has died away," one wrote in 1885, "because the most strenuous efforts of conscientious people cannot affect more than the choice of some one or two officials, whose voice and character are obliterated by a great mass of others." [19]

As early as 1871 Godkin had suggested a remedy which later municipal reformers employed with considerable success: make city elections less frequent; reduce the number of elected officials; give them broad power and responsibility for city-wide administration. He got nowhere with it until the 1890's. "We are all occupied here with the latest attempt to purify the City government by giving the Mayor more power," he wrote from New York in 1884. "I have been advocating it warmly, but it is about the twenty-fifth cure for city mismanagement which I have advocated since I came to the United States, and [I] am consequently not much excited about it." [20]

From the 1860's to the 1890's city government remained impervious to correction by the gentry. Cosmopolitan reformers lacked the organizational resources and technical skill to fashion instruments of overarching, metropolitan control against the local interests of skilled professionals rooted in the wards. The swift spread of electric transit and communication facilities in the late 1880's helped inspire the first real surge of metropolitan planning. Meanwhile reformers were reduced to occasional rebellions from the periphery of city politics, membership on city park commissions, "scientific" charity work, friendly visiting committees to the urban poor, and a steady sputter of outrage over their own isolation.[21]

The play of national politics yielded still less satisfaction. To cosmopolitans whose thoughts gravitated to Washington in the mid-1860's, the triumph of the Union seemed a vital chance to impose the discipline of trained intelligence on postwar issues. The need for discipline was urgent. While the war largely resolved the moral issues around which Republican passions crystallized in the 1850's, it unexpectedly swelled the authority and responsibilities of the federal arm. The war also fostered a decisive return, under Republican auspices, to whiggish policies of neo-mercantilism which now required careful supervision and adjustment. And the quality of public officials being sent to Washington by state and local party organizations to grapple with these new tasks certainly gave pause. For all their swagger they seemed poorly fitted to cope with delicate problems of southern reconstruction, western development, and eastern commercial stability.

What seemed like an abrupt convergence of the grass-roots revolution in political leadership with the revolution of priorities in national politics deeply disturbed the cosmopoltan elite. Congress faced a critical new era innocent of expertise or relevant knowledge of the past. "The class from which our public men are drawn," Godkin lamented, "are perhaps less given to study or reflection than any other in the community. They are generally men of quick sympathies, fond of crowds, fond of moving audiences, and to whom readiness of tongue is the highest of gifts." Their training in complex economic affairs would come, if ever, only through hard public experience. "And experience in this case may be awfully costly." Curtis felt similar pain at the "want of education, of actual knowledge of the course and conduct of other people and times in similar circumstances, among our legislators and leaders of opinion." Cox thought radical reconstructionists wanted to perpetuate the war spirit to avoid thorny fiscal issues. "Demagogues who hope to rule the country by the passions war has engendered don't want a finality," he wrote. "The return to questions of economy and finance would expose their ignorance too soon." He hoped an early end to Reconstruction would clear the air and fill Congress with "men who would rival Huskisson, Canning and Peel" in economic statesmanship. The alternative was continued disorder in the Republic's affairs: "Men's minds become familiar with revolutionary thoughts when they do not see established laws regulating every part of their concerns." [22]

The triumph of settled statesmanship in Washington was a long way off. The almost comic failure of Boston cosmopolitans to remove the burly radical Ben Butler from Congress in 1868 exposed the major difficulty. Edward Atkinson helped organize the challenge by sending that scion of the Massachusetts gentry, Richard Henry Dana, Jr., to oppose Butler. Henry Adams noted the risks involved. If Butler beat Dana he would return to Washington with the scalps of Boston's most respectable gentlemen. "You must crush him now," Adams told Atkinson, "or he will grind your faces in the dirt." The misgivings were confirmed. Butler's popularity with the shoemakers of Lynn and the clamoring support of the city's mayor, police, and firemen let him flick poor Dana aside. Atkinson shrugged off the defeat, but Dana's failure verified for Adams a deepening pessimism about politics. "You in Massachusetts are not in the Union," he lectured Atkinson. "Butler is the only man who understands his countrymen and even he does not quite represent the dishonesty of our system. The more I study its working, the more dread I feel at the future." Butler's ensuing career traded heavily on the opposition of the Boston gentry, confirming Adams' gloom. As Harvard's President Charles Eliot noted ruefully when Butler won the Massachusetts governorship in 1882, "The educated classes have always been apt to grease the wheels of demagogues when they meant to upset their chariots." [23]

The Grant years vindicated Adams' doubts about the wisdom of challenging politicians at the local ballot box. They also snuffed out the elitist dream of controlling national decisions from behind the scenes in Washington. In the late 1860's, cosmopolitans thought this tactic was succeeding. Atkinson had the ear of men in the Treasury Department. Wells was appointed Special Commissioner of the Revenue and, at Atkinson's urging, began to examine the tariff. Wells brought in the able young Francis A. Walker to manage the Bureau of Statistics; Cox arrived to become Grant's Secretary of the Interior; Schurz returned as senator from Missouri; Godkin and Bowles visited periodically on journalistic missions. From his rooms on G Street, lobbying quietly for selected goals on Capitol Hill, Adams nursed a momentary illusion that he touched the sources of power and felt response. It quickly passed. Before Grant's first term ended the cosmopolitans had been put to rout. Wells's office was eliminated; Walker took a post at Yale; Cox was sacked and returned to Ohio; Adams was teaching history at Harvard. Curtis, more stubbornly loyal to Grant than the rest, graced the administration as civil service commissioner for a while, but departed in disgust in 1873. Two years later, having battled Grant and his party to the point of open rebellion, Schurz lost his seat in the Senate. The exodus was complete.

As Grant's crowd spurned reformers, the gentry lost enthusiasm for positive government through leaders like Grant. Expectancy gave way to chagrin at the opaque and oddly unpredictable process of decision-making in Washington. Reformers laced talk of congressional misman-agement with expressions of growing anxiety over the excesses of arbit-rary, "personal" government. "If we are to have the dogma of infallibility set up in this country I prefer the Pope," Horace White commented to Schurz, "because he is neither ignorant nor corrupt." Talk of corruption in Washington was not misplaced, as Grant's regime soon proved. But the thrust of the reformers' indictment aimed mainly at the capriciousness of unrestrained personal power, not personal dishonesty. Centralization of political responsibilities in Washington dramatized the need for reliable structures of public procedure. The institutions of power were inadequate to the uses of power. Henry Adams defined the problem with artistic hyperbole in 1871. "I was at Washington last week and found anarchy ruling our nation," he told Norton. "I don't know who has power or is responsible, but whoever it is, I cannot find him, and no one confesses to more knowledge." The very inaccessibility of the decision-making process plagued reformers' efforts to comprehend what went wrong. They could never quite decide whether over-centralized authority or ignorant mismanagement was the worse evil. In some combination, however, these blights spoiled their faith in federal authority and verified the need to contain it.[24]

The gentry had never defined the creative functions of government very generously. Like the great majority of their contemporaries, including leaders of both parties, the judiciary, and business spokesmen, they held that Washington should play a marginal role in the lives of ordinary Americans. They differed from the majority in doubting the capacity of elected politicians to exercise power equitably through party government. That skepticism deepened sharply in the decade after the war. For the rest of the century they trumpeted a fervent desire to reduce the margin of government to a thin edge.

This prophylactic approach to power was as much the result of specific political experience as any youthful indoctrination in abstract theories of laissez faire. The preference for minimal government did not spring full-blown from textbook acquaintance with the natural laws of classical economics or Herbert Spencer's *Social Statics*. The process of conversion was more subtle. If the wisdom of Adam Smith and Spencer seemed increasingly relevant to liberal reformers, the course of postwar American politics made it so.[25]

Wells's experience in Washington illustrated the point. Originally a disciple of the Philadelphia protectionist Henry C. Carey, he approached the revenue question believing in the clear utility of a tariff barrier for American industry. Dismay at the tactics of protectionist congressmen triggered his turn toward free trade. "I have changed my ideas respecting tariffs and protection very much since I came to Washington," he confessed to Atkinson in 1866, "and am coming over to the ground you occupy. I am utterly disgusted with the rapacity and selfishness which I have seen displayed by Penn[sylvania] people and some from other sections on this subject." A few months later he added, "I get so despondent at times in view of the manner in which legislation is conducted, that I

feel as though it was no use, and that I had better retire." When protectionists dashed his dream of becoming Secretary of the Treasury, Wells
left Washington, abandoned the Republican party, and became a political
pariah in the 1870's. Isolation released his bent for theory. Preference for
low tariffs and sound money grew into rounded dogma. Meanwhile he
yearned to return with his friends and manage the national economy:
"Oh, if some half dozen of us had the absolute control of the finances in
one year we could put new life into the whole country." [26]

The reformers' ejection from policy-making had interesting effects on
group morale. Discouragement and frustration over specific evidence of
their exclusion dogged them constantly. Yet freedom from the prosaic
responsibilities of office allowed their imaginations to sweep the horizon
of abstract possibilities. Their vocabulary was both imperious and plain-
tive as they surveyed an ideal world uncluttered by the work of politicians. Surely they possessed the formulas to make the ideal a reality. "I
tell you I feel like Peter the Hermit," Wells insisted once to James A.
Garfield, "as if I was called to preach the gospel of a financial crusade
and regeneration, and as if nothing could stand against me." From Germany, where he summered in 1883, Atkinson reported a similar surge of
certainty: ". . . under all this sight-seeing an undercurrent of thought has
been working and I could state our case more clearly and with more
force than ever before. . . . Good gracious what a field! I could hold the
biggest audience so that a pin dropped would be heard—but it may not
be." [27]

Meandering congressional tariff and currency policy only strengthened their faith in classical theory. "We shall have free trade and a specie
currency before long," Bowles consoled Wells in 1876, "and after they
are secured Congress will recognize them by statute. How slow is statute
law; how sure is natural law!" But Wells and Atkinson were more impatient; arbitrary congressional fiscal policy was thwarting national
prosperity. "This country is rolling in wealth at the present time but welfare does not ensue," Atkinson fumed. "Why? Because bad laws are making knaves faster than preachers can make saints." Charles Francis
Adams, whose postwar career involved him deeply in practical problems
of rail regulation, shared this belief in the higher truth of theory. "At a
mighty interval and with unequal steps we are the followers of Copernicus
and Galileo and Bacon and Newton and Adam Smith and Bentham," he
informed Wells. "How does it concern us that the mass—the mighty
majority—of our fellow voters are ignorant and stupid and selfish and
short-sighted? That's the practical statesman's affair. . . . Don't you talk
to me of popular acceptance. The moment you and I begin on that we are
lost." [28]

Meanwhile, earthbound politicians in Washington struggled with the grimy chores of year-to-year fiscal management. The messiness of the performance seemed ever more appalling to reformers. A mounting federal surplus opened new fields for political misconduct. By the mid-1880's the condition of public extravagance seemed beyond remedy:

> Schemes for depleting the Treasury, by dividing it among the states, by expending it in wild projects of useless or premature "improvements," by usurping the duties of the states or cities, by building ships that cannot sail, by subsidizing steamers to carry ballast to foreign ports, or finally, by opening the Treasury to a general scramble, in which every man may carry off a dollar or two, to console him for having been taxed ten dollars, are constantly before Congress, and often succeed. The general degradation of the public conscience which such projects engender is more to be deplored than even the waste and loss which they cause to the public wealth.[29]

The apparently mindless game of grab and barter suggested that congressional leaders also suffered from a divorce of theory and practice. Lacking a broad programmatic rationale for national economic development, they relied increasingly on prowess in party management to alleviate their intellectual isolation. Solutions to most economic issues depended on the mastery of shifting configurations among rival factions. These solutions rarely accorded with the prescriptive wisdom of current economic orthodoxy. While the most respectable theories of the day called for minimal public interference in the private economy, contemporary political reality saw the federal government committed to a bewildering variety of promotional subsidies, tariff protections, pensions and special services. A chasm of misunderstanding had opened between doctrinal texts and legislative action. To those like the reformist gentry whose minds accepted the grooves of theory, the sprawling deviations of congressional policy plainly spelled the triumph of corruption over principle. To politicians grappling with the next item on an endless agenda, the reformers' critique seemed like the fastidious carping of silly academic theoreticians. The opposing images of "corrupt politician" and "theorist" which cropped up repeatedly in the angry rhetoric of the 1870's and 1880's were not idle invective. They betrayed a central dilemma of the age, the polar isolation of political reality and formal economic thought. The most powerful developing economy in the world lurched toward maturity without a theory to guide the national politicians who promoted it.

Nothing revealed the gentry's alienation from prevailing political practice more vividly than their high regard for Godkin's *Nation*. Launched in New York in 1865, the *Nation* remained for the rest of the century the elite's primary public medium of group communication and morale. It served as a resonating echo chamber for cosmopolitan thoughts and tastes. While its subscription list always remained small, it connected widely scattered readers to a national community of thought. Hundreds of isolated gentlemen across the country lit their pipes at the end of a busy week to receive Godkin's Friday pronouncements in the mail. "The *Nation* is a weekly comfort and satisfaction," Norton told Godkin. "I always read it with that sort of warm interest with which one reads the letter of a friend. It seems like a personal message from you to me; as if printed for my sake." William James's oft-quoted estimate of Godkin, in a gentle letter to his widow in 1902, called him the "towering influence in all thought concerning public affairs" for the postwar generation.[30]

The tribute was overly generous. Godkin was less a national leader of public opinion than the intellectual strategist of the gentry's reluctant withdrawal from practical politics. His influence was perhaps more precisely captured by the civil service reformer Silas Burt, who thanked Godkin in 1899 for his clarity in reporting "the progressive political and civic degeneracy you have observed in this country since you made it your home." Godkin's knack for lacerating political criticism was clear, and readers found peculiar solace in his surveys of Americal degeneracy. His frankly patrician and anti-mercantilist liberalism endowed the critique with a splendid intellectual authority. While English origins and tastes made Godkin a lonely and rootless American, they nicely legitimized his mordant dissection of American mores.[31]

But this was not the *Nation*'s original purpose. The title caught Godkin's mission at the outset: like Henry Adams he wanted to create a cohesive force of *national* opinion. The idea of a new journal for this purpose surfaced slowly during the Civil War. Charles Francis Adams had suggested it to Olmsted as early as 1861. Olmsted took it up with his friend Godkin in the summer of 1863, shortly before the battle of Gettysburg, and the two men prepared a brochure to spell out their concern.

They perceived an alarming threat to national unity in the spread of states rights views and the derogation of popular institutions of national power. These pernicious ideas were not confined to the South. They pleased many northern businessmen. The disintegration of the Union was being rationalized in precisely the terms used to oppose the adoption of the Constitution eighty years before. "The dangers of concentrated power . . . are painted in frightful colors—the overwhelming importance of local interests is energetically and insidiously preached." Some even advocated separating the city from the state to strengthen local politicians. The hour had come to oppose these views. The nation faced postwar problems too vast for small, partisan minds. "It is a necessity of the country that studious men should take hold of public affairs, and be felt as a power; it is important that they should come closer and more constantly together—should be organized and possess means which they have not hitherto had of making themselves heard and their influence felt." On this ground Olmsted and Godkin sought support for their journal.[32]

The purpose narrowly survived Godkin's first months as editor. Dismay among stockholders and readers over his coolness toward abolitionist radicals and his ambiguous tariff views threatened an early end to the project. Atkinson, one of the Boston backers, decided Godkin had sold out to the protectionists and tried to remove him as editor. Norton, a prolific contributor to the *Nation*'s columns, and Olmsted, who helped edit the paper in the late 1860's, remained Godkin's sturdiest supporters. Godkin tried to take a philosophic view of his troubles. The effort to mobilize opinion on a national plane exposed the depth and variety of parochial bias among intelligent men. He would try to give them a first-class journal, whatever their views. "We have no party backing as we aim to be an independent paper," he noted. "Radicals, conservatives, free traders, protectionists, infidels and evangelicals have all some reason for finding fault with us." [33]

As the years passed, Godkin and his audience aligned their basic assumptions, though succeeding presidential campaigns provoked sharp dispute over tactics. Meanwhile Godkin's ability to identify positive national goals and programs to rally his friends diminished. Concern for the plight of freed blacks, at no time uppermost in his mind, soon disappeared. The journal quickly took on a low-tariff cast as he vented anti-mercantilist preferences. An early, tentative sympathy for worker's co-operatives gave way to hostility toward the aims and tactics of organized labor. Politicians from Tammany Hall to the White House rarely gained anything but his cold mistrust. Civil service reform was almost the only national cause to enjoy his militant approval. By the 1870's, Godkin's function as a leader of elite opinion had narrowed to defining the proper boundaries of reform enthusiasm. His journal, in Bowles' phrase, had become a "moral policeman"; Curtis called it "a sanitary element in our affairs." Godkin's bleak political conclusions did not always go down smoothly with his audience. Like the Social Darwinist essays of William

Graham Sumner, his views had an astringent, purging quality, calculated to rouse men from normal expediencies of thought and habit. Many readers could not bring themselves to share his harsher estimates of American impurity.[34]

When Godkin retired in 1899, President Eliot of Harvard praised him for the bubbles and windbags he had punctured, and duly noted the *Nation*'s sway among educated Americans. If Godkin's opinions were sometimes unconvincing, at least he forced people to study their reasons for disagreeing with him. Eliot's own careful reservations illuminated the meaning of the *Nation*'s career since 1865:

> I have sometimes been sorry for you and your immediate coadjutors, because you had no chance to work immediately and positively for the remedying of some of the evils you exposed. The habitual critic gets a darker or less cheerful view of the social and political state than one does who is actively engaged in efforts to improve that state.[35]

The *Nation* reflected the fate of the gentlemen who conceived it. They tried hard to make an imprint on the political system. Long after their rejection by the Grant administration they fought for party leverage, first among Republicans and, after 1884, among Democrats. The long campaign for civil service reform was a measure of their unabated concern to improve the federal bureaucracy. Yet they found few chances to affect the important decisions of their time. Oppressed by a sense of lost control, they lavished gloom on those in charge. The conviction that American democracy would suffer for rejecting them took on aspects of a self-justifying prophecy. Here Godkin's experience in the United States was emblematic: he made that prophecy his message. Like the Puritan jeremiads of seventeenth-century New England, his angry editorials called the country to account for thirty years of error, and so provided therapy for a small but important class of disappointed Americans. Godkin shared their disappointment. As a young man in the 1860's he had reached for something more.

Rebuffs in the party arena suggested the wisdom of building social cohesion and stability through work beyond the rim of formal politics. Some of the gentry, like Cox, followed the impulse of Eliot and others and turned to academic administration. The historical inquiry of the Adams brothers reflected a common urge to measure present confusion against the lessons of the past. Olmsted swung away from politics in disgust in the 1870's and returned to landscape architecture, a craft he transformed almost singlehandedly into a distinguished American profession. With obsessive, brooding passion he labored to organize the values of order, tranquility, and harmony against the ugly planlessness of urban America. His parklands, suburbs, campuses, and boulevards were quiet witness to the vision of a good society he shared with his friends.[36]

Others strove to develop a national fabric of quasi-reformist agencies, magazines, professional clubs, and public-affairs leagues, which might contain and guide the democratic impulse. The cosmopolitan journalism of Curtis' *Harper's Weekly,* and the more somber *North American Review* under Henry Adams' hand, shared this purpose with the *Nation.* The formation in 1865 of the American Social Science Association (the nursery of modern professional societies among social scientists) opened a chance, which the gentry avidly seized, to air the ethic of graduated change among educators and philanthropists. The ASSA, whose charter stressed the "responsibilities of the gifted and educated classes toward the weak, the witless, and the ignorant," was a profoundly conservative body, reacting against the utopian mood of antebellum social theory. As Whitelaw Reid observed, it was "in no way tainted with Free Loveism," and enjoyed a "large amount of College respectability." The gentry often found its meetings dull and cheerless, preferring more purposeful agencies like the American Free Trade League and the National Civil Service Reform League, two fairly effective reform lobbies. The founding of the Cosmos Club in Washington in 1878 provided the scientific friends of Henry Adams an intimate setting on LaFayette Square to help promote their solidarity and influence.[37]

The weaving of a broad associational network among like-minded men across the country consumed vast intellectual energy. It also paradoxically enforced a certain static, didactic quality in the cultivated thought of the 1870's. The infrequency of face-to-face meetings, the difficulties of regularizing collective views in an age of slow communication, the constant concern for status and good credentials, all lent a heavy tone to group proceedings. Men devoted long hours to reiterating basic assumptions, embroidering first principles, and appealing to mutually recognized authority. The repetition of old beliefs was endless, and the pace of change still defied men's understanding. Yet, for the politically isolated gentry, the network broadened the available audience. It created a national make-weight against the tough, tight organizations of the political specialists they confronted in party conventions. An editorial in the *Brooklyn Daily Eagle* in 1877 discerned this purpose among reformers "who from the journal, the review, the Social Science Congress and the pulpit as pedestals are continually addressing the people." The editorial went on to note that for reformers, conventions were occasions, not means. "In conventions, to be beaten is to them just as much of a

success as to win. They make their appeal to the country as a whole
and they calculate upon the effect of their views upon society rather
than on the mechanism of the party." [38]

In the 1880's a fresh crop of middle-class reformers decided this
was not enough. The age of forlorn protest and counterbalance was
passing. Evidence of restlessness was everywhere as new men challenged
settled habits and presumptions. The young recruits included a high
proportion of lawyers, clergy, and businessmen—professions poorly
represented among the gentry. In contrast with the older men, they were
characteristically committed to one job and one community. Cosmopolitan in view but rooted in their locale, they were more at home in the
new age of career specialization and impatient with the tactics of patrician isolation.

Their influence was visible in the sudden spread of the civil service
reform movement in the early 1880's among men who muttered at the
ineffective ways of the older "dilletanti." It was seen in the Mugwump
bolt from the Republican party in 1884, and more particularly in the
willingness of young Mugwumps to plunge into state and local Democratic politics. A concerted new interest in local community politics inspired civic reform clubs in major cities, beginning in Baltimore in 1885
and culminating in a National Municipal League in 1894. The new
ethic of the settlement house, appealing especially to young college
women, and of the Social Gospel among young Protestant clergy, roused
middle-class awareness of the city slum as human neighborhood. Such
diverse popular phenomena as the Single Tax cult and the Chautauqua
tent revealed a rash of eager social consciousness among Americans
previously uninvolved in associational activity.

Goals varied among the restless, but a distinctive new mood set
them off from the older cosmopolitans. They rejected the peculiar philosophic faith of the gentry that the ultimate end of an orderly universe
was spontaneous human harmony. Harsh labor troubles of the 1880's,
the appalling compaction of slum life in big cities, the new visibility of
difference between rich and poor, suggested that the normal result of un-
tended social change was cleavage and combat. The perception inspired
a remarkable appetite for unvarnished information about "conditions,"
contact and communication among rival interests, and candor in talking
out differences. Where the gentry sometimes treated serious intellectual
controversy as a symptom of moral disorder and defective personal
character, the young men of the 1880's thrived on debate and intellectual
variety. Their activist exhilaration was distinctive. They brought to organizational work a fresh mix of realism and enthusiasm, a willingness
to get involved, to use old machinery for new purposes, to join a party

and win an election, to accomplish practical results. "The great work of the present and future is not to justify ourselves, to free ourselves from unjust aspersion," a rebellious young Mugwump lawyer told Schurz after Cleveland's victory in 1884, "but to bring the first promise of this election to realization. Do you think this work can be done best by our standing outside as critics . . . ? I don't." A young Indiana civil service reformer castigated the ingrown, priggish tone of traditional reform tactics, and urged "the necessity of an active propaganda among the common people, and the absolute need of securing the cooperation of intelligent farmers, mechanics, and the like in this gospel work. We must no longer even seem to be an aristocratic body." [39]

None of this was wrenchingly radical. It urged a change in style, mood, and behavior. It anticipated only by faint promise the more fundamental break with nineteenth-century formalism which punctuated the 1890's. The gentry, for the most part, could live with it. They often welcomed it. As early as 1874, Bowles was running articles in the *Springfield Republican* advocating a new dispensation. "We have got to go through hay-seed, possibly ignorance, most likely inexperience, to light," he told Wells. "At any rate, the old must pass away and all things become new—through granges and young men's reform clubs and disgust, generally. Primary schools for political education are in order."

The gentry lauded the fresh vigor in the fight for old goals like civil service, tariff reform, and the frustration of James G. Blaine's presidential ambition. They happily lent prestige, rhetoric, and experience to the Mugwump bolt. They were even willing to hear out heretics among the new voices. Wells corresponded sympathetically for years with Henry George before rejecting the Single Tax. "I want all you want, *and more,*" George told him. "And it will be a long time before we get where you want to stop." Schurz, who ultimately broke with Godkin on the labor question, befriended the obscure immigrant socialist, Lawrence Gronlund, helped him find a job, and debated the merits of his socialist manifesto, *The Co-operative Commonwealth.* The older men stretched their powers of communication taut in an effort to comprehend new thoughts. [40]

The most provocative challenge broke out within the institutional setting they helped foster, as young, university-trained scholars began to question the cherished precepts of orthodox political economy. This jeopardized the inner sanctum of conventional wisdom. The leaders of the rebellion, Richard T. Ely and Simon Patten, both came from rural homes west of the Appalachians. They resisted the static preachments of professors, went abroad for graduate training, and returned excited by the expanse of German university thought. But their profession remained dominated, in Ely's words, by a "small clique of men" who "constituted themselves as its special guardians and . . . attempt to exercise a sort of terrorism over the intellect of the country."

To crack this monopoly, Ely and Patten launched the American Economic Association in 1885, open to all comers. Warm-blooded and pugnacious, Ely wanted to liberate his craft from sterile classicism and connect it to the pulsations of real life and the wants of real men. Patten, the more fertile theoretician of the two, challenged orthodoxy even more profoundly by stressing the need for regulated oversight of America's economic abundance. Both men squarely repudiated laissez faire. As their views took hold in the profession and the structure of outworn assumptions gave way, the champions of orthodoxy grew defensive and waspish, betraying psychic turmoil. They dismissed Patten's support of the protective tariff as a sell-out to the manufacturers and told him he was "wholly wrong." They called Ely a sentimentalist and warmed themselves over the *Nation*'s blazing reviews of his books. When Ely left Johns Hopkins for the University of Wisconsin, Godkin congratulated Hopkins' President Gilman on his departure. "Professors of Political Economy preaching their own philanthropic gospel as 'science' are among the most dangerous characters of our time," Godkin wrote, "and Ely was one of them." [41]

Once again the prophecy fulfilled itself: intellectual deviation brought public degeneracy in its wake. By 1896 Godkin proved to his own satisfaction that every labor and currency craze of the past decade, from the Chicago riots to the free silver campaign, had been promoted by "men of education," "ethical professors," and "instructed cranks." The crisis of the 1890's had reduced the gentry's prophet to shrill reaction. [42]

In their last years the gentry stared out at an America almost past recognition. Letters to surviving friends reeked of melancholy, self-indulgent pessimism. They gathered to talk ruefully of better days long ago, "like a lot of old crows holding an inquest over the relics of past times." [43] The artistry of their gloom seemed to confirm the ultimate eclipse of their relevance. But defeat spelled more than the passing of sapped men: it completed the rout of America's last generation of eclectic moral amateurs before the thrust of political and professional specialization. Moreover, acute problems of social dislocation still plagued the nation which had sloughed them off and transformed them into intellectual refugees. American society had yet to achieve the institutional order and cohesion which the gentry had identified as its sorest need. The elitist terms of the gentry's order were undesired and discarded. The search for more satisfying terms was far from over.

ARI HOOGENBOOM

⪎ 5 ⪍

Civil Service Reform and
Public Morality

THE REACTION OF AN AMERICAN HISTORIAN to the phrase "Gilded Age" is nearly as predictable as that of one of Pavlov's dogs to a bell. Thoroughly conditioned, the historian thinks of corruption. He will condemn (often while enjoying) Senator Roscoe Conkling's affair with Kate Chase Sprague, abruptly terminated when Senator Sprague ran Conkling off his property with a shotgun; the Reverend Henry Ward Beecher's success at seducing his lady parishioners that resulted in the most spectacular trial of the nineteenth century; or capitalist Jim Fisk's insane infatuation for Josic Mansfield that led to his murder on the steps of the Fifth Avenue Hotel. A notorious libertine, ravisher of railroads, and corrupter of governments, Fisk achieved immortality thanks largely to two reformers, Charles Francis Adams, Jr., and his brother Henry, who described in intimate detail Fisk's sordid relations with both the Erie Railroad and public officials.[1]

Ever since the Adams brothers wrote their essays, the immorality, especially the political immorality, of the Gilded Age has attracted historians. Using Fisk as an example, they insist that public and business morals matched private ones. On the municipal level there was New York's spectacularly corrupt Tweed ring, overshadowing the more modest activities of Philadelphia's gas ring and Washington's Boss Shepherd. State governments were also corrupt. The *Nation* reported in the spring of 1867 that votes of New York legislators were bought and sold like "meat in the market."[2] And corruption was not limited to the Northeast. Southern governments, badly tainted during Reconstruction, found the Bourbon restoration only a slight improvement. In the West, United

77

States Senator Samuel Clarke Pomeroy of Kansas failed of reelection in 1873 after allegedly attempting to buy a state senator's vote for $7,000.[3] And in the federal government itself, Oakes Ames bribed fellow congressmen with Credit Mobilier stock, the whisky ring of internal revenue agents and distillers defrauded the country, and the Star Route frauds cost the Post Office Department millions. In textbooks and lectures the Gilded Age consistently out-scandalizes any other age in our history.

These familiar misdoings, and others, account for the free association of corruption with the Gilded Age. But should the association be so free? Were these scandals typical? Are Jim Fisk and the Tweed ring full-blown symbols of an age or are they symptoms, traces of a disorder that was by no means general?[4] Was this age as corrupt as historians have implied, or was it a prim age whose scandals have been exaggerated by contrast? More basically, what is corruption?

If political corruption is the violation of duty for a consideration, usually monetary, many frequently cited examples of Gilded Age corruption are questionable. President Ulysses S. Grant's participation in Jay Gould's and Jim Fisk's scheme to corner the gold market, for instance was naive, not corrupt; ignorant, not immoral. The Salary Grab Act of 1873, while perhaps greedy, was not illegal. Indeed, salaries of high federal officials needed to be increased. John D. Sanborn's contract to collect delinquent taxes for a 50 percent fee was not an invention of Secretary of the Treasury William A. Richardson but a new application of the ancient moiety system. Far more significant than the collection of moieties during this period was the public reaction resulting in their elimination in 1874. The resentment aroused by the Sanborn contract should be cited as an example of growing administrative efficiency.

And if, like George Washington Plunkitt, one differentiates between honest and dishonest graft, he further reduces the ranks of the corrupt. Honest graft, that estimable Tammany Hall politician said, was the profit that flowed from advance inside information on future government action. Why not make a little money on real estate or paving blocks, if one could?[5] And while one usually does not speak of George Washington Plunkitt, Andrew W. Mellon, and George C. Humphrey in one breath, they are perhaps spiritual brothers, with Plunkitt exceeding the other two in candor if not in profits. Before rejecting Plunkitt's distinction between honest and dishonest graft, one should observe that twentieth-century conflicts of interest more than match nineteenth-century honest graft. The Gilded Age has lost some of its dubious distinction.

The typical historian has been too loose in using the term "corruption." He labels a politically partisan civil service corrupt rather than inefficient, and equates the spoils system with corruption when honest spoilsmen far outnumber dishonest ones. He pronounces Gilded Age politicians guilty of corruption for associating with corruptionists even while attacking guilt by association in his own day.

One apparent reason why the historian has exaggerated the corruption of the Gilded Age is his desire to enliven lectures and writings. All the world loves a scandal, and the historian is loath to abandon the pleasure of dispensing vicarious "sin." More basically, historians dislike the dominant forces in the Gilded Age. The historian is usually liberal, more often than not a Democrat. He is hostile to big business, an advocate of government regulation, strong executive leadership, and an expert civil service. The post–Civil War era stands for all the historian opposes. It was an era of Republicanism, big business power, ineffectual attempts at government regulation, weak executives, and an essentially nonprofessional civil service.

Another reason scholars have exaggerated corruption in this period is the bias of sources. The most articulate individuals in this age were its severest critics. Their enforced inactivity gave them both a cause and the time for writing, while their enemies managed conventions and built railroads. Reformers' letters and writings, their journals and newspapers, dominate footnotes with good reason. Take, for example, the *Nation* under the editorship of the hard-hitting reformer Edwin Lawrence Godkin. Outstanding contributors made the *Nation,* to quote James Bryce, "the best weekly not only in America but in the world." [6] When not quoting the *Nation,* the historian turns to George William Curtis' graceful editorials in *Harper's Weekly,* America's leading illustrated paper. For a quarter of a century Curtis was the most conspicuous civil service reformer in America. Among monthly magazines, both *Harper's* and the *Atlantic* reflected reformism, while the venerable old quarterly the *North American Review* was at times a reform organ. Reformers dominated newspaper sources such as the New York *Evening Post* and the younger *New York Times*—in fact, opposition to civil service reform by distinguished papers was almost limited to Whitelaw Reid's *New York Tribune.*

Finally, reformers are usually quotable. Even though Jim Fisk could coin a beautiful phrase, the area of his interests and the level of his perception limits application of his words. Contrast his broad humor with the acid wit of Henry Adams' superb and readily available letters and his autobiography, *The Education.* Enraptured with Adams' prose, readers accept his prejudices.

Reformers exaggerated inefficiency and corruption. A typical instance was the estimate in January, 1866, by President Johnson's Revenue Commission that the New York Custom House lost $12,000,000 to $25,000,000 annually. Six years later the Grant Civil Service Commission, under the leadership of George William Curtis, projected the earlier figures and estimated that one-fourth of the annual federal revenue was lost in collection. In the ensuing presidential campaign, liberal Republican Senator Lyman Trumbull, citing the commission's report, calculated that the corrupt Grant regime annually lost $95,830,986.22 of the nation's revenue. When an enraged Grant supporter protested and demanded to know the origin of these figures, the commission explained that its estimate was designed to provide the "most forcible illustration of the mischief of the system" and actually dated from "the administration of Andrew Johnson when the evils of the 'spoils' system culminated." The loss was not money collected and then stolen but money due the government and never collected.

The commission also claimed that during Grant's administration deficiencies and defalcations under the internal revenue law had been reduced to one-seventh of those suffered during Johnson's term of office. "We regret," the commissioners concluded, "that in our desire to divest our report of any partisan character whatever and to make it as concise as possible, we failed to explain this statement, more in detail, & to show how ingenious and successful were the efforts of the administration to prevent the loss to which we alluded." [7] Quite obviously the commission painted the bleakest picture possible to demonstrate a need for reform. The commission knowingly used an obsolete estimate, since it testified that the internal revenue system was seven times more honest under Grant than under Johnson. The commission could hardly afford to have the spoils system reformed by spoilsmen.

Along with exaggerating corruption in the civil service, reformers embraced a devil theory respecting their enemies. Grossly overrating the organization of satanic spoilsmen, reformers referred often to conspiracies and rings. In November, 1871, Charles Eliot Norton wrote Godkin from Dresden, Germany, "The whole country is, like New York, in the hands of the 'Ring,'—willing to let things go, till they get so bad that it is a question whether they can be bettered without complete upturning of the very foundations of law & civil order." So great was Norton's revulsion against rapacious capitalists that he questioned the further validity of the "systems of individualism & competition. We have erected selfishness into a rule of conduct, & we applaud the man who 'gets on' no matter at what cost to other men." Norton even approved the recent attempt of the Paris Commune to redress its grievances by force, and, although he shared the typical reformer's aversion to violence that would overturn social order, he advocated "occasional violent revolutionary action to remove deepseated evils." Norton's radicalism, a temporary romantic aberration, revealed a man deeply distressed and frustrated by repulsive politicians and capitalists. In his frustration Norton advocated violent revolution to make men "more conscious of their duties to society." [8]

Norton revealed more of himself than of America. The whole country was not in the hands of the "Ring"—Tweed, whisky, or otherwise. All capitalists were not buccaneers like Jim Fisk, and there was no revolution. American reformers were content to espouse civil service reform, revenue reform, and hard money, a program they hoped would recreate the golden age of the past. But men with a program to reform society were hardly unbiased observers. Obviously reform came through "knocking" not "boosting." The historian, however, faithfully reflects the reformers' dim view of the Gilded Age.

The cause of reformers' jaundiced view and their espousal of civil service reform can be found in their careers. Their morality, their heritage of Puritan virtue cannot be denied, but reformers recognized the evils of the spoils system only after it thwarted their ambitions. The career of the temporary revolutionary, Charles Eliot Norton, serves as an example. Son of Andrews Norton, Harvard Divinity School professor, and cousin of Charles W. Eliot, future president of Harvard University, Charles Eliot Norton was born into the "best" Cambridge circles. After graduating from Harvard, he attempted and later abandoned a career in business. Literature and the arts enthralled him; account books did not. Norton traveled widely abroad where he met George William Curtis, a lifelong friend, and hobnobbed with the Brownings, Thackeray, Ruskin, Carlyle, and the pre-Raphaelites. Before the Civil War he contributed to the *Atlantic,* sympathized with the antislavery cause although he personally did not care for abolitionists ("the most self righteous set of radicals"), and supported the Republican party. During the war he edited the Loyal Publication Society broadsides, which for three years helped shape northern public opinion by supplying editorials to local newspapers. With James Russell Lowell, Norton became co-editor of the *North American Review* in 1864, and in 1865 he joined Godkin and others to found the *Nation.*[9]

The postwar world disenchanted Norton. He was suspicious of democracy, observing that it contributed to the unfortunate national "decline of manners." Norton had no use for Andrew Johnson but even less for radical Republican politicos. He opposed the impeachment of Johnson, reasoning that "three months of Ben Wade are worse than two years of A.J." Johnson's acquittal encouraged him only because it enhanced reformers' opportunity to capture the Republican party. "I think," he wrote Godkin, "we have a better chance now than we had any right to expect so soon for reforming the party & freeing it from the burden of the sins of the extremists who have tried to usurp the leadership."

As the election of 1868 drew near, Norton, like everyone else, fell under Grant's spell. " 'Honesty & Grant,' 'good-faith & Grant' must succeed," he wrote from Manchester, England. "Grant grows daily in my respect & confidence," Norton wrote Curtis after the election and rapturously described the president-elect as "so simple, so sensible, so strong & so magnanimous." Assuming Grant would be especially generous to the reform element, Norton added, "If you see a perfectly fit and easy opportunity, I should be glad to have you use it to suggest my name as that of a suitable person for the mission to Holland or Belgium." Although Curtis wrote to newly appointed Secretary of State Hamilton Fish in Norton's behalf, nothing happened. The reformers' hope to reestablish themselves in their old stronghold, the diplomatic service, proved futile. A few months later, bitterly disillusioned after his season of hope, Norton wrote Curtis: "Grant's surrender, partial though it may be, to the politicians was an unexpected disappointment, but a very instructive one. His other mistakes were what might have been expected,— what indeed we ought to have been prepared for. But some of his appointments are disgraceful,—personally discreditable to him. . . . The question seems to be now whether the politicians,—'the men inside politics,'—will ruin the country, or the country take summary vengeance, by means of Jenckes's [civil service reform] bill, upon them." [10]

Norton's disappointments paralleled those of his friends, particularly those of George William Curtis. Exposed early to transcendentalism at Concord and Brook Farm, Curtis never escaped its influence. After the grand tour abroad, he embarked on a literary career, becoming one of the most popular writers of the 1850's and associate editor of *Putnam's Monthly*. After this magazine collapsed, Curtis repaid a debt he was not legally responsible for by lecturing on the lyceum circuit. An ardent Republican, he supported the Lincoln administration from his editor's post on *Harper's Weekly*. He soon became a power in the New York Republican party, unsuccessfully ran for Congress in 1864, attempted to influence patronage distribution during Lincoln's administration, and was offered a diplomatic post in Egypt. Curtis was not opposed to the spoils system until it ceased to function satisfactorily for him and his friends.[11]

Politicians in general snubbed Curtis and his peers. In the fall of 1866 Charles Eliot Norton launched a campaign to elect Curtis United States senator from New York. Although Curtis' sensitive nature was not a political asset, the *Nation* and several other journals strongly supported him. Success, however, did not follow. "Conkling is undoubtedly to be the man," Curtis wrote Norton in January, "but his friends and [Noah] Davis's and [Ira] Harris's—the three real contestants—have each declared for me as their second choice. Still even that would not bring it because I am not enough of a politician for the purposes of the men who make Senators." As if to prove his point, Curtis "declined absolutely" to unite with the weakest candidate against Roscoe Conkling, who was elected. A few weeks later Curtis, in answer either to public opinion or to personal frustration with politics, wrote in *Harper's Weekly* favoring the passage of the Jenckes civil service bill by the expiring Thirty-ninth Congress. Although tardy, Curtis' espousal of civil service reform lasted until his death twenty-five years later. In this period he became its most conspicuous leader.[12]

Politicians continued to snub Curtis and each cut made him more of a reformer. In September, 1870, he played a prominent role in Conkling's behalf at the New York State Republican Convention. To give convention proceedings an air of respectability, Conkling men elected Curtis temporary chairman. Having won by a wide margin, Curtis delivered an impressive address, which he hoped would stampede the convention into nominating him for governor. When William Orton, head of Western Union and one of Conkling's chief allies, approached him about the nomination, Curtis, feigning disinterest, replied: "If it is evidently the wish of the Convention I will not decline. But I don't want the office and I entrust my name to your honorable care." Professional politicians made short work of the Curtis candidacy. An efficient Conkling lieutenant, Charles Spencer, nominated Curtis but later voted for another candidate, effectively confusing and dividing Curtis supporters. "In one word, my dear boy," Curtis wrote Norton, "I was the undoubted choice of the Convention and I had been disgracefully 'slaughtered' by my friends!" Curtis attempted to convince himself he was "glad" that he would not have to run. "The only real harm the affair can do me," he confided to Norton, "is that my influence will decline with those who think I want office!!"[13]

Politics held further disappointments for Curtis, who remained loyal to the Republican party, headed Grant's Civil Service Commission, and supported Grant in the campaign of 1872. The President, however, snubbed Curtis after 1872. When the New York surveyor vacated his position, reformers considered the nomination of his successor a test case. Grant hesitated but, prodded by Curtis, nominated the deputy surveyor in accordance with the new civil service commission rules. Although reformers tasted victory, they again grew apprehensive when members of the Conkling machine bragged that Grant would withdraw the nomination. Two weeks later the nomination was indeed withdrawn, with the assurance that reform methods would be used in selecting the new surveyor. A committee of three, including Curtis and Collector Chester A. Arthur, was named to select the custom house employee best fitted for the post.

Once more reformers' suspicions were allayed. But spoilsmen were the final victors. Curtis' serious illness kept the committee from holding an examination or making a report. In mid-March, George H. Sharpe, an active politician and the local United States marshal, was appointed without the committee's knowledge. Sharpe's appointment goaded the ailing and testy Curtis into action. Three days after it was announced, he published a letter in the *New York Tribune* emphasizing that Sharpe's appointment was made without his knowledge or consent and ominously adding that "men do not willingly consent to be thus publicly snubbed." On March 18, 1873, Curtis resigned as chairman of Grant's Civil Service Commission.[14]

Curtis was more aggressive when he returned to editorial work after his illness and resignation. Ignored by the administration and unable to realize his political ambitions, he vigorously attacked Grant's civil service policy. Curtis relished his new independence and was proud when the anti-administration *Springfield Republican* called one of his articles "another Bomb Shell." He acknowledged in an editorial that "public disbelief of the reality and thoroughness of the reform" was not surprising. "The President forbids political assessments upon subordinates, and issues an executive order virtually reproving the political officiousness of officers of the service. But, in total contempt of his orders, they levy assessments, desert their posts of duty, assume the management of all party assemblies, and continue to use patronage as a party lever." Grant could have inspired confidence in his administration, Curtis contended, if he had fired his corrupt brother-in-law who was collector of New Orleans, dismissed the postmaster at St. Louis for levying political assessments, filled New York Custom House posts according to the rules, and required civil servants to attend to their duties instead of their party's needs. "Unless these things are done, constantly and consistently done," Curtis concluded, "the work of the Commission, faithful, able, and devoted as we know it to be, will be in vain, and the Republican party will have no right to claim that it has really reformed the civil service."[15]

Unlike Curtis, Henry Adams expected little from Grant and very quickly learned to expect nothing. "We here look," Adams wrote from Washington in February, 1869, "for a reign of western mediocrity, but one appreciates least the success of the steamer, when one lives in the engine-room." Two months later, Adams wrote with the satisfaction his family always seemed to feel when it suffered defeat: "My hopes of the new Administration have all been disappointed; it is far inferior to the last. My friends have almost all lost ground instead of gaining it as I hoped. My family is buried politically beyond recovery for years. I am becoming more and more isolated so far as allies go. I even doubt whether I can find an independent organ to publish my articles, so strong is the current against us." And a few days later Henry wrote his brother Charles Francis, Jr., the treasurer of the Social Science Association, which was agitating for civil service reform, "I can't get you an office. The only members of this Government that I have met are mere acquaintances, not friends, and I fancy no request of mine would be likely to call out a gush of sympathy." Nor could Henry obtain anything for himself. The administration was presumptuous enough to ignore the Adams family.[16]

With their ambitions thwarted, the Adams brothers forsook the conventional methods of political advancement and espoused civil service reform. In February Henry had recognized that the struggle against "*political* corruption" was more basic than free trade and its eradication would be more difficult than the antislavery crusade. By June he was writing an article called "Civil Service Reform," which he described as "very bitter and abusive of the Administration." Although Adams expected it to get him into "hot water," he believed he had "nothing to lose." Henry and his brothers, Charles Francis, Jr., and John Quincy, were "up to the ears in politics and public affairs, and in time," Henry hoped, "we shall perhaps make our little mark."[17]

The *North American Review* published and the *Nation* applauded Adams' article. In it Adams revealed reformers' disdain for the new men of politics and their concern over the passing of a more compatible political age. Two members of Grant's Cabinet, Ebenezer Rockwood Hoar and George S. Boutwell, epitomized the change. Boutwell, Adams stated, was "the product of caucuses and party promotion," but Hoar was "by birth and by training a representative of the best New England school, holding his moral rules on the sole authority of his own conscience, indifferent to opposition whether in or out of his party, obstinate to excess, and keenly alive to the weaknesses in which he did not share. Judge Hoar belonged in fact to a class of men who had been gradually driven from politics, but whom it is the hope of reformers to restore.

Mr. Boutwell belonged to the class which has excluded its rival, but which has failed to fill with equal dignity the place it has usurped." [18]

The careers of Norton, Curtis, and Henry Adams demonstrated that the civil service reform movement fitted a pattern of those out of power versus those in power. Reformers invariably wished to curtail the appointing power after they thought it had been abused. Abuse occurred when men of their own social station or political faction were not appointed to office. The post–Civil War political world was not what the "outs" expected it to be. In their disappointment they turned to reform.

The civil service reformer's political impotence accurately reflected his loss of social and economic power. He was out of step with the rest of society. The post–Civil War industrial transformation made obsolete his laissez-faire philosophy. He favored free trade in an age of growing protectionism. He demanded hard money when cries for currency expansion grew louder. He hated monopoly and rapacious capitalism when big business triumphed. He disliked unions, strikes, and radicals, but these all became more common. An increasing flood of immigrants from eastern and southern Europe engulfed him in the city of his fathers. He opposed imperialism but in the twilight of his career witnessed America's most hypernationalistic war. The reformer stood for little government in a period when the civil service proportionately grew faster than the population. The reformer was an outsider, philosophically as well as politically.

Like its proponents, the civil service reform movement was essentially conservative. Its leaders were not interested in revolutionizing anything or even in recognizing the fundamental alteration industrialism had made in American society. They were prosperous and to some extent led society, but their anticipations were higher than their achievements. Without sacrificing the material gains of the present, civil service reformers wished to return to the attitudes of the good old days before Jacksonian Democracy and the industrial revolution, when men with their background, status, and education were the unquestioned leaders of society. In their frustration, reformers attacked the hated spoilsmen's conspicuous source of strength, the civil service.[19]

If zealous reformers exaggerated the corruption of government in the Gilded Age, what was the actual condition of the civil service? In 1865 it was at its nadir, thanks to the Civil War which swelled its ranks abnormally and provided Republicans with an excuse, that of disloyalty, for firing more officeholders than ever before. There was more than rhetoric in Julius Bing's complaint, "At present there is no organization save that of partisanship; no test of qualification save that of intrigue." [20]

Like most reformers, Bing, the clerk of the Joint Select Committee on Retrenchment who helped Thomas A. Jenckes lay the groundwork for the civil service reform movement, took a dim view of the civil service. Actually, the government would not have functioned at all if corruption and incompetence were as universal as reformers alleged. Nevertheless, professionalism was almost nonexistent in the civil service, and politics permeated it.

At the end of the Civil War the federal bureaucracy was subdivided into seven departments employing 53,000 workers whose annual compensation amounted to about $30,000,000. Uncle Sam was the largest employer in the United States. The Post Office Department, with an office in nearly every village, employed more than half of all civil servants. Next in size and in political importance was the Treasury Department with a large office in Washington, sizable custom houses in major port cities, and internal revenue agents throughout the country. The somewhat smaller Interior Department was also politically significant because of the Land, Patent, Indian, and Pension bureaus. The remaining War, Navy, State, and Justice departments controlled less patronage.[21]

The civil service lacked system. Uniformity in personnel policy outside of Washington was by accident rather than by design, and only a loose personnel system existed even in Washington where clerks were divided into four grades, compensated accordingly, and examined for competence upon appointment. Other evidences of a personnel system were the formal provision for supervision of clerks, the fixing of hours by Congress, the experimentation with efficiency ratings, and the tendency to reward the proficient with promotion. In practice, however, the personnel system was primitive. Examinations were farcical, nepotism was common, no real promotion policy existed, and there was neither a training program for new recruits nor provision for retirement.[22] In these respects the American bureaucracy was not unique. British personnel practices, despite progress toward reform, were also primitive, and those of private business were even more backward.

Tenure of civil servants was short and uncertain in the 1860's. Although every department could point to civil servants who had been in office for many years, these workers were the exception. They formed the working core of the civil service, provided continuity and consistency in administration, and trained new recruits. An example frequently cited is that of William Hunter, the second assistant secretary of state, who in 1868 had been employed in the State Department for thirty-nine years. Unlike Hunter, most civil servants held their positions only a short time and anticipated early dismissal. Tenure varied, with offices requiring a high degree of technical knowledge retaining their employees the longest. In 1868, twenty-seven of the fifty-five officers in the New York assay office had been employed more than ten years, and forty-five of them had worked there more than six years. The office of the United States treasurer, however, was more representative. A tally taken in December, 1867, found that 219 of the 282 employees had been appointed within the preceding four years. Only five individuals had been employed over ten years.[23]

The training and backgrounds of civil servants differed widely. For positions requiring technical competence, such as jobs in assay offices and in the Patent Office, men of ability were secured and retained. In other offices, standards were less exacting. The 282 employees in the treasurer's office, for example, were a motley group. They numbered in previous occupations "7 accountants, 13 bankers, 18 bookkeepers, 27 clerks, 1 detective, 2 druggists, 1 editor, 5 farmers, 1 hackdriver, 1 housekeeper, 1 hotel steward, 16 laborers, 1 lawyer, 1 machinist, 1 manufacturer, 8 mechanics, 14 merchants, 2 messengers, 1 minister, 1 page, 1 porter, 1 postman, 2 salesmen, 1 sculptor, 12 students, 1 surveyor, 24 teachers, 2 telegraphists, 1 county treasurer, 1 waiter, 1 washerwoman, 1 watchman, and of no particular occupation, 112." [24] These appointments were not the result of haphazard policy. They were the fruit of the spoils system.

The spoils system, though hoary in some aspects, had grown with democracy. With frequent elections decided by large numbers, the democratic system forced politicians to build elaborate organizations to influence voters. The best assets in building a "machine" were local, state, and federal employees whose jobs depended upon politicians. With the application of pressure, these civil servants would contribute both time and money to their patron's political wars. Frequent elections, however, meant frequent changes, for winning politicians would force enemies out of office. By 1865 the spoils system rested firmly on three major principles: selection primarily for political considerations, congressional dictation of most appointments, and rotation of officeholders.

The Civil War contributed both to the rise and to the fall of the spoils system. Although the spoils system controlled more offices more completely than ever before, the stress of war exposed its deficiencies and stimulated interest in reform. The needs of the public service itself and the prodding of obstreperous reformers like Norton, Curtis, and Adams, resulted in slow but steady improvement dating from the immediate postwar years. Public service under Grant was actually more efficient than under Lincoln and Johnson. During the Grant regime the internal revenue service improved and Congress abolished moieties. Although Grant earned the dubious distinction of abandoning civil service reform, no previous president had even experimented with it. Grant was not a civil service reformer, but he was more interested in reform than his predecessors, just as his successors were far more committed to reform than he.

In Grant's Cabinet the most maligned administrator was George S. Boutwell, the secretary of the treasury whom Henry Adams singled out as the personification of the spoils system. Yet from 1870 to 1872 Boutwell administered stringent tests in his department. He also appointed E. B. Elliott, a friend of reform who later became a civil service commissioner, to the treasury board of examiners. Elliott helped prepare a guide for treasury clerkship examinations designed to aid in hiring competent workers. These examinations stressed arithmetic, but included a knowledge of weights, measures, bookkeeping, grammar, spelling, geography, history, and law. According to Elliott, admission to the Treasury Department under Boutwell was "invariably" at the lowest level and written examinations were "invariably" required for promotion. Elliott testified that enforcement of these rules was "steady & regular & firm, the standard moderate but persistently enforced examination in no case merely formal." He also stated that Boutwell's system, unlike competitive examinations, "took cognizance of special qualifications derived from experience in previous employment and of other special attainments." The first competitive examination in the United States civil service was held in Boutwell's department in 1870, when six third-class clerks were examined for vacancies in the next class. Although competitive, this examination was not open to all applicants.[25]

Inherent demands of the civil service necessitated reform in Boutwell's department. His connection with competitive and stringent examinations seems strange considering his opposition to civil service reformers and their dislike of him, but it was Boutwell's job to administer a large office. As a responsible official, he recognized the need for skilled employees, a need which increased as government functions multiplied and became more complex. Like reformers, Boutwell desired efficient workers and was prepared to use examinations to obtain them, but unlike reformers, he wished to continue making political appointments. Historians, relying mainly on such partisan sources as the *Nation*, have overlooked Boutwell's reform activities. What was actually an enlightened regime from the standpoint of personnel administration has been magnified as a blatant example of the spoils system.

The most important, the most publicized, and consequently the most maligned office in the country was the New York Customhouse. There, as in government service elsewhere, conditions gradually improved during the Gilded Age. In January, 1866, the New York Customhouse was the scene of frauds, waste, and incompetence; during the next five years removals numbered 1,678, the equivalent of twice the entire force or more than one removal per secular day. Daily collections of $480,000 (the chief source of federal revenue) and the intricacies of tariff legislation required a sensitive business organization, which the customhouse did not have. The cost of collecting revenue in the United States in 1874 was three, four, and five times that of France, Germany, and Great Britain, respectively.[26]

The administration of the New York Customhouse improved steadily after Chester A. Arthur replaced Thomas Murphy as collector in 1871. Since Murphy and Arthur both belonged to the Roscoe Conkling faction of the New York Republican party, Arthur's political dirty work had already been accomplished. The change of collector brought no change in faction; tenure became more secure. A series of investigations kept Arthur on his mettle, and he was an able administrator who brought a measure of efficiency to the customhouse.[27]

While hostility to the Conkling machine usually motivated New York Customhouse investigations, inquiries helped reform long-standing abuses such as the general-order warehouse system. This system required merchants to pay duty on their goods and to take possession of them within forty-eight hours after a ship entered port. Goods remaining beyond this inadequate period were discharged from the vessel under a general order by the collector. Once in the custody of customhouse officials, general-order goods were sent to a specially designated warehouse where, besides cartage, a month's storage was charged even if the goods were removed immediately.[28] Congressional hearings in January and February, 1872, completely aired the general-order business and acquainted the public with the activities of two shadowy figures, George Leet and Wilbur T. Stocking.

A one-time chief clerk in a Chicago freight depot, Leet enlisted as a Union private in 1862 and emerged from the Civil War a colonel attached to Grant's staff. While still holding his army commission, he secured a War Department clerkship in 1868. When Leet informed President-elect Grant that he wished to settle in New York, Grant wrote a letter of recommendation to Moses Grinnell, a prominent New York merchant. Leet knew that Grant intended to appoint Grinnell New York collector and informed Grinnell of that fact when he presented his letter. Overwhelmed by his good fortune and by the coincidence that Leet brought both news of his appointment and a letter from Grant, Grinnell asked Leet what he wanted. Leet promptly demanded the general-order business, from which he expected to clear $60,000 annually.

Somewhat intimidated by this demanding friend of Grant, Grinnell gave Leet supervision over the general-order business which Cunard and North German Lloyd had formerly handled themselves. After farming out his newly acquired plum for $5,000 a year and half of all profits over $10,000, Leet returned to Washington and kept his transaction under cover by using a New York agent. During the years 1869 and 1870, Leet resided in Washington, roomed and boarded with Grant's private secretaries, Generals Horace Porter and Orville Babcock, maintained an army commission, and retained his War Department post, where he filed Grant's army papers. Even while drawing three salaries, Leet used his intimacy with Grant's official household to threaten Grinnell with dismissal unless he received a larger share of the general-order business. Grinnell's successor, Tom Murphy, gave Leet and his friend Wilbur T. Stocking, former army sutler, the whole North River general-order business. At this point, George Leet moved to New York and openly took charge of his customhouse interests.

Revelation of the circumstances under which Leet gained his sinecure compounded New York merchants' dissatisfaction with the general-order business. Their earlier complaints about the rise in rates accompanying Leet's monopoly had not been answered. Even when Grant told Murphy in May, 1871, to sever Leet's connection with the customhouse because of hostile criticism, Murphy successfully defended him by saying that the attack was engineered by the steamship companies. Publicity from the investigation in early 1872, however, proved too much for Leet. He testified that in twenty months he and Stocking had netted only $55,000, but refused to corroborate his statement with his firm's books. The value of his plum will never be known, but a recent investigator, William Hartman, accepts as reasonably accurate the $172,000 estimate by the Democratic minority of the investigating committee. Even before the committee presented its report, public opinion forced Grant to instruct Murphy's successor, Arthur, to reform the general-order business. Storage rates were lowered by 35 to 40 percent, and the public careers of Leet and Stocking ended.[29]

The January, 1872, customhouse investigation also exposed the moiety system, and the issuance of general search warrants. Merchants, however, were plagued with these abuses for two more years. Designed to provide incentive, the customs service used the moiety system to uncover fraud. When a shipment was confiscated one-half went to the government, one-quarter to the informer, and the remaining quarter was divided equally among the collector, naval officer, and surveyor of the port. Although the moiety system had been under periodic attack for twenty years, it did not come under heavy fire until the exposure and publication of the Phelps-Dodge case in early 1873.

A disgruntled clerk, who had been fired for dishonesty, accused Phelps, Dodge and Company of undervaluing certain shipments. A special treasury agent investigating this charge (aided by broad powers enabling him to search the company's books) and concluded—or at least alleged—that it was true. According to law, the whole shipment had to be forfeited. The undervaluations were made on items in shipments totaling $1,750,000. The value of the property on the invoices was $271,017. The undervaluation itself came to $6,000, and the duties the company avoided paying came to about $2,000. Phelps, Dodge and Company settled out of court for $271,017. Merchants and reformers thought "knavish politicians" searching for personal and party funds were responsible for the Phelps-Dodge predicament. They complained that seizures of books and papers were outrageous and that the moiety system drove treasury agents to excess. When attempts were made in Boston and in New York to repeat the Phelps-Dodge success, so great was the reaction that in January, 1874, even Ben Butler—who probably shared in the moieties from Phelps, Dodge and Company—introduced a bill to end the moiety system.[30]

By June, 1874, a bill abolishing the moiety system and placing restrictions on the right of search became law. Although the bill raised the official salaries of collectors, their incomes sharply decreased. New York Collector Chester A. Arthur's salary dropped from approximately $56,000 to $12,000 a year. The office of collector was no longer the political plum it had been. Merchant reformers were largely responsible for the ending of the moiety system, a significant step toward civil service reform. This important group of reformers had practical reasons for supporting reform. It enabled their businesses to function more smoothly during their constant contacts with customhouse employees.[31]

Under President Hayes the administration of the New York Customhouse further improved. Hayes attacked the Conkling machine by attempting to remove Arthur and Naval Officer Alonzo Cornell. After a long battle, Hayes prevailed. The original objective of displacing Conkling men appears not to have been reform but the building of an administration party from the remains of the old Reuben Fenton machine. The administration stood to gain doubly by attacking Conkling—not only would reformers be pleased, but it would also eliminate a hostile faction that failed to deliver the New York vote in 1876. Whatever Hayes originally intended, the struggle continued so long and its publicity was so great that he had no alternative but to make the customhouse a showcase for reform. "My desire," he wrote Arthur's successor, Edwin A. Merritt, "is that your office shall be conducted on strictly business principles, and according to the rules which were adopted on the recommendation of the civil service commission by the administration of General Grant. In making appointments and removals of subordinates you should be perfectly independent of mere influence. Neither my recommendation, nor Secretary Sherman's, nor that of any member of Congress, or other influential persons should be specially regarded. . . . Let no man be put out merely because he is Mr. Arthur's friend, and no man put in merely because he is our friend." [32]

Publication of Hayes's letter to Merritt brought praise from reformers, and this praise grew louder with publication of the new rules. These rules applied to all New York Customhouse and sub-treasury appointees except a few officers of special trust. Appointments were to be made from the three candidates ranking highest on a competitive examination to be administered by one of three examining boards and observed by "well-known citizens." New appointees were to enter only at the lowest grade; other vacancies were to be filled by promotion within the customhouse.

Naval Officer Silas W. Burt, an early and ardent civil service reformer, was the dynamic force behind the new customhouse rules. Although not opposed to competitive examinations, Collector Merritt believed the experiment would be short-lived and asked Burt to enforce the rules. "If you can revive this corpse you are entitled to all the glory," Merritt assured Burt. It was Burt's idea to invite prominent citizens, particularly editors, to observe examinations, an idea that George William Curtis enthusiastically approved. Twelve citizens were invited to each examination, and Curtis attended them all to explain the proceedings. "The editors who attended," Burt later recalled, "were specially interested and their impressions, always favorable, were reflected in their papers." Editors favoring the spoils system, however, invariably declined invitations. [33]

Despite his lukewarm attitude toward the competitive system, Merritt pleased reformers. Even the *New York Times* (highly critical of Hayes) admitted in July that "after four months' experience, it is simple justice to say that the reform has been applied there [the New York Customhouse] in good faith, and with a degree of pertinacity, a patient attempt to make it successful, and an enlightened appreciation of its nature and

its scope, which have been an agreeable disappointment to the doubters."
An energetic civil service reform leader, Dorman B. Eaton, later reported
to Hayes that Merritt's administration of open-competitive examinations
was highly successful. Never before, according to Eaton, had so much
time been given to proper work and so little to partisan politics. Economy, efficiency, promptness, and high morale characterized the service.
Even though political activity had not been entirely eliminated, its decline
encouraged Eaton. Reformers rightly thought that Burt was responsible
for the success of the president's pilot program.[34]

The New York Customhouse was not the only federal office in the
nation showing improvement. Under Thomas L. James, a Conkling Republican, reform in the New York Post Office was in certain aspects even
more advanced than in the customhouse. When James was appointed in
March, 1873, "incompetency, neglect, confusion, and drunkenness" that
staggered "credulity" prevailed in the post office. James found 400 to
600 neglected bags of mail scattered throughout the building, and on one
occasion a book clearly addressed to Vice-President Schuyler Colfax was
delayed for months. James replaced this chaos with system. He dismissed
drunkards and incompetents but conducted no partisan proscription. He
set up examinations and despite political pressure refused to hire unworthy applicants. By May, 1879, he decided that noncompetitive examinations were not adequate and instituted open-competitive examinations
a few weeks after they were established in the New York Customhouse.
Eaton and New York businessmen were proud of their post office. In
1880, the volume of mail had increased one-third over 1875, yet the
mails were delivered for $20,000 less, and collections and deliveries were
increased.[35]

Despite improvement of government service and a growing awareness
even among spoilsmen that further improvement was necessary, the
civil service in the Gilded Age was not yet reformed. Until 1883 it was
basically nonprofessional and was characterized by lack of training, in-
secure tenure, and low morale. Politicians whose interests were local
dominated the civil service, and the government worker, frequently owing
his position to the turn of events in a congressional district, was understandably provincial in outlook. A civil service reform law requiring
that appointments be made on the basis of open-competitive examinations could not pass Congress. The charges of corruption leveled by the
reform press usually failed to convince most Americans. Rising industrialists, urban laborers, and rural farmers did not support civil service reform. Not until an insane office seeker assassinated President Garfield did
reformers have a simple, emotion-packed illustration which the previ-

ously uninterested masses could easily understand. The spoils system equaled murder. An aroused public opinion goaded Congress until it approved the Pendleton Act in 1883.

Under the Pendleton Act the trend toward improvement accelerated. The power of the Civil Service Commission grew with the steady increase of classified positions. An unprofessional civil service became more professionalized. Better-educated civil servants were recruited and society accorded them a higher place. Thanks to secure tenure, local political considerations gave way in civil servants' minds to the national concerns of a federal office. Business influence and ideals replaced those of the politician.[36]

Although these changes outlined the future development of American bureaucracy, the roots of change were in the Gilded Age. Curiously, the reformers, the assiduous cultivators of those roots of change, frequently refused to recognize that improvements in the public service had resulted indirectly from their labor. Prior to the Pendleton Act, the more improved the public service became the more shrill were reformers' protests over public immorality. Their noise obscured improvements and gave the profession of politics a disreputable name it does not deserve, a reputation that even now discourages the reform-type from entering politics. It is indeed ironic that the Gilded Age is indebted to reformers for its tarnished reputation as well as for its improvement in public morals.

Andrew Carnegie.
Library of Congress.

Jay Gould.
Library of Congress.

Dining room of the *St. Louis*, an Atlantic Seaboard pleasure steamer.   *The Chautauquan, July, 1897.*

Interior of railroad directors' car, around 1870.   *Courtesy of Chicago Historical Society.*

Rustic Politics: Governor R. B. Hayes (left) greets constituents and an ox before the roasting. *Rutherford B. Hayes Library.*

President Hayes defends Fort Civil Service from the Spoilsmen.
Harper's Weekly, October 20, 1877.

A Northern view of Southern politics.   *Harper's Weekly, October 18, 1879.*

John Sherman.   *Rutherford B. Hayes Library.*

"Boy Bryan on the Burning Deck."   *Judge, August 8, 1896.*

William Jennings Bryan (left) and Mrs. Bryan (right) greet supporters from the platform of the campaign train, 1896. *Library of Congress.*

A Negro homesteader and family in Oklahoma Territory, 1889. *Western History Collections, University of Oklahoma Library.*

Pioneer farm women gathering buffalo chips. *Kansas State Historical Society.*

Kansas wheat harvest in the 1880's. *Kansas State Historical Society.*

WALTER T. K. NUGENT

❧ 6 ❧

Money, Politics, and Society:
The Currency Question

THE SET OF MEASURES comprising the money question in the Gilded Age,
looked at strictly as a matter of public finance, was worth considering
and solving. Money, banking, and credit were poorly organized and
relatively inefficient; as weak spots in the economic fabric, they required
mending. Ironically, preoccupation with the money question, as it
formed in the late nineteenth century, inhibited repair work, but from
the late sixties to the late nineties, the money question was never confined to public finance. It became a national political issue, not so much
between major parties (until the Bryan-McKinley campaign of 1896) as
among factions within parties. It became a social issue, dividing and
polarizing economic, sectional, and ideological groups within the society
And it was a moral issue, constantly raising concerns about value, worth,
"honest" repayment of debt, the measurement of and reward for labor or
invested property. This immediately aroused the intransigent righteousness of everyone who considered the problem.

Principally for the latter reason, not for purely financial reasons although they were serious enough, the money question was perennially
debated and perennially insoluble. The other major political issues of the
Gilded Age were less hardy. Reintegration of the South into the nation
and the establishment of political and other rights for the freedmen was
the burning issue into 1868, but rapidly dissipated.[1] Civil service reform,
a pet issue of liberal Republicans until their abrupt engorgement in 1872,
exercised only a small number of reformers until, in the wake of the Garfield assassination, the Pendleton Act (1883) removed the edge of controversy from the issue. The tariff, an important issue for its catalytic ef-

fect in helping to define the group constituencies of major political parties, and for other reasons, was prominent only in the eighties. Even then it was becoming too complex for reduction into effective electoral black-and-whites. And the tariff lacked the moral and ideological super-structure which made the money question such a towering troublemaker. Those issues and others were serious and important. They engaged the attention, sometimes the passions, of opinion-makers, politicians, and the electorate. But it does not detract from their importance to point out that the money question, in its various segments and phases, had a longer life, touched more raw nerves, and produced fewer fruits other than bitter ones.

Financial and economic events, some a legacy of the Civil War and some the products of the protean modernizing society, demanded responses. Conventional wisdom and the prevailing orthodoxy, formulated in a less complicated era, focused upon money, and particularly a fixed, immutable, "natural" standard of money, as the basic answer. A highly unorthodox alternative, greenbackism, was available. But for various reasons, as much the ingrainedness of the opposing political-economic ideology as for any pocketbook consideration, greenbackism was unattractive to most decision-makers and voters. A moderately unorthodox alternative, free silver—in some important ways a compromise between greenbackism and the prevailing orthodoxy—attracted many, though never a national majority. The consequence was an ideological and economic struggle, sufficiently clarified by the mid-seventies to be fought out in national politics. In the depression following the Panic of 1873, the struggle became polarized. Both sides were pushed by events and blinkered by ideologies. Fates they did not understand and could not control impelled them. They became locked in combat, first in the late seventies and, after a truce emergent by 1879 which lasted through most of the eighties, again and on much the same terms in the nineties. As befits a tragedy, neither side won. Free silver lost, most palpably and finally, in the election of 1896. But with that break in the tension of opposites, after more than twenty years, the conservative orthodoxy itself began to crumble, a victim of superannuation in the context of hitherto muted problems of turn-of-the-century society.

The money question emerged as a result of specific dislocations engendered by the Civil War. It was complicated by the conflict between the strong and understandable desire of most people concerned with it to seek prewar "normalcy," and their grudging discovery that the clock could not be turned back. The money question was also directly affected by trends and events outside the United States.

Governments, private persons, and companies engaged in international trade or investment recognized the need for a common standard by which to measure articles of trade, means of payment, and credit. They also agreed that gold and silver were best suited for that required standard. In all commercially and industrially advanced countries, gold and silver were traditional standards. But with the spread of the Industrial Revolution and complex patterns of trade and investment, pressure continued for a more precise and fixed standard. Something had to perform the functions of money. It had to be a unit of value which parties to trading or investment contracts recognized as equivalent to a certain quantity of merchandise. It also had to be an acceptable device to pay for merchandise or bonds. And if a purchase were made on credit, the device had to have the same value relative to other goods when the payment was ultimately made as it had when the contract was signed. These functions of money were the same whether trade was international, within a single country, or purely local. The key qualities of these functions, therefore, were acceptability of the monetary device to all concerned, and an unchanging value, over time, in relation to merchandise.

Nineteenth-century political economists agreed on such an operational definition of money. Most accepted a logically unnecessary, but practical, definition of it as gold and silver coin or bullion. Bullion was traditionally so used. National laws sanctioned it within countries. No international authority or treaty defined a fixed ratio between the two metals, though an agreement to that end was sought through the last half of the century.[2] No custom endowed another substance or credit arrangement with monetary life. In a day when commerce and industry grew rapidly, but when steamships, the transatlantic cable, and in some areas even railroads were yet to come, the bullion basis of national currencies fortunately provided some common denominator.

There were differences in the application of the bullion principle. Some countries, often large but all relatively unindustrialized, used silver alone as a standard, including most Asian and Latin American nations, and the German states until unification in 1871. One very important country, Great Britain, and some smaller ones, were gold monometallist. Britain in the sixties, partly because of her preeminent role in world economic affairs, was riding the wave of the future. The United States, with France and a few other countries, legally recognized both gold and silver as monetary standards and had done so since the days of George Washington. Shortly after the Civil War, traditional American bimetallism was to be abolished. The struggle over whether to restore it became the most controverted political aspect of the money question after the mid-seventies.

The general agreement throughout the economic world on the operational definition of money, and widespread practical agreement that bullion fulfilled money's function, served the purposes of international commerce in a rough-and-ready way. The fact that some countries were silver monometallist, others gold monometallist, a few bimetallist, bothered theorists more than bankers and merchants. But the international system, and bimetallism in any single country, depended on the fragile general stability that had existed for some time in the relative quantities of available gold and silver bullion.

Great discoveries of gold and silver had occurred at intervals throughout history. But their effects were gradual, and the balance between the two monetary metals was not abruptly disturbed, since it took months or years for the bullion to arrive fully into market circulation. This beneficent effect of primitive communication and transportation waned in the nineteenth century. Large-scale discoveries of gold in California and Australia in the late eighteen-forties did not destroy the international bimetallic system, but they had enough impact in a bimetallic country such as the United States to lower the relative value of gold sufficiently to push silver coins out of circulation. For gold and silver—and this was a profound flaw in a monetary system which used them as standards— were always marketable as commodities. The relative quantity of gold and silver was becoming subject to abrupt change as never before: from possible future discoveries, from the ease of circulating new bullion by rail and steamship, and from improved mining technology. Even political events such as the war reparations by which Germany took gold from France after 1870, or legal demonetizations, as happened in several countries in the early seventies, affected this rate of change.

The United States, a traditionally bullionist country and a willing participant in the world economy, operated in this context at the beginning of the Gilded Age. The Civil War added several critical particulars to the American situation. Before the war, the United States was on the bullion standard in law and in fact. State and private bank notes were widely used as currency, but these notes had to be convertible into coin at the bearer's demand. Such "specie payment" was a test of a bank's solvency. Gold coin, however, was the only specie ever paid or seen. Since Jackson's day, because of a coinage law of that time whose effect was reinforced by gold discoveries of the forties, silver was worth more as a commodity than as coin. Silver coins disappeared as they were melted down for commodity use or sale. By 1860, no one saw and few remembered silver dollars; for practical purposes specie meant gold coin. Then came the war, and the country's banks suspended specie payments.

The government, faced with large war expenses for which the coun-

try's skeletal financial structure was inadequate, instituted a set of interlocking measures to meet the emergency.³ In some cases, they also satisfied political pressures which the seceding Southerners had blocked. New
taxes and raised rates on those already established were to bring in cash.
The scarcity of cash was remedied in part by the issuing, as a temporary
war measure, of a "national currency." These United States notes were
familiarly called greenbacks, and were neither supported by bullion nor
redeemable in specie.

Lacking a tie to gold, the greenback dollar fluctuated below face
value in terms of gold. By the war's end, holders had to pay a premium
of roughly half again their face value to secure a gold dollar. But the
greenbacks were recognized at par by the Treasury in payment of most
taxes, though not customs duties, and in the purchase of government
bonds. Congress passed a series of acts through the war years authorizing
bond issues. Rates of interest, the terms of the bonds, and the mode of
repayment of principal or interest all varied in these acts. But the rates
were often high, the terms short, and the question of whether repayment
would be in gold or greenbacks left vague. Jay Cooke & Co., the government's agent in the bond sales, let buyers believe that they would ultimately be repaid in gold even though they were purchasing bonds with
inflated greenbacks.

The government's final measure was the authorizing of a system of
national banks, which ingeniously served several purposes. Scarce gold
would flow into the Treasury as groups of private individuals seeking
national bank charters bought, as the National Banking Acts provided,
U.S. bonds with a certain portion of their capital. Then, on the security
of those bonds, the national bank could issue currency—the "national
bank notes"—for general circulation. National bankers could thus draw
interest on their bonds and on their own bank notes as they lent them;
but this double-interest effect, plus a provision in the law placing a 10
percent tax on notes of non-national banks, seemed desirable in order
to encourage applications for charters. Applications came to the Treasury
rather slowly anyway, and were granted mostly in the Northeast, where
gold was available for such investment.

With the end of the Civil War a widespread yearning for "normalcy"
arose. But obdurate problems remained. "Normalcy," given prewar practice and the international context, meant specie resumption on the gold
basis. But nearly half a billion dollars in greenbacks circulated at a high
premium over gold. Over two billion dollars in floating bonds, some
redeemable within a very few years, threatened the government's solvency. National bank notes, which along with the greenbacks were one

of the two major forms of available currency, circulated adequately in the northeastern seaboard states but not in the South and West where, as developing regions, currency was chronically scarce.

The initial phase of the post–Civil War history of the money question began in this context and lasted into 1879. At first there was little serious argument about ends, means, priorities, or theory. Bankers, businessmen, political economists, members of Congress, and Treasury officials wanted to resume specie payments on the gold basis. Treasury Secretary Hugh McCulloch, having received the approval in April, 1866, of substantial majorities in Congress, moved toward specie resumption by retiring greenbacks from circulation. He tried at the same time to preserve and increase the Treasury's gold reserve to support greenbacks continuing to circulate.

McCulloch was a Democrat, a one-time state banker from Indiana, and an impeccable bullionist. Like many people, he was devoted to rapid resumption of specie payments not because he was a fanatic about gold or because he wished consciously to aggrandize, through Treasury policy, bankers, bondholders, or wealthier groups in general. Instead he saw resumption on the gold standard as the clearest means to the great end of social stability and harmony. Inflation meant speculation, immorality, and diversion from solid and honest production. True economic and social progress came only from observing the laws of nature, a return to a stable standard of gold, whose value McCulloch and many others considered to be "intrinsic."

McCulloch chose a bad moment to seek these goals through contraction. Contraction intensified the postwar deflationary trend. Many manufacturers, some bankers, and a few mercantile people complained that the pressure of contraction was too great. In early 1868, after not quite two years of contraction, Congress under moderate Republican leadership repealed the authorization of 1866.

Agreement on broad purpose and disagreement on specific policy always characterized the money question. The debate over contraction was only the first instance. John Sherman of Ohio, already the leading Republican financial statesman, managed the Senate repeal bill. Sherman's argument for repeal was not inflationary. He did not oppose resumption or the gold standard, but rather pleaded for stability in the business cycle. The question in Congress in early 1868 was not whether to resume, but how and when. The answer of Republican leaders, though not always of Republican congressmen, was less rigid than that of Secretary McCulloch and the Democratic rump in Congress.

The campaign of 1868 actively began several weeks later. It brought the money question forward as a major campaign issue and demonstrated a persistent political pattern. Republicans appeared unified, moderate, but apparently "sound" on the money question, while Democrats appeared rigid, disunified, and untrustworthy. Seldom was confusion more rife than in the Democrats' handling of the money question at their 1868 convention. They nominated for president ex-Governor Seymour of New York, whose campaign utterances represented traditionalist northeastern Democrats close to Hugh McCulloch's positions. But the campaign platform was almost "heretical" on financial questions. It embodied the "Pendleton Plan," named after a one-time Ohio manufacturer, which pledged to repay the Civil War government bonds in "lawful money" (i.e., greenbacks), unless the bond contract stipulated repayment in coin, which many did not. However, the impression was strong across the country that the government intended at the time of sale to repay in gold. Any alternative was already being called "repudiation" by the Republican platform and press. Both parties in 1868 contained representatives of almost every shade of opinion on the money question. By talking specifics, the Democrats went on the defensive and widened their internal divisions. Apparent zeal for a vague orthodoxy gave Republicans a freer hand in the campaign. It also kept harder-money elements happy, while leaving their substantial greenbackish faction—usually radicals—to exult in the nomination of General Grant and the progress of Reconstruction.

After the election, Republicans helped the Democratic party smear itself further with the tarbrush of "financial heresy" and "repudiation," as they passed a bill pledging ultimate payment of Civil War bonds in coin, and specie resumption as soon as "practicable." The bill received two-to-one majorities in each house from most Republicans and some eastern Democrats. Western and southern Democrats, and the most greenbackish radical Republicans, opposed it. The lame-duck but intransigent Johnson vetoed the bill in one of his final acts; Congress re-passed the measure and the newly inaugurated Grant signed it almost immediately. The Public Credit Act of March 18, 1869, was merely a pledge to redeem greenbacks and bonds in coin. The date and method were unspecified. But it was another major step toward establishing the GOP as the party of sound and honest money, despite its deep inner divisions.

In control of the Treasury Department and both houses of Congress, Republican financial statesmen moved to settle the two outstanding questions of public finances then pending—the funding of the ominous interest-bearing debt, of which much of the $2.1 billion total was already redeemable, and stabilizing the paper currency. Rapid resumption of specie payments seemed unlikely and undesirable. Minds had not changed on that point since contraction repeal in early 1868. Senator Sherman and Secretary of the Treasury George Boutwell agreed on the main policy requirements. They must create stable economic conditions conducive to stable business expansion, continue solidifying investor confidence in public credit, and end the gold premium and resume specie payments. To achieve these goals, they drew up three bills, which Sherman introduced into the Senate early in 1870.

The first was a currency stabilization bill. It would maintain the greenbacks at their existing level, about $356 million, neither contracting them nor issuing more. And it would replace $45 million in "temporary loan certificates," paper bearing 3 percent interest but which circulated as currency, with the same amount of national bank notes issued by newly chartered banks. The bill, like so many others Senator Sherman helped design and present during his long career, carefully delineated the limits of political compromise. While achieving currency stabilization, it answered midwestern pressure for more currency, and midwestern dissatisfaction with the concentration of national bank charters in the Northeast. The limit of new bank note issue was small enough for northeastern Republicans to accept.

Greenbackish Republicans could console themselves that the bill did not contemplate replacing greenbacks with national bank notes, as others urged. Nor did it expand the greenback issue. Sherman's bill preserved the image and substance of "sound money" while alleviating politically dangerous sectional discord. The bill passed the Senate nearly intact. The House measure embodied a much less limited bank note expansion, with the new notes to replace greenbacks. But conference committees substantially agreed to the Senate version, and the final votes in July, 1870, followed party rather than sectional lines.

The second bill proposed to re-fund the national debt. It would exchange high-interest, short-term floating bonds issued during the wartime emergency for new bonds bearing lower interest and terms of up to thirty years. The new issues, unlike many of those they would replace, clearly stated that principal and interest would be paid in "coin of the present standard value." Debate over the funding bill was long and intense. The discussion focused very heavily on public virtue, national honesty, and avoiding "repudiation" on the one hand and unearned reward to speculators on the other. Members generally agreed that an investor should finally receive no more and no less than he lent on a contract at the beginning. They did not agree that paper currencies achieved that principle. The bill passed both houses in July, again after conference committees arrived at most of what Sherman's Senate bill had originally proposed. The Funding Act of 1870 and the Currency Act of 1870 successfully dealt with critical war legacies in ways which both soothed businessmen and solidified the Republican party.

Sherman introduced a third measure in April, 1870, which did not reach the floor during that session. In the context of the other two measures, it proposed to rectify an inconvenient fossil in the existing statutes. This coinage bill, in addition to affecting the administration and operation of the U.S. Mint, would abolish silver as one of the two traditional American monetary standards. In this unobtrusive way, silver made its entrance on the public stage of the money question, the stage it was eventually to dominate in the final acts of the drama.

The rationale for abolishing the silver standard was not complicated, given the widely accepted policy lines laid down by McCulloch, Boutwell, and Sherman. The 1870 funding bill, and the Public Credit Act of 1869, stated that principal and interest of public obligations would be paid in "coin." Under existing statutes, "coin" meant either silver or gold dollars, but for a generation no one had used silver dollars. Bond buyers during the war thought of repayment in gold. The confidence of investors, many of them foreigners who expected repayment in gold, had to be maintained. A shift to the gold standard already commanded strong support in bimetallic France and silver-monometallist Prussia. American policy-makers, notably Sherman but including most others, thought the trend highly progressive. Sherman had been deeply involved in a successful effort to commit the Paris International Monetary Conference of 1867 to a unified international gold coinage, and in 1868 had brought a gold standard bill before the Senate. American and European policy-makers agreed that silver was an anachronism and bimetallism a confusion unworthy of a scientific and enlightened age.

Bimetallism threatened stable business conditions as long as it remained on the statute books. Although silver had been slightly scarcer for years than the American statutory mint ratio of sixteen to one stated, and hence had not circulated even in the prewar days of specie payment, new discoveries and new technology could make it less scarce. Gold could then be driven out of circulation. The basic problem was not whether a cheaper or dearer metal would circulate, but to keep as the standard the same metal, the one people had confidence in and believed had "intrinsic value." Stability, investor confidence, and sound public credit would follow.

Silver's reappearance, moreover, was neither theoretical nor unappreciated. Treasury investigations, made in 1866 and after under direction from McCulloch and Boutwell and support from Congress, revealed the probability of large silver discoveries. Railroad and mining improvements would rapidly bring that new silver to world markets and the U.S. Mint. American silver production was climbing steadily. Experts and officials in Europe and the United States understood and discussed this threat to gold circulation in bimetallic countries as early as 1867.

This was the basis for Sherman's coinage bill. In listing what were to be American coins and their metallic content, it omitted the silver dollar. John Jay Knox and Henry Linderman of the Treasury pointed out in a supporting report that the exclusion ended the silver standard. Almost three years passed before Congress enacted the bill in February, 1873. But the sporadic debates never came to grips with silver demonetization, its fundamental reform. Special interest groups were concerned with its content. Yet the "bloated bondholders" of later legend, and indeed even silver producers (at least to the extent of urging retention of silver as a standard), were not among them. Pressures came from gold producers to have their mint charge reduced, from a nickel refiner who wanted more of that metal used in minor coins, and from the Treasury to revamp the Mint administration. Silver demonetization became law virtually without notice in the general or financial press. There was nothing surreptitious about it; it was not newsworthy.[4]

The Sherman-Boutwell policy of currency stabilization and debt refunding proceeded reasonably well from mid-1870, amid a climate of prosperity that heated inflationarily in 1872 and 1873. Specie resumption was still distant, but seemed less urgent in those prosperous years. The gold premium dropped to a new and steady level of only 10 to 15 percent in 1870. No new important financial legislation, except the delayed Coinage Act, appeared.

But as the country slid into depression after 1873, latent divisions within the major parties and society sharpened. In 1874 and 1875, Sherman preserved the fragile Republican coalition on paper currency that had lasted since the summer of 1870, despite sectional and economic-group stresses greatly intensified by the depression. In the spring of 1874, a bipartisan group of western and southern congressmen, responding to constituent pressure to relieve currency tightness, pushed through the House an "inflation bill" raising the limit on greenback issue from $356 million to $400 million. Sherman could not prevent Senate acceptance, together with an authorization of another $46 million in national bank notes. Grant vetoed the bill, rubbing raw the sectional wounds of many Republicans. Sherman then moved through the Senate a "free banking" bill already passed in the House. It removed limits on the number of national bank charters and thus raised the potential bank note issue, securing expansion in a conservative way palatable to most Republicans. Grant signed the "free banking" bill, but Republican sectional disarray was only a little less than complete.

The Democrats captured the House in the fall elections, and Sherman made the most of a last lame-duck opportunity. In December, 1874, after a Republican caucus, he pushed through the Senate a bill removing sectional limits on free banking, setting a minimum level of greenback contraction but pledging to resume specie payments on January 1, 1879. Thanks to the latter provision and Sherman's shrewdness, the bill became, after nearly straight party-line votes, "An Act to provide for the resumption of specie payments." It was if anything more inflationary than deflationary, more political than financial.[5] It preserved the Republican image as the guardian of sound finance and honest money. But the depression was so ravaging the conventional wisdom of gold monometallism and specie resumption that an "inflationist" stance, which the Democrat-controlled House was about to take, was becoming less an onus than an opportunity.

Until 1876, virtually every advocate of "soft money" concerned himself with expanding the paper currency, either national bank notes or greenbacks. The most "conservative" position under the "soft money" heading until that year was "free banking," the removal of all or part of the legal limits on national bank charters and note issues. These notes seemed tied, however tenuously, to gold because of the banks' charter requirements. To the left were those who wanted to expand the greenback issue. Both groups and their later variants gave at least lip service to specie resumption at an unspecified future date. A vocal minority occupied the radical pole of "soft money." Breaking fundamentally with the whole bullionist theory, they advocated a permanent inconvertible paper currency—maintenance of greenbacks in their pristine unbacked state.

The theory of greenbackism had several sources, including Henry Charles Carey, often acclaimed as America's ablest political economist, who influenced manufacturers in his native Pennsylvania, and leaders of the National Labor Union such as Alexander Campbell and William Sylvis. Careyite and labor greenbackism differed in certain details, but agreed that production was the source of economic life and growth. Money existed to facilitate production, and its form mattered little as long as it performed that function well. Inconvertible paper was a more satisfactory form than specie because it was not a marketable commodity. Greenback theory was not truly inflationist, and attempted to tie public indebtedness and circulating currency to productivity. But it attracted economic groups interested in "easy" or "soft" money, some labor elements, a considerable number of manufacturers in expanding industries such as iron and steel, and, after 1875, farmers.

Greenbackism was too much at odds with conventional wisdom, and too theoretical, to attract a mass following. Some Radical Republicans in the late sixties espoused the Careyite version. In 1876 a Greenback National party, running Peter Cooper for president, polled about 1 percent of the vote. By then, however, a new "soft money," free silver, was attracting more followers than greenbackism ever would. Free silver stood on tradition and bullionist principles, with attractive monetary results for the "producing classes." It would restore the silver dollar demonetized in 1873, coined without limit at the old mint ratio of sixteen to one.

From the spring of 1876 to mid-1878 the money question occupied much of the Congress' time, in the form of bills to repeal the Specie Resumption Act and to reenact free silver. Resumption repeal had the support of the House Democratic leadership, and passed. In December, a free silver bill sponsored by the Careyite Pennsylvania Republican, William D. Kelley, and the Missouri Democrat, Richard P. Bland, passed with overwhelming bipartisan support. Both measures died in the Republican Senate, but passed the House again late in 1877. By then, resumption repeal was understood to be a more moderate step than free silver, but the House elected in 1876 was more strongly silverite than its predecessor. Greenbackism waned in Congress and among manufacturing interests, but resolutions of respectable chambers of commerce and state legislatures augmented agrarian and labor demands for free silver. The debate on both sides carried vituperative, almost demagogic tones. Ideological lines were emerging sharply.

Clearly, the Senate had to deal with the Bland free silver bill in early 1878. Sherman was by then secretary of the Treasury, but his Republican financial colleagues carried on the tactic of compromise while preserving the substance of "sound money." Since 1876, Sherman and others had discussed two variants of bimetallism which superficially resembled free silver but would preserve the gold standard. These were "limited bimetallism"—the coinage of a fixed maximum of silver dollars—which would not drive gold from circulation, and "international bimetallism"—the unlimited coinage of silver provided that a treaty defined an international gold-silver ratio—thus preventing any one nation from having its gold stock depleted. Silver was so plentiful and relatively cheap that unlimited coinage on the old sixteen-to-one ratio would drive gold from the United

States, and defeat specie resumption and the stabilization and re-funding policy secured over the preceding decade.

With these considerations in mind, the Senate majority added two amendments to the Bland free silver bill. One limited the number of silver dollars to be coined in any month to between two and four million. The other called for an international monetary conference to seek a treaty ratio between gold and silver. The bill, thus amended, became law over President Hayes's veto as the Bland-Allison Act of 1878.

The Senate then debated repeal of the Specie Resumption Act for almost two more months. It passed a bill which put a higher floor under greenback circulation than the 1875 act provided, but left the resumption-day pledge intact. The gold premium was edging toward zero. Secretary Sherman was building the Treasury's gold reserve, and resumption was a few months away. An International Monetary Conference convened in Paris in August, but it was doomed from the start. Germany and the smaller nations in her economic orbit had switched from silver to gold monometallism in the early seventies. France was only nominally bi-metallic, having suspended silver coinage in the mid-seventies as silver prices dropped. The participating nations would not shift monetary standards to accommodate an American faction.

The first phase of the history of the money question in the Gilded Age ended in early 1879 with the resumption of specie payments and the gradual return of prosperity. The per capita public debt was about half the 1865 level, per capita interest about 40 percent. The debt and the currency were stable and funded. But the debates, particularly over free silver in 1876–78, had revealed stresses, provoked economic group coalitions, developed conflicting ideologies about society in general, and fixed people's minds in these ideological ruts. Nothing had really been solved. Adverse economic conditions would trigger another campaign. The major parties occupied firm positions, as the platforms of 1880 showed. Republicans were self-congratulatory over achieving par with gold; Democrats called for paper convertible into silver as well as gold coin. With the return of a more favorable climate, manufacturer greenbackism dissipated.

The manufacturers who ten years earlier seemed to be part of the "producing classes" began to identify themselves as capitalists, especially since agrarians, generally silent on the money question until the free silver debate, were appropriating the "producer" self-image and provided much of the mass support for free silver. The two ideological coalitions—free silver and greenback; gold monometallist and limited or international bimetallist—accepted a body of dogma and rhetoric. Both proceeded in a very few steps beginning from the stuff of currency, to the proper monetary standard, to the "only" honest, natural, legal, rational way to meet public and private contracts, to find fundamental moral views about society. By 1880, almost anyone considering the money question put on his respective dogma as a buckler and a shield. People were ready to convert. They were seldom ready any longer to be converted.

Agitation over the money question subsided during most of the eighties. There was no lack of greenback or free silver bills in the congressional hopper. Another international monetary conference in 1881 attempted, again unsuccessfully, to deal with the glut of silver threatening the stability of countries with a silver standard. But the money question remained chiefly visible in the electoral activities of a dwindling band of greenbackers. General James B. Weaver received 3 percent of the popular vote in the 1880 presidential election, as a greenbacker, and several greenback congressmen were elected in 1878, 1880, and 1882. But greenback support, which in the early seventies had come from manufacturing and radical labor sources, was chiefly agrarian in the eighties. The major parties were occupied with other issues.

Depression overtook western and southern agriculture in 1888 and after. Further declines in the domestic and international silver price, and another panic in 1893 followed by general depression, produced the second and final phase of the money question's history. A remarkable expansion of agriculture in the Great Plains during the early and middle eighties became a speculative land boom by 1886–87. One bad season for wheat and cattle in 1887–88 depressed land prices severely, drove investment funds out of the area, made cash scarce, and created a heavy economic burden for small farmers. Mortgage obligations assumed in good times, often for farm improvement and with reasonable expectations of repayment, became dreadful weights. As farm income was gripped in a deflationary cycle, existing mortgages and otherwise normal operating costs such as freight rates drove many farmers into bankruptcy and others, barely surviving, into despondency.

In the South, depression did not come with such surprising suddenness, but conditions among small farmers, both Negro and white, were often worse than in the West.[6] Distressed and angry farmers in the two regions joined the nonpolitical Farmers' Alliances in droves. By early 1890 thousands of local alliances functioned vigorously. Serving as discussion forums, the alliance meetings produced a consensus among farmers as to what their problems were—money, land, and transportation—and how to attack them. A political party was the chosen weapon.

In 1890 the People's party became a reality, and did well in state and local elections, much better than the Greenback party had ever done.

The party's leadership was liberally sprinkled with free silver men and former Greenbackers who, Bourbon-like, had learned little and forgotten less since the late seventies. The mass electoral base of populism was aroused by concrete economic conditions and was more interested in relief of those conditions than in formulating any elaborate ideology.[7] Populism scarcely had an ideology, selecting instead from available and appealing rhetoric, ideology, and issues. The Omaha Platform of 1892 advocated both a "national currency" to replace bank notes and free silver, and was aimed at political union of the "laboring classes," the "producers." This meant farmers and workers, rather than laborers and manufacturers.

Radicals in the Populist party criticized maldistribution of wealth and other social and economic inequities growing out of material progress. But most rested their case on established values and beliefs, such as democratic individualism, the "producer philosophy," anti-monopoly, and the centrality of the money question. The shrillest denounced silver demonetization as the "Crime of '73," railed against the 1870 bond refunding in coin, and branded the "double-interest" national banks a monopolistic public enemy—all of which had been said many times over in 1876–78. Populist ideologues and Populist voters in general were not reactionary or "retrograde." Their critique of the political and economic order, especially on the money question, was simply not very new or profound. This was not surprising; they were politicians, not political economists.[8] Having cast their movement in the form of a political party, the Populists attracted a substantial following. General Weaver received more than triple the popular vote as the Populist presidential candidate in 1892 than he had in 1880. But the decision to exist as a political party carried fatal liabilities.

As western and southern agrarians increasingly identified a shortage of currency as the basic cause of economic distress, the world price of silver in relation to gold continued its downward slide. Whether, and under what conditions, silver was to serve a monetary function became again a major conundrum for policy-makers by 1890. Free silverites among congressional Democrats, no longer under wraps after Cleveland's defeat in 1888 and augmented in 1889 by Republicans from the silver-producing "omnibus" states, mounted a powerful drive for their cause. Harrison's Treasury secretary, William Windom, called for legislation authorizing Treasury silver purchases above the Bland-Allison level. In January, 1890, a bill was introduced to raise purchases of silver to roughly the annual domestic output. "Treasury notes of 1890," redeemable in gold or silver, would be issued against that silver bullion.

The bill passed the House, where Speaker Reed held a slender Republican majority in line. But in the Senate, free silver Democrats and western Republicans passed a free silver substitute, 42 to 25. The House did not concur. Eastern Republicans swapped support for limited silver expansion for western votes for the McKinley tariff bill, and the Sherman Silver Purchase Act became law. Senator Sherman, then and later, said that he supported the measure only to circumvent free silver. In 1890, as in the 1870's, he settled upon a device which preserved party harmony yet avoided hard- and soft-money extremes.

The Act temporarily buoyed silver prices, but did not offset a contractionary cycle which fluctuated from 1891 to 1897.[9] An international monetary conference at Brussels in 1892 produced no results, as Britain still opposed real international bimetallism. The Austro-Hungarian Empire demonetized silver, and in the summer of 1893 Britain closed the mints of India to silver. These events further depressed silver prices. The widening gap between the market price of silver and the old American mint ratio intensified charges that the silver dollar was dishonest, and that its demonetization had been an immoral enrichment of bondholders. Neither internationally nor domestically were financial statesmen dealing adequately with the silver problem. But the intensely uncompromising positions on the question, in and out of Congress, forbade careful and moderate action.

Parallels between the first and second phases of the money question appeared in other ways besides the repetition of dogmas. Money agitation among particular interest groups occurred in 1887–90 as in 1867–70, followed by package settlements, silver purchase and tariff in 1890, re-funding and currency stabilization in 1870. Three years of implementation, quieter in 1870–73 than in 1890–93, succeeded these compromises, whereupon financial panics intervened. The ensuing depressions aroused sectional and group hostilities, most markedly within the party in power. Both phases culminated in bitter struggles over silver. The first, from 1876 to 1878, ended in the truce of the Bland-Allison Act. The second ended more abruptly with silver's defeat in the 1896 presidential campaign and the return of prosperity. But the last years of the second phase were more intense and final than those of the first.

The Populist party, which attracted over a million votes in 1892, seemed to be growing. The sectional and ideological fissures within the major parties were widening. The Democrats had the bad luck, in this context, to win the 1892 election. Cleveland, like Grant twenty years earlier, took a conservative path. The Treasury's gold reserve dwindled as holders redeemed Treasury notes in gold. Sharing the orthodox view that the gold reserve was the source of public credit, and that the silver purchase policy threatened it, Cleveland called Congress into special session in the summer of 1893 to repeal the Silver Purchase Act of 1890.

But no Democratic Sherman came forward to preserve party harmony and the substance of "sound finance." The exhausting and torrid repeal session lasted from early August to early November. Like so many over the preceding quarter-century, the debate touched less on the technical effects of repeal or defining a workable substitute than on whether gold or some kind of bimetallism represented "honesty" in exchange and deferred payment. The argument was completely irresolvable by 1893.

History worked havoc with theory. Silver values had changed drastically. Hundreds of millions in government bonds had been bought and sold since the Civil War, besides re-funding, silver demonetization, and specie resumption, whether or not buyers had paid in greenbacks and been promised gold redemption. Silver was a fact, an American product, possessed in quantity by the Treasury, the white hope of depressed groups and sections chronically short of circulating medium. Yet the gold standard was also a fact, more unchangeable because so many people in the world were utterly convinced of its ineluctability. Their great oversimplification was to have made the preservation of the public credit identical with preservation of gold monometallism.

Sherman and other senators who participated in the legislation of the early seventies vehemently asserted that silver had been demonetized to protect the public credit, not to enrich bondholders. Repeal of silver purchases was now necessary, they said, for the same end. On August 28, 1893, the House voted for repeal by a majority of more than two to one. Except for a small band of westerners, Republicans were united. The Democrats split, in a ratio of about seven in favor to four against repeal. All eight Populist congressmen voted against repeal. On October 30 the Senate balloted 43 to 32 for repeal; again Republican defections came from the silver states. Cleveland had his wish. But repeal did not end the presentation of Treasury certificates for redemption, and the gold reserve kept declining. The President had to deal with the very group which silverites denounced as public enemies, the "international bankers." A syndicate headed by J. P. Morgan accepted new Treasury bond issues which replenished the gold reserve. The syndicate resold the bonds within hours at a 7 percent profit; so much for doubts about investor confidence in continued specie payments in gold.

The Cleveland repeal policy proved useless, and antagonized interests which split the Democratic party. The frustrated silverites moved steadily toward a single-issue national campaign in 1896. The Populists, especially westerners, concentrated on the single issue of free silver in 1895 and 1896. They accepted the financial and electoral logic that currency expansion with free silver would solve their other problems and gain wide support.[10] Private pressure groups such as the National Executive Silver Committee and the American Bimetallic League disseminated silver propaganda widely. Gold monometallism had its lobbyists too, such as Professor J. Laurence Laughlin of the University of Chicago.

The money question was inevitably the major issue in the 1896 campaign. Their recent history predetermined the positions of the parties. The Republican platform, adopted in June, advocated international bimetallism. In view of the negligible success of several international conferences on the subject, and current or impending moves away from silver by Russia, Japan, and some Latin American countries, this clearly meant preservation of the gold standard. Obstreperous western silver Republicans split off, but hurt the McKinley ticket little. Opponents of the Democrats' free silver position were even fewer. When the Populists nominated Bryan and focused on silver, the two sides were clearly drawn.[11]

Silver had come a long way from the quiet congressional committee rooms of 1870 to the center of national attention in 1896. Its departure was much quicker than its advent. Bryan's defeat, by the largest popular margin a Democratic presidential candidate had suffered since 1872, effectively ended the money question. In his re-match with McKinley in 1900, Bryan vainly attempted to revive the issue. The result of 1896, followed by a return of prosperity, the appearance of new gold on world markets, and the continued expansion of non-currency money within the United States dramatically broke thirty years of accumulated tension.

Bryanites, crushed, assumed that their depressed conditions would continue. Gold standard men rejoiced, their dread of a panic and depression attendant upon an extinction of the gold standard by free silver having been lifted. Free silver, even international bimetallism, might well have proved unworkable. The gold standard itself failed some years later under the pressure of another world depression. The tragedy of the money question was not in the feasibility of any one position or the harmfulness of another. Good money, as the Greenbackers had said, is anything people think is good money. The tragedy lay in the compulsive preoccupation of Americans with the money issue itself. Technical questions of financial policy became fixed and interminably explicated systems of dogma. Compromise was impossible; a solution could come only with the defeat of one of the polar positions. The result of the campaign of 1896 was a national blessing. If Bryan had won, the money question would probably have blighted American politics for a few more years. As it happened, the money question, and an era, came to an end.

R. HAL WILLIAMS

$\backsim$ 7 $\backsim$

"Dry Bones and Dead Language": The Democratic Party

ON MARCH 4, 1885, jubilant Democrats from throughout the country gathered in Washington to witness the inauguration of the first Democratic president in twenty-four years. For southern party members the event had special meaning, and they came in large numbers to celebrate the symbolic restoration of their section to national political power. After a day of rebel yells, "Dixie," and loud cheers for a Confederate general who rode in the inaugural parade, a Georgia reporter noted "a feeling here to-night stronger than I ever saw it before, that the war is over." Democrats from other areas shared the southern jubilation, for they believed the day's ceremonies meant the end of a quarter-century of political impotence and the beginning of a long period of Democratic hegemony. As one party spokesman had earlier declared: "The election of Grover Cleveland to the Presidency of the United States marks the dawn of a new era in our national history." [1]

To thoughtful Democrats, Cleveland's inauguration also brought new worries and an unfamiliar sense of accountability for the country's welfare. The party must demonstrate, after the Republican charges of the previous two decades, that it could safely be entrusted with national office. It would also have to shed its accustomed role as the party of opposition and assume, as House Speaker John G. Carlisle reminded fellow Democrats, "responsibilities which have heretofore rested on our opponents." Some observers questioned the party's ability to make such a transition, to turn from obstruction to formulation of a coherent policy. "The Democratic party," warned the *Nation* in 1886, "has for the first time in years found itself charged with the full responsibilities of govern-

ment. It comes to this task not as a united body, having a clear pro-
gramme and a settled platform of principles on the leading questions of
the day, but with very marked divisions in its ranks on all the leading
issues. This division is so marked that the leaders of the party are not
even agreed on the question what is the leading issue." [2]

By the mid-1880's, as the *Nation* suggested, internal fragmentation
was a hallmark of the Democratic party. Its organization, splintered in
successive crises over slavery, secession, and the Civil War, continued
to deteriorate during the postwar Republican supremacy. Imbued with
a governing philosophy of states rights, decentralization, and limited
government—doctrines which also found expression in the party structure—the Democratic party became less a national organization than a
loose grouping of state parties. Even in the South and other areas where
it possessed strength, the party depended on relatively informal alliances
between individuals rather than on a tight organizational framework.
Although Democrats often expressed admiration for the "more compact
and effective discipline" of their Republican opponents, they remained
unable to rectify this fundamental Democratic weakness. In 1878, the
prominent Kentucky editor Henry Watterson lamented the absence of
"cohesion" and "discipline" in the party. "On the other hand," noted
Watterson, "we see the Republicans deploy like a phalanx. It is enough
to make a cat howl." [3]

Lacking a strong organization, Democratic leaders before 1885 continually found it difficult to impose unity on their followers or even
among themselves. The party's tenure in opposition—when it drew
those who, for one reason or another, opposed the policies of the dominant Republicans—accentuated this problem and left it more than ever
a complex coalition of groups with differing, and often conflicting, interests. Critics in one state labeled it "a sort of Democratic happy family,
like we see in the prairie-dog villages, where owls, rattlesnakes, prairie-
dogs, and lizards all live in the same hole." The rural South and the
Democratic machines of the urban Northeast formed its most reliable
bases of strength, and the party claimed among its membership farmers
and industrial laborers, natives and immigrants, and small businessmen,
as well as merchants, bankers, and railroad magnates. This diversity, and
the disparity in outlook it entailed, fostered internal conflict and frequently made the Democratic coalition unstable. [4]

Unfortunately, the Democratic party consistently failed to attract
the type of leadership needed to unify its diverse membership and steer
it in a constructive direction. The party's undistinguished record during
the Civil War, its determination to restrain the federal government, and

a tendency to venerate tradition combined to convince ambitious, national-minded, and innovative men that they would find a more congenial home within the Republican organization. Moored firmly in the states, the party did gather a cadre of able and powerful local leaders, but they received little national exposure and were more parochial in outlook than Republican counterparts. Too often they proved unwilling to subordinate local objectives in the interest of a national party victory. Presidential campaigns raised a few Democrats to national stature, but the propensity to bestow nominations on such relatively obscure and inexperienced figures as Samuel J. Tilden, Winfield Scott Hancock, and Grover Cleveland provided a measure of the party's weakness in this regard.[5]

In the absence of vigorous leadership, the Democratic party in these years generally reflected the views of its conservative or Bourbon wing. An informal union of like-minded men throughout the country, the Bourbons believed that human society functioned according to immutable natural laws with which government should not interfere. The primary task of government, they thought, was to remove any man-made obstacles that might hinder the natural operation of these laws. Thomas F. Bayard, a prominent Delaware Democrat, concisely expressed the Bourbon philosophy when he recalled a visit to a busy canal near the Great Lakes: "I can still shut my eyes," Bayard declared, "and see the stately procession of majestic vessels, freighted with the native products of the vast Mid-west moving noiselessly along the pathway of beneficent exchanges. What a lesson is here against governmental interference! How wisely the well instructed spirit of self interest works in self directed channels, and is developed by natural competition without fear of contact with maleficent [sic] statutes!" If this echoed the rhetoric of the antebellum Democracy, Bayard and his fellow Bourbons did not resent the comparison. Temperamentally bound to the past, they offered a negative and simplistic guideline for the nation's future: a return to individualism and an end to "governmental interference" through a low tariff, sound currency, and administrative economy.[6]

Sizable elements within the party resisted the Bourbon demands. Many Democrats did not share the conservatives' confidence in the "well instructed spirit of self interest" and doubted the wisdom of such rigid restrictions on governmental activity. Alarmed by the inequities that accompanied the country's economic development, these members organized and led extensive anti-monopoly movements which attempted to regulate large corporations. Bitter intraparty differences also arose over the money question as Democrats from economically depressed areas in the South and West periodically demanded inflation in the form of paper currency or silver coinage. In these same sections, and in the cities of the Northeast, Democrats sought federal subsidies and appropriations with a persistent zeal which belied the party's pronouncements in behalf of frugal government. Urban Democrats in particular, aware that their power rested on a continuous flow of jobs and money, scorned "this cheap loaf of economy" and agreed with one Boston boss who asserted: "I never saw a man in my life who made economy his watchword who was not always defeated before the people." [7]

Democratic disunity was most apparent on the tariff question. Men like Kentucky's Henry Watterson, convinced of the futility of further agitation of Reconstruction issues, early seized on tariff reform as a way to refurbish the party's image and enlist new recruits. Diligent work by the reformers resulted in the inclusion of tariff-for-revenue-only planks in the Democratic platforms of 1876 and 1880. But Watterson and his allies met stiff opposition within the party. Most Democratic leaders, mindful of protection's economic and emotional appeal, exhibited a profound distaste for the issue. One segment of the party, represented in Congress by Pennsylvania's Samuel J. Randall and about forty followers, fought any significant reduction in duties. Even such ostensible reformers as Thomas F. Bayard wavered when reform threatened to touch home industries. In an attempt to straddle the issue, many Democrats simply called themselves "incidental protectionists" and took awkward refuge in expressions of support for both reform and protection.[8] An indication of the party's confusion came in 1880 when its presidential candidate, General Winfield Scott Hancock, virtually repudiated the platform's revenue plank, dismissed the tariff as a "local question," and assured manufacturers they would receive "just as much protection" from his party as from the Republicans. Reformers withdrew from the canvass in disgust, and a cartoonist later depicted the bewildered general on a campaign platform whispering to a companion: "Who is Tariff, and why is he for revenue only?" [9]

By 1885, and the inauguration of Grover Cleveland, the Democratic party seemed woefully unprepared to rule, tired and fragmented, lacking focus and discipline, with neither a coherent national purpose nor experienced leadership. Despite the gradual passing of Civil War memories, many northerners still distrusted the Democratic party: "they dread the restoration of the democratic party to power," a pro-Cleveland newspaper acknowledged. Twenty-five years of supremacy had left Republicans with less fear than contempt for a party which one called "a hopeless assortment of discordant differences, as incapable of positive action as it is capable of infinite clamor." In candid moments, Democrats also questioned their party's capacity to govern. "It was a bad thing for the South," a disheartened Henry Watterson once remarked, "that its fortunes were in any way tied to the lumbering bag of dry bones and dead language, which at the close of the war, was labeled the Democratic party." Grover Cleveland assumed a difficult and discouraging legacy as he moved into the White House in March, 1885.[10]

Optimistic Democrats, on the other hand, cited several major advantages which helped offset their party's weaknesses. Foremost among these stood the continuing Democratic appeal to the electorate. By almost any measurement, the party made a rapid recovery after the war. As early as 1868 its presidential nominee carried four northern states, including New York. During the 1870's, with economic depression, the waning of Reconstruction, and the Grant scandals, the voters turned in increasing numbers to the Democratic party. In 1874, less than a decade after the war, the party gained control of the House of Representatives, which it maintained for all but four of the succeeding twenty years. Of the five presidential elections between 1876 and 1892, it won a plurality of the popular vote in all except one. To Democrats, conscious of the handicaps under which they labored, the party's electoral strength proved its "indestructible vitality." "This is not accidental," contended William L. Wilson of West Virginia. "It can have no other rational explanation than that the party has been, from the beginning, the guardian and defender of some fundamental principle, or principles, of free government, in whose truth and permanence it has found its life and its growth." [11]

Democratic campaign strategy in these years always began with the "Solid South." A sizable Republican vote, persistent local factionalism, and frequent independent movements worried Democratic politicians and made the South less solid than it seemed. But the Democrats, using their own, more successful version of the "bloody shirt," managed nevertheless to defeat every Republican attempt to loosen their political hold on the section. Between 1880 and 1892, none of the fifteen southern and border states gave an electoral vote to a Republican candidate for the presidency. Democratic strategists could rely on these states to furnish their presidential nominees with approximately 135 electoral votes, only about fifty short of the number needed to win.[12]

From the relative security of its southern bastion, the party stretched into the crucial northern states which, during the last two decades of the century, supplied the margin of victory or defeat in national elections. Despite its fundamental dependence on the South, the Democratic party rested on a less sectional base than did the Republican party. While identification with Negro rights and military rule stunted Republican strength below the Potomac, the Democratic principles of states rights, administrative economy, and limited government won adherents everywhere. Roman Catholics, German Lutherans, and other non-moralistic ethnic groups gravitated toward Democratic ranks in resentment against the prohibition, public school, and sabbatarian legislation demanded by the pietistic wing of the Republican party.[13] Through the activities and influence of such organizations as Tammany Hall in New York City, the foreign-born also formed a large reservoir of Democratic voters in the North. "When he first landed in New York with his wife," ran Mark Twain's exaggerated characterization of the typical immigrant, "he had only halted at Castle Garden for a few minutes to receive and exhibit papers showing that he had resided in this country two years—and then he voted the democratic ticket and went up town to hunt a house." [14]

Above all, the Democratic party appealed to those throughout the country who longed for a return to simpler ways. To people weary of Reconstruction commitments, distrustful of Republican activism, troubled by a rapidly changing society, Democratic orators offered the comfort of a simple remedy: "the master-wisdom of governing little and leaving as much as possible to localities and to individuals." Democrats on the state level consistently demonstrated the fruitfulness of this approach, making major advances in the areas of labor legislation, political reform, and business regulation.[15] Unhappily, most party members failed to recognize that these achievements, however significant, were limited and temporary, that a nation's complex problems demanded complex national solutions. But in the 1870's and 1880's the Democratic philosophy attracted those who believed, in the words of William L. Wilson, that "it is better for some things to be done imperfectly and clumsily than to set up a paternal and bureaucratic government to do them." It remained to be seen whether this philosophy could survive a national crisis, if it could answer the needs of an increasingly urban-industrial society, whether in fact it provided a suitable foundation on which the Democratic party, under Grover Cleveland, might construct a national political majority.[16]

The man to whom the party had entrusted its immediate future initially displayed considerable distaste for his new duties. "I look upon the four years next to come as a dreadful self-inflicted penance for the good of my country," Cleveland told a friend before his inauguration. "I can see no pleasure in it and no satisfaction, only a hope that I may be of service to my people." Always cautious, Cleveland seemed to realize that his swift rise to national prominence, including brief service as mayor of Buffalo and governor of New York, had not prepared him for presidential responsibilities. A reputation for conservatism, political independence, and official integrity, together with a full measure of luck, had carried him to the White House.

At the outset of his presidency Cleveland made it clear that he sought no sharp departures from established Democratic policy. In words reassuring to his fellow Bourbons, his inaugural address proposed only an economical government, a sound financial system, an "unstrained" interpretation of the Constitution, and appointments based on "merit and competency" instead of "party subserviency." The address carefully skirted the tariff issue. "The people," Cleveland declared, "demand reform in the administration of the Government and the application of business principles to public affairs." [17]

In the four years that followed, Cleveland's stubborn and courageous pursuit of these goals won widespread public acclaim and earned for the Democratic party a new respectability. By 1888, as the *New York Times* argued, the President had "destroyed forever the superstition that the Government could be safe only in the hands of one party." The 1886 midterm elections produced such limited Republican gains that they virtually amounted to a victory for the administration. The Democrats retained control of the House, losing only fourteen seats, and sliced their opponents' margin in the Senate. The party also performed satisfactorily in most state contests.

As public esteem for Cleveland grew, Republicans were openly fearful about their prospects in 1888. A friend warned Benjamin Harrison of Indiana that "the people are well satisfied with the administration of Cleveland." Franklin K. Lane, a young California journalist and later a member of Woodrow Wilson's Cabinet, agreed: "The people admire old Grover's strength so much, he is a positive man and an honest man, and when the people see these two exceptional virtues mixed happily in a candidate they grow to love and admire him out of the very idealism of their natures." [18]

One significant element did not join in the general praise. Behind Cleveland's personal triumph lay a party in open rebellion against the administration's patronage policy. It would have been difficult for any president to quench the voracious demands of an organization that had been excluded from federal spoils for twenty-five years, but Grover Cleveland, whose short career had not included training in the symbolic and practical importance of the patronage to local party structures, made no attempt to conceal his contempt for office-seekers. As he once remarked, "when a man begins to talk about office I begin to get irritable and my head begins to ache." Sound advice on patronage came from Samuel J. Tilden and others, but Cleveland generally ignored it and instead pursued a confused and capricious patronage course.

The resultant criticism from Democratic leaders often took an extremely bitter tone. The party, charged the Nebraska Democratic Chairman, had been "mugwumped to a state of idiocy. The President has a big belly. His brains are not proportioned to it." "Faithlessness is a passport to recognition by this mass of Presidential fat," added the head of the California party. "Our people are howling against him over the whole country. With this feeling existing, can it be possible he is again to be our nominee[?] God grant otherwise." [19]

The party's patronage troubles only symbolized its larger misfortunes between 1885 and 1887. James G. Blaine and other Republicans were busy remolding their party to face fresh challenges and to fit new constituencies, but the Democratic party lingered in its antebellum past, preoccupied with spoils, splintered by the conflicting objectives of local chieftains, preferring time-honored negativism to constructive innovation. The President displayed a penchant for details rather than an awareness of the larger concepts of national and party policy. His early, rigidly narrow view of the presidency precluded active political leadership. His well-known inability to accept advice or delegate responsibility —Tilden called him "the kind of man who would rather do something badly for himself than to have somebody else do it well"—hampered the growth of a cadre of experienced Democratic policy-makers. Cleveland's task, in effect, had been to create a national party, to unify and revitalize the aging Democratic party. Instead, he adopted an individual approach to the presidency, which enhanced his own stature but did not cure his party's deep-seated ills. "The Democratic party isn't in power," complained a disgusted Vice-President Thomas A. Hendricks. "Grover Cleveland is making a party of his own." [20]

Then, on December 6, 1887, the President took the first decisive step of his administration. Alarmed by the growing surplus in the Treasury and perhaps conscious of the need to rally his party for the coming election, he devoted his entire annual message to an attack on the present tariff laws, "the vicious, inequitable, and illogical source of unnecessary taxation." In one stroke, Cleveland committed himself and his followers to reform the protective system. Tariff revision, Democrats knew, had major drawbacks as a political issue. Protectionist sentiment within their own party was still strong. Opponents would ignore the President's promise of "safe, careful, and deliberate reform" and his plea against "bandying epithets" like free trade. The Democrats would be branded as free traders, accused of unsettling the country's economy, and could suffer serious losses among Irish voters who linked tariff reform with English interests. Above all, they would have to overcome the long-established Republican argument which tied the tariff to prosperity and patriotism in a national framework of protection for manufacturers, farmers, and laborers. Rumors that Cleveland intended to take a firm stand on the issue brought warnings to "go slow" from cautious Democrats. As one wrote: "The danger of alienating large bodies of workmen, whose ignorance is crass, who are thoroughly organized, and whose employers are extremely jealous of any danger of loss of profits, is to my mind the danger of the situation." [21]

Shrewder observers, however, realized that Cleveland's message was an astute political move. A determined campaign to lower the tariff offered the party a much-needed opportunity to expand its electoral base. Adroitly used, the reform issue could gather new recruits from eastern importers and merchants, southern and western farmers, and New England manufacturers who desired cheaper raw materials. Throughout the country, Democratic speakers could argue persuasively that high duties meant high prices for consumers and that the tariff dampened economic growth by accumulating surplus funds in the Treasury. Mindful of the narrowness of Cleveland's 1884 victory over James G. Blaine, party strategists saw the issue as a way to penetrate Republican areas of the Midwest and unite New England, New York, and the Democratic South in a powerful and permanent anti-tariff coalition. Exploited with skill and vigor, tariff reform would place the Republicans on the defensive and lay the foundation for Democratic hegemony.[22]

For a time at least, Cleveland's message also fostered a spirited sense of commitment and cohesion within the Democratic party. To a party uncertain of its future and disrupted by civil service reform, the message came, in the words of the *Washington Post,* as "a ringing reminder of duty to be done." It inspired some party members, rejuvenated others who had despaired of tariff revision, and gave to all Democrats the popular war-cry of ending subsidies to special interests. Tariff reform had a positive and constructive sound, although in reality it fit neatly into the traditional Democratic demand for the separation of government and business. Democrats like West Virginia's William L. Wilson thought the President had revolutionized the party. Heretofore, Wilson frankly admitted in 1888, "the Democratic party, made up of all the elements of opposition to the practices and policies of the past twenty years, [lacked] something of the homogeneousness and organic unity of a party organized upon clear and definite lines of public policy." But now it had become "a great living organism, instinct with life, with enthusiasm, and rallied upon great principles which it understands, believes in, and is eager to champion." It "has been transformed from a party of opposition into a party of positive policies and aggressive courage." [23]

Unfortunately for the party, Wilson's assessment of its "aggressive courage" was premature. Instead of a vigorous defense of tariff reform, the Democrats soon lapsed into their customary disunity and indecision. Appropriately enough, Cleveland headed the retreat. Growing fearful of the political hazards of his tariff position, he decided to press for an evasive revenue plank in the 1888 Democratic platform. Carried to the convention by Maryland Senator Arthur Pue Gorman, the President's proposed plank ignored his recent message and did not even include the word *tariff*. Unaware of Cleveland's role in the affair, bewildered reporters noted that "this little game is not easy to understand." But Gorman and his allies were unable to stem the new-found enthusiasm of the tariff reformers led by Henry Watterson of Kentucky. To Cleveland's equivocal draft the convention added a direct commendation of his message and a strong endorsement of tariff reduction. Enraged, the President attempted to modify the party's stand in his letter of acceptance.[24]

Democratic indecision extended into the 1888 presidential campaign. Although Cleveland recognized that a favorable outcome depended on "information and organization," the Democrats failed to match the skilled efficiency of the Republican canvass under Benjamin Harrison of Indiana. The President himself, apparently convinced that his educational task had ended in 1887, refused to campaign and remained at the White House or his summer home throughout the crucial contest. He also acquiesced in the selection of two high-tariff Democrats to direct the canvass. "What a predicament the party is placed in," lamented a Texas Democrat, "with revenue reform for its battle cry and with a known protectionist and the head of the great copper trust of this country as our chairman and leader."

The election results reflected Democratic lassitude. Cleveland won two northern states—New Jersey and Connecticut—and a 90,000-vote national plurality based largely on increased Democratic majorities in the South. Harrison won New York, Indiana, and the election. A marginal Republican performance in the Midwest suggested the possibility of a different outcome had the Democrats waged a united and vigorous campaign. But with Republicans in control of the presidency and both houses of Congress, Democratic defeat seemed complete.[25]

Yet, in the course of the next four years, a succession of major victories revived the party's hopes and convinced jubilant Democrats that an "extraordinary political revolution" had occurred across the nation. Several developments led to the marked Democratic resurgence after 1888. In the Midwest, the party profited from the activities of local Republican pietists who sought legislative implementation of their moralistic goals. Temperance agitation momentarily overturned the Iowa Republican organization and enabled the Democrats to capture the governorship in 1889 and 1891. In Wisconsin and Illinois, Republican efforts to restrict parochial schools resulted in similar gains for the Democrats. Minnesota Democrats likewise benefited from their opponents' evangelical zeal, and in 1890 Nebraska elected its first Democratic governor. Throughout the Midwest, as angry German Lutherans and Catholics deserted the Republican party, it appeared that the Democratic party might at last become the region's dominant political institution.[26]

An even greater boost to Democratic fortunes came in the nationwide reaction against the Republican Fifty-first Congress. Labeled the "Billion Dollar Congress" for its appropriations, subsidies, and pension grants, the session discredited the Republicans and gave the Democrats an opportunity to attack Republican expenditures and governmental activism. The high-tariff McKinley Act, passed in the fall of 1890, raised fears of higher prices and underscored the Democratic demand for tariff reform. An abortive attempt to enact a Federal Elections bill aroused antagonism in the North as well as the South.

From his New York City law office, Grover Cleveland watched the Republicans "getting deeper and deeper into the mire" and advised party leaders to "let them flounder" rather than propose alternative policies. It was sound strategy, for the 1890 elections displayed the enormous increase in Democratic strength. Republican representation in the House dropped from 166 to 88, while the Democrats won 235 seats. Traditional Republican strongholds like Ohio, Illinois, Michigan, and Kansas witnessed Democratic victories. The Democrats achieved their first significant penetration of New England in three decades. Massachusetts chose a Democratic governor and seven Democratic congressmen. In a letter to his state committee, one Massachusetts Democrat expressed the sense of wonderment felt by party members across the country: "I think we can with a good deal of *Modesty* ask for some of your *Congratulations,* as our town went Democratic for the first time in the History of the *World.*"[27]

The 1892 presidential election was another impressive triumph for the Democratic party, confirmed its new electoral appeal, and indicated the possibility that a permanent change had occurred in American politics. With Cleveland again their nominee, the Democrats carried the South, New York, New Jersey, Connecticut, Indiana, and part of the electoral vote of several other states. Cleveland also took Wisconsin and Illinois, the first Democratic candidate to do so since the 1850's. A large share of the labor vote and increased strength in the cities imparted additional significance to the party's achievement.[28] For the first time since before the Civil War the Democrats captured control of the White House and both branches of Congress. It was the most decisive triumph won by either party in twenty years. When inauguration day arrived, Democrats believed they had ended the stalemate which had characterized American politics for two decades. Confident leaders even predicted that the Republican party would soon disintegrate and disappear. "Democratic victory this time," declared the *Atlanta Constitution* on the day after the election, "means the inevitable dissolution of the republican party, and the splendor of yesterday's democratic victory is proof positive that the day of republican dismemberment is not far distant." "It is a revolution," agreed the *New York Times,* "and no Republican can even hope to see his party again in power for a long term of years." [29]

As in 1885, however, thoughtful observers noted flaws behind the Democratic façade. Internal confusion and dissension continued to beset the party. Cleveland's drive for the nomination had involved him in a bitter fight with New York Senator David B. Hill. The 1892 national convention reenacted the 1888 struggle between Cleveland and ardent tariff reformers. A strong reform platform and concentration on the tariff in the campaign fostered unprecedented unity on the issue, but Democrats still exhibited uncertainty over actual rate reductions.[30] The silver question also promised to be troublesome. Cleveland's overt hostility to the white metal contrasted with the free silver platforms adopted in Democratic state conventions throughout the South and much of the West. The swift spread of agrarian discontent, expressed in the Farmers' Alliance and later the People's party, alarmed Democratic leaders and threatened to disrupt the party's southern bastion.[31] Above all, the Democratic party's victories in 1890 and 1892 had rested largely on a negative foundation, based on popular opposition to Republican policies rather than on the advancement and public acceptance of a coherent Democratic program. Whether the Democrats could implement such a program, and convert new voters into permanent supporters, was the major question of the second Cleveland administration.

Unfortunately, the Democratic party after 1893 possessed neither the favorable conditions nor the skillful management needed for this task. Within a short time of Cleveland's inauguration, tested by a severe economic depression, the party was thoroughly divided and discredited. Its leadership, inept and ineffectual when confronted with the problems of the decade, enfeebled the party organization and alienated the electorate. For these related developments Grover Cleveland bore a large responsibility. To his party he provided no possibility for compromise and accommodation; to the nation he offered no hope for escape from economic hardship. His inflexibility and tenacity, qualities which had won praise during the more placid years of his first administration, became serious liabilities in a situation which demanded experimentation, innovation, and bold leadership.

Most important, Cleveland's approach to the depression gave rise to a general belief that the Democratic party was unresponsive and unsympathetic to the economic plight of the people. This belief, which grew steadily during the currency, labor, and other controversies of the mid-1890's, was the largest single influence in the popular repudiation of the President and his party by 1896. While the country demanded positive action, wrote one embittered observer, "this 300 pounds of fat, called Cleveland, sits astride the Nation, pulling and rowelling his steed, and thinking he is a devil of a rider because it kicks so." [32]

Against a background of unemployment, suffering, and discontent, the Cleveland administration demonstrated the fatal inability of Democratic negativism to cope with a national crisis. As members of a "depression party," faced with unusually complex problems and armed only with rudimentary economic knowledge, the Democrats could hardly have achieved a complete measure of success and popularity. But a wide field for effective action and spirited leadership existed in the economic and political conditions of the 1890's. Many Democrats on the state level, where constant contact with the electorate taught the value of flexibility, made the necessary adjustments in party philosophy. Cleveland and other national leaders did not. Dogmatic, stubborn, and self-righteous, determined to resist "the unwholesome progeny of paternalism," they clung unwaveringly to the ancient Bourbon faith in "the inexorable laws of finance and trade" which governed human society.[33] "In times like these," explained one Cabinet member, "when every citizen is striving to reduce expenses, the Government, which is merely a collection of citizens, must do the same thing." Another of the President's advisers phrased it more vigorously: the administration's primary task, he declared, was to oppose the unfortunate impulse toward "High Daddy government," to hold fast against " 'reforms' which mean that the Government is to rock the cradle and drive the hearse, weep over the grave and sit up with the widow, and pay every man for cracking his own lice." [34]

This outlook fostered policies which resulted in a rapid decline in

Democratic fortunes from their high point in March, 1893. Repeal of the Sherman Silver Purchase Act, pushed through Congress in the fall of 1893 as the Cleveland panacea for the nation's economic ills, failed to relieve the depression, split the party, and evoked resentment against the President's negative approach to economic hardship. A tactical error of vast consequence, Cleveland's demand for immediate and unconditional repeal focused national attention on the money question and ended Democratic hopes of submerging their currency differences in a campaign to reform the tariff.[35] The subsequent use of bond sales to buttress the gold standard, including an 1895 issue to a private syndicate headed by J. P. Morgan, added to growing discontent and increased suspicions that Cleveland had succumbed to the influence of Eastern financiers. In March, 1894, moreover, the President sternly rejected a chance for compromise when he vetoed a bill to authorize the coinage of the silver seigniorage in the Treasury. Ignoring advice that the silver Democrats considered the bill "a great opportunity to unify the party by doing something for their side of the question," Cleveland angered supporters of the white metal and once again raised charges that he followed a "purely obstructive" policy toward the depression.[36] The President's actions throughout had been consistent and courageous, but they had little effect on the economic situation and exacerbated the divisions within the party. Unhappily for Cleveland, they also intensified the silver sentiment he had intended to dampen.

An abortive effort to lower the tariff in 1894 furnished the final blow to Democratic prospects. The opportunity for genuine reform, seasoned politicians knew, had vanished the previous year with Cleveland's decision to place the currency before the tariff. A troublesome matter at any time, tariff reform demanded a spirit of unity and enthusiasm which the party, torn and discouraged by the silver controversy, no longer possessed. Recent events had encouraged a revival of Democratic localism which now found expression in an emasculated tariff bill. Cleveland's one attempt to provide national leadership and inspiration, a public letter to William L. Wilson which bluntly accused Democratic congressmen of "party perfidy and party dishonor," overlooked his own responsibility for the party's tariff difficulties and embittered Democrats who pointedly reminded the President of his past evasions on the issue. Speaking for many of his colleagues, Maryland's Arthur Pue Gorman told the Senate that "the limit of endurance has been reached." In mid-August of 1894 the unpopular Wilson-Gorman tariff bill passed Congress, and Cleveland let it become law without his signature. A product of Democratic divisions, the law supplied a dismal conclusion to the party's tariff reform crusade.[37]

The extent of popular disenchantment with Democratic policies became evident in the 1894 state and congressional elections. Party leaders had early recognized the likelihood of a major setback, but few anticipated the magnitude of the Democratic party's defeat. Promising protection and prosperity in contrast to the "utter imbecility" of the Cleveland administration, the Republicans profited from a countrywide reaction that buried the Democratic party in state after state. In the largest transfer of congressional strength in American history, the Democrats lost 113 House seats, while Republican totals rose from 127 to 244. A gain of five seats gave the Republicans a chance to control the Senate. Twenty-four states elected no Democrats to national office; six others chose only one Democrat each. A single Democrat represented the party's once-bright hopes in New England. The election virtually destroyed the party in the Midwest. Of the eighty-nine representatives from that region, only three now bore the Democratic standard. Everywhere, the Republicans recaptured their 1892 losses and cut deeply into traditional Democratic sources of support.[38] In the aftermath of the election, the divisions within the party hardened as administration and anti-administration forces each blamed the other for defeat. Democratic unity and confidence disappeared. The expectations of political dominance that had accompanied Grover Cleveland's victory in 1892 had not materialized.[39]

A marked economic upturn after 1894 might have enabled the Democrats to salvage something from the wreckage, but the depression continued to feed popular discontent and the Cleveland administration became ever more conservative and rigid. Its adherents saw themselves as the last remaining bulwark in defense of the Constitution and sound government. Massed against them, they believed, were the forces of radicalism, the "silver bullionaires, industrial tramps and train wreckers, dreamers, dunces, cracked women, bums, bullies and loafers, who want to repudiate their own debts and divide the property of the thrifty and well-ordered." If unpopular now, the conservatives constantly reassured each other, history would vindicate them and their beleaguered President. "That his integrity of purpose and his wisdom will endure to the end no one doubts," exulted an ardent Cleveland man, "and his name will gain in splendor in the high company of the great who have held fast to the eternal verities in crises when the weak, venal and ignorant have clothed themselves in dreams, or profited by pretenses." Alone in a hostile world, convinced of their righteousness, the Cleveland Democrats battled in the nineties for the "eternal verities": property, sound money, limited government, and the Constitution. For many of them it was an exhilarating experience.[40]

The administration's continued resistance to change, the spread of silver sentiment, the tariff fiasco, and the party's crushing 1894 defeat created a worrisome dilemma for individual Democrats. Under attack from every direction, identified with the President's unpopular actions, some Democrats early succumbed to the temptation to repudiate the head of their party and place themselves in harmony with the views of their constituents. But to most party members, however much they disagreed with Cleveland's policies, a break with the national leadership was a misfortune to avoid. The vast majority of Democrats strove continuously in the mid-1890's to find common ground with the Cleveland administration. "We either have a party," declared one Democratic senator, "or we constitute an affair that cannot be called either an organization or a democratic institution, and if we pretend to be a party we will be forced to stand by our administration." The history of Cleveland's second term was in large part the story of the earnest efforts of individual Democrats to remain loyal to Grover Cleveland and his administration.[41]

No single event between 1893 and 1896 caused the failure of these efforts. Inept handling of the patronage, the decision to postpone tariff reform, administration rigidity on the currency issue, suppression of the Pullman strike, repeated bond sales—each had a different impact on different Democrats. Cleveland demanded strict obedience from Democratic followers, frequently asking them in effect to endanger or forfeit political positions at home, but his own actions plainly displayed an unwillingness to make comparable concessions.

Finally, at various points after 1893, individual Democrats reluctantly concluded they could no longer compromise with an uncompromising administration. At first one by one, and then in droves, they deserted the President, leaving him the spokesman for an ever smaller coterie of fervent supporters. The Democratic party was deeply "fractured" at least two years before 1896, and William Jennings Bryan's candidacy only formalized a process that had begun as early as 1893. Cleveland, not Bryan, compelled Democrats to commit themselves in the nineties. In the end, the 1896 Democratic National Convention revealed, to Cleveland's dismay, the nature of the party's new commitment.[42]

The nomination of Nebraska's William Jennings Bryan in 1896, on a free silver platform that denounced nearly every measure pursued by Grover Cleveland since 1893, completed the party's break with the administration and created a "New" Democratic party. "Now," lamented a member of Cleveland's Cabinet, "we find perverts where we least expected them, and a madness that cannot be dealt with or, indeed, scarcely approached." [43] Bryan's nomination revived Democratic hopes for success in the election. The young and handsome Nebraskan, waging an evangelistic cross-country campaign, brought the Democrats closer to victory than any other candidate could have done. Although the nominee of a divided and discredited party, Bryan, with the aid of the Populists still attracted almost 48 percent of the popular vote in the nation. His emotional crusade for silver capitalized on agrarian discontent and won voters who otherwise would not have supported the Democratic ticket.

Bryan's terse explanation for his defeat—"I have borne the sins of Grover Cleveland"—ignored the basic weaknesses of his own one-issue canvass and the effectiveness of the deft tariff-centered campaign waged by the Republicans under William McKinley. But in the 1890's, the explanation seemed accurate and suggested that the election's significance lay in how close Bryan came to winning despite grave handicaps. The Nebraskan was "beaten in advance," as one Democratic newspaper noted. "Three years of Clevelandism had reduced the Democracy to a hopeless wreck." [44]

Such reflections consoled defeated Democrats, for careful study of the returns also revealed that the election had confirmed the political revolution of 1894. In gathering a 600,000-vote plurality, the largest for either party since 1872, McKinley and the Republicans consolidated a massive electoral coalition which imprisoned the Democratic party in the South and scattered sections of the West. The appearance of Maryland, Delaware, West Virginia, and Kentucky in the McKinley column testified to the party's loosened hold on areas of former strength. The urban centers of the Northeast and Midwest, which generally went Democratic in 1892, now furnished part of the base on which the Republican coalition rested. Extending the pattern that emerged two years before, the Democrats in 1896 carried only one midwestern city with more than 45,000 inhabitants, lost normally Democratic New York and San Francisco, and won only seven of Boston's twenty-five wards. A single county in New York State, and none in all of New England, gave a plurality to the Democratic candidate. Devastating losses in the cities, and among labor, immigrant, and some farm voters, reflected the continuation of the 1894 anti-Democratic trend, as well as William Jennings Bryan's lack of appeal to these elements. More than ever dependent on the South, the Democrats were again the familiar party of opposition. Their search for a permanent majority, seemingly so close to realization in 1892, ended in total failure. [45]

The elections of 1894 and 1896 together closed a distinct era in American political history. They terminated the politics of equilibrium which had prevailed since the Civil War and laid the foundation for a generation of Republican rule. For the thirty-five years after 1894, broken only by brief resurgence under Woodrow Wilson, the Democrats remained the minority party. The advent of McKinley prosperity, the Spanish-American War, and the popularity of Republican policies all contributed to this development, but the electorate also discovered that the "New" Democratic party differed surprisingly little from the old. New leaders brought fresh ideologies to the party, and William Jennings Bryan espoused a more active brand of reform than had Grover Cleveland. But in general, the party after 1896 remained firmly rooted in negativism, clinging to outdated ideals of states rights, retrenchment, and limited government. Another free silver platform in 1900, and the nomination of a Cleveland Democrat in 1904, advertised the continued Democratic inability to adjust to the needs of a changing society.

In the critical task of party management, Bryan was as inept as his predecessor. To voters in the early twentieth century, concerned with the problems of advancing industrialism, the Democratic party seemed a ramshackle, almost irrelevant array, lacking the national outlook and cohesion needed to govern effectively. They distrusted a party which had never learned to unify and organize diverse followers in behalf of constructive programs. Only in the 1920's and 1930's, when the party produced leaders attuned to an urban-industrial society and when the Republicans, in turn, failed to alleviate a severe depression, did the mass of voters decide to entrust their future to the Democratic party.[46]

As they surveyed the ruins of their party in the late 1890's, Democrats naturally recalled the bright prospects with which they had begun the decade. Two successive elections repudiated the Republican party and seemed to presage the establishment of permanent Democratic hegemony. Yet within a few years the party had completely squandered its hard-won gains. The depression was the basic cause for the reversal, but Democrats questioned whether the disaster was inevitable, whether in fact the party could have retained unity and a measure of public confidence even in economic hardship. They speculated in particular on the outcome for the party if Cleveland, like William McKinley in 1897, had sidestepped the volatile currency issue and called a special session of Congress devoted to tariff reform. "Nearly all of the other blunders by the Democratic party grew out of this one fatal mistake," contended the *Chicago Herald,* expressing a conclusion common to most Democrats. "Started wrong, it went wrong, and at every turn it was given a further impetus in the wrong direction by some mischievous utterance from the White House." Party members wondered if a skillful president might have drawn much of the sting from the silver movement. Cleveland's dogmatic approach clearly had transformed the white metal from simply an infla-

tionary instrument into the symbol for a wide range of popular grievances. Above all, these Democrats recognized, the critical events for the
party had occurred between 1893 and 1895 when Cleveland emasculated
it and shaped American politics for decades to come. In a fundamental
sense, the actions of Grover Cleveland and the national Democratic
party had thrust the Republican party into power.[47]

Cleveland's real weakness during his second administration was not
his failure to solve the depression—no one could have fully accomplished
that—nor was it his stubborn pursuit of principles. The weakness was the
manner in which the President had approached the task, his retreat
into unthinking rigidity, the failure to provide positive leadership, and
growing isolation from popular sentiment in the country. His inability to
accept advice stifled criticism, however constructive, and produced a
small band of loyal adherents who, in their enthusiasm, constantly misled him about the political and economic situation in their states.

Cleveland had indulged in a dangerous tendency to classify members
of the party as either "statesmen" or "politicians," assigning to the
former category those who unreservedly supported his policies. He had
never recognized the existence of a middle rank of Democrats who sought
to unite principle and party. To this latter group, the large number of
party members who conscientiously endeavored after 1893 to maintain
the middle ground, Cleveland had to appeal if he hoped to preserve the
party and perpetuate its principles. His failure to make such an appeal,
to provide a basis for united action, polarized the Democratic party.

Because he delighted in being viewed as superior to his party, it was
ironic that much of Cleveland's troubles stemmed from an inability to rise
above the party's outdated doctrines. Neither he nor the national party
kept pace with a changing country. By the mid-1890's Democratic localism and negativism no longer served as satisfying answers in an increasingly industrialized, interdependent society. In a time of national crisis,
Cleveland demonstrated the sterility of the Democratic ideal of negative
government. As bond issue followed bond issue, unaccompanied by
spirited leadership, the people lost faith in an administration and a party
which appeared irrelevant to their needs and callous to their plight. In
growing numbers they accepted the Republican tenets of economic nationalism and governmental activism which they had repudiated only a
few years before.

For this development Cleveland and the Democrats had only themselves to blame. Awarded national power in 1892, they failed to meet the
challenge in a way that would satisfy the voters, strengthen the party organization, and insure continued Democratic electoral victories. If the

voters turned after 1894 to "the party of progress, prosperity, and national authority," they also turned against the party and principles of Grover Cleveland.[48] This was Cleveland's main legacy to his party and the nation.

H. WAYNE MORGAN

∽ 8 ∾

Populism and the Decline
of Agriculture

MANY COMMENTATORS noted the summer heat in 1890. High humidity plagued the South, and "dust-devils" crossed the Plains States, but much of the atmosphere was emotional. Politicians, editors, observers on city stoops and small-town porches detected a public desire for change, especially among farmers. Weary congressmen who had sat in Washington since December, 1889, recognized the signs, but their unusual activity did not seem to change the mood. The dominant Republicans passed a flood of major legislation in the Fifty-first Congress: the Sherman Antitrust Act, the McKinley Tariff, the Sherman Silver Purchase Act. They almost secured a federal election law, and scores of unpublicized bills improved the public service. But expensive internal improvement projects, pension legislation, and expanded services all cost money. And more and more people thought tariff protection raised consumer prices. Whatever the diverse reasons, the November congressional election results were disastrous for Republicans, who declined from 166 to 88 House members, while the Democrats rose from 156 to 235 members. Fourteen newcomers wearing the label "Populist" would sit in the new House; two "Alliancemen" went to the Senate. Politicians caught the sounds of approaching trouble. For a generation, both parties had contested every national election as a matter of survival, each trying to forge a national coalition. Voters defeated many Republicans in 1890 on local issues concerning temperance, school curricula, and regulatory legislation, but agrarian discontent impressed national commentators. The Republicans seemed to be gaining, but the present repudiation could be a major setback if discontented farmers left GOP ranks. In an era of balanced politics, they could make the difference in the presidential election of 1892.

149

James S. Clarkson knew this better than most men. As editor of the *Des Moines Register*, an original Republican and fierce partisan, he carefully analyzed voter sentiment. Iowa seemed safe, but farmers liked panaceas. Clarkson sensed a potential farm uprising that might become bipartisan, allying an angry West and South in a threat to both major parties. Clarkson did not quite know how to meet this unrest. Most midwestern farmers had responded to the GOP's nationalistic program of land division, internal improvements, and tariff protection, but Republican policies seemed inapplicable directly to farm debts and overproduction. Agrarian resentment also increased as politicians paid more attention to industrial interests. Business moved inexorably into trusts that supposedly raised the prices farmers paid without benefit in the prices of what they sold. Politicians hoped to combat this feeling by bringing farmers into local affairs. People liked ritualistic, secret societies, Clarkson noted. "The Farmers' Alliance is in itself more the product of social hunger than political thought or action," he wrote President Harrison. "The farm neighborhood has little social life, has none of the secret societies, nothing of clubs, scarcely a church sociable. We propose to put a Republican club into every farm neighborhood possible, as soon as we can, and make it a social and literary as well as political force." [1] His attitude reflected myth, reality, and a frank desire to avoid political dissension.

But it was not an illogical notion. The nation was familiar with the "Granger movement" and similar organizations. They gained national recognition through railroad regulation, especially in the depressed 1870's, but prosperity let the societies emphasize social and educational activities that buttressed the myths of virtuous rural life. Grangers were important in state and local politics, largely Republican in the West and Democratic in the South in national politics. In the mid-1870's, forty-four states had Granges or similar organizations. Towns on Kansas prairies and in Vermont hills centered on a Grange hall, where Sunday afternoon picnics and week-night dances relieved rural drabness.[2] Books and newspapers extolled the virtues of new planting methods, modern machinery, and market information; but this reading perpetuated the farmer's basic philosophy of self-help. The increasing desire to glorify and preserve the small independent farmer had roots deep in American life, but also signaled his passing. An age of collectivized "business farming" was at hand. The Granger movement was essentially reactionary, trying to segregate the farmer from society, raising his standard of living without contamination from alleged urban vices.

Many farmers feared the glamorous appeals of education that widened youth's horizons to include the city or a nonagricultural career. They often saw higher education as a pillar of a caste system in economics and politics. Favoring "technical education" that involved knowledge useful in the field and corral, they opposed the "frills" of languages, history, or pure science. Larger school grants also meant higher tax levies.[3]

Behind romantic popular views of agrarian life loomed steadily increasing economic problems. In 1885, a New York paper warned that "Future storms will come not from the South, but from the West." [4] As the age of eager subsidy for transportation passed, farmers away from cities increasingly grumbled at excessive government support to industry, without apparent aid to agriculture. Discontented western farmers threatened the connections that politicians of both major parties had laid between the East Coast and the land beyond Pennsylvania. Southern agrarians stirred within the Democratic party. Some openly suggested a new politics, involving a West-South alliance, with cooperation between farmers and workers on the theme of hard work and low pay.[5]

Events baffled the farmer. He worked hard, produced more, yet received a declining share of the national income. Cotton, wheat, corn, and meat products flooded the home market and sought outlets abroad. A multitude of individual producers faced inflexible marketing arrangements that profited middlemen, and made each year's income uncertain. Science improved fertilizers, and the farmer grew more for a lower price. Machinery lightened daily toil, but the temptation to plant more land fed a cycle of overproduction. Twenty years after the depression of the 1870's, the price of corn and cotton had halved. In 1894, growers received less income from 23 million acres of cotton than from 9 million in 1873. The farmers' share of the total national income in 1860 was about 30 percent, and declined to 20 percent in a larger system in 1900. Agricultural wealth accounted for some 40 percent of the national total in 1860, but only 16 percent in 1900. The price of silver, a staple "crop" in the Far West, also fell. In 1872, an ounce sold for $1.32; for $1.11 in 1884; and for $0.63 in 1894.

In a tradition of vivid stump oratory, with biblical colorations of apocalypse, the farmers' rhetoric sounded increasingly radical, but few farmers wanted socialism. They would grant individualism a still larger role by regulating the marketplace. Like most Americans, they wished to even out man-made inequalities of opportunity, not destroy the prevailing system. Railroad regulation, currency inflation, and price supports would reduce "special privilege." Competition had not raised debts, or reduced income. They mixed faith in material well-being and belief in man's rationality; people made the economy and could remove its flaws.[6]

By the late 1880's a variety of organizations offered solutions, blend-

ing into the "Alliance Movement." The National Farmers' Alliance attacked railroad discrimination, mortgage combines, interest rates, and
low prices. Further south, in Lampasas County, Texas, a movement that
became the "Southern Alliance" grew rapidly. By 1886 it absorbed frag-
mentary groups and resembled a new national party. Leonidas LaFayette
Polk of North Carolina typified the changes, style, and rationale in
many farm groups. A compelling speaker, with an engaging personality,
Polk was a genial small-town booster with vision and ambition. He
dabbled in real estate and defended most of the southern mythology. But
he also traveled tirelessly among neighbors with the good news of scientific farming and cooperation. In 1877, he became the state's first agricultural commissioner, pushing scientific training and practical mechanization, trying to unify farmers. In the mid-1880's, his voice reached beyond
North Carolina in the farm press. At decade's end, he was president of
the national Farmer's Alliance.[7]

Polk worked with farm clubs to pressure the state legislature for special programs, but he also valued cooperation that might combine the
blessings of individualism with the advantages of collective buying and
selling. If bigness and efficiency produced stability and profits, let the
farmer combine like business and labor.[8] A Michigan Grange newspaper
offered similar advice. "We note the success of united effort, and as each
class labors for its own interests, unless the agricultural class meets combination with combination, they will be overwhelmed in the conflict." [9]
These critics asked for equal economic rights in the existing system.
"Grant to agriculture the same privileges and benefits that are given to
manufacturers, banks, railroads, and other great factors which enter into
production and distribution," a farm journal said in 1891. "When this
is done, and the farmer has his rights, the country will retain its people
and the cities will not be crowded as they are at present." [10]

These national spokesmen, and a thousand local leaders, turned enthusiastically to cooperative societies in the 1880's. Farmers could pool
capital to buy seed, fertilizer, and equipment at reduced prices. They
could market produce through cooperatives at higher prices than as individual sellers, and might also break monopolies in ginning, retailing,
processing, and transportation. Some cooperatives succeeded, but the
total experiment failed. Few men had the capital, talent, or time to be
both businessmen and farmers. Cooperatives also alienated local merchants and the middle class, whose support farmers needed for larger
goals. But the cooperatives illustrated most farmers' belief in regulated
competition, and aimed at higher individual profits, not collective socialism.[11]

Some thought the answer to weaknesses that defeated cooperatives was a broadly based subsidy program. Charles Macune of Texas presented the "Sub-Treasury Plan" at the December, 1889, meeting of the Southern Alliance in St. Louis. It seemed captivatingly simple. The national government would establish a sub-treasury, warehouses, and grain elevators in every county that offered for sale in a given year at least $500,000 worth of nonperishable staple commodities like cotton, wheat, corn, sugar, oats, barley, rice, and wool. The government would issue on deposit a legal tender loan at 1 percent interest, to an amount equalling 80 percent of the goods' current market value. The sub-treasury would sell unredeemed products a year later at public auction. The idea aroused controversy among reformers, and opponents used it to ridicule all agrarian ideas. It smacked of socialism, they said, and would create yet another unstable form of currency. The government would be receiver for huge farm surpluses, and prices would certainly decline as they were sold. Farmers would merely use the income to plant more staples, increasing the market glut. Many could make a case for land and bond subsidies to railroads, which served and developed a national constituency, but the sub-treasury scheme would perpetuate existing problems at public expense.

Farm organizers crossed long distances in dilapidated buggies and astride weary horses to leave pamphlets at lonely homesteads. They brought contact with a larger world, fortified hopes for the future, and enlivened the present. They often drew large crowds, but left little permanent legacy. In the West, farmers had neither time nor money for a permanent organization. In the South, Democrats charged that agrarian unrest would bring Negro rule. And such a widespread collection of individualists seldom agreed on much. In 1891, the alliances boasted 35,000 speakers and organizers, but most were part-time amateurs.

Many farm leaders avoided politics; even poor men did not lightly abandon old allegiances. But by the 1890's, the divided agrarian effort moved toward a national political crusade. Party politics might unify the movement, where piecemeal cooperation and preachment failed. "We don't want a farmer's party," Polk said in 1888, "but we do want to see the farmers of this country take sufficient interest in political matters and political action to keep a strict eye on all that their party does." He was more candid a year later: "Plainly, we will not consent to give indefinite support to men who are unfriendly to our interests. . . . If this be party treason, make the most of it." [12] And veterans of other reform crusades, like Ignatius Donnelley, noted candidly that nonpolitical Granger organizations resembled guns "that will do everything but shoot." [13] Journalists might call discontented agrarians "hogs in the parlor" of polite society, but farmers had disproportionate power. If they built an organization to embrace all disaffected groups, American politics might take a new turn. Many farmers would now ask why their share of the American dream had not quite come true.

The rapidly developing and profitable western expansion of agriculture during the mid-1880's well illustrated the farmer's belief in that dream. Thousands of families moved onto the apparently rich plains after the war, eager to take free public land or buy cheaply from railroads that overemphasized the area's soil and climate. The market for wheat, corn, and swine seemed firm, and with adequate rainfall, farmers could see a newfound promised land. In a land of far horizons and immense fields, a boom spirit became the accepted tone. Prosperous farmers in specialized crops, or on eastern plains where rain was more predictable, frowned at rumors of agrarian radicalism that frightened investment capital. It was wiser to play the tunes of expansion and profits for farmer, money-lender, and merchant. This produced a smug rhetoric. "Nothing causes the Nebraska farmer more dismay than to return from town after spending a few hours there, and find that his farm has been converted into a thriving city with street cars and electric lights during his absence," the *Nebraska State Journal* assured readers in 1887.[14]

This web of plans and monotone of optimism brought eastern capital. Though debtors complained of high interest rates and mortgage combines, many eastern firms poured money into marginal investments which failed with a resounding crash in the mid-1890's, and hardly merited a "Shylock" portrait. In the new plains and mountain states, forced economic growth caused overexpansion. Every likely spot became a town, surveyed with numbered lots at a hundred times their true value. Each river bend would produce a teeming port. All flat terrain was ideal for railroad tracks. And river junctions grew on paper into great cities, controlling the commerce of whole regions. It was all in the grandest American style, and when the crash came, ruined men sought scapegoats east of the Mississippi River.[15]

Appeals to caution seemed unreal in an area isolated from the main currents of business life. It was like a separate country, and developed "a fever of speculation in real estate which affected the whole population, destroyed all true senses of wealth, created an enormous volume of fictitious wealth, infected with its poison all the veins and arteries of business, and swelled the cities to abnormal proportions." [16] In weak agrarian economies, all the pieces fitted together. Men holding unstable railroad stock invested in equally uncertain cattle or land schemes to develop the railroad's present business and future growth. And in small communities, a banker often extended credit to doubtful risks who went begging in less personal money marts. Economic softness in one sector endangered subsidiary business, and there was no diversified system to absorb depression's shock.[17]

But however genuine and pressing the problems of daily economic life became as agrarian prosperity thinned in the late 1880's, much of the discontent reflected a growing disenchantment with the ideals that had carried farmers west. The higher the goals, the harder the fall. The rains did not come on time; someone should have said so. Mortgage rates were higher on dry plains than in eastern Iowa or Kansas; somebody was at fault. Freight rates on Kansas wheat differed from those on Minnesota wheat. It all produced unusual bitterness. In the drought year of 1886, travelers in Blanco County, Texas, read on an abandoned farmhouse floor: "200 miles to the nearest post office; 100 miles to wood; 20 miles to water; 6 inches to hell. God bless our home! Gone to live with the wife's folks." [18]

Many farmers had realized just enough affluence to deepen hostility into a desire for revenge. Advertising, new communications, better transportation all made the farmer desire luxuries undreamed of twenty years earlier. He went into debt for a new barn, fresh house paint, a piano, magazine subscriptions. He added luxuries to the table—meats processed in distant cities, fresh fruits and vegetables shipped in new refrigerated cars, goods preserved in sugar. And on terrain suited to mechanization, farmers accepted costly chattel mortgages to buy reapers, plows, and combines. No one could blame them; and no one warned them.

Of course, it was not easy to accept personal responsibility for or live with poverty. Mortgage companies often extended credit rather than repossess valueless farms. Eastern lenders were not generally more exorbitant than local agents, but it was easy to think otherwise. That general interest rates were actually declining made no impression on farmers who produced more staples for less income to pay stationary debts. And high rates on chattel loans, secured with property that was usually either a necessity like machinery or a symbolic luxury like a piano, especially embittered debtors. Hostility toward mortgage companies, railroads, and processors coalesced into a conspiracy view of an integrated economy that seemed to use the farmer for other men's advantage.[19]

A Populist speaker summed up the dilemma. "We were told two years ago to go to work and raise a big crop, that was all we needed. We went to work and plowed and planted; the rains fell, the sun shone, nature smiled, and we raised the big crop they told us to; and what came of it? Eight cent corn, ten cent oats, two cent beef and no price at all for butter and eggs—that's what came of it. Then the politicians said we suffered from overproduction." [20] It seemed pointless for the farmer "to make two spears of grass grow where one grew before. . . . Now he is struggling hopelessly with the question of how to get as much for two spears of grass as he used to get for one." [21] The process created a politically dangerous resentment: "The farmer fed all other men and lived himself upon the scraps." [22] The long range looked no better. The farmer now seemed integrated near the bottom of an economy whose virtues he had always extolled. He thought himself the nation's mainstay, source of its values, but occupied a minority economic status. The system that lightened labor and increased productivity extended his reach but not his grasp.[23]

Few men could easily accept the obvious answer—elimination of the small independent farmer. "The logical conclusion from the evidence offered, is that the troubles of the farmer are due to the fact that there are altogether too many farms, too many cattle and swine, too many bushels of corn, wheat, rye, oats, barley, buckwheat, and potatoes," a reporter noted in 1890, "too many tons of hay, and too great a production of nearly all other farm products for the number of consumers." [24] The quickest way to emphasize the point was to feed the stove an ear of corn. "And if while we sat around such a fire watching the year's crop go up the chimney," Vernon Parrington recalled, "the talk sometimes became bitter . . . who will wonder?" [25]

Agrarian unrest was sharpest in the South. Much of the war's legacy of destruction remained virtually untouched in hills and along rivers, despite a few glittering showcase city sections. Indexes of railroad construction, bank deposits, port shipping, did not hide the starker realities of sharecropping and crop liens. A narrow tax base resting on real property increased the farmer's burden and made him sometimes oppose expenditure for education and social service. Isolation, ignorance, and sterile one-party politics heightened the tensions in southern life.

The agricultural decline of the late 1880's swept away thousands of optimistic, marginal farmers. The stubborn, genuine farmers remained, ready to demand political solutions for economic problems. After 1890, talk of a "People's Party" met greater interest. Most western farmers did not leave traditional party attachments, yet there were enough discontented agrarians, as the elections of 1890 showed, to turn areas if not whole states from Republican to Democratic allegiance. The farmer likely to change parties was heavily in debt. If laws might give him debt relief and raise prices, he would vote for those material self-interests.[27]

This marginal farmer was not yet typical, but he could be the catalyst for other dissatisfied elements like cattlemen, sheep-herders, professional reformers, and some immigrant groups.[28]

Above all, agrarian spokesmen used appealing rhetoric that voiced a growing unrest among many Americans who liked the fruits of cohesive economics but feared impersonality and declining individualism. Few farmers looked back to a lost Eden, or forward to a socialist commonwealth. They wanted the existing system, with protected advantages, but they were more certain of anxieties than remedies. In 1891, a Kansan combined material problems with emotional distress in words that summed up the foundations of a farm revolt:

> At the age of 52 years, after a long life of toil, economy, and self-denial, I find myself and family virtually paupers. With hundreds of hogs, scores of good horses, and a farm that rewarded the toil of our hands with 16,000 bushels of golden corn we are poorer by many dollars than we were years ago. What once seemed a neat little fortune and a house of refuge for our declining years, by a few turns of the monopolistic crank has been rendered valueless.[29]

"A neat little fortune," and "turns of the monopolistic crank" revealed personal motivation and a temptation to blame frustration on unseen forces.

Agrarians were not united in discontent. The farmer serving urban populations with dairy products, vegetables, poultry, and fruits shared little with men growing wheat or cotton. It was hard to compare the rich farms of Delaware, Pennsylvania, or Maryland to risk-farming in Dakota and Nebraska. The vacationer in upstate New York, central Ohio, or Wisconsin, seeing prosperous dairy herds, fruit, and vegetable crops, could hardly imagine the grinding poverty of back-country Alabama. The settled farmer near city markets, with a light debt burden and varied crops, distrusted western and southern brethren. Talk of monopoly was not persuasive, when the industrial system consumed his products. Back-country farmers disliked railroads, but suburban dwellers were less inclined to harsh regulation or blanket condemnation. Eastern growers disliked the long-haul freight advantages western producers enjoyed. Farmers near cities suspected currency inflation and liked tariff protection that eliminated Canadian imports. As western corn, wheat, and beef overwhelmed eastern farmers, states like New York and Pennsylvania established experiment stations to help diversify agriculture. Sorghum, beet sugar, grapes, fruit, poultry, and dairy products sustained eastern farm income as eastern wheat and corn production became unprofitable. In states like Illinois and Ohio, agrarian discontent never matured into viable political movements.[30]

These developments fortified western views of sinful cities that corrupted the young and made good farmers serve a bad system. Tangible factors increased the age-old emotional conflict between town and country. Whole counties bore the cost of city government, but reaped few benefits. Banks often favored urban investment, further curtailing farm credit. State and federal funds usually went for urban improvements. There were no custom houses in the countryside. River and harbor appropriations seldom immediately helped dirt farmers. Farm organizations underlined this hostility by excluding merchants, professionals, stockholders in corporations, and even business clerks. Populists tried to unite disaffected urban elements and agrarians, ignoring ancient and fundamental hostility between the two groups.[31] Few insults carried greater sting than to call a city dweller a "hick," or a farmer a "dude." This clash of emotions and differing economic self-interests thwarted any lasting unity between workers and farmers, but few political dreams have had such long life with so little substance.

Old sectional suspicions also increased. The East symbolized oppression to men who borrowed from its bankers, paid railroads with offices in New York and Boston, elected politicians who moved in its circles. The feeling worked both ways. As the land boom collapsed, the Northeast attacked western big talk. But most of the hostility came from the prairies and hills. Agrarian politicians, vented hatred of established power in lurid talk of exploitation and revenge. Demagogues like South Carolina's Ben Tillman raged against "the bond-holding, blood-sucking East." Midwestern radicals welcomed a new politics based on western interests and attitudes.[32]

This agitation reflected western and southern resentment at being "left behind" in national wealth and power.[33] An alternating attraction and revulsion for city life ran through all this talk as farmers hoped to be independent, yet enjoy an industrial system possible only with urban populations. "The tendency is away from the farm and away from the rural districts," James B. Weaver lamented in 1887, "the trend is toward the city, where the needy congregate and where crime becomes organized and where the Republic is stabbed." [34] Trips to cities and towns often fortified agrarian distrust of urban values and peoples, even as the young folk escaped to its alleged vices and luxuries.

Human agents of an impersonal system fared poorly at agrarian hands. Isolation bred the ironic twins of neighborliness and suspicion of human nature. Men who worked long hours in hot fields or herded cattle in freezing weather naturally both envied and disliked soft-handed salesmen, mortgage agents, and "drummers" who discussed how things were done in the respectable East. Middlemen living off commissions, riding in fancy rigs, traveling in first-class train coaches, sitting in elegant offices, angered farmers. The drummers' flashy clothes and glad-handing manner mixed fears of city contamination and subconscious longing for bright lights and forbidden fruits. This attitude also prevailed toward intellectuals and experts. Ben Tillman's venom was not typical, but his hostility represented southern farmers. He called the public school system "an abominable humbug," flayed Charleston, thought the state university a den of aristocratic agnostics, and labeled The Citadel a "military dude factory." [35] It was an unhappy agrarian legacy in areas that needed expertise, education, and acceptance of broad social change. It was useless to praise the whole economic system, when a major part endured both real and fancied grievances that touched men's ideals and goals in life. To tell angry farmers they were in a period of economic transition was folly. They would know the reason why. If there must be a fall, someone should provide a cushion.

Attitudes focused among discontented farmers in the hot summer of 1890. Off-year elections were notoriously faction-ridden, and often pivoted on whimsical local issues and personalities. Angry farmers showed their power in local contests by attacking regular party candidates.[36] In June, 1890, Kansas farmers organized the first major People's party, and began talk of a national third-party movement for the presidential contest in 1892. Populist speakers created awesome noise, firing verbal grapeshot at the financial interests that supposedly dominated "old parties." [37] The talk was a kind of therapy for people who aired repressed grievances.

The voters took greatest pleasure in the oratory a handful of vivid leaders poured out like lava from long-dormant volcanoes. Mary E. Lease climbed to temporary fame. Hard experience with drought and grasshoppers qualified her to discuss a brand of economics and view of life that appealed to those from a similar pattern. Critics ridiculed her as "Patrick Henry in Petticoats" and "The Kansas Pythoness," but she had attractive answers. "You may call me an anarchist, a socialist, or a communist. I care not, but I hold to the theory that if one man has not enough to eat three times a day and another has $25,000,000, that last man has something that belongs to the first." [38] She touched in bright stereotypes the humdrum desires that made up a million hidden lives, and enjoyed her role. "Mrs. Lease . . . was sometimes a bit of a demagogue and was not without a letch for money and the fleshpots thereunto pertaining . . ." noted that critical bourgeois, William Allen White.[39] There was truth in *Judge*'s assertion that like most reformers, she wanted place and power. "Mary Lease will never consent to be saved unless she leads the heavenly band." [40]

Ignatius Donnelley moved steadily toward prominence in the developing Populist movement. His checkered career reflected alternating urges for respectability and a desire to dominate a crusade. As a member of the national House from 1862 to 1869, he gained a taste for office and power that his radical talk never quite covered. Donnelley touched the bases of greenbackism, farmer-laborism, and republicanism without losing a nervous personality.[41] He dabbled in real estate, believed in the lost continent of Atlantis, thought Francis Bacon wrote Shakespeare's plays, and printed his visions of apocalyptic punishment and utopian salvation as novels. Like most radicals, he thought to reform the world, but only revolted against his origins. He enjoyed the role. "For my part, I rather like this walking on volcanoes," he once said in a revealing insight.[42]

That was also true of other men now taking the lead in populism as 1890 passed into history. The respectable James B. Weaver of Iowa watched the world behind a set of whiskers and calm glance worthy of an establishment politico. But as greenback candidate for president in 1880, and an ally of various reform groups, he was a natural Populist leader to combine moderation and energy. William A. "Whiskers" Peffer won a Kansas Senate seat in 1890, and Jerry Simpson, "Sockless Socrates of the Prairies," would represent a Kansas House district. These and other leaders were not all of populism, and most rose to the crusade's top because of their writing and speaking. They were merely reformers with a Populist phrase, but they symptomized a restless urge for change, and liked to live in the shadows of tall words and big promises. They did not represent a majority of the nation's farmers, and were not the only reformers stirring the receptive West. Believers in labor rights, railroad regulation, temperance, and local control of schools competed with Populists, but with suitable leadership and an appealing central issue, Populists had the best chance to control agrarian states and gain national influence.[43]

Life was inevitably harder for reformers in the South where any threat to Democratic rule raised the bogey of "Negro domination." But in poverty-stricken areas like interior Georgia, men like Tom Watson were desperate enough to risk life and limb to fight sterile one-party rule representing the past. In most of the South, populism appealed to genuine human needs but conflicted with old emotions around the Democratic party, and a guerrilla war raged between the two groups. Western agrarians employed the ammunition of speeches, but in the South both sides used real bullets, nightriders, and the torch. Ballot boxes vanished in mysterious fires, or drifted down sluggish bayous. Poor leadership, lack of time and money, and a long tradition of violence hampered every southern Populist move toward success on any level.[44]

As populism gained momentum with scattered but impressive election victories in 1890, nervous opponents used the time-honored weapon of ridicule. Professional reformers, the drifters and bummers of politics, found a ready haven in populism and even sincere agrarians admitted the movement became "an asylum for all the cranks in the universe." [45] Grover Cleveland feared agrarians would make the Democratic party "a sort of political cave of Adullam to which would report 'everyone that was in distress, everyone that was in debt, and everyone that was discontented.' " [46] Democratic Governor James S. Hogg of Texas ridiculed the movement in effective rural language. It threatened states rights and white rule, he said; its members were incompetent malcontents. Populist spending proposals, including funds to promote rain-making, totaled an alleged $35 billion. "Such fellows could not drive a wagon and team without running over every stump within range of the road. They could not operate a windmill without bursting every joint of the machinery. Many of them could not set a mousetrap. Yet they go around telling you how to run the government." [47] This stereotype of crankiness was a major factor in defeating the agrarian crusade in a nation seldom radical in hard times.

By midsummer of 1890, the agrarians would have "the satisfaction of having caused almost a panic in the Democratic party of the South and the Republican party of the West," the *New York Sun* prophesied.[48] In December, 1890, the Southern Alliance, Colored Farmers' Alliance, and other groups gathered at Ocala, Florida, to plan political action. Demands included free coinage, and expanded government banking system, tariff reduction, a graduated income tax, and more railroad regulation. In May, 1891, a national Populist movement began to form with a convention in Cincinnati. A gathering in St. Louis in February, 1892, formally organized the People's Party.

The program rising from these organizational moves blended belief in individualism and equal opportunity with controls on competition. Men fearful of business influence in politics assumed that a regulatory government would remain both personal and modest. Populists saw government both as a negative force to restrain enemies and a positive element to subsidize their livelihood.[49] They talked loosely of removing "special interests" from government, but had little idea of how government thus purified would function. Nothing in their doctrine better illustrated their optimistic, typically American thinking than the notion that progress through law was automatic.

Debt relief was the center of political populism. Most men, of whatever occupation or status, worried over home mortgages, future expenses, and unexpected costs. Pious exhortations about frugality and self-denial seldom altered the normal human proclivity to spend all income. Human pride magnified debt in a thousand ways. To owe the bank was not disgraceful or unusual, but for an individual to say he could not pay his bills was humiliating and compounded hostility. For every debt collected under duress, a local creditor overextended loans to a neighbor in temporary distress. For every grocery or doctor bill refused extension, many others quietly disappeared as "bad debts" or silent charity. These were the normal acts of communities where men dealt in personal terms. In a unifying economy, with large investment necessarily in the hands of central agents, it was easier to blame financial woe on mysterious combines and distant conspirators than to admit bad personal judgment. Rural debt was especially poignant. Farmers registered debt not merely as mortgages, or in columns of figures. A new bonnet, a comfortable retirement, a suit of clothes, a trip to a fair, or table luxuries were the apparent differences between success and failure not only in farming but in life.

Like urban dwellers with home mortgages, farmers expected to pay debts on land and houses. But borrowers felt the pinch of debt most in chattel mortgages for short-term or "luxury" credit, where rates were erratic and excessive. A year's credit to buy new machinery or horses in Kansas could cost from 40 percent to 375 percent, and many counties were mortgaged to full assessed valuation. Farmers protested special fees, commissions, and discounts for short-term loans in tight money markets. The mortgage company was usually reluctant to repossess a homestead or acreage, but movable property was at the mercy of an interest deadline. A man watching agents drive his horses to auction or hauling away a reaper naturally liked the idea of paying notes with depreciated dollars.[50]

Hostility easily created human villains. "The average land owner and farmer, though exercising the most consummate skill and practicing the most rigid economy, cannot hope to achieve fortune in a lifetime," Leonidas Polk wrote in 1891. "The speculator in 'futures' and the manipulator of stocks, with no knowledge of frugality and without legitimate skill, achieve fortune in a day." [51] This resentment blazed at "millionaires" whom the press discussed with a mixture of contempt and envy. Populist agitators led growing bands in a new anthem:

> There are ninety and nine who live and die
>   In want, and hunger, and cold,
> That one may live in luxury,
>   And be wrapped in a silken fold.
> The ninety and nine in hovels bare.
> The one in a palace with riches rare.[52]

Believing that the basic economic and political system was sound, Populists naturally attacked those who turned it from automatic progress for everyone to benefit a few. "A bold and aggressive plutocracy has usurped the government, and is using it as a policeman to enforce its insolent decrees," James B. Weaver declared.[53]

Acceptance of conspiracy made order of apparent chaos, removed personal responsibility, and magnified self-importance by increasing the power of unjust adversaries. Invisibility was a kind of opulence that fed starved emotions. To fight against mortgage rates was one thing. To free mankind from the grip of a "money monster" was a more compelling rationalization for both frustration and economic grievances. How well this savored of biblical dramas familiar to rural audiences: "We must expect to be confronted by a vast and splendidly equipped army of extortionists, usurers and oppressors marshalled from every nation under heaven," Weaver said.[54] It simplified things to discuss an "invisible government, whose throne room was Wall Street, [that] controlled the visible government in nation and state, in spite of statesmen's warnings and popular protests."[55] A flushed patriotism enlarged the view. Frequent attacks against absentee ownership and foreign investment filled Populist pronunciamentos and platforms, with Britain the chief culprit.[56]

Orthodox explanations of cyclical depression were unconvincing. "There is something besides overproduction that has caused [hard times]," Leonidas Polk argued. "I believe that it is not God's fault that we are in this bad condition. Congress could give us a bill in forty-eight hours that would relieve us, but Wall Street says nay."[57] A historic American belief in the virtues of simple legislation, the values of agrarian life, and the force of conspiracy combined to make currency manipulation a compelling issue for debtors. "There is more potentiality for evil in the country today, in the present condition of the silver question, than there is in the tariff question," Boston's elegant Edward Atkinson warned as early as 1882.[58] Increased investment in silver mining, its solid constituency in the Far West, and overrepresentation in national politics, made silver a logical rallying cause. Though Populists committed to deeper reforms protested against shallow currency panaceas, free coinage swept all before it because people could grasp what it promised to do.

An expanded volume of currency, resting on tangible silver dollars rather than fiat paper money, promised to raise prices and equalize debts. Populists wished to repay the kind of dollars they borrowed. William J. Bryan later summarized the argument's attractive logic:

> The mortgage remains nominally the same, though the debt has actually become twice as great. Will [the farmer] be deceived by the cry of "honest dollar"? If he should loan a Nebraska neighbor a hog weighing 100 pounds and the next spring demand in return a hog weighing 200 pounds, he would be called dishonest, even though he contended that he was only demanding one hog—just the number he loaned.[59]

That the creditor often extended funds on risky collateral naturally escaped notice.

In usual American fashion, distressed farmers wanted government action. "It is the cardinal faith of Populism, without which no man can be saved, that money can be created by the government in any desired quantity, out of any substance, with no basis but itself," a reporter noted.[60] Silverites argued that adequate government recognition would stabilize the white metal's price, and regulate the purchasing power of all dollars. Patriots ignored gold's presence as the world's standard of value and drew an unbalanced picture of America as a world power. "Standing among the nations of the world as a giant among pygmies," Richard P. Bland argued, "why should we ask the aid or advice of baby England, baby Germany, or Lilliputian France, in establishing for ourselves a bimetallic system?"[61] It was easy to remember good times— when gold, silver, and paper remained reasonably stable—forgetting the flight of gold in periods of doubt and depression. By the 1890's, free silver had wide appeal. High school boys abandoned afternoon baseball for pamphlets on the money question. In poverty-stricken Alabama a hill family heard of its blessings and, equating free silver with free lunch, dispatched a runner with a bucket to gather their share.[62]

The crusade enfolded its members. Like all earnest men in the grip of need, Populists fancied themselves alone in a hostile world. The sunburned farmer on the hot plains of Kansas or Iowa and the despairing tenant in the brooding South believed they alone felt an impending crisis. But many intelligent men in business and politics had long sensed imbalances in the system. In the mid-1880's, there was a wave of nervous speculation about the triumphing industrial system. Books, articles, government reports, and laws reflected concern. But it was easier to describe the malady's symptoms than its cure. "I may be wrong, but from my point of view it appears that machinery is constantly making capital more independent of labor," a New Yorker wrote a friend in 1885. "[And] that while labor has shared in the benefits of the great forces that now control the world, its wants, owing to the march of education, have increased much faster. There was a time when ignorance was bliss and men were content to be the slaves of capital. Now men are generally educated to the belief that they are the equals of others in their natural rights; and yet they find the opportunities to employ those natural rights for their own benefit greatly abridged." [63] William Henry Smith of the Associated Press agreed, writing his friend Rutherford B. Hayes: "The great question of the relations of capital to labor, that is now at our doors, must be met. Woe betide the Party or the man that trifles with it." [64]

But what to do? Laws did not seem to control the economy. The American people clearly did not wish to dispense with big business, only to make it responsive to personal demands and remove it from politics. But no body of men was able to draft or enforce economic decrees. The disciplines of economics, sociology, and statistics were only beginning. Most businessmen were not shortsighted materialists or bloated bondholders, but accepted a system that inevitably produced both speculation and solid economic building. Who could correct evils without threatening virtues? Wharton Barker, a Pennsylvania businessman, disliked the "aggression of concentrated capital," but could only predict that "the conflict between capital and the working classes has become irresistible." [65]

Practical men with a sharp sense of life's just rewards, like former President Hayes and Congressman William McKinley, worried over the problem. Years of managing Ohio politics broadened their view without eroding their humanity. They believed in laws, but knew that only individual human response produced social stability. "My point is that free government cannot long endure if property is largely in a few hands, and large masses of people are unable to earn homes, education, and a support in old age," Hayes said.[66] McKinley often publicly condemned the "mad spirit for gain and riches which is so prevalent in American society . . . by gambling in stocks, speculation in wheat, by 'corners' and 'margins.' " [67]

No system had ever produced so much material wealth for so many people, but the whole production process baffled politicians who tried to even out its impact. Senator Cullom of Illinois praised the Sherman

Antitrust Act, but knew it could not arrest the trends of life itself. "The inevitable tendency seems to be for the big fish to swallow up the little ones. There is no doubt about the fact that the aggressions of capital have been very great, and nothing is accomplished, apparently, that puts a check upon it, or has so far. And while the prices of manufactured articles are not increased by the concentration of capital above what they were when more people were proprietors of business institutions yet, after all, I think it is unfortunate for the country that the control of the business of the country is concentrated in so few people." [68] He saw that ethical and moral considerations, involving both man's highest and lowest aspirations, would enter any national debate on the system's merits and weaknesses. Republicans and Democrats felt the time's curious changes as much as Populists. They were uncertain of law's efficacy, not quite convinced that men who made the system could always control it with government regulation that also became impersonal.

Political action inevitably intrigued Populists when their economic condition failed to improve. As 1892 brought the familiar rites of spring surrounding a presidential contest, worried regulars saw an agrarian party develop around a program and vocal leadership. The Republicans would clearly renominate President Harrison, an able but dull man. Democrats would choose former President Grover Cleveland, who was not popular with farmers anywhere. As the most vocal champion of laissez faire in public life, he spurned demands for government aid and bitterly opposed currency inflation. His astute managers insured that he could head a diverse constituency on the lofty theme of tariff reduction and curtailment of Republican spending. Thus both parties were really committed to industrial issues, for the Republicans championed tariff protection, federal subsidy, and "sound currency."

Democratic leaders could not expect enthusiastic endorsement either of Cleveland or tariff reform at the expense of the currency question and economic regulation. No new party would be likely to dispossess the Republicans or Democrats in 1892, but leaders reported that the Farmers' Alliance was "a demon in their rear." [69] Talk of another party naturally prompted soothing syrup from regulars. In the South, Democrats counseled against splitting the white vote. Cleveland was sure to win, and opponents could expect little from his new administration. Anyway, in time-honored fashion, everyone had better get together in a loose crusade, settling for a little of the loaf. But more and more Populists like Leonidas Polk opposed fusion that would blur their image. His followers staged a national convention in July, 1892, a "Second Independence Day," to choose national candidates and write a platform to define present goals and provide rhetoric for a future coalition of the dissatisfied.

This platform sounded radical, opening with Ignatius Donnelley's lurid preamble that divided Americans into two stark classes, Haves and Have-nots, foretelling immediate apocalypse unless agrarian demands triumphed, and simplifying history into two conspiracies, one for and one against the people. But the document cleverly mixed altruism and practical politics. Various planks demanded a sub-treasury, free coinage, an income tax on the middle and upper classes, government ownership of communication and transportation, and regulation of railroad and land companies. This sounded new but had many roots in state and federal regulatory laws. Much of the text was an essay in hedging, favoring generous pensions for veterans, internal improvements, a free ballot but without all-important federal regulation, and restriction of foreign contract labor. It avoided a serious stand on tariff protection, and as an afterthought asked organized labor to join the crusade. Despite the excited attention of some newspaper reporters and political editors, the document contained little outside the American reform tradition.

Leonidas Polk's death early in the summer had left Judge Walter Q. Gresham—formerly of Indiana, now of Chicago—as the new party's most popular presidential leader. But Gresham, whose anti-railroad and mugwump bias pleased many Populists, was not ready to abandon all old party ties. The delegates turned instead to General James Baird Weaver of Iowa, greenback candidate for the presidency in 1880, former member of Congress, and veteran of many a good crusade. The managers shrewdly balanced the ticket with "General" James G. Field of Virginia, actually a former Confederate major.[70]

The inevitable nominations of Harrison and Cleveland signaled a dull campaign, in which Populists could gain a disproportionate hearing simply because they were unusual. Industrial violence at the Homestead steel works in Pennsylvania was another signal of dissatisfaction, and Populists hoped to gain labor support. They were most active in the South, the Plains States, and the silver mining areas of the Far West. The South naturally produced the campaign's most vivid moments, where Democratic regulars battled fiercely against Populist invaders, raising the cry of Negro domination. Many Southerners faced an ugly choice. Those who cut Democratic ties risked ostracism from neighbors, penalty from the country storekeeper who extended credit and bought crops, and physical violence.[71]

But Populists dodged rocks, bottles, and verbal assaults to campaign. They financed train rides between stops with meager contributions from the faithful, and counted on the rural press to spread the good tidings of coming reform. Many a farmer put his last nickel into Mrs. Lease's laundry basket, after agreeing with her violent denunciation of the bloated East and its hideous money power.[72] General Weaver naturally met the worst reception. In Georgia, mobs of Democrats made his tour a bitter gauntlet. After suffering the indignities of rotten eggs, tomatoes, profanity, and manhandling, he canceled the trip.

Despite their sincerity, Populists never shook off the crank image that unnerved some potential supporters. Their often lurid talk and big promises let others emphasize their shallowness and sectionalism to a people who valued individual responsibility for economic well-being and suspected regulatory bureaucracy. As one acid pundit noted:

> Why should the farmer delve and ditch?
> Why should the farmer's wife darn and stitch?
> The government can make 'em rich,
>   And the People's Party knows it.
> So hurrah, hurrah for the great P.P.!
> $1 = 7$, and $0 = 3$,
>   A is B, and X is Z,
> And the People's Party knows it! [73]

Throughout the South, fear of Negro domination, or of helping Republicans, kept many from voting for Weaver. The Populists simply lacked the money or organizational skill to combat the representative Democratic party's blunt intention to count them out. Weaver gamely toured the West, but behind the scenes, Democratic leaders undermined Populist strength with local fusion arrangements and promised rewards from a new Cleveland administration. Ironically, the Populist threat also helped solidify both major parties.

Cleveland won the election easily with 277 electoral votes and 5,500,000 popular ballots to Harrison's 145 electoral votes and 5,180,000 popular votes. Weaver polled over 1,000,000 votes, winning 22 electoral votes, carrying Kansas, Idaho, Nevada and Colorado, with 1 vote each from North Dakota and Oregon. As in the off-year elections of 1891, the new party scored numerous local victories. But though radical commentators saw future national success in the returns, the Populists were at their maximum strength. They had failed to break the solid South, and carried western states interested in silver rather than reform. They won many contests only by fusing with Democrats. And the party's candidates made no appreciable impact east of the Mississippi or in the upper Midwest.

After Cleveland took office in March, 1893, the country moved into a bitter depression that seemed to offer Populists a great opportunity. Cleveland's ruthless use of patronage and power to repeal the Sherman Silver Purchase Act, his refusal to recognize fusion arrangements, and deflationary fiscal policies destroyed the Democratic party. The climactic social upheavals of 1894 seemed to prove Populist assertions that the system was breaking down, but actually sent doubtful voters back to established parties. The bitterly contested congressional elections of 1894, in which Republicans swept the board, sealed Populism's doom. The electorate preferred the GOP's soundness and familiarity to tinkering. And the voters' repudiation of Cleveland's party opened the way for new Democratic leadership that would neutralize or enfold Populist appeal. Voters also identified populism with the violence at Pullman and with Coxey's Army. Cries for free coinage seemed dangerous to both property owners and wage workers. Populist disinterest in tariff protection, which Republicans used brilliantly, also unnerved voters seeking prosperity. And the income tax, sub-treasury, and other economic panaceas seemed illogical and dangerous amid depression.

Populist leaders hoped to win national power in 1896, but the electorate turned overwhelmingly to constructive republicanism and its moderate candidate, William McKinley. The Democrats repudiated Cleveland, embraced free coinage, and accepted a new leader, William Jennings Bryan. In a confused campaign, most Populists reluctantly supported Bryan rather than divide the reform vote. Populism continued as a force on the edge of politics, with shadow presidential campaigns in 1900 and 1904. But local officeholders and national spokesmen disappeared as "McKinley prosperity" arrived and the nation moved into a popular expansionist phase, toward respectable reform in a "Progressive Era." Leaders naturally sought external causes for their defeat, and the movement's dissipation in the sun of good times. But populism failed primarily because it appealed to a single class. No lasting union with organized labor or the urban dispossessed was ever possible. The movement represented both immediate economic grievances, which prosperity removed, and rural hostility to the urbanization and industrialism which inevitably triumphed. The election of 1896 was the symbolic moment when industrialism began to dominate the nation's development.

Most farmers returned to historic party allegiances, though a few radical leaders drifted into a futile socialism, bitter that free silver had overridden their hopes for a more profound crusade to change American life. But much of Populist rhetoric expressing hostility to cities and factories did not die; nor did the farm sector's political power wither. Agrarians dominated most state governments and remained heavily over-represented in national affairs. Populistic subsidy programs won acceptance under the pressure of depression in the 1930's, and after World War II, but did not solve the "farm problem." Expensive price support programs only cushioned the small farmers' fall, as agriculture took on the attributes of big business.

The movement's place in the mainstream of American history was hard to assess. The most facile view put Populists ahead of their times in demanding economic regulation. Sympathetic scholars made them precursors of progressivism and the New Deal, but relied more on the pronouncements of a few leaders than on the demands that briefly united angry marginal farmers. And the farmer's secondary role in progressivism actually widened that movement's appeal. Reform seemed respectable in middle-class hands away from the heresies of free silver and agrarian sectionalism. The New Deal built on precedents, but reacted more to general economic collapse than to any Populist heritage. Expensive price support programs are a greater testament to the Farm Bloc's congressional power than to any planning, and have not saved the small farmer. Little in Populist doctrine was unique or new, and most of the later acts ascribed to its influence would have come without the stirring events of the 1890's. The movement was firmly in the mainstream of American reform, advocating public action to redress material grievances. Populism generally attacked the existing system's operations, not its purpose. Its great achievement was twofold: to advertise significant discontent with the way industrialism distributed favors, and to signal the passing of agriculture as the dominant element in American life.

LEWIS L. GOULD

📚 9 📚

The Republican Search for
a National Majority

IN THE TWO DECADES AFTER 1877 the Republican party established itself
as the clear choice of the majority of the nation's voters. The GOP's
decisive triumph in 1894, confirmed by William McKinley's victory in
1896, ended a generation of political equilibrium and overturned the
national Democratic majority that had persisted since the 1830's. Since
Republican dominance continued until the onset of the Great Depression
in 1929, an understanding of how the party captured the allegiance of
the electorate after 1877 is the key to political history in the Gilded Age.

Victory did not come easily. Building a successful Republican coalition required the patient effort of determined and resourceful party leaders who faced resolute and skilled opposition. Public life enlisted the
talents of politicians in both parties whose abilities compare favorably
with men of any other era of American history. They resorted, on occasion, to the tested weapons of influence, bribery, and corruption; yet
excessive emphasis on the less savory aspects of the politician's craft
obscures the degree to which they debated real issues, grappled with
genuine problems, and sought workable solutions.

By 1877, political management had become especially arduous for
Republicans. Reconstruction had checked the natural strength of the
Democrats in the South, but the election of 1874 produced a resurgence
of Democratic power both below the Mason-Dixon line and in other
sections. A narrow defeat in the presidential election of 1876 underlined
the Democratic party's new vitality. Securely based in the South and
strong among German and Irish Catholics and other northern non-
moralistic ethnic groups, the Democrats retained the votes to compensate

for the party's weak national organization. In contests for the White House, they could count on approximately 135 electoral votes from the southern and border states and needed only New York and Indiana to be within reach of victory. The party's dedication to states rights and limited government gave it popularity in all sections. Its ability to control the House of Representatives for sixteen of the twenty years between 1874 and 1894 testified to a continuing hold on the electorate. Thus, as the memory of the war dimmed, the Democrats anticipated a renewal of their antebellum dominance.[1]

The Republicans faced troublesome internal problems beyond the Democratic revival. The GOP remained sectional, confined to the Northeast and Midwest, confident of victory only in secure bastions like the states of upper New England. In the 1850's and 1860's the party won pietistic Protestant ethnic groups in New England and the Midwest. Drawn by the union between moral reform and antislavery, these groups gave the Republicans their initial victories. But in the 1870's these voters tended to slip into third-party movements that emphasized local issues like prohibition. The Republican share of the popular vote markedly declined in crucial states in the Midwest. Unless the party broadened its national base of support, or appealed to other ethnic voters, the Democrats would probably reemerge as the majority party.[2]

To complicate matters, traditional Republican ideology seemed increasingly irrelevant to this task of political rebuilding. A dozen years of Reconstruction had wearied the public of the complexities of the Negro problem. While most Republicans still believed in the principle of black advancement, they shared the growing skepticism about the methods used to achieve it. Party leaders doubted that Reconstruction issues could sustain a majority coalition. Assistance to the black man demanded extensive government action. The Democrats responded with their popular war cry against federal power, and invoked racist slogans against Republican sponsorship of civil rights for the Negro. Party members and strategists, aware of public apathy and equivocal in their own racial attitudes, muted their earlier commitment to the Negro cause.[3]

Republicans did not think it necessary to abandon the Negro altogether. While Democrats flaunted their own bloody shirt in the 1880's, prominent GOP leaders like William E. Chandler and James G. Blaine continued to excoriate voting frauds in the South and, within the narrow limits of public interest, sought to consolidate and expand the gains of Reconstruction. The Republicans blended calculation of political advantage with genuine concern for the Negro; this equivocal endorsement put them far ahead of the Democratic position of repression and segregation. The Republicans supported an honest ballot in the South from 1880 to 1890. Once in office, the Democrats repealed federal legislation that protected the Negro's right to vote.[4]

The erosion of the party's ethical position after the Grant years vexed Republican leaders. Whiskey rings, Indian frauds, and corrupt officeholders tarnished the GOP luster as the party of morality, a renown originally associated with winning the war and securing the peace. As practical men, the professional custodians of Republican fortunes did not regard civil service reform as an answer to this dilemma. Overhaul of the spoils system would divide rather than unify, and hardly provided a rallying point to arouse the electorate and secure converts. When pressures built up for an enlarged civil service, Republicans bowed to them, but most leaders viewed the issue as of secondary importance.[5]

The internal organization of the Republican party displayed grave weaknesses by 1877. The incompetent leadership of President Grant accelerated the centrifugal tendencies within the GOP. Dedicated to nationalism but imbued with the Whig tradition of a weak president, the Republicans found it easy to succumb to the demands of state and congressional leaders after 1868. Yet, as the career of Senator Roscoe Conkling of New York emphasized, this situation presented ominous possibilities for divisive and self-centered activity. Personal infighting made good newspaper copy and satisfied Republicans who nursed grudges, but it did little to restore the morale and impetus that the party had misplaced during the Grant years.[6]

Finally, their doctrine of an active state continued to handicap Republicans. Nineteenth-century Americans distrusted a government that collected taxes, promoted enterprise, and intervened in local affairs. With that easy tolerance for inconsistency that has characterized the politics of the nation, Americans sought and accepted government largesse but endorsed Democratic warnings against the positive state. Republican activity that brought increased expenditures touched the electorate on an exposed nerve.

Manifestations of this governmental activism on the local level also weakened the Republican electoral position. Midwestern party members, eager to enact their religious pietism in prohibition and sabbatarian laws, alienated potential sources of support like German Lutherans. This "moralistic crusading" divided Republican voters and lessened the party's chances for victory in local elections. To establish a secure national majority, the Republicans needed to unify the party's divergent impulses for social change.[7]

After the disputed election of 1876, the Republican party resembled an ailing adolescent. The one-time radical, George W. Julian, reviewed Grant's presidency and the decline of Republican fortunes, and concluded in 1878 that the party "lies wallowing in the mire of its apostasy, the helpless victim of its leaders and the spectacle of the nation." [8] The editor of the *Nation* attributed Republican malaise to the cumulative disadvantages of its extended tenure of power. The party was "steadily losing from the defection of those who want a change for the mere excitement it will bring; of those who are dissatisfied with something it has done or failed to do; and of those who think that four or five Presidential terms is enough for one party, and that the other ought now to have a chance." [9]

Such ominous predictions obscured persistent advantages that the Republican party enjoyed despite its weakened condition. Association with the triumph of the Union gave the party a claim on the emotional loyalties of citizens for whom the conflict had been the great experience of their lives. For Julia B. Foraker, "The Republican Party had saved the Union. It was the Union." Invocation of the memories of the struggle on the campaign trail was not mere "waving the bloody shirt." This stereotype discounted a genuine and continuing source of Republican strength.[10]

As the party of the Union, progress, and morality, the Republicans gained an aura of respectability and stability during Reconstruction. In many sections of the North, Democrats bore the stigma of disunion, copperheadism, or outright treason. Senator George Frisbie Hoar gave this sentiment its classic expression:

> The men who do the work of piety and charity in our churches; the men who administer our school systems; the men who own and till their own farms; the men who perform skilled labor in the shops; the soldiers, the men who went to the war and stayed all through; the men who paid the debt, and kept the currency sound, and saved the nation's honor; the men who saved the country in war, and have made it worth living in in peace, commonly, and as a rule, by the natural law of their being, find their place in the Republican party; while the old slave-owner and slave-driver, the saloon-keeper, the ballot-box-stuffer, the Kuklux, the criminal class of the great cities, the men who cannot read or write, commonly, and as a rule, by the natural law of their being, find their congenial place in the Democratic party.[11]

The Republicans gathered more than respectability from their years in office. The experience of governing taught party members the virtues of positive action and promoted a sense of internal cohesion. Faced with the responsibility of enacting legislation to deal with the conquered South and the currency question, the Republican party achieved a unity that made its leaders and rank and file more willing to subordinate their own interests to the cause of common victory. Because of its minority status in at least one House of Congress for most of the years after 1874, the GOP learned to rely on discipline and self-denial as the means to legislative success. Similar tendencies carried over into campaigns. One veteran observer of the Washington scene found the Democrats a "headless undisciplined force," while the Republicans composed "an organized, well-disciplined army." [12]

As the Republicans dealt with national problems, they developed a cadre of national leaders. With their traditional reliance on state machines and decentralization, Democrats produced few politicians with national reputations after 1870. But the Republican party drew on the talents of men like James G. Blaine, James A. Garfield, Benjamin Harrison, and William McKinley. Given their first opportunity for advancement during the Civil War, such individuals found the GOP receptive to men of youth and energy. The party's national emphasis drew them toward the House and Senate. Ambitious Republicans used these forums as springboards to higher offices. This process of competition and upward movement kept Republican hopefuls in the public eye and gave the more popular and successful among them a national following that Democratic counterparts never achieved.[13]

When Rutherford B. Hayes entered the presidency in March, 1877, the Republican party owned enough political assets to invalidate forecasts of imminent decline. Yet new issues and tactics were necessary if the party wished to move from uneasy parity with the Democrats to dominance. From 1877 to 1892 the Republicans tried to construct a majority coalition in all sections of the country. Their efforts to penetrate the South with new approaches to the Negro question failed, but their campaign to make the tariff the basis of a unified party laid the foundation for eventual Republican success in the 1890's.

As president, Hayes followed a policy of conciliation toward the South to promote genuine Republican organizations in that region. The GOP "must in some judicious way divide the Democratic party of the South and make the Republican party better than it is." In practice, this policy only united southern Democrats against Republican invasion and did little to rehabilitate the feeble party structure in the South. Democrats persistently refused to grant the Republicans equal access to their electoral stronghold. By 1880 the dream of establishing a wing of the GOP in the South had virtually expired, though it remained a residual aim of Republican leaders until 1890.[14]

While Hayes chased the will-o'-the-wisp of southern Republicanism, he did not check the deterioration of the party's position in the North. Economic depression after 1873 combined with Republican factionalism to give the Democrats both houses of Congress after 1878. GOP prospects improved as the election of 1880 approached, largely because of an economic revival and the continuing inability of the Democrats to compose their differences and find an attractive national candidate. Nevertheless, the Republicans found the campaign of 1880 a testing experience, even with their popular standard-bearer, James A. Garfield, a reasonably united party, and divisions in Democratic ranks.[15]

During the 1880 canvass, the Republicans turned away from the southern question as the liabilities of that tactic became apparent in the Maine election in September. Garfield and James G. Blaine agreed that concentration on tariff protection would rally the party's disaffected elements, produce campaign funds, and exploit Democratic confusion on the issue. In crucial states like Indiana, the Republicans stressed their consistent advocacy of higher duties, as contrasted to General Winfield Scott Hancock's indiscreet comment that the tariff was a "local question." Republican ability to brand the Democrats as the party of free trade in 1880 helped James A. Garfield eke out a narrow victory. The GOP had found the issue that could alleviate its internal dissensions and lead to creation of a new national majority. Under the intellectual leadership of James G. Blaine in the 1880's and William McKinley in the mid-1890's, the Republicans made protection the central issue of American politics.[16]

The tariff played a crucial part in the era's party battles. In addition to their very real relevance to the economic interests of the nation, "Tariff arguments were ideological instruments of voter mobilization and party combat." [17] By emphasizing protection the Republicans did not evade the important questions of their time. The tariff offered them a means to win a national majority and to implement their economic program for the country. Protection ultimately was too narrow a basis for continued Republican success in the early twentieth century, but the doctrine was a vital issue in the years after 1880.

The tariff's political potency arose from the deft way Republicans blended the issue's economic and emotional appeals and disseminated them on all levels of the party structure. As an economic doctrine, protection reached out to all segments of American society. While stressing the encouragement that the tariff offered to developing industries, Republican orators also carefully underlined the benefits to workers of higher wages under protection. Within a closed market, every element of society would prosper. As Blaine told a Milwaukee audience in 1884, "Under the Protective system, agriculture, manufactures, and commerce have flourished in equal degree." [18] In their endorsement of the tariff, as in their support of aid to education, irrigation projects, and speedy distribution of the public lands, the Republicans minimized group conflict. Instead, they conceived of "The economic system of the country . . . as a vast cooperative productive enterprise, in which the social or the public economic interest was promoted by energetic and promiscuous stimulation of productive agencies in private hands." [19]

For many participants in the American economy in the late nineteenth century, this argument for the tariff seemed valid. In the agrarian sector, more prosperous and specialized farmers in the East and Midwest, challenged by Canadian wheat, beef, lumber, and wool, wished to protect "the home market." Urban workers noted "the steady rise of real wages during the last three decades of the century" and endorsed McKinley's plea to "stand by the protective policy, stand by American industries, stand by that policy which believes in American work for American workmen, that believes in American wages for American laborers, that believes in American homes for American citizens." Elements of the business community may have defected from the protectionist coalition when reduction of duties on their product or necessary raw materials seemed prudent, but tariff protection won their general support in promoting the nation's economic expansion.[20]

Republicans also clustered symbolic appeals around the economic arguments for the tariff. Protection meant prosperity, contended GOP candidates, and their elaborate historical analyses traced the misfortunes that had befallen the United States under the low-tariff policy of the Democrats. "In 1860," William McKinley told the House of Representatives in 1890, "after fourteen years of a revenue tariff . . . the business of the country was prostrated, agriculture was deplorably depressed, manufacturing was on the decline, and the poverty of the Government itself made this Nation a byword in the financial centers of the world." [21] Reasoned Democratic rebuttals never eclipsed the effectiveness of linking protection with prosperity.

Republicans attacked Great Britain as the major enemy of the tariff and successfully identified protection with patriotism and American nationalism. Free trade and tariff reform were evidence of Democratic subservience to English exporters. To a generation still sensitive to the lingering animosities between the United States and Great Britain, these considerations carried much weight. For Republican politicians harried by questions like prohibition, assaults on the English helped minimize divisive issues within party ranks and assisted in courting normally Democratic ethnic groups.[22]

GOP emphasis on the tariff after 1880 did not spring from cynical or opportunistic motives. A pragmatic response to practical realities, it represented the kind of intelligent accommodation to necessity that enables political organizations to survive and prosper. To a party beset with ideological disagreements on other matters, and plagued with a diminishing hold on the voters, the issue revived Republican enthusiasm, divided the Democrats, and ultimately helped produce a national majority after 1893.

More than any other party leader, James G. Blaine engineered this transformation. The most popular politician of his day, Blaine used his oratorical power and a brilliant mind to emphasize the need for party unity on the doctrine of protection. Blaine was no mere spoilsman, consumed with an ambition for the White House and heedless of the means used to attain higher office. In fact, in the 1880's he performed the vital function of a national political leader by educating his party on the tariff issue and thus laying the groundwork for Republican success in 1888 and beyond. The arguments and rhetoric on which Republican orators relied in discussing protection owed much to Blaine's skilled exposition.

The furor over his personal morality, especially in the election of 1884, obscured his central role in the revival of Republican fortunes in the 1880's. More moderate than critics conceded, more attuned to the changes reshaping American life than most colleagues, Blaine sought the center of the political spectrum for his party. He believed that protection offered both the means to partisan victory and a reasonable solution to the problem of economic growth. For a generation of Republicans Blaine symbolized inspiration and commitment in public life and his followers, a majority of the party's rank and file, paid little attention to his detractors. These workers and voters applauded Blaine when he urged them to endorse "the principles and the policies" that had made the United States "in manufacturing, in agriculture, the leading Nation of the world, not merely in a material sense, but in a moral and philanthropic sense."[23]

The election of 1884 underscored Blaine's value to his party. Anticlimax and confusion had followed victory in 1880 when President Garfield, in the midst of his campaign to grasp the leadership of his party, fell victim to an assassin's bullet. Under the reputable but uninspired direction of Chester A. Arthur, the Republicans lost the unity of 1880 in squabbles over the tariff, pork-barrel legislation, and the civil service. In the congressional elections of 1882, Republicans were on the defensive throughout the Northeast and Midwest, and the Democrats made substantial gains in the House and some gubernatorial contests. Passage of the Pendleton Act to reform the civil service did little to revive Republican hopes as 1884 drew near and, as economic indicators turned downward, party leaders resigned themselves to a Democratic triumph.[24]

The choice of Blaine in that year, however, gave the Republicans a fighting chance for success. Party factionalism, the defection of the erratic Mugwumps, and the indiscreet alliteration of the Reverend Samuel Burchard did not help Blaine's cause, but these were less significant than the vigor and enthusiasm Blaine brought to the Republican campaign. His emphasis on the tariff, his canvassing of the Midwest, and his popularity nearly overcame the Democratic party's inherent advantages. Although Grover Cleveland won the White House in 1884, Blaine slowed the downward trend of Republican performance at the polls, helped improve the GOP's positiion in the House and Senate, and provided his party with the opportunity to regain the presidency in 1888.[25]

Happily for the GOP, President Cleveland did not establish the Democrats as serious challengers for majority-party status during his first term. Obsessed with patronage and bereft of any viable program, the Democrats languished during the late 1880's while the Republicans regrouped. The congressional elections of 1886 produced Republican advances in the House, though seasoned observers questioned whether this presaged a renewal of party control of the presidency. To recapture the White House, Republican leaders stressed unity and organization while the Democrats held power.[26]

Once again the tariff proved precisely the issue to unite the diverse elements of the Republican coalition in 1888. Grover Cleveland, in his annual message of December, 1887, dared the GOP to make the presidential campaign turn on this issue. Blaine quickly responded that "The Democratic Party in power is a standing menace to the prosperity of the country." Taking their cue from this retort, Republicans accepted the tariff challenge of the Democrats. At its convention in June, the party selected an intelligent supporter of protection, Benjamin Harrison of Indiana, whose ability to carry his native state blended successfully with his shrewd campaign for the nomination. There were no bolts by Republican rebels in 1888, and Harrison matched his pre-convention maneuverings with his carefully controlled presidential canvass.[27]

Where Cleveland mishandled the tariff all through 1888, Harrison embellished the standard appeals for protection with graceful language and a pleasing presence for the crowds that gathered at his home. While Cleveland lazed away the season in torpid inactivity, Harrison expended his energies with efficiency. Democrats suffered from division and dissension over the tariff; Republicans endorsed protection almost to a man. Although Cleveland's expanded southern majorities helped him to a 90,000-ballot lead in the popular vote, Harrison carried New York and Indiana, and with them the electoral college. Equally important, the GOP controlled both houses of Congress and could begin to implement their apparent mandate for protection.[28]

Republican success in 1888 owed much to a sluggish adversary. In addition, within the framework of an older military style of campaigning, the GOP had tested techniques and practices for future political canvasses. As the phasing out of the spoils system dried up the customary sources of campaign funds, the party sought to tap the business community. This tactic increased the possibility of undue influence on the political process by private interest groups, but, in the absence of alternative forms of campaign revenue, reliance on business contributors became a necessary expedient. Moreover, Republican leaders displayed a striking ability to retain their independence and keep the new donors at arm's length.[29]

Creation of the National League of Republican Voters in 1887 marked another innovation in the process of marshaling electoral support and was a highly useful device in maintaining party enthusiasm between elections. Harrison's adoption of the tactic of addressing visiting crowds from his front porch in Indianapolis let the party reach voters in a controlled situation that retained the trappings of spontaneity. The widespread distribution of pamphlets, as well as the increased use of newspaper boiler plate, enabled the Republicans to present their case to large numbers of the electorate at a relatively low cost. Voters read and digested this literature avidly in an age when politics claimed the attention of most literate Americans. These new techniques influenced the outcome in 1888 more than highly publicized but comparatively unimportant events like the "Murchison" and "Dudley" letters.[30]

Republican cohesion carried over into the Fifty-first Congress. Effective leadership, particularly by Thomas B. Reed as Speaker of the House, produced a series of forward-looking enactments designed to carry out the party's programs for economic growth and political reform. The Sherman Antitrust Act represented a genuine attempt to meet the consequences of industrial combination within the limits of the common law. The Sherman Silver Purchase Act sought a workable middle ground on the perennial dilemma of bimetallism. Even the much-maligned McKinley Tariff contained the promise to adjust the protective system in its provisions for reciprocity. This was a Blaine solution, and illustrated once again his efforts to make the tariff a workable answer to American economic problems. The Republicans enjoyed less success with their Federal Elections bill, a moderate attempt to safeguard the ballot in the South and foster the GOP in that region, that fell prey to a coalition of Southerners and silverites. Nevertheless, the "Billion Dollar Congress," so called because of its alleged extravagance, left a record of constructive legislation unequaled until the Wilson administration.[31]

Republicans found it difficult, however, to translate legislative achievement into political success after 1889. On the national level, President Harrison was as inept a party leader as he had been a superb campaigner. His aloof manner and austere personality, which the waspish Reed likened to a "dripping cave," negated most of his patient attempts to strengthen the party's structure. The chill that Harrison imparted to the presidency spread throughout the GOP and caused a subtle, but dangerous, deterioration of morale among Republican leaders.[32]

The strenuous campaign of 1888 also left troublesome legacies for the Republicans in local contests. Across the Midwest, Republicans who believed in prohibition and public control of parochial education, resumed efforts to use the party to realize ethno-cultural goals. In Iowa, temperance-minded, pietistic Republicans alienated ethnic support and allowed the Democrats to win control of the governorship. Wisconsin Republicans, like counterparts in Illinois, found that enactment of laws requiring the teaching of American history and other subjects in English irritated German Lutherans and Catholics and drove these groups toward the Democratic party. Party professionals in the area, such as John C. Spooner in Wisconsin, saw that voters would not support campaigns to use government to buttress the moral beliefs of Republican evangelical elements.[33]

Erosion of GOP strength in 1889 continued into the next years as the Democrats, happier in their familiar and less demanding role of opposition party, criticized increased expenditures, and the activities of local Republican pietists. Racist assaults on the Federal Elections bill also served the Democrats well. Passage of the McKinley Tariff gave the Democrats their final selling point in the 1890 elections. Attacks on the higher prices that would allegedly come when the new law took effect became a staple of Democratic oratory in October.

The result in November devastated the Republicans. Their representation in the House dropped from 166 to 88, while the Democrats elected 235 congressmen. Maintenance of party dominance in the Senate provided small consolation. After a decade of exertion, the Republican party fell back into the perilous situation of the late 1870's. The party's condition did not improve in 1892. President Harrison's renomination pleased few Republicans and the Democrats, even with Cleveland heading the ticket, rolled to a clear triumph. With a plurality in the popular vote of nearly 400,000, and a secure margin in the electoral college, Cleveland had carried his party to heights that it had not attained since before the Civil War. The result was so decisive that astute commentators like Professor Woodrow Wilson concluded that "the Republican party is going, or at any rate may presently go, to pieces; and signs are fairly abundant that the Democratic party is rapidly being made over by the stirring and disturbing energy of the extraordinary man who is now President." [34]

The active and innovative program of the Republicans after 1888 accounted in large part for the Democratic resurgence. The GOP did not become "the party of energy and change" in the 1890's; it had played that role since the 1860's. From Congress to the most lowly precincts, Republicans sought to mold America in their own vision of the good society. Their solutions ranged from the moralistic goal of the pietists in local temperance contests to the Whig-oriented economic policies of Blaine and William McKinley. Achievement of these diverse aims required one common ingredient—a vigorous government with enhanced powers to affect the lives of private citizens. Between 1889 and 1892, the voters recoiled from this prospect. They relied instead on the traditional Democratic doctrines, and repudiated Republican activism. In the absence of basic change in the political and economic situation, the electorate would not accept the spending, higher prices, and religious moralism that had become the popular hallmarks of the GOP. [35]

The onset of a severe depression in 1893 dramatically altered the prospects of the Republicans and enabled them to emerge as the nation's majority party. To some extent, the GOP gained simply because the voters deserted the Democrats. The mean Democratic vote in the Midwest, for instance, dropped nearly ten percentage points between 1892 and 1894. As factories, banks, and railroads collapsed into bankruptcy or receivership, the voters north of the Mason-Dixon line turned away from their earlier allegiance to the principles of the Democrats. In the context of economic crisis, ethnic affiliations or previous voting habits became less important than the desire to repudiate the party of hard times.[36]

Republicans also enjoyed the luxury of an inept and stubborn President leading the opposition. Cleveland's dogmatic approach to the money problem in his fight to repeal the Sherman Silver Purchase Act, his ruthless use of the patronage in states like California, Colorado, and Nebraska, and his general insensitivity to the plight of party leaders hastened the Democratic party's collapse. In many states the GOP merely stood by while the Democrats destroyed themselves.[37]

Although pleased with what one western party member called the "almost heaven born opportunities" presented by Democratic division, Republicans were not content with victory by default. They used the customary weapon, tariff protection, to dramatize the contrast between the economic situation of the Harrison and Cleveland administrations. Once again, the Cleveland Democrats played into Republican hands with a clumsy performance over the unpopular and ill-constructed Wilson-Gorman Tariff of 1894. This act, which satisfied neither protectionists nor reformers, let Republicans denounce "tinkering" with the tariff in hard times, and, in particular localities, criticize specific provisions for harmful effects on the local economy.[38]

By the summer of 1894, Republicans could predict substantial increases in congressional and senatorial delegations outside the South. Democratic attempts to rekindle the ethnic tensions of the 1880's by associating their opponents with the anti-Catholic American Protective Association could not counteract the cumulative impact of a year of economic depression. Thomas B. Reed forecast that "The Democratic mortality will be so great next fall that their dead will be buried in trenches and marked 'unknown.' " The magnitude of the Republican success, however, astounded even the most optimistic party professionals. GOP strength in the House rose from 127 seats to 244, while the Democrats lost 113 representatives. In the Senate, Republicans picked up five new members. The election of 1894 marked the largest reversal of congressional political strength in American history. The election's significance transcended the immediate effect on party alignments in Washington. The result in 1894 ended the politics of equilibrium that had existed since the conclusion of the Civil War. With the exception of the Wilson interval, reflecting Republican disunity and Democratic good fortune, the GOP dominated Congress and the presidency for the three and a half decades after 1894.[39]

The Panic of 1893 was primarily responsible for this change, but this explanation does not account for the persistence of Republican hegemony

after the economic climate had improved. In the early years of the twentieth century, an industrializing America found Republican policies more
relevant than sterile Democratic negativism. Tariff protection, subsidies,
and the tentative beginnings of the regulatory state made the GOP the
more progressive and innovative of the two parties within the existing political framework. As the more cohesive of the parties, the Republicans
governed in a fashion that pleased the electorate.

Republicans drew the sources of their political supremacy after 1894
from many segments of American society. In the larger cities of the
Northeast and Midwest, Republican majorities became a commonplace
until the middle of the 1920's. More important, the GOP won supporters
among previously unreceptive ethnic groups like German Catholics and
Lutherans, in part because of the party's diminished reliance on its
pietistic wing. To its strong base among the professional and entrepreneurial elements of the North, the Republicans added the allegiance of those
religious and national groups, in both rural and urban settings, whose
absence from the party's coalition had been so damaging in the 1870's
and 1880's. These new members of the Republican majority left the
Democrats during the depression, but remained within the fold after
1894 because Republican programs and policies appealed to their personal concerns and group aspirations.[40]

As they prepared for the presidential election in 1896, the Republicans could not know that they had ended their long search for a national
majority. Party strategists did realize that Democratic losses in 1894
had made the task of winning the presidency substantially easier, and the
bright prospects for victory prompted numerous hopefuls to take the
field. In the course of the contest for the nomination, William McKinley
emerged as the embodiment of forces that had reshaped his party and
altered the structure of national political life.

The inheritor of the policies that Blaine first advanced in the 1880's,
McKinley mastered the complexities of the tariff in the hard school of
Ohio politics and in ·countless congressional intrigues. He was more
adept in his personal relationships than the mercurial Blaine, even if he
lacked the intellectual power that the Maine statesman had displayed.
McKinley's service in the House, his efficient tenure as governor of Ohio
from 1891 to 1895, and his popularity within the party placed him in an
ideal position to capitalize on the improved chances of the GOP after
1894. His association with the McKinley Tariff, an act that acquired
added luster with the hindsight born of depression, made it convincing to
describe him as "the advance agent of prosperity." [41]

McKinley's public personality particularly appealed to ethnic and economic groups on which the new Republican majority rested. As governor of Ohio he did not oppose organized labor, and his recognized empathy for the workingman enhanced his attractiveness to urban voters. In the confused politics of his native state, McKinley avoided antagonizing traditionally conservative ethnic groups. He represented moderation and compromise on these sensitive ethno-cultural matters and was well suited to win the backing of the segments of the population that had hitherto been cool to GOP candidates. The attacks of the American Protective Association on McKinley's candidacy produced beneficial side effects for the Republican presidential aspirant which the authors of the onslaught hardly contemplated.[42]

McKinley was no innovator, but his campaign for the nomination and the White House drew with great skill on the abundance of political tactics that his party had accumulated since the days of Blaine. His front-porch appearances recalled the first Harrison canvass, while his reliance on business contributions and a "campaign of education" elaborated on techniques first tested in 1888 and 1892. The imposition of order on the hurly-burly of the campaign accorded with a general Republican tendency, but McKinley, and his able lieutenant, Marcus A. Hanna, extended these rationalizing trends. The large amounts of money raised for the campaign disturbed those who legitimately feared the effects of cash in politics. A national campaign required substantial expenditures, but the total was less important than the ways in which the money was spent in 1896. McKinley and his managers helped to set a pattern—centralized organization, controlled exposure of the candidate, saturation of the organs of public opinion—that has prevailed to the present.[43]

The nomination of McKinley in St. Louis did not occur because of the monetary resources of Mark Hanna or through corrupt understandings with purchasable delegates. From late 1895 through the opening of the convention, the McKinley forces organized a bloc of votes that accurately reflected the candidate's standing within the party. In the West, McKinley's connection with the tariff and his moderation on the silver issue enabled him to outdistance the regional hopeful, Senator William Boyd Allison of Iowa. Thomas B. Reed, arch-defender of the gold standard, lacked a secure power base in his home area of the Northeast and never displayed significant national strength. Attempts to stop McKinley with a coalition of favorite sons collapsed in the spring of 1896. As the only genuine national candidate of his party, McKinley achieved his first-ballot triumph on merit.[44]

The Republican party organization in the 1890's was not a closed corporation. Precinct and county conventions that selected delegates to state conclaves responded readily to pressure from the party faithful. One of the reasons for the rise of pietism in the late 1880's was the very openness of the party structure; determined groups could make their influence felt. Thus McKinley's success in his fight for the nomination was not a shadow victory, won by fraud or subversion. Had the majority of Republicans desired an alternative, they possessed the means to find one in 1896.[45]

Republicans had every reason to anticipate an easy campaign for the presidency. The departure of Henry M. Teller of Colorado and the other western silver men from the convention had damaged the party only slightly, and the strong gold plank in the platform buttressed the GOP in the East. Meanwhile, the Democratic front runners lacked national standing and the ability to compete with McKinley's popularity. By stressing the tariff and playing down the money question, McKinley and Hanna envisioned decisive success in November.

The nomination of the young, fiery Nebraskan, William Jennings Bryan, forced the Republicans to revise their strategy to deal with the challenge of free silver. The strongest candidate in his party, Bryan went out on the hustings like Blaine in 1884 and waged a vigorous, evangelistic crusade for silver and Democratic victory. For voters, weary of four years of hardship and social unrest, Bryan's campaign had a novel and captivating aura that buoyed up the Democrats during the summer and early fall. Ironically, Bryan's moralistic tone won over some normally Republican pietists who found that a Democrat was now talking their language on ethno-cultural issues.[46]

Republican advisers did not panic, and their countermoves deflected much of the force of Bryan's offensive. In farm states, Republicans argued that tariff protection was a better guarantee of future prosperity than an inflated currency. Urban voters heard Republicans note that expansion of the money supply would harm workers on fixed income and would damage the international position of the American economy. Among the traditionally Democratic ethnic groups, McKinley's mild tone compared favorably with Bryan's strident approach. The Democratic crusade for silver palled by mid-autumn and the enthusiasm that Bryan had built up ebbed away by election day. Hanna's quip that Bryan was "talking silver all the time and that's where we've got him," underscored the limitations of the Democrat's one-issue campaign and the correspondingly larger appeal of McKinley's program.[47]

The election results solidified the revolution of 1894. McKinley's majority in the popular vote of some 600,000 ballots represented the largest margin since Grant's victory in 1872. The GOP candidate consolidated the Republican hold on northern industrial states and confined the Democrats to the South and parts of the West. In the major cities McKinley far outdistanced his adversary and perpetuated the gains made two years earlier. The Democrats inevitably recovered somewhat from the poor showing of 1894, but their inability to crack the strongholds of new Republican power, the cities of the Northeast and Midwest, indicated that their future prospects would depend more on the mistakes of the GOP than their own inherent assets as a party.

Disappointed Democrats have persuaded historians that Republicans in 1896 used economic coercion and vote frauds to swell McKinley's total. This explanation ignores both the relative honesty of American national elections following the adoption of the Australian ballot, and the continuation of Republican majorities for thirty years after 1896. Perceptive studies of voting behavior place less weight on such alleged incidents of political corruption and correctly stress the importance of issues and convictions in determining the outcome of these elections. In the context of political developments of the 1890's, the election of 1896 becomes less the dramatic confrontation of opposing approaches to the future development of the nation and more the outgrowth of previous events that had revolutionized American politics.[48]

In acquiring its position as the majority party after 1894, the GOP undeniably benefitted from economic depression and Democratic mistakes. But the Republicans prevailed because they more nearly met the needs and desires of the mass of American voters than any other party. As the nation became industrialized, interdependent, and cohesive, Republican doctrines provided plausible solutions to the dilemmas of economic expansion. The electorate's perception that GOP policy had more relation to its problems than Democratic alternatives ultimately explained the outcome of these crucial party battles. In an era of serious public debate over important issues, the triumph went to an organization that acted in the best traditions of the two-party system. Republicans like McKinley and Blaine had labored with unremitting effort to secure the opportunity to govern effectively. After 1894 the voters gave the party its chance. The quest for a national Republican majority had ended.

Senator James Gillespie Blaine,
"the Man from Maine."
Library of Congress.

President Grover Cleveland.
Library of Congress.

"Too big a job for the little tugs." The Cleveland Administration's promised good times are stuck on the mudbank of fiscal uncertainty. *Judge, May 4, 1895.*

Market Street in Canton, Ohio, during the campaign of 1896.   *Ohio Historical Society Library.*

Marcus Alonzo Hanna.
Library of Congress.

President McKinley in Canton, Ohio.   *Ohio Historical Society Library.*

"Who is Tariff, and why is he for revenue only?" A famous cartoon commenting on General Hancock's defeat in 1880.   *Harper's Weekly, November 13, 1880.*

Carl Schurz.
Library of Congress.

Secretary of State John
Hay radiates confidence.
Library of Congress.

Settling the Tariff Question, a country store debate.
New England Magazine, October, 1894.

William James.
Fogg Museum, Harvard University.

Henry Adams in middle age.
Fogg Museum, Harvard University.

Hamlin Garland, 1903.   *Library of Congress.*

William Dean Howells
in relaxed old age.
Library of Congress.

Mark Twain.
Library of Congress.

PAUL S. HOLBO

◦◦ 10 ◦◦

Economics, Emotion, and Expansion:
An Emerging Foreign Policy

THE BURDENS OF AN ERA are often traced to the past. In American foreign relations, the late nineteenth century appears as the fountainhead of
subsequent triumphs or tragedies. The belief that the United States
emerged as a "world power" or became an "imperialist nation" in 1898
is a cliché. Scholars continue to examine these events, however, and
sometimes shape thinking about past and present foreign affairs. Understanding these interpretations contributes to a better appreciation of the
patterns and development of foreign policy.

One of the first careful historians of this period was Eugene Schuyler,
a pioneer American professional diplomat. In university lectures, published as *American Diplomacy* in 1886, he emphasized issues of neutral
rights on the high seas, navigation on various waterways, fisheries disputes, and commercial treaties.[1] These questions seemed trivial to later
generations, but several recent diplomatic historians have focused upon
incidents not far removed from Schuyler's themes. They have written
about low-keyed quarrels with the European powers over Samoa, arguments with Germany over the sale of diseased American meat, and incidents stemming from the attacks of American mobs on Italian and
Chinese immigrants. Their general picture of foreign relations in the
Gilded Age is one of "diplomacy in low gear," or of "awkward years,"
when little was accomplished but when somehow the way was prepared
for the more exciting events at the end of the century.[2]

Quite a different and more immediately significant interpretation appeared in the 1920's. The influential "progressive" historian Charles A.
Beard, who had previously gained attention by claiming to have revealed

199

profit-seeking by the authors of the Constitution, published a widely
heralded economic interpretation of the nation's history, *The Rise of
American Civilization* (1927). In the chapter on the post–Civil War
years, Beard and co-author Mary Beard traced American foreign policy
to "a resumption of the old solicitude for the promotion of foreign commerce." They argued further, with little evidence, that "manufacturers
and merchants still had an appetite for new markets beyond the seas and
officers of the Navy were as eager as ever to sail to fame and power in
the wake of Commodore Perry." They also alleged mischief and malice
in the conduct of policy in 1898 by officials such as Assistant Secretary of
the Navy Theodore Roosevelt.[3] Beard developed the thesis about the economic roots of American foreign policy in two provocative books of
1934, *The Idea of National Interest* and *The Open Door at Home*. He
argued again that attempts at "expansion in foreign markets" had persistently distorted United States foreign policy, especially under Republicans from the time of William H. Seward to Herbert Hoover. Beard's
interpretation contributed substantially to the isolationist mentality that
inspired the New Deal neutrality legislation. He specifically recommended
that the country abandon all engines of war and diplomacy, sink its
merchant fleet, forego foreign trade, ignore the world, and engage in
centrally planned domestic reform.[4]

Other historians in the 1930's enlarged upon another lead from
Beard, though the new vogue of interest in "public opinion" and "propa-
ganda" was also influential. The "yellow press" of New York publishers
William Randolph Hearst and Joseph Pulitzer allegedly inspired a "mar-
tial spirit" in the American public, which drove a reluctant but weak
President William McKinley to war in 1898.[5]

Professor Julius W. Pratt vigorously rejected the key Beardian notion
that businessmen were warhawks in April, 1898, or expansionists before
Commodore George Dewey defeated the Spanish fleet at Manila Bay.
Drawing heavily from the new field of intellectual history, Pratt contended that ideas, not economic interests, had led Americans to expansionism, which in turn produced the war with Spain. He found the roots
of empire in the views of American clergymen, intellectual proponents
of Social Darwinism, and naval theorists such as Captain Alfred T.
Mahan.[6]

Despite Pratt's onslaught, Beard's economic interpretation was
widely popular in the isolationist 1930's. It faded gradually from the
textbooks, if not all classrooms, during the 1940's. It disappeared almost
completely with the sweeping scholarly rejection of Beard's work in the
1950's.[7] A combination of the "yellow-press" interpretation, focusing on

overheated "public opinion," and Pratt's expansionist intellectuals survived in both textbooks and teaching.[8] Students who attended high school and college during the postwar decades absorbed that version of events, but its foundations visibly crumbled in the early 1960's under diverse new interpretations.

A controversial younger generation of Beardian historians accepted the master's economic determinism and Pratt's intellectual factors but minimized the "yellow press" and a militant public or Congress. Walter LaFeber pointed out in 1963 that the sensational newspapers existed prior to 1898 and questioned their importance in bringing on the war. They possessed no monopoly of circulation even in New York City and had slight impact on the militant Midwest. And he found little effect on McKinley, who sharply criticized them. He might have added that the "yellow journals" were not only disreputable but Democratic, which further diminished their reputation with the Republican administration. The President determined policy, argued LaFeber, but expansionist business interests generally guided him.[9] LaFeber and other historians of the New Economic Determinist school contended that war came in 1898 because the United States had suffered severe depressions in the 1880's and 1890's. Economic "overproduction" also inspired warnings from intellectuals and led to a desperate search for markets for "surpluses" in such places as Brazil, Venezuela, Nicaragua, and China. Americans did not seek colonies in the European sense but engaged in "imperial anticolonialism" with a foreign policy and tariffs based on an "open door" for trade. Similar expansionist policies resulting from economic considerations allegedly warped American foreign relations from the 1850's to 1898, and to the Vietnam War.[10]

The New Economic Determinists treat American economic motives and ideology as invariably expansionist, in contrast even to Beard who recognized a conflicting isolationistic "Jeffersonian" strain. Their interpretation of the role of economics in American history is one of monolithic expansionism. But the late nineteenth century fairly bristled with exceptions, and the economic interests were divergent and often conflicting. Ironically the New Economic Determinists have undermined the economic interpretation of history by greatly oversimplifying it.

There are substantial elements of validity in their arguments, however. American production was booming. Sharp and sometimes prolonged depressions occurred, especially in the 1870's and 1890's, and prices often dropped abruptly.[11] A high percentage of businessmen failed, and so did many farmers. Even such ultimately successful entrepreneurs as John D. Rockefeller suffered intense anxiety about their businesses.[12]

And some theorists warned of "overproduction," such as the economist David Ames Wells, a former commissioner of revenue and Republican free trader, who wrote of the "stagnation" of the economy. But each of these factors had other aspects: the economic determinants in American society, and hence in foreign policy, were extremely complex.

The productive capacity was not seen primarily as an economic problem, but evidence of strength and prosperity. Every president and most politicians, including Greenbackers and Populists, boasted about the land of plenty and the promise of American economic life. Businessmen and farmers generally sought to increase production. Panics left disturbing emotional, economic, and political legacies, but their results were diverse, and did not all move the country towards expansionism. Some inclined Americans to look inward.

The periods of stringency always passed; new concerns took the place of firms that failed. Boom followed bust. Success was in the air, and there were fortunes to be made. Good times, not panics, were normal—at least if one's own party held office. The "outs" blamed incumbents for depressions, and were charged in turn with creating "distrust and uncertainty." [13] The incumbent party invariably claimed that its policies were ending the depression; only the agitation of the opposition hindered recovery. Representative James Garfield of Ohio put it well in 1878, some months before the Panic of 1873 had really passed, when he criticized the Democrats for proposing "infinite mischief at this time, when the country is just recovering itself from a long period of depression." [14]

Politicians such as Garfield who favored high tariffs occasionally numbered proponents of the overproduction thesis among the mischiefmakers; these theorists tended in the 1870's to be free traders. The overproduction theorists also drew fire from men with alternative explanations and different solutions for hard times. Early in the Panic of 1873, Republican congressional leaders insisted that the United States maintain its credit. Strict economy and sufficient revenue from high tariffs would accomplish this. One intentional result was the closing of a number of consular offices and the hampering of foreign trade and travel. Republican Representative James Monroe of Ohio, a former consul in Brazil, protested vainly: "The whole of South America is without a consular clerk." [15]

At congressional hearings in 1878 and 1879, dozens of witnesses suggested dozens of theories about the hard times. A wholesale grocer criticized big capitalists for squeezing out little men. A financial expert thought speculation caused the trouble. An importer called for lower tariffs. And so the hearings went, displaying the wild variety of American economic thought and interest.

Congress wrangled over the form and quantity of money, sometimes relating it to foreign trade. Republican Senator Justin Morrill of Vermont protested in December of 1873 that American commerce suffered because of national bank notes and greenbacks issued during the Civil War. "We are yet content to waste our energies in the vain attempt to compete with paper against the hard money of the world," he told Congress. "We might as well challenge steam with sails, or a Toledo blade with a sword of lath!" [16] Morrill was an arch-protectionist, and his appeal may have derived more from an equally ardent interest in "sound money" than from solicitude for foreign trade.

Republican Senator John Sherman of Ohio, who managed most money bills in the mid-1870's, also was greatly concerned about the public credit and feared free silver. Sherman devised legislation to provide for specie resumption in 1879 and for silver coinage without making silver a monetary standard. Most Republican congressmen, including some who favored greenbacks, voted for his compromise bills. But soft-money Democrats charged that the demonetization of silver constituted the "Crime of 1873." Tight money was their explanation for the country's ills, and they advocated more greenbacks or the unlimited coinage of silver. The bitter feelings and curious notions the currency issue aroused primarily affected domestic politics. But they also colored opinions on foreign policy, and became entangled in every discussion of foreign trade and the tariff. The panacea of free silver even affected advocates of the overproduction thesis, for it overshadowed their pet theory and divided potential supporters.

The solidly established protective system was the most obvious obstacle confronting advocates of foreign markets. By the early 1880's there was not a single Republican free trader in the Senate, and William D. "Pig-iron" Kelley managed the formidable GOP protectionist forces in the House. Kelley derided the "preposterous assertions" of "school-men and the organs of these foreign commercial agents that [we] are suffering from 'over-production.' " [17] A prominent fellow Pennsylvanian, Democratic Representative Samuel Randall, agreed. Some members from both parties worked energetically to preserve American markets for domestic products. Republicans generally favored high tariffs, which became an ideological, emotional, and partisan position. They championed the interests of "workingmen"; low-tariff Democrats espoused the cause of "consumers." Passionate invocation of the ideas in these political labels, not interest in new foreign markets, typified congressional debate on tariffs in the 1870's and 1880's.

Efforts to revise the tariff after 1880 did not result from a depression or fears of overproduction, but from two years of prosperity after 1878.

Almost $600,000,000 of customs revenue in the Treasury created a troublesome surplus. Congress characteristically responded by establishing a special tariff commission, which undertook an investigation that was so leisurely that it provoked public protests. Then hard times struck, with rising complaints about Republican tax policies. But nothing induced a divided Congress to do more than enact the "Mongrel Tariff" of 1883, which changed few rates significantly.

Far more was involved in the tangle of tariff politics than a search for foreign markets. The intricacy of issues became apparent again when protectionist Republicans joined low-tariff Democrats to delay Senate acceptance of President Chester Arthur's reciprocity treaties. The lame-duck administration had negotiated pacts with Spain and several Central American nations to increase trade. This goal doomed them, at least for most protectionists. The new Cleveland administration finally withdrew the treaties in 1885, saying they provided "illusory" tariff relief and would cause "new and large drains" upon federal revenue.[18]

The hard times of 1882 to 1886 did not inspire economic expansionism. Some commentators saw a connection between the depression and industrial surpluses. Wells once more traced the difficulty to a "saturated" economy and called for lower tariffs and new markets. But other men opposed Wells's pet theories. Commissioner of Labor Carroll D. Wright could not see how low tariffs and foreign sales would relieve surpluses, especially if all producing countries sought recovery in the same way. Wright advocated greater statesmanship and international attention to the costs of armies and disruptive wars.

Some economic analysts, such as Edward Atkinson and Henry George, flatly rejected Wells's argument of overproduction, which George termed "preposterous when there is actual want among large classes." A writer in the Banker's Magazine argued that "our wants are indefinite." Protectionists wanted to restrict imports, while the new American Economic Association called for action by "church, state, and science." Edward Bellamy, author of Looking Backward (1888), proposed utopian reforms; social workers demanded better organization of charity; and Henry Demarest Lloyd advocated control of monopolies. Still others spoke for or against more homesteads, cheaper money, or restricted immigration.[19] Advocates of foreign markets were only some of many voices wailing in the economic wilderness.

The tariff and the person of James G. Blaine figured importantly in the campaign of 1884, which Grover Cleveland won. But the new President revealed slight interest in foreign markets. He rejected Arthur's reciprocity treaties, except where there existed "a common border line [as with Mexico] incapable of being guarded." He defined a proper tariff in his annual message to Congress in December, 1887, which inspired the Democratic Mills bill.[20]

The President attacked the "indefensible extortion" of protective tariffs and bemoaned the stifling of competition by "trusts" that benefitted from high duties. He referred briefly to "glutted domestic markets," but only as one argument among many reasons for tariff reform. He chiefly recommended the "free importation" of certain raw materials, which the Mills bill defined as lumber, flax, hemp, and wool. The object was not to secure foreign markets, but to aid domestic consumers by helping American manufacturers to produce goods more cheaply. Cleveland's immediate object was political, since Republican protectionists who controlled the Senate would defeat the Mills bill. The Democratic tariff program was mainly a "reform" to unify the Democratic party in the campaign of 1888.[21] Cleveland rallied some "importing interests" to his side and gained the support of "a large body of manufacturers who wished cheap raw materials and knew that foreign competition would help to provide them." [22] But the President's strategy, which attracted some eastern businessmen, did not help him at the polls, and contributed to later Populist and Bryanite hostility to his leadership.

The triumphant Republicans, who won the election of 1888 partly as a result of their tariff stance, felt they had a mandate to raise duties. But first they enacted Senator Sherman's long-debated antitrust measure, temporarily offsetting Democratic complaints that protective tariffs were responsible for monopolies. The next step was to increase tariffs on both farm and manufactured products and, at the same time, do something about the Treasury's surplus. Chairman William McKinley of the House Ways and Means Committee removed the tariff from raw sugar, which produced much federal revenue. Cheaper sugar would also please the average housewife and business firms that imported Caribbean raw sugar. The foremost of these was the Sugar Refineries Company, soon incorporated as the American Sugar Refining Company and notorious as the "Sugar Trust." McKinley planned to check the big refiners by retaining a limited duty on refined sugar.[23] He placated domestic producers with a bounty to compensate for their loss of protection.

Little in this draft of the McKinley bill revealed interest in markets abroad.[24] This disturbed Secretary of State James G. Blaine, who especially opposed admitting Cuban sugar free of duty without getting concessions in return. Blaine submitted to President Benjamin Harrison the report of the First Pan-American Conference, which had recently met in Washington and recommended negotiation of bilateral and multilateral reciprocity treaties.[25] Harrison urged that McKinley's bill be amended, and Blaine pleaded for reciprocity with former colleagues in the Senate. He also wrote an open letter to Senator William P. Frye of Maine, asserting that the McKinley bill was "a just measure and . . . in accordance with the wise policy of protection," but that there was "not a paragraph or a line in the entire bill that will open the market for another bushel of wheat or another barrel of pork. If sugar is now placed on the free list without exacting important trade concessions in return, we shall close the door for a profitable reciprocity."

Blaine had to overcome opposition to reciprocity from extreme protectionists and Democratic skeptics, and convince Congress to let the President negotiate trade agreements. Democratic congressmen and a few Republicans insisted that the proposed executive agreements were unconstitutional. But the Secretary secured modified reciprocity in the bill by winning McKinley's support. Congress established a special duty-free classification of commodities known as the tropical list, including sugar, molasses, coffee, tea, and hides. The President could impose duties on these items if the exporting nations did not extend corresponding privileges to the United States.

John W. Foster, who shortly succeeded Blaine as Secretary of State, undertook the necessary discussions with Latin American governments and colonies. His first agreement, with Brazil, reduced duties 25 percent on various American agricultural and manufactured goods. Spain made a similar arrangement for Cuba, and its exports of sugar to the United States increased dramatically. Hawaiian planters watched unhappily, for their sugar enjoyed special freedom from American tariffs under a reciprocity treaty of 1875. They wanted heavy tariffs on Caribbean competitors and correctly feared that the McKinley law's bounties would enlarge the infant American beet-sugar industry.

President Harrison signed the McKinley bill on October 1, 1890, and most parts of it went into effect a few days later, just a month before the congressional elections. At once Democratic politicians took up Cleveland's complaint of 1887 that high tariffs fostered monopolies. They also echoed the discontent of importers and clever hucksters with goods to sell, especially tinplate, who harped on the theme that the McKinley tariff would increase the cost of living.[26]

Overconfident Republican congressmen were suddenly at the "Hell Gate" prophesied by Democratic Representative Roger Mills. Fear rather than facts swayed the public, since the new law's real economic effects were quite unknown. But the results of the election of 1890 were dramatically clear. A political revolution reduced Republican ranks in the

House from 166 to a mere 88, while the Democrats garnered an overwhelming 235, though they did not control the Senate until 1893. In 1894 they overturned the McKinley tariff and abruptly nullified the Republicans' reciprocity agreements.

This sequence of events might seem to show that Blaine's tenure as Secretary of State in the generally prosperous years after 1889 marked high point of economic expansionism. This appears all the more so because the Republicans who resumed office in 1897 quickly enacted the stratospheric Dingley tariff, which contained a restricted tropical list. As a result, Brazil alone was again willing to make a reciprocity agreement with her flighty northern neighbor. The Senate, meanwhile, rejected new reciprocity treaties, despite President McKinley's approval. Reciprocity was dead except with Brazil and Cuba after 1901.

The New Economic Determinists, however, minimize the partisan rivalries of the early 1890's and the virtual end of reciprocity in 1894. The severe depression after 1893 and concern over "surplus production" allegedly compelled even the anti-imperialistic Cleveland administration to seek economic expansionism. Thus the Democrats helped set the stage for the famous Republican actions of 1898. According to LaFeber, they sought revision primarily "to help American manufacturers compete in foreign markets," and they rejected the McKinley tariff "not because they liked Republican reciprocity less, but because they loved unlimited reciprocity more." Secretary of State Walter Q. Gresham, a key figure in this interpretation, "concluded that foreign markets would provide in large measure the cure for the depression and its attendant labor troubles." Gresham fixed his foreign policy upon the principle of "averting economic and political disaster at home by commercial expansion abroad." He thus ceases to be a forgotten and inconsequential Secretary of State and becomes "the purest example of the economic expansionist, anticolonial attitude of the new empire." [27]

This thesis has the compelling appeal of simplicity. But its authors misread American political history and fail to note emotional and ideological ingredients that affected foreign policy. The Cleveland-Gresham policies did not originate in the depression of 1893, but in Cleveland's famous tariff message of 1887. The recommendation of free raw materials he made then became the chief ideological principle and battle cry of his party for the next six years.

In 1891, for example, the House Democrats introduced a series of "pop-gun bills," which had no chance to pass the Republican Senate but kept the Cleveland policy of free raw materials before the public. At the Democratic convention in 1892, the delegates echoed Cleveland in denouncing the "trusts and combinations fostered by republican policies." They proclaimed that tariffs were unconstitutional "except for the purpose of revenue only," and predictably endorsed the principles of "free raw materials and cheaper manufactured goods." Cleveland accepted the nomination with a promise of tariff reduction, though not "impossible free trade," and pledged to support "freer raw material," a minor modification that reappeared in final discussion of the Wilson tariff in the Senate in 1894. The President declared in 1894, in a trenchant public letter, that free raw materials was "the most Democratic of all tariff principles" and "gave us a rallying cry in our day to triumph." But by then his position on the tariff had contributed, along with the related trust question, to the disaffection of Democrats and Populists whose unhappiness had begun with the silver issue.

Before the Cleveland administration could enact the principle of free raw materials, it faced a serious crisis in federal revenues and the onslaught of the depression of 1893. The President's solution was to repeal the Sherman Silver Purchase Act. When repeal had little effect on the depression and divided his own party, Cleveland did not seek new approaches to the hard times and social unrest. Instead of focusing on foreign markets to relieve surplus production, he doggedly pushed familiar policies and his followers voiced oft-stated arguments.

The conventions of thought were solidly established in the early 1890's after years of repetitious debate. In December, 1893, the President turned to the tariff, and in a message to Congress stressed again the importance of providing "cheap materials" for our manufacturers and lessening costs to consumers.[28] He paid little more attention to foreign markets or surpluses than in 1887, before the depression. And even these brief references merely buttressed his basic proposal about raw materials.[29]

But the New Economic Determinists point to statements by the President's spokesmen: Chairman William L. Wilson of the House Ways and Means Committee; Senator Roger Q. Mills, who managed the tariff legislation in the upper house; Chairman Daniel Voorhees of the Senate Finance Committee; and Secretary Gresham.[30] Here the evidence is highly selective. Too frequently, only those parts of statements are quoted that seem to support the interpretation, and they appear without the context necessary to understand them. Wilson referred to foreign markets in only three sentences in a *Forum* article on the tariff in January, 1894. He wanted free raw materials, "the really great and beneficent reform of the bill," whose aim also was to give workingmen "untaxed materials to work with." He further tried to assuage public fears about foreign invasion of the American market and praised the bill's technical features. More important, he asserted that it was "*a mockery to talk of overproduction*" because of the hungry and ill-clad.[31] In a major speech to the House, which extended into two days, Wilson referred to foreign markets but also spoke of many other reasons for adoption of the Cleveland program. Wages seemed to be the main point; at other times, he attacked "monopoly," or the menacing influx of immigrants coming to work in protected industries, or the "evils of powerful wealthy interests." [32]

Senator Mills's article in *The North American Review* in February, 1894, provides more evidence for the argument about foreign markets, though his brief references emphasized free raw materials and the need for continued tariff reduction. In his two major speeches to the Senate, Mills concentrated on the technical advantages of the Wilson bill and alleged benefits for agriculture. He argued that there were wheat surpluses, but he opposed the Republican system of "reciprocity between farmers principally." He did not argue for new trade with Latin America or Asia but for selling grain to Britain. Mills was concerned about little but farming, and hardly created an impression of the Cleveland administration's interest in expanding economic frontiers generally.[33]

Senator Voorhees said nothing about foreign markets in his lengthy major address. The aged Indianan attacked big businessmen and "the power of hoarded money," wept for toilers and consumers, and flayed the McKinley tariff as "a gigantic crime . . . so rotten in morality, and so ravenous in its exactions." [34] Similar heated speeches by other Democratic congressmen during the highly partisan debate amounted to a screeching refrain against monopoly and wealth that often obscured the administration's other arguments for the Wilson bill. Tension in Congress reflected and contributed to the fragmentation of the Democratic party. Protectionist Democratic senators and others unhappy over Cleveland's politics now joined to emasculate the Wilson bill. When they finished, duties almost reached the level of the McKinley tariff. More bitter still for Cleveland men, the key principle of free raw materials disappeared except for "free wool." This helped devastate the western sheep-raising industry and contributed to the rise of Bryanism. Any hopes the administration had of encouraging foreign trade in this way suffered a crushing setback. Democratic Senator Arthur Pue Gorman of Maryland, responding to sharply critical exhortation from the President, even charged that free raw materials was a departure from Democratic dogma.[35]

Gorman's protest was the first of many to come from both wings of the party. By 1897 the Democratic minority leader in the House, Joseph Bailey, bitterly attacked "this Cleveland heresy," which he attributed to "the same influences which came so near pledging our party to the maintenance of the single gold standard." It was a "strange infatuation," he complained, that sought to win "Mugwump votes" and to please eastern manufacturers by giving them "the valuable privilege of buying their materials at free-trade prices and selling their finished products at protection prices." [36] Bailey's speech marked a sullen epitaph for tariff reduction by the Cleveland administration. Many Democrats after 1894 moved toward protectionism as they abandoned Cleveland's policies.

Secretary of State Walter Q. Gresham occasionally expressed concern about labor unrest and interest in foreign markets.[37] But he said different things to different people, and his position dovetailed closely with the legislative progress of President Cleveland's programs. In the summer of 1893, he did not focus on surplus production, but held that "false notions as to the true meaning of the word 'money' and the function of the Government to it are at the root of our troubles." Repeal of the Sherman Silver Purchase Act "would do much good" by "relieving senseless fright" and releasing hoarded money.[38] A year later, as LaFeber pointed out, he wrote of the nation's seeming inability to "afford constant employment for our labor." However, LaFeber failed to quote his next sentence, in which Gresham said, "This is owing, in part, to the rapid increase of labor-saving machinery, but *in greater measure to high protective tariffs*." [39] At that moment the fate of the Wilson tariff bill was still undecided. In another letter of the same period, Gresham linked free raw materials to foreign trade, but also to the need to combat "special interests" and "trusts." He added, "I am at times very serious and anxious" over the labor situation. A week later he complained that immigration was the problem and that the Republican tariff had "attracted to our shores hundreds of thousands of laborers, many of them vicious and dangerous." Still, he was "not so discouraged" over conditions.[40] LaFeber also cited a lengthy *Harper's* article by Carl Schurz in October, 1893, and his correspondence with Gresham. But this material in fact focused overwhelmingly on the great foreign policy question of Hawaii, which was Gresham's immediate responsibility and growing concern. Only one paragraph dealt with foreign trade.[41] Thus it is misleading to claim that Gresham was "obsessed" by the problem of "glutted wealth" or that he "concluded that foreign markets would provide in the large measure the cure." [42]

The important story of tariffs in the Gilded Age was by no means largely the revelation of a depression-driven search for foreign markets. The tariff was an exceedingly complicated subject involving special economic interests, sharp and growing partisanship, and political ideology laced with emotion. These elements created a subtle and variegated tap-

estry in great part designed for home consumption, not a single strand
that drew statesmen abroad or tethered American diplomacy to illusory
commercial hopes.

Historians who favor an economic interpretation of American foreign policy also cite evidence of pleas and petitions from commercial conventions and organizations. But in tariff debates, congressmen almost
automatically discounted the importance of business associations dominated by importers and others engaged in foreign trade. Legislative action involving the American merchant marine provided a comparable
case. As in intricately related tariff policy, advocates of expanding the
merchant marine made little headway because of the complex interplay of
politics and opposition from other economic interests.

The shipping question arose because of the decimation of the merchant marine after 1861. Before the Civil War, American merchantmen
had almost rivaled Great Britain's ships and transported about 70 percent
of the country's total foreign commerce. But by 1900 they carried less
than 10 percent. "The merchants and the peoples of foreign lands [are]
familiar with every emblem but our own," Republican Senator Chauncey
Depew of New York complained in 1901. An observer of 1907 noted
that not a single American ship went regularly to or from Germany,
Sweden, Norway, Denmark, The Netherlands, Russia, Greece, or
Turkey.[43]

Americans were wedded to the antiquated ways of wood and sail,
while Europeans began to convert to steel and steam even before the
Civil War. The merchant marine never recovered from the wartime
depredations of Confederate commerce destroyers. After the war, capitalists often preferred to invest in subsidized railroads or protected industries. Those still interested in shipping could not purchase less expensive foreign-built ships for American registry because of an old law of
1817. A retaliatory act of 1866 prohibited the return to American
registry of ships that had sailed under safer flags during the war.[44] Congress also laid prohibitory duties on European steel plate for ship construction, thus aiding American foundries. It compensated shipyards for
the high cost of steel plate by giving them a monopoly of construction
for American registry, and it induced 90 percent of all American ships
to concentrate on the coastwise trade by banning foreign vessels from
this important traffic between American ports and on inland waterways.[45]

American exports to Europe multiplied even without a merchant
marine, and foreign tramp steamers might have served elsewhere if a
steady traffic had existed. But businessmen learned that ocean transportation to new markets was neither quick nor reliable, and sometimes

not even available. Foreign firms frequently had subsidized tramp steamers and contract lines at their disposal. But Congress, which would not even support the diplomatic corps or reform the decrepit consular service, refused to assist American shippers as it aided manufacturers and railroads. Democrats usually headed the opposition to subsidies for "special interests," and countered pleas for bounties with proposals for lower tariffs on foreign steel plate and for "free ships"—meaning the purchase of European ships. Midwestern Republicans accepted their contention that bounties to shippers would penalize farmers.

James G. Blaine, however, persistently tried to secure assistance to shipping, particularly for a line between New York and Rio de Janeiro. He contended that subsidies were a way to keep tariffs and aid exports simultaneously. But scandals in three experiments with mail subsidies, differences between shipbuilders and shipowners, and tariff politics frustrated his efforts. During the Spanish-American War, the government had to purchase or register foreign vessels to transport troops and supplies. Following the war, Senators William P. Frye of Maine and Depew of New York again pressed for a subsidy bill, shrewdly promising that it would provide auxiliary ships in case of war and promote shipbuilding. They spoke prophetically of the proposed Nicaraguan canal and the possibilities of markets in Japan and China, and the needs of farm and industry. But they stressed national defense in order to pass the bill.

Democratic Senator George Vest of Missouri led the rebuttal, as he had done for over twenty years. "All this talk about auxiliary cruisers," he sneered, "is the merest subterfuge, a mere glamour, an appeal to the old flag in order to cover an unjust appropriation." The formation of a new set of trusts, including the United States Steel Corporation, that would benefit from bounties inspired more harsh words from the measure's opponents. Vest especially damned the Standard Oil Company, which was interested in tankers, and the "Chicago trust" of meat packers, who would obtain all the "enormous bounty, under pretense of benefiting the cattle raisers of the country whom this syndicate is daily robbing." [46] Such economic and ideological opposition doomed the subsidy bill, despite the war's dramatic lessons.

The Navy fared better at the hands of Congress than did private shippers, but it too was in sad repair following the Civil War. Many editors and congressmen considered a Navy unnecessary or a pork-barrel project, which was substantially true. Supposedly, the fleet served as a coastal-defense force, but it could not perform even this modest function. As late as 1885 the Secretary of the Navy reported, "We have nothing which deserves to be called a Navy." One concerned congressman remarked that the Navy was a mere alphabet of floating wash-tubs, an insult that could be believed after a coal barge ran down the U.S.S. *Tallapoosa*.[47] Officers were embarrassed to show visitors their rotten, sail-powered wooden hulks. In 1881 a Chilean naval officer allegedly told a visiting American squadron to mind its own business or he would sink the entire United States fleet.

Some improvement occurred in the early 1880's, owing to such energetic naval officers as Rear Admiral Stephen B. Luce and President Arthur's determined Secretary of the Navy, William E. Chandler. They actually added only three steel cruisers with two-thirds sail power to the fleet, but they established the Naval War College, which survived the hostility of the Cleveland administration. By 1890 a dozen light cruisers and three second-class battleships were authorized. The nation's strategic concept nevertheless remained the same. Congress approved these vessels to provide coastal defense and break foreign blockades in case of war. Even the new *Maine* was still designated a "sea-going coast-line battle-ship" and joined nine wooden vessels that remained in service in 1893.

Prominent officers of this era, such as Commodore Robert W. Schufeldt and Admiral David Porter, argued for naval development as a corollary to commercial expansion. This tack sometimes had negative effects in Congress because of implications for tariff or shipping policy. But protectionist congressmen occasionally exercised an economic influence upon naval development, especially in the 1880's, by favoring appropriations to reduce the Treasury's surplus and preserve high tariffs.

Historians who have found ideas more important than economics in shaping foreign policy note that navalists also employed political and philosophical arguments. These involved national history and honor, the defenselessness of the country, the Monroe Doctrine, world events, and Darwinian ideology. The beneficial struggle for power between great national forces was a favorite theme of Admiral Luce and Captain Alfred T. Mahan. Mahan also is known today for moralistic advocacy of national expansion and for "realistic" analysis of international affairs. In the 1890's, he was much more influential in Great Britain, Germany, and Japan than in the United States. Still, he reached American audiences through a series of magazine articles, and was widely quoted. And his friends included Senator Henry Cabot Lodge and Theodore Roosevelt.

Mahan's influence in this country, however, has been exaggerated. It is questionable that the public really accepted his ideas; even the Navy was skeptical.[48] He was essentially a historical and semi-philosophical publicist who reflected rather than influenced events. He modestly admitted in *Retrospect and Prospect* (1902) that his articles traced "not

my development, but the progress of national awakening from 1890 to
1897." His chosen task was to analyze and rationalize what had been
done, not to propose bold new policies.

His expansionist themes also obscured his conservative position on
specific issues. Mahan opposed the acquisition of a naval base in the
Dominican Republic. While he favored acquiring the Hawaiian Islands,
he was not a pioneer annexationist. Mahan actually had serious doubts
about taking the Philippines because they might prove difficult to defend.
At most, he told Lodge, the United States should retain Luzon. Three
years later he concluded that "such oversea expansion as the United
States has so far made has not been primarily for military purposes,"
though it contributed incidentally to naval power. Perhaps further expansion would come, for "other than military or naval reasons . . . but in fact
no such undue expansion has yet occurred." [49]

Senator Lodge had not worked closely with Mahan until 1898,
though he began to quote him in 1894. Lodge was an ardent nationalist
before the Spanish-American War, but not a scheming imperialist. He
took little interest in foreign relations during the early 1890's, objected
to territorial acquisitions overseas until late 1894, and believed in August,
1898, that Hawaii should be the outer limit of American expansion in
the Pacific. At that time he apparently accepted Mahan's modest recommendations about the Philippines, and transmitted this view to the
Department of State.[50]

Theodore Roosevelt, in contrast, was early in accord with Mahan's
thought, partly because of mutual interest in naval history. But Roosevelt did not play a significant role in national affairs until after the Spanish-American War. The action for which McKinley's young Assistant
Secretary of the Navy has become best known, sending Commodore
George Dewey to the Philippines, was really the result of routine con-
tingency planning by naval officers. Their aim was to deprive Spain of
Philippine revenues in case of war, not to acquire the islands. The President himself personally gave final approval for Dewey's move to the
islands, contrary to the popular legend that Roosevelt did it at a moment
of temporary authority. Roosevelt received undue credit for the planning
because his friend Lodge, one of the first historians of the war, found
that the Navy's bureau chiefs preferred not to have their work noticed.
Roosevelt did not suffer from such hesitation.[51]

Roosevelt's views on international affairs, race, and national progress
were complex, but he generally fitted the stereotype of the imperialistic
Social Darwinian.[52] As a young man he often seemed to spoil for a fight;
and in the 1890's he favored a belligerent posture towards Great Britain,

Germany, and Spain. But such aggressiveness was not characteristic of other prominent Social Darwinians, inaccurately portrayed as warhawks and expansionists. They generally were anti-militarists. Herbert Spencer held that human society would evolve from militancy to industrialism, and that the military were wasteful and destined to wither away. The prominent historian, John Fiske, argued that industrial progress made warfare also less endurable. Fiske spoke of spreading ideas and institutions, but his famous lecture "Manifest Destiny" said nothing about territorial expansion. He also favored a form of world federalism and an international tribunal to preserve peace.[53] The Reverend Josiah Strong, whose thought actually was Christian and not Darwinian and who defined an Anglo-Saxon as anyone who spoke English, wanted to spread evangelical Protestantism, not the American political system. "I do not imagine that an Anglo-Saxon is any dearer to God than a Mongolian or an African," he wrote in 1893. Reviewers and readers of his books were more interested in his views on home missions than in his remarks on world leadership. But Strong may have indirectly fostered expansionism with appeals for evangelism and his argument that communication had brought the world closer together. When war came, he supported acquiring Hawaii and Puerto Rico and retaining the Philippines. Yet he condemned talk of the "white man's burden," insisted on the employment of proper means in foreign policy, and said that world not national interests must be consulted.[54]

Professor John Burgess of Columbia University was a consistent anti-imperialist after 1898, when he sharply criticized his former student Theodore Roosevelt. Burgess, who once had lectured on the significance of expansion, now viewed it as "disastrous to American political civilization." President David Starr Jordan of Stanford, a Social Darwinian biologist, believed that the white man was superior but that war was degrading. And Andrew Carnegie, one of the few identifiable Social Darwinians among prominent businessmen, was a major contributor to anti-imperialism and the organized promotion of peace. The general influence of Social Darwinism upon businessmen and leaders of public opinion, and its impact on foreign policy, is questionable.[55] But if this philosophy actually was important, it might have led Americans away from war and the acquisition of territories.

The fear that foreign ventures would be costly or valueless also contributed to the forces resisting expansion. So, too, did feelings of racial superiority, though historians have often mentioned only their expansionist side.[56] From 1870 to 1900 Southern Democrats and many other Americans objected to the acquisition of territories with Negro, Latin, or "tropical" populations. Or they argued, as did Carl Schurz in opposing the acquisition of Hawaii in 1893, that democracy could not survive in such climes.[57] Partisanship also created many vigorous if inconsistent critics of expansion. The *Seattle Daily Times* in January, 1900, dismissed the "wiping out" of Philippine tribes and even "the loss of our own brave soldiers" as simply "the survival of the fittest." But six months later, after the Democrats opened their presidential campaign on the theme of anti-imperialism, this strongly Bryanite organ scored the McKinley administration for employing the army "to subjugate those identical people in the island of Luzon who had fought Spain for half a century . . . to gain their liberty." [58]

Ernest R. May has suggested that European liberal thought was another important influence upon American policy, at least upon local and national leaders of opinion. In the 1870's respected English liberals such as William E. Gladstone, John Bright, and James Bryce impressed their anti-imperialist views upon influential American politicians, editors, preachers, and professors. President Ulysses S. Grant expressed interest in the Dominican Republic for trade and as a place of refuge for American Negroes. He wanted at least to obtain Samaná Bay as a naval base. But Americans with transatlantic connections, such as Senators Schurz and Charles Sumner, led the successful battle against the President's proposals. Sumner subsequently boasted to John Bright of his stand against colonialism. May adds that a majority of the observable opinion leadership upheld the sophisticated anti-colonial tradition into 1897, when they stalled President McKinley's efforts to revive the project for Hawaiian annexation that the Cleveland administration had throttled in 1893.[59]

The mainstream of debate over American foreign policy flowed from less elevated heights, however. In Grant's time, politicians, editors, and civil service reformers quarreled peevishly over alleged waste and corruption in government. There was little respite from denunciation. The *Nation* observed in January, 1870, that quiet had been expected after President Andrew Johnson left office, but that a "scandalous and utterly unpardonable attack" was opened on President Grant within two weeks after Congress returned. A month later this journal greeted the President's Dominican treaty by exclaiming: "What a splendid field will be thrown open by the purchase to all unemployed collectors, assessors, appraisers, postmasters, consuls, and district attorneys." [60]

But the onslaught had just begun. In March of 1870 the House of Representatives passed a resolution asking the Department of State for information about "lands, mines, franchises, and privileges of all kinds by the Dominican Government; also, the amount of money paid out by our Government preliminary to and concerning the negotiations of said treaty, to whom and for what purposes, and out of what fund paid." [61] Controversy increased when it became known that the President had sent his aide de camp, General Orville Babcock, to negotiate with the Dominican president, Buenaventura Báez, and that Babcock had associated on his several trips with two unsavory American speculators, Joseph Fabens and William Cazneau. The two Americans proposed to make a place for Babcock in their Dominican schemes, while the unscrupulous Báez offered him land near Samaná Bay. Babcock refused the offer, but he brought arms and $100,000 to support Báez' government.

Several American newspapers reported the activities of the speculators. Senator Sumner and others apparently raised the issue of corruption in the Senate's executive sessions on the Dominican matter. Sumner supposedly told a reporter: "Why, a friend of mine, who has been down there, says that the whole coast of the bay of Samaná is staked off into lots, and marked 'Cazneau' and 'Babcock' and 'Baez,' and that one or two particularly large ones are marked 'Grant.' " [62]

Grant's supporters, particularly Senators Oliver P. Morton and Roscoe Conkling, responded by attacking their Republican colleague, Sumner. Taking the unusual step of publicly discussing the previous secret debate, Conkling scored the President's detractors: "Loathsome charges were sown broadcast throughout the land. It was alleged that the treaty was hedged about with jobs on every side. Lands were said to have been staked off . . . and it was whispered that the restless foot of guilty and venal adventure had been set upon the soil of Samaná. These unclean vaporings were breathed upon the Chief Magistrate and upon members of his official family." Sumner unfortunately refused to affirm or deny the validity of the accusations. He asserted only that the interview had not been authorized and alluded vaguely to the "real character" of the negotiators. [63] This simply compounded the insinuations.

Sumner and the Democrats next assaulted the Grant men's modest proposal for a commission to visit and report on the island. Flamboyant Samuel "Sunset" Cox complained of the "arcana" and "secret recesses" of the administration, which, he sneered, was "run by aid-de-camps and military people." Morton tried to halt the charges of corruption by suggesting that the new commissioners not be paid. But Senator Thomas Bayard asserted that only those who sought "illegitimate gains" would be willing to serve. [64] Congress narrowly authorized the commission, and Grant appointed three men who were above suspicion. The Grant men also deposed Sumner from the chairmanship of the Foreign Relations Committee. But the Dominican venture was dead, never to be revived

in the Gilded Age. The reaction was so severe that American businessmen with legitimate grievances against the Dominican government were
often unable to obtain help from the Department of State.

Similar charges of corruption again occasionally entered discussions
of foreign policy in the 1880's. There were suspicious allusions to
railroad promoters and to former President Grant in debates over a
reciprocity treaty with Mexico, and to California sugar refiner Claus
Spreckels in discussion of renewing a reciprocity agreement with Hawaii.
But far greater controversy over alleged profiteering flared in 1893,
when the Hawaiian Revolution occurred, partly because of tariff politics
and the presence of Spreckels and the Sugar Trust.

President Harrison, a reluctant expansionist, responded cautiously to
annexationists who overthrew Queen Liliuokalani's unpredictable regime
with the aid of the American minister and marines. He sought to avoid
intimations of imperialism or of favoritism to the sugar planters.[65] Before the Senate could ratify his carefully drafted annexation treaty, the
new Cleveland administration withdrew it for reconsideration. Secretary
of State Gresham believed that the revolution was the "dishonorable
scheme of a lot of adventurers," and soon appeared increasingly hostile
towards the provisional Hawaiian government headed by Sanford Dole.[66]
This became the position of many Cleveland Democrats, who opposed
annexation until it was consummated in 1898.

The press reported that Claus Spreckels, originally identified with
the revolutionaries, opposed annexation because the United States might
halt the flow of Oriental contract labor. This introduced the bogey of race
into the debate. The bumbling German-born "Sugar King" also unwit-
tingly advanced the cause of annexation by lobbying against it late in
1893. Annexationist papers angrily exploited his opposition. Even the
moderate *Washington Evening Star* listed the anti-annexationists as "a
corrupt queen seeking to enlarge her powers, her paramour, the lottery
ring, the opium smugglers and Claus Spreckels." Annexationist politicians stirred the same syrupy pot, which President Cleveland heated by
condemning the Republicans' proceedings and giving the issue back to
Congress. "Mr. Spreckels appears to be unusually pleased with the policy
of the Administration," asserted Republican Senator Joseph Dolph.[67]
The Democrats countered effectively by charging that the equally notorious Sugar Trust *favored* annexation, and that the Hawaiian revolutionaries had simply been after the bounty given sugar growers by the
McKinley tariff "in order that they might plunder the pockets of the
people of the United States." [68]

The debate was absurd because Spreckels and the Sugar Trust,
portrayed as devils on opposite sides, had recently merged some in-

terests.[69] The complex connections between their beet-sugar and cane-sugar operations, and their roles as purchasers of raw sugar for refining, made the issues even more confused. The Hawaiian matter became hopelessly complicated and still more impassioned because it was entangled with simultaneous discussions of the Democratic Wilson tariff bill of 1894. Disclosures followed that some congressmen were speculating in sugar stocks—the insinuations touched Cleveland himself—and that the Sugar Trust's lobbyists were effectively at work on Capitol Hill. The political clamor mounted when the Wilson bill left the sugar refiners in a fairly good position and also restored the advantages that the McKinley bill had taken from the Hawaiian planters. Chairman Wilson himself concluded the stormy tariff debate with a pathetic speech asking whether this was a government of, by, and for the people *or* the Sugar Trust.

The emotions swirling around these economic issues affected foreign policy. They help to account for the persistence of anti-imperialism in the late 1890's. Infuriated western Democrats such as the influential Senator Mills, and outspoken silver Republicans and Populists such as Senators Richard Pettigrew of South Dakota and William Allen of Nebraska, were relentless foes of Republican annexation. They associated the policy with the sugar bounty, privileges for Hawaiian planters, Oriental contract labor, handicaps for beet-sugar farmers, and profits for sugar refiners. "What nonsense to talk about the sugar trust being opposed to annexation," Pettigrew stormed in July 1898.[70] So strong were their feelings that on this issue they stood with the despised Cleveland men. Together they blocked Hawaiian annexation until Commodore Dewey's presence in the Philippines allowed the McKinley administration to argue that the islands were needed to supply him, though in fact Hawaii was not on the best line of transit.

Ironically the suspicious, if humanitarian, critics of Hawaiian ventures helped to call attention to the events that finally made annexation possible. Dissidents such as Senator Allen, who had been discussing the Cuban revolution since 1895, vigorously advocated policies friendly to the forces fighting Spain. The new McKinley administration was soon under fire for being too cautious on Cuba. In May, 1897, a coalition of Democrats, Populists, and rebellious Republicans interrupted discussion of the Dingley tariff bill and passed a joint resolution calling upon the President to recognize Cuban belligerency. The United States had become a "quasi-partner with Spain in the conduct of this brutal and atrocious war," exclaimed Senator Joseph Foraker of Ohio.[71]

The stand of the Populists, silver Republicans, and Bryanites revealed the impress of their recent fight for free silver. They regularly accused

President McKinley of conspiring with European financial interests to prevent Cuban independence, avoid war, and shackle the United States or Cuba with Spain's heavy bond debt. One product of their new crusade was the now-famous Teller amendment. The real purpose of this originally inconsequential measure was to disclaim American responsibility for any such bond debt, not to forestall United States acquisition of Cuba. Pettigrew and some of its backers were anti-expansionists, but Foraker and Teller wanted to obtain Spain's territories in the Caribbean and Pacific. The various opposition elements shared little more than an interest in Cuba, a record of political rebellion, and extreme alienation from McKinley.

The imperialists among them may have been influenced by Europe. In the 1880's, according to May, European thought and example caused expansionist as well as anti-expansionist currents to appear in the United States. By the time of the Spanish-American War, elite opinion had become ambivalent on expansion and the old anti-imperial leadership was shattered. Consequently an expanded new public expressed opinions on foreign policy; and new, more numerous, and less sophisticated opinion leaders asserted their aggressive views. The outcome was a brief interval of expansion after 1898, though the Republicans still dealt cautiously with the Philippine issue. By 1900, however, Democratic charges impelled even vice-presidential Theodore Roosevelt to deny that Republicans were imperialists. Public interest in foreign policy soon lagged, notes May, and the old anti-colonial tradition was reasserted.[72]

There certainly was a European example for expansion. Men such as Teller and Foraker typified the new opinion leadership, though their motives and attitudes differed sharply from those of the young orator, Senator Albert Beveridge, who grandiloquently defended McKinley's policies. But none of these men substantially influenced the President, who made the crucial decisions for war and acquisition of territory. Teller, Foraker, and their allies lost their challenge to the President for leadership in April, 1898. Beveridge and the young Republican warhawks rarely ventured beyond the President's policies, talking of duty, destiny, and markets in China, but actually advocating only the wisdom of what McKinley had already done. The politicians closest to the President, such as Senators Marcus Hanna of Ohio and John C. Spooner of Wisconsin, were not in any new opinion establishment but neither were they warhawks or expansionists. They invariably supported McKinley, whether on the issue of peaceful negotiations with Spain or ratification of the peace treaty.

The President had assumed charge of diplomacy well before the outbreak of war. He had persevered in negotiations with Madrid until it became clear that the Spanish government would not grant the crucial point of Cuban independence, owing to opposition from liberals, right-wing Carlists, and other elements of public opinion.[73] McKinley had long favored the acquisition of Hawaii, but never advocated taking Cuba, and soon shored up its independence. He sent an outspoken anti-imperialist, President Jacob Gould Schurman of Cornell University, to report on the condition of the Philippines. Schurman concluded that the United States would have to remain for a time.

While McKinley sampled opinion on the accomplishments of the war, he decided that the United States must assume responsibility for the Philippines because no other solution seemed practicable. The islands could not be given back to incompetent Spain, turned over to another power, or left adrift in an imperialistic world. When the Philippine insurrection erupted, he conceded that ratification of the treaty of peace now was assured. But he ordered an investigation to determine if Americans were responsible for the outbreak of fighting, and his administration took pains to ease public concern. He also agreed to recommendations from Schurman and others that a civilian government replace military rule in the islands.[74] Hawaii might not have been annexed but for the war, and Philippine annexation came by the narrowest of margins.[75] The President probably could not have secured more territory if he had wanted it, despite the war's momentum. The American political system with its conflicting interests and emotions was a formidable obstacle.

But McKinley did not retreat in the campaign of 1900, because he had not previously advocated expansion for its own sake. Expansion was simply a legacy of the war. "The war was no more invited by us than were the questions which are laid at our doors by its results," he told an audience at Omaha in October, 1898. "Patience" would be required for the "duty" that lay ahead. The term imperialism also, for the majority of Republican editors and orators, was little more than a verbal embellishment of what the administration had already done and not a prospectus for the future. When the label became a liability, McKinley and his party disavowed it without embarrassment. Before the election of 1900, Americans generally considered their accidental empire more than enough. Pleased with recent triumphs but unwilling to take on further responsibilities, the country returned to its customary frustrating ways.

ROBERT FALK

$\mathcal{S}$ 11 $\mathcal{Q}$

The Writers' Search for Reality

THE SERIOUS WRITERS OF ANY AGE are in search of reality, the real thing, the genuine article valid for their time. What make the difference between literary movements and periods are the special historical characteristics of the age and the particular literary form which embodies that reality and contemporaneity. In the Gilded Age literature increasingly expressed a vision of reality in the novel form, as distinguished from the "romance" of Cooper, Hawthorne, and Melville. The decades following 1865 were a blend of the old and the new. The older established writers of the mid-century—Longfellow, Whittier, Lowell, Bryant, Holmes, and Hawthorne—were still powerful spokesmen of romanticism. Their voices merged with those of younger writers beginning to be heard. Of the early realists in fiction, three indelibly stamped the Gilded Age: Howells, Mark Twain, and Henry James. Hawthorne's influence was strong in the early work of both Howells and James. Melville, by a strange and ironic commentary on the critical taste of the period, was relatively unknown. Poetry during the postwar decades was derivative, except for Emily Dickinson and Whitman, both of whom had to wait for the critical understanding of later generations. After 1890, a younger group of writers began to express in fiction a different and stronger variety of realism called naturalism which drew upon French and Russian fiction, native agrarian protest, and Populist ideas. Literature combined the inherited tendencies of romantic thought and expression with the newer methods of realism. This combination was further altered by the naturalistic mode of the nineties in the work of Hamlin Garland, Stephen Crane, and Frank Norris.[1]

Twentieth-century critics have emphasized the negative and corruptive factors of politics and society during The Gilded Age. It is difficult now to avoid certain of the preconceptions about that period of American culture which emerged during the 1920's and 1930's in the historical writings of Charles Beard, V. L. Parrington, Van Wyck Brooks, and others. These men saw the age as the source of economic and cultural disparities adversely affecting their own time. Rugged individualism, the "gospel of wealth," the railroad barons and oil magnates, corrupt politicians, the uncontrolled exploitation of the material resources of the nation, the survival of the fittest were the elements they used to castigate the decades after the Civil War. Historians dismissed morals and manners as "genteel" and "innocent," neo-Puritan in the general refusal to admit the facts of life. *Victorian* became a word to devaluate the taste and manners of The Gilded Age. To George Santayana "The Genteel Tradition" meant that American life then was characterized by a decadent Calvinism, merging with transcendental idealism and a kind of wishful idealism at odds with the pragmatic and materialistic forces of the nineteenth century. Others, like Edith Wharton in her novel *The Age of Innocence* (1920), dramatized the period's effeminate culture and hypocritical high-mindedness. She pictured the 1870's and 1880's as an orthodoxy of factitious purity and false delicacy which shielded wives and daughters from the reigning vulgarity and bad taste. Much of this pejorative criticism needs revaluation. We have proceeded far enough beyond the Menckenism of the twenties and the Marxianism of the thirties to see that some of this flagellation was motivated by the need to disparage the Gilded Age to justify the deficiencies of those later decades. We should go beyond the negative implications of such historical tags as "The Gilded Age," "The Genteel Tradition," and "The Age of Innocence."[2]

Such phrases have only limited validity in accounting for the climate of ideas which helped produce Henry James, Howells, Mark Twain, Henry Adams, and Stephen Crane. Like all men of exceptional gifts they were both of their age and apart from it. James, the most truly original and talented artist of the period, was an American Victorian despite his distrust of much of the American scene and his rediscovery of Europe as a source of value. Howells, old-maidish and conservative to a later generation, was a literary radical in his own time. Henry Adams felt alienated from the politics of the Grant administration, yet he was clearly a product of the intellectual milieu in which positivism, science, and evolution were leading doctrines. The ideas of such original minds as William James, Chauncey Wright, John Fiske, and Charles Peirce were closely woven with the cultural texture of that generation. In short, the literary and intellectual accomplishments of the period were a subtle mingling of new ideas and ways of expression with the public tone and flavor of that much-belittled era of history.

Seeming to have exhausted the possibilities for analysis of Henry James and Mark Twain, criticism has recently turned to lesser writers such as Howells, John W. DeForest, Bret Harte, George W. Cable, and Edward Bellamy. These men had distinguished careers and popular followings, and it would be inappropriate to reassess the period without estimating their accomplishments. Talented and now neglected writers of regional fiction such as Edward Eggleston, Constance Fenimore Woolson, Joel Chandler Harris, Hamlin Garland, and Sarah Orne Jewett were also important. If we include those writers of the 1890's such as Harold Frederic, Stephen Crane, and Frank Norris the literary portrait of the age takes on still larger proportions.

Influential editors directed flourishing literary periodicals. Howells of the *Atlantic Monthly,* R. W. Gilder of the *Century,* G. W. Curtis of *Harper's Weekly,* and J. G. Holland of *Scribner's* were all tastemakers charged by later critics with perpetuating the canons of propriety. The literary essay was an art, and men like T. W. Higginson, Thomas Bailey Aldrich, and H. H. Boyesen carried on the tradition of Lowell and O. W. Holmes. Criticism was slow to develop from conventional book reviews and provincial judgments, but in the hands of James, Howells, and a few liberal-minded men such as Thomas Perry, W. C. Brownell, and E. C. Stedman, it emerged as a literary genre, independent of didacticism. The best of this criticism helped to provide a rationale for the novel of realism.[3]

Popular and sentimental fiction also flourished, a sign of the generally low level of taste among the juvenile or somewhat-arrested-adult readers of boy-books, dime novels, romance, and the kind of fiction once described by Henry James as depending on "a 'happy ending,' on a distribution at the last of prizes, pensions, husbands, wives, babies, millions, appended paragraphs, and cheerful remarks." There were "good" and "bad" boy or girl stories. Frances H. Burnett's *Little Lord Fauntleroy* was a best seller, making a snob-appeal to the American worship of titles. "Juveniles" varied in juvenility from *Tom Sawyer,* a book for adults about boys, to George Peck's *The Story of a Bad Boy and his Pa* and Harriet Stone's *The Five Little Peppers and How They Grew.* Foreign imports such as Stevenson's *Treasure Island,* Blackmore's *Lorna Doone,* Anna Sewell's *Black Beauty,* and Madame Spyri's *Heidi* all found eager readers, along with the adventure novels of Ouida, Rider Haggard, Marie Corelli, and Jules Verne. Native writers indulged in sermonizing and sensation, chivalry and romance, tears and laughter, westerns, and

dime novels. The Reverend E. P. Roe struck a new vein of popularity in
Barriers Burned Away, inspired by the great Chicago fire of 1871. Lew
Wallace's *Ben Hur* established a vogue for historical romance in the
nineties shared by F. Marion Crawford and others. Edward Westcott's
David Harum made bad grammar and "hoss-sense" a highly lucrative
product and a patriotic fashion for thousands of native readers in the
1890's.

But the most enduring juveniles of them all were the boy-success
novels of Horatio Alger. They reflected a taste for mawkish sentiment,
faith in hard work, no smoking, and obedience to elders as sure ways
of acquiring a fortune. Alger wrote with incredible speed, turning out
109 books between 1868 and 1898, averaging about 50,000 words each
and marketed at from ten cents to $1.50. Young readers apparently
could not get enough of Alger's painting of the rainbow possibilities of
wealth amid degradation and poverty. But farm boys were less impressed
by his moralizing than by his fascinating and realistic details of street
life in New York.

The Alger books were not merely an adolescent form of the gospel
of wealth or a juvenile ethic of acquisitiveness. This interpretation of
their historical role is a tempting, but easily exaggerated thesis. For the
Alger hero, wealth and success were rewards for duty, patience, and
resignation. But the emphasis upon luck and pluck placed the formula
more clearly in the traditions of Protestant piety and romantic melodrama. Alger's own evangelical background combined with the popular
romance of the period to produce his money-and-happiness endings.
These rewards were not the result of struggle and competition, but gifts
of providence, chance, virtue, and good fortune.[4]

To many later observers the Gilded Age was a "golden age" of
business. The illusion of ever-increasing fortunes was a powerful incentive to divert attention from harsher realities. American innocence, for
one thing, was too often mistaken for a virtue, while European experience
was considered corrupt. It was flattering to regard the evolutionary philosophy of Darwin and Herbert Spencer as leading upward to infinite
progress and development, particularly in material things. Not until
later did critical spirits recognize that Social Darwinism contained the
seeds of uncontrolled individualism and the worship of strength over
equality and humanity. The inequities of a rising urban and industrial
civilization were obscured in the general optimism and meliorism. National
pride and nativism led to an unwarranted complacency with the dogmas
of democracy. It was enough for patriotic spirits that the nation, a century before, had professed in political documents that all men were

created equal. Obvious indications to the contrary were dismissed as exceptional; all would be well in the end. There was a western frontier, still waiting to be exploited, a place where men were men, out of the reach of oppressive institutions of church or state. The nation was unconcerned by approaching middle age with its responsibilities and troubling problems.

Such was the general mood in 1870. But it was not the whole story. It established the socio-cultural background for the paradoxical character of Victorian realism. Literary and intellectual life, however, contained a direction and a purpose of its own. What was meant by realism in the fiction of that period? What did the best writers intend to accomplish? What theories and methods did they follow? In the major authors of the time, the disparate and often contradictory forces of the age formed a center which we can regard as the essence of literary realism.[5]

Realism as a literary phenomenon formed in the late 1860's as a protest against mid-century romantic attitudes and conventions. During the 1870's it was in a transitional and experimental stage, and by 1880, there was an authentic movement of realism in the novel; that decade produced the most characteristic writing of the period. After 1890 a different climate of ideas altered the character of realistic fiction when a new and younger generation, sometimes influenced by darker, deterministic philosophies, explored the naturalistic mode. But the gradual beginnings of realism around 1870 may be seen in the early stories of Henry James, in Howells' Italian sketches, De Forest's best novels, especially *Miss Ravenel's Conversion from Secession to Loyalty* (1868), Twain's *Innocents Abroad,* and Bret Harte's *Tales of the Argonauts.* A time of hesitation, the seventies was a decade of nationalism, and a merging of lingering romantic attitudes with newer realities. Henry James described the tone as "a romantic vision of the real." The mood was one of hope and anticipation of the coming dispensation combined with considerable innocence about its form and nature. A spirit of progress, based in part on the lure of material improvement, helped America move on from the tragedy of war. Walt Whitman expressed this somewhat vague idealism: "All goes onward and outward, nothing collapses." Whitman was one of the few who sensed the dangers of materialistic expansion and the neglect of other ideals. The public mind in 1870 was impatient of restraints, unwilling to brood over the human condition. Three factors mainly preserved the illusion of effortless growth: mid-century idealism, positivistic science and evolution, and the buoyant optimism of an expanding nation.

William Dean Howells succeeded in 1871 to the editor's chair of the

Atlantic Monthly, the leading national literary periodical.[6] In this influential position, he was responsible for the persistence of certain earlier attitudes, but he was also sensitive to the fresh current of realism and contemporaneity apparent in the contributions he accepted for the magazine.
His own fiction was at first a blend of "romance" with deft strokes of
what he called "real life." Howells was still a decade away from writing
convincing studies of manners and social analysis, but his style was flexible and carried the conviction of a genuine artist who could skillfully
record authentic dialogue and convincing characters.

The *Atlantic* in the 1870's moved cautiously away from classical
moorings toward the fascinating and untried waters of Darwinian controversy, adding the word *science* to its subtitle in 1868. *Appleton's
Journal,* edited by E. L. Youmans, the *North American Review,* the
Popular Science Monthly, and other periodicals discussed new ideas
emanating from Darwin, Spencer, Huxley, Tyndall, and Mill. Chauncey
Wright, John W. Draper, John Fiske, and other spokesmen of the new
science brought positivism and evolution to support a teleological compromise between religious orthodoxy and a naturalistic explanation of
man's origin. Instead of God, they substituted the preexistence in the
mind of moral reason and self-consciousness. William James urged that
emotional and semiconscious states of mind were active elements of
reality, emphasizing the validity of desire, feeling, love, aspiration and
habit. From the concept of the spontaneous variation of species which
William James derived from Darwinian thought, variations from the
norm came about mysteriously. But once appearing, they could be eval-
uated in the direction of useful and valuable ends, thus supporting a
conventional ethical system.

Such pragmatic relativism affected fiction, especially in the handling
of character. The mind was no longer a static and unitary fact, but was
changing and complex, subject to environmental conditions. The brave
hero and the virtuous heroine of romantic fiction and literary tradition
gave way to the ambiguous and the complex personality—Howells'
young women with pretty faces and neurotic psyches, James's highly
sensitive individuals, or De Forest's scheming coquettes.

The naturalistic implications of the new science were temporarily suspended in postwar idealism. Nervous critics complained that the novels
of James and Howells lacked old-fashioned passion and were too ironic
and analytical, too "realistic." Daisy Miller was an outrage on American
womanhood; Howells failed to create "noble" women. While there was
still a reluctance to grapple with the more violent aspects of human
perversity among the lower orders of society, there were important chinks

in the façade of what Howells called "the large, cheerful average of health and success in America." Strokes of non-genteel dialect, hill-country speech, and anti-romantic views appeared in the work of such local clolorists as Sarah Orne Jewett, Mary E. Freeman, and Constance Fenimore Woolson. Greater fidelity of language and verisimilitude informed the pages of Joel Chandler Harris and George Washington Cable in their sketches of Negroes and Creoles. In tentative ways realism entered select eastern circles and periodicals, where it mingled with tears and laughter, regional eccentricities, humor and sentiment.

In the West and on the middle border, a new and stronger literature of realism heralded a fresh beginning for an indigenous American literary style.[7] Mark Twain and Bret Harte opened this campaign during the late 1860's with *The Celebrated Jumping Frog of Calaveras County* and *Condensed Novels*. The tall tale, a special western kind of humor laced with exaggeration, laughter, and crudity characterized Twain's early writing. *Innocents Abroad* (1868) deflated romantic pretensions and struck a blow at romantic sentiment, flattering the American middle-brow tourist by looking at the Old World with a "show me—I'm from Missouri" attitude. Bret Harte imitated Dickens, Cooper, the Brontës, Dumas, with near-parody and burlesque. In 1870 *The Luck of Roaring Camp and Other Stories* gave its author tremendous and immediate popularity. Harte mingled romantic and realistic elements in a para-doxical way which typified the era's transitional character. His stories were melodramatic and the philosophy behind them meretricious. His people were burlesque variations of the real thing, his style elegant and precious. But in skillful juxtaposition of East and West, in "fine" writing about degraded scenes and frontier scamps, in humor mixed with con-descension, and in realism compounded with romance, Harte's volume summarized the 1870's. His Dickensian contrasts of frontier types, card sharks, and prostitutes possessing heroic traits of idealism and self-sacrifice, struck a responsive chord typical of the reigning social and cultural nexus.

Sentiment, artifice, decorum, and gentility, which editors and readers in polite eastern circles accepted, were affronted by the weapons of a frontier psychology bent on puncturing romance, effeminacy, and prud-ishness. The horse sense, misspellings, and earthy humor in the work of Mark Twain, Bret Harte, Bill Nye, and Artemus Ward were not quite realism, but were a powerful antidote to lingering romanticism. Harte parodied Whittier's "Maud Muller"; Mark Twain burlesqued Franklin's earnestness, Cooper's noble scouts and savages, and rebuked the culture-seekers. Yet in many ways even the most intransigent of these iconoclasts belonged to the genteel tradition. Rarely did they overstep the bounds of propriety in relations between the sexes. A generation which could be shocked by Whitman's "indecency" preferred Tom Sawyer's harmless flirtations with Becky Thatcher, or the conventional court-ships of popular fiction. If Bret Harte went somewhat further in "The Luck of Roaring Camp," it was overlooked or else disguised by the delicacy of his style. And Henry James's hinted adulteries in *The American* and *The Portrait of a Lady* went almost unnoticed, partly because of the readers' innocence, and partly because James concealed them behind the "fig-leaf" ambiguity of his impeccable prose.

The fiction of Howells and James chiefly revealed the gradual forma-tion of a theory and, more importantly, a method of realism in literature. During the seventies their work was tentative and experimental, but showed a gradually evolving esthetic of the novel considerably in advance of critical theory. They had much in common, despite strong individual differences. They agreed that the writer's first responsibility was to illuminate character. Both were conscious of the need to describe an evolving American type. Almost simultaneously they discovered the *jeune fille,* the innocent but unconventional "heiress of all the ages," whose self-conscious Americanism and pretty face were significantly re-vealing in a European situation. She was a product of national and regional conditions and the most interesting phenomenon of the novel of realism. Henry James developed the international possibilities of the young American woman in all her complexity—"shocking" independence of manner, idealism, pride, and democratic instincts. Howells treated the type in a variety of domestic situations. His Kitty Ellison *(A Chance Acquaintance,* 1873) was cut from the same cloth as James's Mary Garland *(Roderick Hudson,* 1875) or Euphemia de Mauves or Daisy Miller or Isabel Archer.

Howells differed from James in the importance he attached to the transatlantic novel as a vehicle of realism. He mainly stayed at home. "At my age," he wrote his father in 1876, "one loses a great deal of in-defineable, essential something, by living out of one's country, and I'm afraid to risk it." He stood with American nativism, and his fiction was the story of the commonplace, of "poor Real life."

The real dramatic encounter, for both novelists, was always between two or three persons—in short, "romance," but romance controlled and delimited by a firm sense of stern realities. Their novels frequently left heroines in unresolved dilemmas. James especially preferred the incon-clusive ending with a near-tragic, or at least a strong renunciatory ges-ture. Howells, sensitive to the growing scientism of the age, mingled love of New England country inns and picturesque surroundings with shrewd and subtle observation of the moods and whims of Puritan maidens who titillated, but did not quite offend, his lady readers.

As editor and critic, Howells was outspoken in championing truth, actuality, verisimilitude, and fidelity to real human motives. He admired the realists who stressed commonplace events—Trollope, Jane Austen, George Eliot, Turgenev. He praised the honesty of Mark Twain, De Forest, and Bret Harte, but disapproved of Dickens' theatricality and Zola's "bad French morality." He avoided "the fetid explosions of the divorce trials" and overemphasis upon the master passion. His early realism was moderate, and he once said that he would never write a novel his own daughters could not read without embarrassment.

After 1880, when he had resigned from the *Atlantic* editorship, Howells revealed a growing awareness of social and economic facts. He became a Christian socialist with strong sympathies for the working man, and admired Tolstoy's humanitarianism. Later critics charged him with old-maidish propensities, but Howells consciously avoided the sensational and abnormal in his reaction against the high drama and bold adventure of the mid-century romantic novel. Reticence remained part of his conscious creed of realism. He rested the theoretical case squarely on faithfulness to the common, average, middle-class experience of his time.[8]

Henry James's relation to realistic fiction diverged from that of Howells. Beginning in the 1870's at about the same point as his friend and contemporary, he rapidly moved toward the French school of Balzac, Flaubert, and Maupassant.[9] Early European travel and exposure to the richer civilizations and traditions of the Old World saved him from some of the parochialism which affected Howells and other native novelists. In many reviews and essays of the seventies and early eighties, James worked out a wholly original and nearly impressionistic position in the conflicting debates between realism and idealism, or between didacticism and art-for-art's-sake, romance and reality, Anglo-Saxon decency and French license, and other literary dialectics. He admired the serious view of art and the technique in Daudet, Goncourt, and Balzac, while drawing back from "the rags, bad smells, and unclean furniture of the Gallic mind." He praised and practiced Anglo-Saxon wholesomeness and idealism, but his artistic sense and cosmopolitan taste rebelled at the too-insistent didacticism of George Eliot.

The best European models guided James in the 1870's. He was flexible, subtle, discriminating in searching for a literary synthesis to satisfy his own sense of morality and idealism without violating honesty and realism. Like his generation, James was not ready for a naturalistic approach to life or fiction. Temperamentally, he could not accept it even in his late years when it had prevailed. His realism was the modified creed of Turgenev or Daudet, and his critical theories were influenced by the impressionism of Sainte-Beuve and Edmond Scherer.

James was a novelist of the highest stature in the great tradition of world literature, admired for experimental methods and an international point of view. Yet he shared the era's esthetic experiments along with some of its Victorian reticences and proprieties. He converted and transcended the limitations of the age through a steady preoccupation with the psychological springs of conduct, an unlimited respect for the potential of the human mind to survive against conventional attitudes and social tyrannies. In his vast curiosity over the techniques of fiction, the subtle, verbal solution to intellectual conflicts, and a strong carry-over into a more scientific age of certain transcendental and idealistic strains of thought, James was the leading realist of fiction during the 1870's. In *Roderick Hudson, The American,* and *Daisy Miller* he explored the theme of international contrast. In Isabel Archer, heroine of *The Portrait of a Lady,* he outlined the young American woman as a generic and symbolic figure of the time. He painted her not in the easy black-and-white contrast of romantic fiction, but in realistic and psychological colors which underlined her complexity.

The Portrait of a Lady (1881), one of his best long novels, marked the culmination of his early international phase. It was a tragedy of manners in a series of portraits, the heroine unifying the whole. The conception was derived from Turgenev, "the beautiful genius," who with George Eliot, contended for the mastery of James's artistic conscience in this novel. It was his first full-length experiment with the method which became his special contribution to the novel form, the use of a central consciousness as an angle of narration to provide dramatic suspense and psychological complexity. Character was his supreme interest, revealed not through action or plot, but through depth and perspective as in a portrait in oils. Isabel Archer filled the center of the canvas, surrounded by satellites arranged in varying attitudes of love, admiration, friendly counsel, or hostility. Deterministic forces entered the situation to compromise her destiny. But the interplay of character and circumstance, equally distributed, produced the dramatic qualities of this externally unexciting story.

The 1880's brought "The Triumph of Realism" in the novel. Howells' *A Modern Instance* (1882) and *The Rise of Silas Lapham* (1885) were his masterpieces. Mark Twain wrote *Huckleberry Finn* (1885) and

A Connecticut Yankee in King Arthur's Court (1889), the former his most sustained work of fiction. There the romancer and poet, the social critic, the humorist, cynic, realist, satirist, and the rich narrator of the American past were all suffused in the imaginative strength of the style and point of view, restricted to the mind and accent of a young narrator-hero. In the eighties James lived in England, produced two purely American novels, *Washington Square* (1880) and *The Bostonians* (1885), and turned out many skillful short stories and a collection of fine critical essays, *Partial Portraits* (1888).

These three major writers had reached a peak in their productive lives. Each in a different way found the moment propitious for fiction. Some of the earlier hesitations and uncertainties of the seventies coalesced to produce a coherence of thought and an atmosphere of literary ripeness. The earlier idealism had mellowed and blended into a more pragmatic tone. Intellectual America seemed more settled after nervous apprehension over Darwinism and evolution had quieted down. A new synthesis of conflicting ideas came into sight. The self-conscious nationalism of the earlier decade gave way to a new confidence. The quest for reality was deepened, but not yet darkened by the industrial conflicts and social upheavals of the nineties. Realism became less talked about and more successfully practiced in the mid-eighties.

In adapting the methods of the English novel of manners to the American scene and by applying his keen sense of emerging national types, Howells made his finest contribution to realistic fiction. Character was still his primary interest, but a growing concern for social problems gave his work in the middle 1880's range and a new depth. In *A Modern Instance* a steady accumulation of circumstantial detail and environmental forces were marshaled to break up the marriage of Bartley Hubbard and his wife, Marcia Gaylord. The story's naturalistic, even deterministic direction, however, was somewhat weakened by a certain quality of ethical righteousness at odds with the main plot. Howells was more successful in integrating idealism with reality and circumstances in *The Rise of Silas Lapham* by placing within the main character a conflict of mind and a combination of moral weakness and social conscience. Silas Lapham was the first self-made businessman to be handled with psychological complexity against a detailed background. It was a muted but convincing portrait, drawn with a mixture of satire and sympathy after the manner of Jane Austen and with touches which recalled Balzac. From Europe, James described Howells as "the great American naturalist," but warned against a tendency toward certain "romantic phantoms and factitious glosses" in his novels. Howells called James the shaper of a new fiction, derived from Hawthorne and the milder realism of George Eliot and Daudet, rather than that of Zola.

James's own fiction failed to show significant technical advances beyond *The Portrait of a Lady*. His work in the eighties moved toward the social fiction of Balzac and Zola, but his true forte was not to be the novel of sociology or determinism. *Washington Square* and *The Bostonians* applied realistic methods to the American scene, but were not his best work. James failed to find in native conditions a coherence or tradition which did justice to his gift for psychological writing. Both novels were concerned with the realism of spectacle and documentary detail, containing multiple characters and descriptions of places and social conditions. Neither was favorably reviewed, and discouragement over their reception turned James away from the American scene. He omitted them from a later collected edition. Indignation in Boston over the brilliant satire on feminine suffragists and bluestockings in *The Bostonians* affected his own evaluation of the novel, and he turned to an English setting in his next long work, *The Princess Casamassima* (1886). This account of London underground socialists and anarchists and his next work about the London world of the theater and of politics, *The Tragic Muse* (1889), completed the cycle of his long novels of social significance. Their enduring qualities lay in skillful psychological portraiture rather than representation of sociological phenomena and naturalistic documentation. Hyacinth Robinson and Miriam Rooth were rounded literary portraits whose destinies were partially controlled by the different worlds that shaped them.

Mark Twain's relation to the Gilded Age has baffled criticism ever since 1920, when Van Wyck Brooks developed his "genius-thwarted-by-commercialism-and-Puritanism" thesis in *The Ordeal of Mark Twain* (1920).[10] Brooks's denigration of the culture which blunted Mark Twain's idealism and turned his satire into crude humor and vulgarity was echoed by later critics and blended with Marxist criticism of the 1930's. Mark Twain was typical of the age whose name he coined. He mirrored its puzzling contradictions and cross-currents, and shared Colonel Sellers' dream of sudden wealth. Money was the theme of many of his stories, but unlike Horatio Alger's his endings were often bitter. He was defensive about art, Europe, age, tradition, culture, and bookishness; yet he was one of the era's most cosmopolitan travelers. He possessed broad humanitarian sympathies and reformist tendencies, but condemned the human race as selfish, cynical, brutal, and deterministic. He was full of ribaldry and profanity,[11] yet he was one of the most sensitive and "exquisite" of men. He detested "novels, poetry, and theology," but defended the authenticity of local color and regional fiction which could be written only by a man who had years of "unconscious absorption" and prepared himself to report the soul of a nation, its life, speech, and thought.

He was not at home in philosophy or in theoretical criticism; his standards were reality, fact, verisimilitude. He did not write from any conscious theory of the novel. Mark Twain was a conscious literary artist, not a spontaneous genius, but he did not believe in schools or doctrinaire definitions of realism. His was a special blend of realism, born of experience and frontier skepticism, schooled by such hard disciplines as the printing office of a newspaper or the pilot house of a Mississippi steamboat. Travel made him conscious of personal limitations and threw him back upon the main affirmation of his life, faith in individual dignity and worth. In two books of the early 1880's, *Life on the Mississippi* and *Huckleberry Finn,* Twain achieved an equilibrium of the varying elements of his nature and talents.[12] It was not the middle zone between romance and naturalism sought by Howells, nor the special "ideal reality" of James, but a balance between the youthful, frontier humorist and the aging misanthropist of the 1890's. In these books he successfully expressed his strain of idealism and love of accurate dialects and local places and people. He could not hold the balance long. *A Connecticut Yankee,* for all its brilliance and bitter satire, exhibited less of the control and sustained writing skill that marked the two earlier masterpieces.[13]

Mark Twain belongs to world literature but he was a village iconoclast with the gift of laughter and a strain of eternal youth and innocence which have especially endeared him to Americans. In his one undoubted literary masterpiece, *Huckleberry Finn,* he raised the rural American past to the level of myth and gave a symbolic quality to the Mississippi River and the Midwest frontier. Miraculously, and seemingly without a conscious theory of fiction, he explored the dramatic potential of a narrating center by endowing the vernacular hero with a conflict between his natural idealism and the hereditary training of the established slave culture of prewar America. Huck thus symbolized the nation's tragic divisions. Mark Twain was also the source of a genuine American idiom in which native humor, dialect, and speech rhythms created a literary style free of British mannerism. He remained part of the Gilded Age, but transformed its commonplace experience and even adolescent emotion into enduring literature. Youth and innocence helped shape his mind, but a powerful presentiment of reality and truth marked his genius.

In the late 1880's, literature began to reflect social and cultural changes. Civil unrest and labor strife increased, signaling intensified class conflict. The great popularity of Edward Bellamy's *Looking Backward* (1887) testified to growing concern over an unbalanced economy. Collectivist protest, which novelists had disregarded as unfit for genteel consumption, entered into the mainstream of realism around 1890 in the works of Howells, Hamlin Garland, and Stephen Crane. Deeply affected by the "civic murder" of the Chicago anarchists convicted after the Haymarket affair in Chicago in 1886 and strengthened by his reading of Tolstoy, Howells changed his private stance from passive humanitarianism to active protest. In *A Hazard of New Fortunes* (1890), *A Traveler from Altruria* (1894), and other novels he displayed a highly developed social conscience in behalf of the working class. His personal philosophy veered sharply in the direction of government control of key industries such as utilities. Garland's *Main Travelled Roads* (1891) voiced the silent suffering of agrarian life, made poignant by the first-hand experience of his family in Wisconsin and the Dakotas. And Stephen Crane, in *Maggie, A Girl of the Streets* (1893), reported with the dispassionate pen of a journalist and the irony of an artist how poverty and drunkenness drove the daughter of a Bowery family in lower New York to prostitution and suicide.

The naturalistic mode in fiction was in its early phase during the nineties, but its concern with social problems of the lower orders of society and its economic determinism dominated fiction well into the next century. Frank Norris' *McTeague* (1899) was the first full-blown naturalistic novel in America, using some of Zola's methods in a San Francisco setting. *McTeague* and *The Octopus* (1901) embodied Norris' special combination of Populist folklore, violence, and melodrama. His powerful prose style, a mingling of scientific documentation and the excessive use of reiterated symbols of natural forces, gave his writing its special quality and identified it with the 1890's. The decade was deeply divided between the new realism of economic protest and a resurgence of romantic interest in brute strength and Darwinian muscle. Norris had lofty notions of the novel as a pulpit from which to preach Truth to The People, and to demonstrate "whole congeries of forces, social tendencies, and race impulses." He felt it should contain violence, vast scenic effects, murder, bloodshed and "variations from the type of normal life" which he associated with the realism of Howells and his followers.[14]

War, poverty, shipwreck, and violence also provided the material for much of Stephen Crane's writing. As a journalist and reporter for a newspaper syndicate, Crane reported two wars, traveled much of the world, and wrote of first-hand experience in a distinctive style beyond reportage. Crane believed in immediacy of experience for the writer, yet paradoxically his masterpiece, *The Red Badge of Courage* (1895), was about a war he never saw. This account of a raw recruit facing battle conditions in the Civil War was a brilliant imaginative reconstruction of war scenes and a profound study in the psychology of cowardice, fear, and bravery. But Crane's technical accomplishments, impressionistic style, and symbolic devices were equally innovative. Myth and metaphor contributed largely to the meaning of *The Red Badge*. The story has suggested to some critics a search for self-identity by a young knight questing through perilous adventures for a holy grail of ancient myth. Much of this mythic ritual was contained in imagery with religious undertones and symbolic colors, and in abstract landscapes and allegorical figures. Like Mark Twain in *Huckleberry Finn,* Crane discovered much of the meaning and ironic complexity of his novel in careful handling of the limited point of view of his young and innocent hero.[15]

In this same decade Henry James turned to writing plays for the London theatre, an experience which taught him new techniques for fiction. In *What Maisie Knew, The Turn of the Screw,* and *The Sacred Fount,* all written in the late 1890's, he used a limited angle of narration to gain dramatic irony and suspense. Only after 1900 did he theorize about a "center of consciousness" in the prefaces to his novels. Both Mark Twain and Stephen Crane followed the course he charted in using a controlled center of narration, to be the single most important discovery of the twentieth-century novel.

The search for reality, begun in the 1870's with the mild and tentative realism of local-color writers and the early travel fiction of Howells and Mark Twain, gradually evolved into the complex novel of psychological and sociological significance during the eighties and nineties. This evolution brought new insights and methods that made *Huckleberry Finn, The Red Badge of Courage,* and the late major novels of Henry James masterpieces of American fiction, and placed them among the great novels in the English language.

PAUL F. BOLLER, JR.

❦ 12 ❦

The New Science and American Thought

IN AN INFORMAL POLL taken by some British scientists in the 1930's, Sir Isaac Newton was rated the greatest scientist to appear since the Renaissance. Charles Darwin's name was second on the list, and Michael Faraday and Albert Einstein tied for third place. The fourth highest was an American: Josiah Willard Gibbs, professor of mathematical physics at Yale from 1871 until his death in 1903. Henry Adams regarded Gibbs as "the greatest American, judged by his rank in science," but Adams was exceptional.[1] Few Americans during the Gilded Age, outside the scientific community, could have identified his name. Science was the rage with middle-class Americans in the late nineteenth century, but science meant chiefly evolution. Educated and informed Americans followed the controversy over *Origin of Species* with zest, and they were proud of the contribution of American scientists, particularly paleontologists, to the advance of evolutionary science. Outside of evolution, though, their scientific knowledge was not extensive. They knew something of American work in the "new" astronomy, and perhaps a little about American chemistry. But the "new" physics was *terra incognita* for the layman trying to keep abreast of the latest developments in science; it was too technical a discipline for popular understanding. There were no articles by Gibbs or about his work in the *Atlantic, Harper's,* the *Nation,* and in the *Popular Science Monthly.*

Even in academic circles, people often confused him with Wolcott Gibbs, the Harvard chemist.[2] Until the Royal Society of London awarded Gibbs its highest honor, the Copley medal, in 1901, his reputation was far greater in Europe than in the United States. Clerk Maxwell very early

239

recognized his genius and acted as a kind of publicity agent for him among British scientists. Wilhelm Ostwald introduced his work into Germany, and Henry Louis LeChatelier made it known in France. Dutch chemists were the first to make practical use of his suggestive formulas in the new science of physical chemistry. When Irving Fisher went to Berlin for study in 1893, he had only to mention Gibbs to German mathematicians to elicit the exclamation: "Geebs, Geebs, jawohl, ausgezeichnet!" Unlike Fisher, however, most graduate students had to go abroad to hear of him for the first time.

Fisher, who later applied Gibbs' concepts to the field of economics, was one of a small group of students who studied with him at Yale. Most students "did not know of his existence, much less of his greatness." [3] To the handful of graduate students able to profit by his instruction Gibbs gave courses of lectures on vector analysis, multiple algebra, thermodynamics, theory of light, theory of electricity, and statistical mechanics. And in a small room in the Sloane Physics Laboratory he worked late at night on the series of remarkable scientific papers in which he applied the laws of thermodynamics to chemistry.

Somewhat shy and modest, though by no means lacking in confidence in the value of the work he was doing, Gibbs cared little for public recognition. His was apparently an aristocratic view of intellectual endeavor: he directed his findings to the small elite of fellow workers in science who could converse in the abstract language of mathematics. His work was "severely mathematical, and incapable of being translated into common language," and few American chemists during his lifetime were sufficiently trained in higher mathematics to comprehend him.[4] Editors of the *Transactions* of the Connecticut Academy of Arts and Sciences, in which his major monographs appeared, confessed that they could not understand what he was saying. When Clerk Maxwell died in 1879, one of the members of the Academy said ruefully: "Only one man ever lived who could understand Gibbs' papers. That was Maxwell, and now he is dead." [5]

Maxwell first became interested in Gibbs in 1878 when the latter published two papers discussing geometrical methods of representing by diagrams the thermodynamical properties of homogeneous substances. The distinguished British physicist did the young professor the immense compliment of constructing a plaster model for water, illustrating Gibbs' diagrams, and sending a cast of it to Yale. Gibbs was doubtless pleased, though he invariably shrugged it off evasively when his students queried him about it. More impressive than his first two papers, however, was his monumental memoir, "On the Equilibrium of Heterogeneous Substances," which appeared in two parts in 1876 and 1878. In this work, which raised him to first rank as a scientist, Gibbs, striking off on entirely new paths, brought physics and chemistry together and laid the foundations for the science of physical chemistry. In this monograph Gibbs introduced his famous "Phase Rule" (which so enchanted Henry Adams), a formula capable of "giving shape to research." By means of the Phase Rule (water, for example, can exist in three phases—vapor, liquid, and ice), it was possible to discover: (1) under what conditions of temperature and pressure different substances (and the same substances in different phases) can exist together in equilibrium and (2) what effect changes of these conditions will have on the composition of various mixtures. By establishing principles by which the heterogeneous substances occurring in nature could be understood and handled most efficiently, Gibbs's formulas were to be of great importance for industry and science.

For years, however, Gibbs's epoch-making monograph was almost completely neglected. Apparently content to leave it to others to make practical use of his formulations in their own good time, Gibbs turned to developing a system of vector analysis for mathematical physicists. Toward the close of his life, he also did pioneering work in statistical mechanics. Ostwald, who translated "Equilibrium" into German in 1892, found "treasures in the greatest variety and of the greatest importance to the theoretical as well as to the experimental investigator" in its pages. LeChatelier, who translated it into French in 1899, was even more laudatory:

> Gibbs was able by a truly extraordinary effort of the scientific imagination and logical power to posit all the principles of the new science and to foresee all its ulterior applications. . . . To Gibbs belongs the honor of having fused the two sciences into one, chemical mechanics, of having constituted a completely defined body of principles, to which additions may be made in the future, but from which the progress of the science can take nothing away.[6]

In time, Gibbs's work had wide application in metallurgy, mineralogy, petrology, and theoretical chemistry. And in the twentieth century his formulas were utilized in the manufacture of hundreds of plastics, drugs, dyes, and organic solvents.

Gibbs was not a prolific writer. "A person who writes so much," he once remarked, "must spread his message rather thin." But almost everything he published ultimately had some relevance to the world of industry which was coming of age during his lifetime.[7] Gibbs's personal life was exceedingly undramatic. A confirmed bachelor, he lived with his sister in New Haven, attended church faithfully, and voted Republican in every election but 1884, when he shifted to Cleveland. One of the few anecdotes about him, probably apocryphal, is that he always insisted on mixing the salad at dinner on the ground that he was a better authority than anyone else on the equilibrium of heterogeneous substances.

Mathematics was his greatest passion. For Gibbs mathematics was no mere intellectual game; it was indispensable for interpreting and thus mastering nature. "The human mind," he told members of the American Association of the Advancement of Science in 1886, "has never invented a labor-saving machine equal to algebra. It is but natural and proper that an age like our own, characterized by the multiplication of labor-saving machinery, should be distinguished by an unexampled development of this most refined and most beautiful of machines." [8] "Mathematics *is* a language," he insisted at a Yale faculty meeting. By speaking this language, Gibbs contributed enormously to modern industrialism.[9]

Clerk Maxwell, who discovered Gibbs, was also among the first to see promise in the gifted young Henry A. Rowland who was teaching physics at Rensselaer Polytechnic Institute in Troy, New York. As early as 1868, while the Erie War was raging, Rowland, not quite twenty, had decided against money-making. "I intend to devote myself hereafter to *science*," he resolved. "If she gives me wealth, I will receive it as coming from a friend, but if not, I will not murmur." [10] In 1873 he submitted a paper on the magnetic properties of iron, steel, and nickel to the *American Journal of Science*. The editors rejected it. Maxwell, however, arranged for its immediate publication in England. Impressed by Maxwell's judgment, Daniel Coit Gilman selected Rowland as first professor of physics at Johns Hopkins University. Before going to Baltimore, Rowland worked several months in Berlin for the great German physicist Hermann von Helmholtz. In Helmholtz' laboratory he investigated the magnetic effect of moving electrostatic charges, and his findings were of some importance in the development of the modern theory of electrons.

At Johns Hopkins Rowland studied the effect of the earth's rotation on terrestrial magnetism, and made improved measurements for certain electrical units which were internationally adopted. After many experiments, he obtained a numerical value for the mechanical equivalent of heat (the "Golden Number" sought by many investigators in the nineteenth century) that was universally accepted. But perhaps his greatest achievement was in spectrum analysis. The exquisitely delicate concave grating which he devised to analyze the solar spectrum produced such magnificent results that scientists in France and England were "actually dumbfounded." [11] With this apparatus, adopted in physics laboratories everywhere, Rowland produced his famous "Photographic Map of the Normal Solar Spectrum" and launched a systematic study of the spectra of the elements. In later years he studied alternating currents and their application to motors and measuring instruments, and invented a printing telegraph which won a prize at the Paris Exposition of 1900.

Rowland "had triumphant joy in intellectual achievement such as we would look for in other men only from the gratification of an elemental passion." [12] His political ideals were high; he disapproved of men like James G. Blaine, whom he needled at a dinner party. Though accepting the basic principles of Christianity, he looked primarily to the "scientific mind" for advances in civilization. "This is the mind," he declared, "which is destined to govern the world in the future and to solve the problems pertaining to politics and humanity as well as to inanimate nature." [13]

For Rowland's somewhat younger contemporary, Albert A. Michelson, science was fundamentally an art. "If a poet could at the same time be a physicist," he told the Lowell Institute, "he might convey to others the pleasure, the satisfaction, almost the reverence, which the subject of light inspires. The aesthetic side of the subject is, I confess, by no means the least attractive to me." [14] Determination of a figure for the speed of light was a lifelong interest of the German-born physicist.[15] While teaching physics at the United States Naval Academy, young Michelson made his first measurements with equipment he built at a cost of about ten dollars. He also published his first paper, "On a Method of Measuring the Velocity of Light" in the *Journal of Science* in May, 1878, and presented to the A.A.A.S. in St. Louis a new figure—186,508 miles per second—which he estimated was correct to within one part in 10,000. With Michelson, the first American to receive a Nobel Prize (1907), came real precision in measuring light speed, and until his death in 1931 he continued to refine his measuring techniques and obtained increasingly accurate figures.

The Michelson interferometer, an instrument which measured small lengths, determined the wavelengths of light, and analyzed a narrow spectrum region, was tremendously important in the development of modern physics. Michelson invented the interferometer in 1881 to ascertain the effect of the earth's motion, as it traveled through the "ether" (a motionless substance, filling all space, postulated by physicists to account for the travel of light through space), upon the velocity of light. The results were negative. "The hypothesis of a stationary ether is . . . incorrect," he concluded.[16] So momentous were the implications of his findings for classical physics that he determined to improve his investigative techniques.

In 1887, with the help of Edward A. Morley of Western Reserve

College, and utilizing an interferometer with a higher order of accuracy, he renewed his efforts. The Michelson-Morley experiment demonstrated that the concept of a "luminiferous ether" must be abandoned. With the abandonment of a motionless ether, in terms of which the motion of the earth and other heavenly bodies might be measured, the concept of "absolute motion" itself had to be discarded.[17] Michelson's experiment, according to Albert Einstein, "showed that a profound change of the basic concepts of physics was inevitable." Einstein partly based his own famous relativity theory, the theory that measurements of space and time are "relative" to some arbitrarily chosen frame of reference, on the Michelson-Morley experiment.[18]

If American scientists played a creditable part in the developing "new" physics, they also contributed to the "new" astronomy. The old astronomy had been concerned largely with position and motion. The new utilized physics to investigate the physical structure of celestial bodies. In the United States, the transition from positional astronomy to astrophysics came when Edward C. Pickering, physics professor at M.I.T., became director of the Harvard Observatory in 1877. Comparatively little was known about the nature of stars, and Pickering concentrated on accumulating data in the new field. A "collector of astronomical facts," he constructed a meridian photometer to measure the magnitude (brightness) of stars as they crossed the meridian, and devised a system of visual stellar magnitudes that was adopted internationally.[19] He was also a pioneer in stellar photography, and created a library of celestial photographs containing thousands of glass plates which recorded the history of stars. He collected the spectra of thousands of stars that yielded valuable information about their composition, temperature, and physical conditions, and worked out a system of classifying stellar spectra that became standard.

At Dartmouth and later at Princeton, Charles A. Young, known to his students as "Twinkle," conducted pioneer studies in solar physics. Edward E. Barnard, astronomer at the Lick Observatory of the University of California and then at the University of Chicago's Yerkes Observatory, applied celestial photography to the Milky Way with excellent results. James Lick, a San Francisco philanthropist who amassed a fortune in real estate speculation, left a bequest in 1875 for "the greatest and most powerful telescope" yet made. The observatory bearing his name, with a 36-inch telescope, was completed in 1888.[20] A few years later Charles T. Yerkes, Chicago traction-system magnate, gave money to found the Yerkes Observatory, with a 40-inch telescope.

In 1875, when the Lick trustees sought advice on the telescope for the California observatory, they naturally turned to Simon Newcomb, chief astronomer with the United States Naval Observatory in Washington, D.C. Two years previously, Newcomb had supervised the construction of the Naval Observatory's 26-inch object-glass. The "success of the Washington telescope excited such interest the world over as to give a new impetus to the construction of such instruments." [21] Newcomb's major field was celestial mechanics. While not indifferent to the newer astrophysical investigations, he worked on mathematical astronomy to prepare the most exact tables possible for the motions of heavenly bodies. The moon's motion was his lifelong concern. To correct errors in the tables of lunar positions, he delved into the old records of European observatories, pushing his researches back to the middle of the seventeenth century.

In 1877, Newcomb became superintendent of the *Nautical Almanac* office, which prepared the *American Ephemeris,* an astronomical almanac containing data on the past and future positions of stars and planets for astronomers and navigators. Distressed by the confusion pervading the field of exact astronomy, he at once launched an ambitious program involving a discussion of all observations of value on the positions of the sun, moon, planets, and bright fixed stars made at the leading world observatories since 1750. The task was tremendous. But for more than twenty years he tried to bring precision into the calculations of the positions and motions of heavenly bodies and to "start the exact astronomy of the twentieth century on one basis for the whole world." [22]

Newcomb's labors won universal respect among scientists. Einstein called him "the last of the great masters who . . . calculated with painstaking care the motions of the solar system" and regarded his work as "of monumental importance to astronomy." [23] Newcomb was offered a position at Harvard and, though urged to escape Washington politics, he remained in government service. "I was still pervaded by the optimism of youth in everything that concerned the future of our government," he explained, "and did not believe that, with the growth of intelligence in our country, an absence of touch between the scientific and literary classes on the one side, and 'politics' on the other, could continue." [24]

Samuel P. Langley, who became secretary of the Smithsonian Institution in 1887, also found work in Washington stimulating. Langley attracted public notice with pioneering work in aviation, but his achievements in astronomy were also notable. Unlike Newcomb, he was interested mainly in the physical characteristics of heavenly bodies, and his specialty was solar radiation. While director of the Allegheny Observatory in Pennsylvania (1867–87), he invented the bolometer, a type of electrical thermometer which attained worldwide use, for measuring the distribution of heat in the spectrum of the sun. With this instrument, capable of measuring differences in temperature as small as one millionth of a degree, Langley investigated the distribution of radiation over the sun's surface and in sunspots, the solar energy spectrum, its extension toward the infra-red, the lunar energy spectrum, and the temperature of the moon. He also became absorbed in the problem of measuring the amount of heat the earth received from the sun, and the effects of fluctuating solar radiation on the earth's atmosphere. His research had a direct bearing on the development of an accurate system of weather forecasting. "If the observation of the amount of heat the sun sends the earth is among the most difficult in astronomical physics," he said, "it may also be termed the fundamental problem of meteorology or the science of weather." [25]

Not long before Langley left Allegheny Observatory for the Smithsonian, a paper on the flight of birds, read at the annual meeting of the A.A.A.S. in Buffalo, aroused his interest in the mechanics of flight. He at once embarked on experiments in what he called "aerodynamics." In 1891, he announced that it was possible "to construct machines that would give such velocities to inclined surfaces that bodies definitely heavier than air could be sustained upon it and move through it with great velocity, and capable of carrying other than their own weight." [26] While in Washington he constructed several model flying machines, flew one successfully for 3,000 feet on May 6, 1896, and confidently predicted that "the great universal highway overhead is now soon to be opened." [27] Assisted by the War Department, he later constructed man-carrying airplanes. His experiments were unsuccessful, and the Wright brothers were the first to make successful piloted flights. But Wilbur Wright freely acknowledged the importance of Langley's pioneer work.[28]

Because he attempted to put his theories about the mechanics of flight into actual practice, Langley was better known to the American public than were his fellow physicists and astronomers. Even more celebrated, both then and later, were inventors like Alexander Graham Bell and Thomas A. Edison. The relevance of the telephone, the electric light bulb, and other practical inventions to everyday living was immediately apparent. But the significance of the fundamental researches of American physicists and astronomers, couched in the abstractions of mathematics, was difficult for laymen to grasp. Scientists like Gibbs and Rowland and Pickering were indifferent to public fame, and since the tradition of popular pride in the achievements of theoretical scientists had not developed in the United States, they were largely unknown outside of scientific circles. Hence the myth that American talents lay almost exclusively in applied, rather than in pure science. But American genius shone brightly in physics and astronomy, though it lagged considerably behind Europe in mathematics and chemistry. And recognition of this frequently came first in Europe.

New ideas appearing in physics and astronomy bypassed the American reading public, but that was not true of the ideas appearing in Charles Darwin's famous books, *Origin of Species* (1859) and *The Descent of Man* (1871). The impact of Darwinism on American thought, popular as well as scientific, was relatively prompt and profound. The importance of Darwin's transmutation theory for botany, zoology, geology, and biology was obvious. Unless American toilers in these fields were to remain simply fact-finders and classifiers, they had to test the natural-selection hypothesis in their own work. The shattering effect of Darwinian evolution upon traditional religious thought about the special creation of the world and the uniqueness of man was also apparent, and American theologians were forced to rethink their positions in the light of the new evolutionary concepts. American philosophers also realized that Darwinism challenged concepts that had dominated Western thought since Greek times. Any American, in short, who thought seriously about the nature and destiny of man had to be familiar with Darwin's work. Where Gibbs's and Michelson's work was too technical for popular comprehension, educated laymen could read and understand *Origin of Species* with no great difficulty. The great debate over Darwinism, which commenced among American scientists shortly after the publication of *Origin,* soon spread to nonscientific circles throughout the land.

Few American scientists of consequence rejected Darwinism outright. As Darwin had expected, the older scientists were least receptive to his conclusions. Edward Hitchcock, Massachusetts geologist and, for a time, president of Amherst College, had published a book in 1852 reconciling geology with the Scriptures, and saw no reason to modify his outlook. He remained a strict creationist and publicly opposed evolution. Timothy A. Conrad, Pennsylvania conchologist and paleontologist, also bitterly opposed evolution and predicted that Darwin's "wild speculations" would soon be forgotten.[29] Matthew F. Maury, the naval officer who helped create and develop the science of oceanography, firmly rejected Darwinism as being incompatible with the Bible: "The Bible, they say, was not written for scientific purposes, and is therefore of no authority in matters of science. I beg pardon: the Bible *is* authority for everything it touches. The agents concerned in the physical economy of our planets are ministers of Him who made it and the Bible." [30]

By far the most famous and influential anti-Darwinist was the Swiss-born Louis Agassiz, professor of natural history at Harvard, whose work in ichthyology, paleontology, and glacial geology had earned him high esteem among scientists everywhere, including Darwin. Agassiz was no biblical literalist like Maury; he had, in fact, little interest in organized religion. His opposition to Darwin rested largely on a philosophy of nature he had formulated as a young man in Europe. For Agassiz, every specific form of plant and animal represented "a thought of God" at the moment of creation and the structural affinities among different species were simply "associations of ideas in the Divine Mind," not evidences of common descent. "The study of nature," he said, "is an intercourse with the highest mind." [31] His exhibits in the Harvard Museum of Comparative Zoology were intended to reflect the permanence of species. Darwin's *Origin* he regarded as "mischievous in its tendency." [32] In lectures, popular articles, and in books, he waged a militant campaign against Darwinism and on behalf of his own version of special creationism. In the last article he wrote on the subject, shortly before his death in December, 1873, he did concede that Darwin "brought to the subject a vast amount of well-arranged information," but he insisted that "there is no evidence of a direct descent of later from earlier species in the geological succession of animals." [33] His Harvard colleague Jeffries Wyman, the anatomist and ethnologist, who regarded the "immediate creation of species" as "preposterous," regretted that Agassiz used his immense learning and prestige to combat Darwin. "He was just the man who ought to have taken up the evolution theory and worked it into good shape, which his knowledge of embryology and palaeontology would have enabled him to do. He has lost a golden opportunity, but there is no use in talking of that" [34]

Wyman was too cautious and reserved to challenge Agassiz publicly, and Asa Gray, director of the Harvard herbarium and pioneer in the field of plant geography, emerged as Darwin's leading American champion. Gray and Darwin began corresponding in 1855, and Darwin found the floristic data Gray sent him helpful in writing *Origin of Species*. Darwin had already confided his theory of evolution, which he first outlined in 1842, to two British friends, botanist Joseph D. Hooker and geologist Charles Lyell, and in 1857 he decided to try out his ideas on Gray. Change, not constancy, he insisted, was the law of nature. A perpetual struggle for existence took place among living organisms, according to Darwin. Those born with variations helping them in the struggle for existence lived to reproduce their kind and transmit favorable variations to their offspring. "Natural selection" described the process by which organisms happening to possess useful variations survived and those lacking them perished in the struggle for life. Later on Darwin borrowed

Herbert Spencer's phrase, "survival of the fittest," to mean the same thing. Gray had reservations about natural selection. As a purely mechanical explanation of the evolutionary process, its implications for religion troubled him. But he was determined that Darwin should have a fair hearing in the United States. His long review of *Origin* for the *Journal of Science* in March, 1860, which Darwin called "by far the best which I have read," was sympathetic and perceptive.[35]

Gray's efforts on Darwin's behalf in the 1860's and 1870's resembled those of Thomas Huxley in England. He debated Agassiz before the Cambridge Scientific Club and at meetings of the American Academy of Arts and Sciences in Boston. He also prepared a series of articles for the *Atlantic* explaining Darwin's ideas to the general public, lectured on Darwinism to Yale Divinity School students, and wrote friendly notices of Darwin's later books for the *Journal of Science*. Gradually, however, he and Darwin parted company over the theory of design in nature. Like the majority of American scientists, Gray was a convinced theist, and the reconciliation of Darwinism with religion was a matter of some urgency. Darwin, who confessed to Gray that he was "in an utterly hopeless muddle" over the problem, eventually became an agnostic.[36] Gray came to believe that the beneficial variations appearing in living organisms were providentially designed. He also regarded the evolutionary process as "the order or mode in which [the] Creator, in his own perfect wisdom, sees fit to act," thus, in effect, transforming natural selection into what might be called "supernatural selection." [37]

The weakness of Gray's reasoning was obvious. The introduction of providential design into evolutionary development, as Darwin pointed out, made natural selection "entirely superfluous." [38] But by teleologizing Darwinism, Gray was able to square his own scientific and religious beliefs, and he became a lucid and courageous expositor of the new evolutionary outlook. As the Darwinian botanist Joseph Hooker told Huxley after Gray's death in 1888, Gray understood Darwinism "clearly, but sought to harmonise it with his prepossession, without disturbing its physical principles in any way. . . . He certainly showed far more knowledge and appreciation of the contents of the *Origin* than any of the reviewers and than any of the commentators, yourself excepted." [39]

More common among American scientists than Agassiz' uncompromising animosity and Gray's consistent friendliness to Darwinism was a gradual accommodation to some limited form of evolutionism. Arnold Guyot, the Princeton geographer, regarded nature as a manifestation of God and at first clung tenaciously to his belief in the constancy of species. But in time, he accepted with reservations the idea of evolution through natural causes, though he excepted man from the process. James Dwight Dana, Yale geologist who led the way in transforming American geology from a collection of isolated facts into a historical science, was similarly slow to assent to the new view of species. "Geology," he declared in 1871, "has brought to light no facts sustaining a theory that derives species from others." In 1874, however, he conceded that the "evolution of the system of life went forward through the derivation of species from species," but he insisted there had been "abrupt transitions between species" and that for man "there was required . . . the special act of a Being above nature." [40] His final position appeared in a letter to a clergyman toward the end of his life: "While admitting the derivation of man from an inferior species, I believe that there was a Divine creative act at the origin of man; that the event was as truly a creation as if it had been from earth or inorganic matter to man." [41]

Joseph LeConte, Georgia-born geologist teaching at the University of California, confessed that as late as 1872 he was still a "reluctant evolutionist." A few years later, however, he described himself as "an evolutionist, thorough and enthusiastic." [42] But his evolutionism, like that of most American scientists, was not pure Darwinism. LeConte regarded the "law of derivation of forms from previous forms" as "certain as the law of gravitation." But he emphasized "paroxysmal" rather than uniform changes in nature, agreed with Lamarck in stressing the inheritance of acquired characters as an explanation for evolutionary change, and relegated natural selection to a relatively minor role in the development of organic life.[43] He also worked out an ambitious religious philosophy, based on both the immanence and transcendence of God in universal evolution, that even the absolute idealist Josiah Royce disliked. The Michigan geologist Alexander Winchell made a similar religious adjustment to evolution. But George F. Wright, the Oberlin geologist-clergyman who was an expert on glaciation and who wrote extensively on religion and evolution, adopted Asa Gray's design argument: "there must be a divinity shaping the ends of organic life, let natural selection rough hew them as it will." [44]

William Keith Brooks, professor of morphology at Johns Hopkins and a specialist in marine zoology, insisted that "the term 'supernatural' is due to a misconception of nature; nature is everything that is." [45] Though pointing out that science throws no light on final cause or purpose, Brooks was an early convert to Darwin and accepted a wide applicability of the principle of natural selection. Chauncey Wright, Cambridge mathematician and philosopher, was an even more thoroughgoing evolutionary naturalist, and vigorously objected to all cosmic generalizations founded on evolution. Fully accepting the naturalistic assumptions of Darwinism, he proposed in 1873 a scientific explanation of the origin of human self-consciousness based on psychological antecedents in animal life. But Wright, who died in 1875 at the age of forty-five, was a rarity. The Gray (design) and LeConte (immanence) versions of evolution dominated the thinking of most American scientists during the 1870's and 1880's. These adaptations of Darwinism also most influenced American theological and popular religious thinking about evolution in the late nineteenth century.

Many American scientists stayed aloof from the conflict between naturalism and supernaturalism. Quietly pursuing researches in botany, zoology, geology, and paleontology, they accumulated indispensable evidence for the validity of Darwin's theory. This was particularly true of American paleontologists. Joseph Leidy, founder of vertebrate paleontology in the United States, was "a John the Baptist for Charles Darwin." [46] Leidy was one of the first to exploit the rich western fossil beds. Even before Darwin announced his theory publicly, he had gathered a mass of information about the ancestral lineage of the horse, camel, rhinoceros, and other extinct vertebrates that pointed unmistakably to evolutionary development. Leidy was an early convert to Darwinism, and upon the publication of *Origin* saw to it that Darwin was elected a member of the Academy of Natural Sciences of Philadelphia. Immensely pleased by this early recognition of his work in the United States, Darwin told Charles Lyell: "It shows that some Naturalists do not think me such a scientific profligate as many think me here." [47]

Even more important for Darwinism was the work of Othniel C. Marsh, who was appointed to the first chair of paleontology in the United States at Yale in 1866. In 1870, he launched a series of expeditions to hunt for ancient fossils in the West that yielded invaluable evidence for the evolutionary theory. His discovery of birds possessing teeth and other reptilian characteristics established a genetic link between reptiles and birds which, according to Thomas Huxley, removed Darwin's theory "from the region of hypothesis to that of demonstrable fact." [48] Of Marsh's monograph on the extinct toothed birds of North America, appearing in 1880, Darwin wrote: "Your work on these old birds, and on the many fossil animals of North America, has afforded the best support to the theory of Evolution, which has appeared within the last twenty years." [49] Equally impressive was Marsh's collection of fossil horses that traced the evolutionary changes which had occurred during the emergence of the modern horse. Huxley, who visited the United States in 1876, spent several days in New Haven examining the collection, which he called "the most wonderful thing I ever saw." [50] As Marsh brought out box after box of fossil-horse material, he cried: "I believe you are a magician. Whatever I want, you conjure up." [51] For Huxley, Marsh's specimens "demonstrated the evolution of the horse beyond question, and for the first time indicated the direct line of descent of an existing animal." [52]

Marsh, known as the "Big Bone Chief" among Indians in the West, regarded his discoveries as "the stepping stones by which the evolutionist of to-day leads the doubting brother across the shallow remnant of the gulf once thought impassable." [53] He was a firm exponent of natural selection. "To doubt evolution today," he told the A.A.A.S. in 1877, "is to doubt science, and science is only another name for truth." [54] Edward D. Cope of Philadelphia, Marsh's great rival in the "boneyards" of the West, was a Lamarckian rather than a Darwinian. But his fossil collections and his classifications of extinct vertebrates in western United States contributed enormously to the advance of evolutionary science.

Reviewing "Fifty Years of American Science" for the *Atlantic* in September, 1898, W. J. McGee pointed out that Darwinism had "wrought, within a quarter-century, the most profound revolution in the history of human thought." Then he added: "Yet the revolution would have been long delayed had Englishmen alone contributed to it, or even men of Continental Europe; for, with a half dozen exceptions, the earliest and strongest apostles were Americans." [55] His appraisal of the achievements of American scientists in other fields, particularly physics (though he overlooked Gibbs), astronomy, geology, and technology, was similarly enthusiastic, though he admitted that European scientists had made the most basic scientific generalizations. But they had been "hastened" in America. "The world has moved forward as it never did before," he concluded. "Yet fully half the progress of the world, during the last fifty years, has been wrought through the unprecedented energy of American enterprise and genius, guided by American science." [56]

McGee wrote partly out of a strong sense of national pride. But he also had a tremendous admiration for "the straightforward and unselfish habit of thought fostered by scientific methods" and he wished to encourage these methods in all areas of American life. His great hope was that the "sense of right thinking" which is the "essence of science" would lead ultimately to "the elevation of moral character" in the United States.[57] Essentially an evolutionary optimist, McGee looked to the future with confidence.

Henry Adams, a conscientious observer of scientific developments in the late nineteenth century, did not share McGee's sanguine expectations.

He was chiefly impressed by the austere implications for human life of new scientific laws. McGee had had nothing to say about the second law of thermodynamics, which states that entropy, dissipation of energy, tends to a maximum in the universe. Adams was more struck by this law, formulated by Lord Kelvin in 1851, than by evolutionary law. Holding, like McGee, that science should be extended to the humanities, Adams proposed to reevaluate human life in the light of the second law. Man, he suggested, was a "thermodynamic mechanism," who by progressively untapping the energies latent in nature for his own use and misuse, was contributing mightily to the dispersion of energy in the universe and hastening the day when energy in the solar system would be at too low a level to sustain life.

Thermodynamics led Adams to Gibbs, and the Phase Rule. For Gibbs's three phases (solid, liquid, gaseous) Adams substituted historical stages (religious, mechanical, electrical) based upon the kind and amount of energy man used. "From the physicist's point of view," wrote Adams, "Man, as a conscious and constant, single, natural force, seems to have no function except that of dissipating or degrading energy. . . . [He] does more to dissipate and waste nature's economies than all the rest of animal or vegetable life has ever done to save them." [58]

For Adams, the twentieth century was to be one of unprecedented violence and destruction as man careened thoughtlessly but inevitably, in accordance with the second law, down the road to ultimate extinction. Few Americans shared his pessimism. Like McGee, most Americans, including men of science, saw in the scientific advances of the late nineteenth century limitless opportunities for human progress. John Fiske's "cosmic philosophy," which saw the "perfecting of Humanity" as the goal of evolution, perhaps best reflected America's exuberant spirit:

> The future is lighted for us with radiant colours of hope. Strife and sorrow shall disappear. Peace and love shall reign supreme. The dream of poets, the lesson of priest and prophet, the inspiration of the great musician, is confirmed in the light of modern knowledge; and as we gird ourselves upward for the work of life, we may look forward to a time when in the truest sense the kingdoms of this world shall become the Kingdom of Christ.[59]

To William James, with his keen sensitivity to the ambiguities and recalcitrancies of the human situation, there was something distasteful, even callous, in the "sunny, sky-blue" optimism of the Fiske variety. But he thought that Adams was indulging in a kind of pessimistic frivolity over a "tragic subject." [60] James, who took his medical degree at Harvard in 1869 and taught anatomy and physiology before moving into psychology and philosophy, had a thorough grasp of the scientific method. His "pragmatico-humanism," as he once called his philosophy, was an effort to apply scientific imagination to basic questions of human existence.

But science, James believed, did not consist of a body of immutable truths about reality. It was a human creation growing out of man's need to introduce useful order into the endless sequence of sense impressions which he experienced and which were the ultimate data for human knowledge. Scientific laws were not "exact copies of a definite code of non-human realities." They were rather "so much 'conceptual shorthand,' true so far as they are useful but no farther." "Our mind," he added, "has become tolerant of symbol instead of reproduction, of approximation instead of exactness, of plasticity instead of rigor." [61] For Adams, abandonment of belief in unchanging laws of nature, discoverable by man and inherent in the structure of things, meant confusion and chaos; for James, it meant challenge and adventure. The universe, so far as man could know it empirically, was open, plastic, unfinished, evergrowing, and not to be confined within the bounds of a closed system of thought.

James had a temperamental aversion to closed systems, scientific, religious, or philosophical, and he called them "block universes." These systems pictured the universe as totally unified and inexorably shaped by a static plan or force, the will of God or Fate or the Absolute or Natural Law. Eliminating block universes, no matter how imposing or attractive, meant freeing man from the bondage of determinism and enhancing his status and dignity as a creative thinker and actor in an ever-changing universe. Evolutionary change was at the heart of James's philosophy. He was one of the first philosophers to realize that the Darwinian vision meant that fixity of natural laws, like fixity of species, must give way to a developmental view.

James stressed the factor of variation in evolutionary development, and was particularly impressed by spontaneous variations in human thinking. The mind of man, he insisted, continually introduced novelty into the universe. When creative thinkers like Newton and Darwin unified certain portions of reality into a law of gravitation and a law of natural selection, they produced something new in the universe with important future consequences. By such acts of creative intelligence, man participated fruitfully in the growth and development of the open universe. Even such commonsense categories as "things," "minds," "bodies," and "causes," James suggested, were creations of "prehistoric geniuses whose names the night of antiquity has covered up; they may have been verified by the immediate facts of experience which they first fitted; and then from fact to fact and from man to man they may have *spread*, until all language rested upon them and we are now incapable of thinking naturally in any other terms." [62] But man's creative insights must be verified by experience. They must put him into fruitful relations with reality and satisfy some human need, physical, emotional, or intellectual. This was James's humanism. The validity of ideas depended upon the degree to which they have satisfactory consequences when put into practice. This was James's pragmatism. Truth in ideas, said James, meant *"that ideas (which themselves are but parts of our experience) become true just in so far as they help us to get into satisfactory relations with other parts of our experience; to summarize them and get about among them by conceptual short-cuts instead of following the interminable succession of particular phenomena."* [63] James also believed that the meaning of an idea consisted of the entire process by which it was tried out in experience. "The truth of an idea," he said, "is not a stagnant property inherent in it. Truth *happens* to an idea. It *becomes* true, is *made* true by events. Its verity *is* in fact an event, a process: the process namely of its verifying itself, its veri-*fication*. Its validity is the process of its valid-*ation*." [64] He was anxious to substitute a dynamic for a static concept of truth.

James believed that man had as much right to adopt "working hypotheses," subject to the test of experience, in religion as in science. Religion was a serious interest to him. Like Asa Gray, he wanted to reconcile religion and science without violating pragmatically validated scientific ideas. The LeConte-Fiske notion of God immanent in creation seemed to imprison man in a closed universe and deprive him of freedom and responsibility. Nor was Gray's argument from design convincing: "from the order of the world, there is no path to God by coercive reasoning, or even by strong analogy or induction." But religion, like science, satisfied certain human needs and the pragmatico-humanist must take it seriously. Science satisfied the intellectual and esthetic passion for order, unity, and economy of thought; religion fulfilled the emotional need for some kind of moral meaning in the universe at large. In times of trouble, religion offered comfort and consolation. In times of heroic endeavor (James's perennial mood), it supplied the assurance that the struggle for high moral ideals, against overwhelming odds, was not pointless:

> That we believe in God . . . is not due to our logic, but to our emotional wants. . . . The world is a datum, a gift to man. Man stands and asks himself, "What is it?" Science says molecules. Religion says God. Both are hypotheses. Science says, "You can't deduce or explain anything by yours." Religion says, "You can't inspire or console by yours." What is *worth* most, is, after all, the question. Molecules can do certain things for us. God can do other things. Which things are worth the most? [65]

Both were worthwhile for James. But though he speculated endlessly on religion, he made no extensive use himself of what he called the "will to believe." He did, however, dislike scientific determinism. It deprived human life of any ethical significance, and erected provisional and approximate scientific formulations about reality into final truths. There were aspects of human life, of which religion took account, that always escaped impersonal scientific generalizations. In the deep privacy of every individual's heart, James felt, there were unsharable experiences and voiceless intuitions that abstract concepts can never quite get hold of. To *be,* he once said, was more important than to *define being.* An unmistakable existentialist strain in James's thinking passed almost unnoticed in his lifetime.

Critics of James have singled out his pragmatic method for special attack. The belief that ideas are instruments of human adaptation to be judged by their effectiveness in coping with reality seemed to denigrate man. But for James the pragmatic method was simply a generalized description of the way in which the modern scientific mind proceeds. Michelson discarded the concept of luminiferous ether because it turned out to be useless for explaining observable natural events. Gibbs found immense "cash value," to use James's expression, in the Phase Rule, when he used it to account for changes taking place in nature. James's pragmatism was primarily a theory of ideas, not an ethical system. But when John Dewey, a young Hegelian who became a pragmatist after reading James's *Principles of Psychology* (1890), applied the new philosophy to moral life, he emphasized the broad consequences for other people of the moral decisions an individual makes, the continuity of means and ends, and the importance of ideals in illuminating present activity and in enhancing its quality.

Vulgarized and caricatured to mean a justification for ethics of sheer expediency and self-aggrandizement, James's philosophy has been interpreted as a perfect reflection of the materialistic ethos of his age.[66] But James, like Dewey, had the highest moral and intellectual ideals.

He was an indefatigable searcher for human understanding, and a courageous champion of unconventional and unpopular ideas and causes. He was at least as idealistic in his outlook as his twentieth-century detractors.

In the booming American economy after the Civil War, the passion for acquisition and enjoyment was widespread. James deplored the "moral flabbiness born of the exclusive worship of the bitch-goddess SUCCESS," and the "squalid cash interpretation put upon the word success" by so many of his countrymen.[67] Henry Adams was similarly repelled by the era's vulgarity. But both James and Adams realized that materialism was part and parcel of modern industrialism, not a peculiarly American characteristic. Many Americans, moreover, stood aloof from the frantic getting and spending of the day and continued quietly to pursue ideals and goals, social and intellectual, that transcended immediate advantage. Scientists like Gibbs, Rowland, Newcomb, Langley, and Gray, were as truly American as "robber barons" like Jim Fisk or Captains of Industry like John D. Rockefeller.

Absorbed in the task of probing nature's secrets, America's scientists labored ceaselessly and selflessly to enlarge man's understanding of the world with little or no thought of economic gain. Their contribution to science was enormous, and the example they set by their lives and work was impressive. Henry Rowland perhaps best stated their credo. "I value in a scientific mind most of all," he wrote,

> that love of truth, that care in its pursuit, and that humility of mind which makes the possibility of error always present more than any other quality. This the mind which has built up modern science to its present perfection, which has laid one stone upon the other with such care that it to-day offers to the world the most complete monument to human reason. . . . It is the only mind which appreciates the imperfections of the human reason and is thus careful to guard against them. It is the only mind that values the truth as it should be valued and ignores all personal feeling in its pursuit.[68]

Vernon Parrington called the Gilded Age a "world of triumphant and unabashed vulgarity without its like in our history." [69] Perhaps. It was also one of remarkable scientific achievement.

Asa Gray.
Fogg Museum, Harvard University.

Louis Agassiz.
Fogg Museum, Harvard University

William Rainey Harper,
dynamic president of the
University of Chicago.
Library of Congress.

Gray Herbarium at Harvard.   *Fogg Museum, Harvard University.*

Edwin Lawrence Godkin. *Library of Congress*.

George William Curtis. *Library of Congress.*

William Graham Sumner.
Library of Congress.

Field class in zoology.   *Popular Science Monthly, September, 1899.*

Chemical laboratory, Ohio State Normal School.   *Popular Science Monthly, May, 1895.*

Mary E. Lease,
"the Kansas Pythoness."
*Kansas State Historical
Society.*

Cartoonist Thomas Nast.
Library of Congress.

Evangelist Dwight
L. Moody, 1900.
Library of Congress.

A "life class" in drawing, 1881.
*Frank Leslie's Illustrated
Newspaper, January 15, 1881.*

League of American Wheelmen in Boston, May 30, 1881.   *Frank Leslie's Illustrated Newspaper, June 18, 1881.*

Circus parade, 1892.   *Library of Congress.*

Typical page of advertisements, 1881.   *Frank Leslie's Illustrated Newspaper, May 7, 1881.*

"AMERICA" AT THE CHICAGO AUDITORIUM: BALLET OF INVENTIONS—TELEPHONE BOYS.

"AMERICA" AT THE CHICAGO AUDITORIUM: BALLET OF INVENTIONS—ELECTRICITY GIRLS.

The chorus line for "America" at the Columbian Exposition, 1893.
Illustrated American, August 26, 1893.

Actor Joseph Jefferson as Rip Van Winkle, 1894. *Library of Congress*.

Actress Ellen Terry. *Library of Congress.*

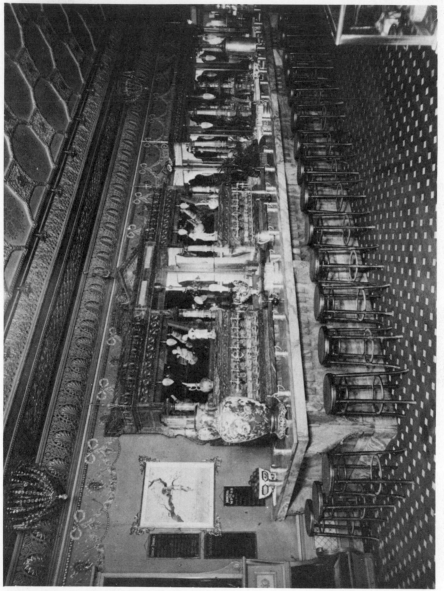

Gunther's Soda Fountain, Chicago, 1888. *Courtesy of Chicago Historical Society.*

Suburban home, Manchester, New Hampshire.   *Library of Congress.*

ROBERT R. ROBERTS

❧ 13 ❧

Popular Culture and Public Taste

POPULAR CULTURE in the hectic and colorful era that followed the Civil War encompassed diverse media. The daily newspaper, enriched with wire service news, the mass revival meeting, the Chautauqua lecture, and the traveling theater troupe all reflected American ideas and aspirations. Publicly accepted painting, sculpture, literature, music, and theatrical entertainment reflected social values. Audiences listened patiently while the actor Joseph Jefferson, the revivalist Dwight Moody, and the lecturer Russell Conwell each said something that touched national tastes.

The traditional values of Western Europe flavored this culture, whatever its variations of style or scope. Though covered with Victorian moralism and propriety, popular novels followed the eighteenth-century English precepts. Charles Dickens was very likely the "world's most popular author," and belonged both to "art" and to the popular culture of America.[1]

The arts were a major part of American life. George Makepeace Towle, a traveler returned to America from England, heard "boys in the street singing and whistling Mozart and Rossini, and hand organs grinding out the arias from *Faust* and *Lucrezia Borgia.*" Towle was also impressed by the lively American theater, including "more performances of Shakespeare in America . . . than . . . in England" and "tragedy, fine old comedy and the 'free and easy' burlesque." [2] Even in the cheap story-papers, authors of accepted stature appeared with the storytellers. Classical actors and actresses such as Edwin Booth and Sarah Bernhardt were immensely popular. The Gilbert and Sullivan musicals were immediate hits. In the theaters Shakespeare preceded *East Lynne*. Samuel Smiles or Mrs. E. D. E. N. Southworth might outsell Thomas Hardy or the Brontë sisters, but the classics were on the same lists and programs.

The traditional culture of the Western world, albeit sometimes in diluted forms, held sway in America, in a healthy mingling of popular and classical taste. One opera house in a middle-sized American town in the 1880's offered the best from the classic tradition in music and drama.

The total society did not acclaim great art, or wholesome popular arts without exception. These years saw the rise of mass magazines and newspapers, and changes in the theater and other forms of entertainment that produced an increasing gap between popular culture and higher standards. Such artists as Albert Ryder and George Inness had a small audience at best. Surviving Brahmins like the Adams brothers believed the American people patronized only shoddy lectures and tasteless magazines. Pre–Civil War monuments such as Longfellow and Emerson lived into the postwar decades and did not find them good. But there was little of the spirit of "épater le bourgeois." The coterie artist and the self-conscious rebel against middle-class values were not dominant. This familiar schism had yet to appear in the Gilded Age.

Traditional and popular culture mingled, and was derivative— England naturally contributed most heavily to American public culture. The common name for the prevailing moral view was "Victorian," obviously not a native product. The most popular style of middle-class architecture was called the "Queen Anne." The arbiter of this building style and of home decoration and landscaping was Charles Locke Eastlake, Englishman and disciple of Ruskin and William Morris.

English standards cast the longest shadow in literature, especially the novel. More copies of Dickens were sold in the 1880's than in the 1860's, and his influence was strong.[3] Thackeray, Anthony Trollope, George Eliot, Jane Austen, and the Brontës regularly appeared on American publishing lists. Good reading was more readily available than at any prior time, and the press and magazines reached huge audiences.

English standards did not apply only in quality literature. The most celebrated novel of the sensational-romantic school, *East Lynne,* was by a Londoner, Mrs. Henry Wood. A second Englishwoman, Mary Elizabeth Braddon, contributed the "preposterously successful melodrama," *Lady Audley's Secret.* A third English lady romancer used the unusual pen name of Ouida, and wrote tales like *Under Two Flags* and *A Dog of Flanders.* The American reading public was not alone in its thirst for melodrama and romance. As literacy increased and, particularly, as more women received education, adventures and romances appealed to readers in Chicago or Manchester or New York or London.

Change and uneven development characterized most activities. The press remained from the 1850's to the 1880's a domain for personal journalism. In the early 1880's the American theater entered a new phase, the "Golden Age of the Road." Equally significant changes took place in minstrelsy and the Chautauqua movement. Popular culture defied exact classification, but generally, culture in the 1870's resembled that of the 1850's; the 1880's were the years of greatest transition.

Changes in architectural design and construction illustrated basic problems in developing a national cultural style. Building in the postwar years obviously continued earlier traditions, but new design in the Gilded Age was not always derivative. The era reveled in color and often mistook display for innovation. As in other sectors of life, a new building style suited for the factory or mass urban housing was slow to emerge. But the overt thrust of this newly rich society was toward an enlarging middle class. The Italianate brownstone in wealthy city areas, and the detached single-family dwelling on a spacious lot were two of the period's best developments. Large windows, high ceilings, decoration, and special functions for each house level provided both comfort and spaciousness.

Exceptional men produced the landmarks of architecture. Richard Morris Hunt designed residences for millionaires based on the chateaux of the French renaissance and a high style. His imaginative and splendid mansions, such as the Vanderbilt house on Fifth Avenue, or the even more successful Ochre Court at Newport, deserve to be remembered.[4] The firm of McKim, Mead and White, did noteworthy work—town houses built for Henry Villard and his friends, "the greatest private residence[s] ever erected in Manhattan."[5] Henry Hobson Richardson's churches, public buildings, and business structures were distinguished and utilitarian. But his most successful domestic design reflected the reigning Queen Anne style.[6] These leaders and such firms as Burnham and Root, or Adler and Sullivan in the Chicago school of business building, were ample evidence of a vital architecture.

Few people could afford distinctiveness in a family dwelling, however, and these men did not redirect the national tone.[7] The three principal influences on mass building all preceded the war: the Gothic revival, mansard roof, and Italianate style. The Gothic had heavily influenced public buildings, churches, and college architecture. But the translation of a traditional Gothic into "Carpenter Gothic" was well under way. This included "steep gables and pointed windows; sometimes they were sheathed with vertical boarding instead of the familiar horizontal clapboard." Decorative matter called gingerbread filled out these

designs. Though the whipsaw might occasionally mar a plan, this ornamentation was basically healthy, and belonged with the "vigorous and
pleasurable folk arts." [8]

The continuity of taste and style were also obvious in interior decoration. The prints of Currier and Ives, dating from the 1830's, continued
to dominate a large national market, and in time became collectors'
items.[9] The sculptor John Rogers was a folk hero of sorts, pleasing many
people with an honest craftsmanship and understandable subject matter.
His first popular work was "The Checker Players," in 1859, and he became "not only a household name but a household ornament." [10]

The novel also reflected this basic continuity. People who emerged
in the 1850's continued to write best sellers. Mrs. Mary J. Holmes,
described a trifle cruelly, if accurately, as "that prolific favorite of the
unthinking," was a case in point.[11] Her publishing career began in the
1850's and continued into the 1880's at roughly the rate of a novel a
year. Her protagonists were paragons of perfection, physically and
morally, and her villains were monsters of evil. The story's outcome was
never long in doubt, and her books belonged in the sentimental-moralistic
school of writing. Publishers and booksellers had long recognized the
market for such writing and welcomed successful lady authors.[12] The
sentimental-moralistic novel was a staple of the weekly story-papers and
the publishers' lists.

Mrs. E. D. E. N. Southworth was the queen of what Nathaniel
Hawthorne called that "d——d mob of scribbling women." She was
easily the "most popular authoress in the annals of American publishing"
no mean achievement in a field where ladies have excelled.[13]

Mrs. Southworth generally set her stories in Virginia or Maryland.
Occasionally a craggy mountain pass might defy the facts of geography,
but usually a fine old plantation served as the background for a romantic
tale. Handsome heroes of slim and graceful carriage, and pure and lovely
heroines won through to true love in spite of fearsome villainies, ancient
curses, and assorted tribulations. In *The Malediction; or The Widows of
Widowville,* a mysterious stranger with patrician features learned that a
noble plantation house, rising above the Chesapeake Bay, was the home
of a beautiful heiress, prevented from marrying by an old family curse
of a peculiar but unknown type.[14] Who could resist a situation fraught
with such peril and promise? Obviously not the reading public of the
Gilded Age who continued to buy Mrs. Southworth's books for over
sixty years. Her works still sold in considerable numbers when she died
in 1899.

The novel with more sensational elements like violence, a hint of sexuality, or exposures of vice in high places, was also popular. The English best sellers, *East Lynne* and *Lady Audley's Secret,* followed this formula. There were numerous practitioners of this style, including Sylvanus Cobb, Jr., and Charles Reade. Cobb began publishing in the cheap story-paper, the *New York Ledger,* in 1856 and was still active in 1885. The more "cultivated and genteel" readers disdained Cobb, but he had a contract for thirty years at $50 per week with the *Ledger.*[15] Reade was also a perennially popular author whose sensational tales appeared on publishers' lists from the 1860's to the 1880's. In *Griffith Gaunt* (1886), and *A Terrible Temptation* (1871), he proved that exposés of vice and sin in high society appealed strongly to the moralistic middle class.

The religious novel had its seed-time before the Civil War and blossomed in the following generation. The persistence of these novels was easy to understand. These were years of challenge and trial for churches, particularly traditional Protestant denominations. Orthodox theologies subjected to liberalizing influences in the prewar decades, now abruptly faced new scientific thought, especially Darwinian evolution. No other topic occupied more time in pulpit discourse or space in the religious press, and this interest carried over to the reading public. The churches' ideals and social programs were being severely tested by the social and economic problems of an urban-industrial growth of nearly frightening proportions. The faith of the fathers and traditional values were sorely tried; people grasped for reassurance in a happy and logical fictional world. This was the case in the three major religious best sellers, Augusta Jane Evans' *St. Elmo* (1859), Elizabeth Stuart Phelps's *The Gates Ajar* (1868), and the Reverend E. P. Roe's *Barriers Burned Away* (1872). In *St. Elmo* a beautiful and brilliant girl convinced St. Elmo to turn from atheism to the ministry. *The Gates Ajar* ignored theological problems and vanquished doubt by describing the beauties of a worldly sort of heaven. And in *Barriers Burned Away* the great Chicago fire and spiritual truths combined in a "sure-fire" formula. These books led publishers' lists throughout the late nineteenth century, testifying to the appeal of simple faith in a complex age.

In the 1880's, one of the major popular novels in American history appeared. In *Ben Hur,* General Lew Wallace combined the appeal of religion, the glamor of a historical setting in the Roman Empire, and sheer melodrama. The book had an immense vogue among people in all walks of life, and became a popular touring stage play.[16] Combining action with purpose, glorifying individualism, and reaffirming the religious verities, "A Tale of the Christ" inevitably appealed to Americans.

In varieties of style the self-help and success theme, with a strong admixture of inspiration, dominated most popular writings. The theme was still emphasized early in childhood through the widely used McGuffey readers. These school readers conveyed the well-known lessons of honesty, industry, obedience, thrift, piety, punctuality, and similar virtues.[17] Fame and fortune would follow strict adherence to these rules of living. The popular Horatio Alger books reinforced this doctrine. The young hero found that a life of virtue and the luck to save the daughter of a rich man from drowning could lead to worldly success. The role of chance loomed large in these success stories, but the American lad with enough gumption to seize that opportunity was firmly in the tradition of self-help and individualism.

By the late 1880's two famous essays had reinforced the gospel of uplift and success. The first was Russell Conwell's *Acres of Diamonds*. This Philadelphia minister insisted that a man could find wealth in his own backyard if he but looked, and that it was every man's duty to acquire riches. The second was Andrew Carnegie's celebration of competitive individualism in selecting those best fitted to prosper—and the obligations of wealth—in *The Gospel of Wealth*. These works suited the dominant middle class, and reflected the ideas of a nation engaged in building an industrial economy. But such tastes were not peculiar to that age or to America. Englishmen were buying Samuel Smiles in as great numbers, and the uplift theme had always been an American favorite.

The public also read and listened to boisterous humorists. Their techniques were not new. The grotesque exaggerations of the Davy Crockett story, the rural parody of the style and manners of "city folk," and the artful mishandling of the English language were all inherited from an earlier time. But there was an increasing consciousness of the peculiar traits of regions and localities. Economic forces were driving the nation toward nationalism, and this produced an audience for writers and lecturers who portrayed unique and disappearing types of American life. The Yankee, the midwestern "hayseed," the rough and ready westerner, and southern types found a public for their brands of humor.

The leaders of this school of humorists included David Ross Locke (Petroleum V. Nasby), Charles Farrar Brown (Artemus Ward), and Henry Wheeler Shaw (Josh Billings). As "hayseeds" or other simpletons, they poked fun at customs and conventions. Josh Billings wrote in his *Farmer's Allminax,* "Most people repent ov their sins bi thanking God they aint so wicked as their nabors." [18] Artemus Ward got off his share of quotable remarks: "I tell you, feller citizens, it would have been ten dollars in Jeff Davis' pockets if he had never been born." And "Old

George Washington's fort was not to hev eny public man of the present day ressemble him in eny alarmin extent." [19]

The sale of their books testified to popular appeal. Billings' *Farmer's Allminax* sold 90,000 copies in its first edition in 1869, and in ten years subsequent versions sold as many as 127,000 copies, and never less than 50,000.[20] These writers served up a pungent humor based on strong characterizations, parody, and broad social satire. In an age of colorful individuals, folk figures did not take a back seat to business barons or political leaders.

Major innovations in magazine publishing came in the 1890's. But in newspaper printing, the 1880's produced a major change, the fall of great editors and personal journalism to syndicates. New business methods, increased costs, lower prices, the demands of advertising, and the need for mass distribution diminished the personal note and encouraged the rise of the news merchant.

The changes that would be called "yellow journalism" had not yet occurred. Sensationalism, the comics, and other attributes of modern newspapers were not overly noticeable in the newspapers of the 1870's and were just beginning in the 1880's. An upstate New York farmer continued, after Greeley's death, to subscribe to the *Tribune* in the belief that Horace was still responsible for its contents.[21] Technical changes occurred rapidly. The telegraph and cable, press associations, expensive new machinery, labor unions, and advertising revenue transformed newspapers from personal organs to a big business. These changes in communication and distribution widened and deepened the content of every major newspaper. The feature article on politics or diplomacy was common, as were special departments and correspondents for social and artistic questions.

In magazine publishing, these were years of "boom." [22] The number of journals increased from 700 in 1865 to some 3,300 in 1885, and circulation figures rose.[23] There was also a major trend toward more dependence on advertising, and in the early 1880's advertising "demonstrated its value and established its place in the general magazine." [24]

Among magazines, the cheap story-papers which held sway before the Civil War continued to attract readers. The *New York Weekly,* the *New York Ledger,* and Frank Leslie's *Chimney Corner* purveyed fiction, poetry, essays, joke columns, and advice columns to a variety of readers. The *Ledger* and *Weekly* claimed a circulation of over 300,000, and the other shorter-lived story-papers had circulation figures in the thousands for a few years. Publishers of these competitive enterprises naturally tried to give the middle class what it wanted. The moral tone was smugly proper. Publishers assured readers that their particular publication was a family paper which the innocent daughters of the household could read safely.[25]

Fiction was the bulk of the material in these papers, largely serialized versions of romantic or historical novels of famous authors. If the publisher was not fortunate enough to have a popular writer under contract, imitators produced remarkably similar tales. Interspersed in the fiction was poetry of the pre–Civil War style and manner, never the unconventional barbarities of a Walt Whitman. There might also be something from Dickens or another noted English author, and for patriotism and inspiration, historical sketches of the Founding Fathers or essays by Horace Greeley or Henry Ward Beecher. There were also regular columns on "Advice to Young Women."

The subheading of the *New York Ledger* proudly announced that it was "Devoted to Choice Literature Romance The News and Commerce." Neither "The News" nor "Commerce" were much in evidence; stories, essays, advice columns, poems, and proper jokes made up the bulk of story-papers. The content reflected the desire for sentimental fiction and the triumph of the accepted values, which might be expected in any popular writing. There was also a taste for uplifting essays and poetic sentiments. An issue of *Frank Leslie's Popular Monthly,* contained a travel article, a sketch of a successful businessman, an episode in a continuing novel, and a poem beginning with the verse:

> Would I could send my spirit o'er the deep,
> Would I could wing it like a bird to thee,
> To commune with thy thoughts, to fill thy sleep
> With these unwearying words of melody,
> Brother, come home.

The "Entertainment Column" might have a coy joke: "Said the sailor to his sweetheart: 'I know that ladies care little about nautical matters, but if you had your choice of a ship, what kind would you prefer?' She cast down her eyes, blushed, and whispered: 'a little smack.' " [26]

Though not so widely read as story-papers, the actual leaders of the magazine world were the genteel aristocrats, *Harper's Weekly* or *Monthly, Atlantic, Galaxy,* and *Scribner's.* Some of these, notably the Harper publications, were popular; all reflected middle-class tastes and ideas. These were journals of "miscellany and opinion," [27] and the dutiful reader ploughed through heavy prose. The upper middle-class reader had time for reading, and a stern sense of the duty of being informed. An article on "The Development of the Steamship, and the Liverpool Exhibition of 1886," complete with diagrams of hulls, super-structures, and engines, was thirty pages long, followed by a scientific article on the "Forests of North America." But perhaps many readers hurried on to "Marse Archie's Flight," a dialect Civil War story, or the last chapter of a long novel of New York family life.[28]

The journals reflected the era's great interest in scientific matters. Economics was another prominent subject. And almost any issue had an article on the evolutionary hypothesis and its significance for religion. *Harper's Weekly* described itself as "A Journal of Civilization." This whole group of periodicals ranged from popular fiction to foreign news, humor, travel, literary essays, editorials, and economic and scientific subjects, with excellent illustrations. Taken as a whole, they were an excellent mirror of the informed mind.

But Americans did not spend their evenings and Sundays solely in reading. They heard lectures, attended the theater, went to curiosity museums and circuses, and participated in self-improvement classes at Chautauqua institutes. They sought escape from reality, the confident proclamation of the "old truths" in a Moody revival meeting, or inspiration at a Chautauqua. They also attended that new phenomenon, organized, big-league baseball.

No revival team compared in popularity to Dwight L. Moody and Ira D. Sankey. Moody in 1875 was "the rising young tycoon of the revival trade as Andrew Carnegie was of the steel trade or John D. Rockefeller of oil." [29] He coupled businesslike methods with the old-fashioned gospel, and his success was enormous. Ira D. Sankey directed the music and contributed stirring solo renditions of popular hymns, many composed by the partners. But Moody was the driving force in this revival movement of the 1870's and 1880's. He used committees to prepare the way, asked for cooperation of the various denominations, made the act of conversion simple and businesslike, and preached in popular language. No learned theological discourse or flowery rhetoric ever marred the simple plea to "take Christ now." There were ties between Moody and popular writing. Magazines and novels were building a taste for "sentiment and make-believe," and the successful revivalist "would have to speak the new commoner's tongue." [30] Moody the lay preacher appealed to the same broad audience that read the story-papers and Mrs. E. D. E. N. Southworth. He was a remarkable combination of a revolution in techniques and a lag in values which characterized so much of popular culture. His methods were modern but the message consisted of forceful repetitions of the "old truths."

There were many other famous preachers, some conservative, a few liberal. Some argued that Christianity should be applied to social problems; others preached on sin and salvation. But one man symbolized the middle-class pulpit, Henry Ward Beecher. Although not a typical preacher, he spoke with tremendous authority from the Plymouth Congregational Church in Brooklyn, New York, and from his editorial position on the *Independent*. He rejected the theology of his Calvinist forebears, influenced in so doing by his father, Lyman Beecher. He preferred a doctrine of love and an ethic of individualism modified by the demands of brotherhood. His sermons were dazzling dramatic displays, more remarkable for emotional appeal than serious content. One notable admirer, Samuel L. Clemens, wrote of the Beecher style: "He went marching up and down the stage waving his arms in the air, hurling sarcasms this way and that, discharging rockets of poetry, and exploding mines of eloquence, halting now and then to stamp his foot three times in succession to emphasize a point." [31]

In 1872, Beecher was accused of seducing the wife of a close friend and co-worker, and the ensuing scandal, aired at two church councils and public trial, was a national sensation. In an era when sexual fidelity was considered an essential bulwark of public welfare, the affair created unique concern and sensation. As much as any other event, it raised serious questions about the prevailing mores in the realm of "private versus public conduct, the function of the evangelical church, and the place of women in the social order." [32]

The Chautauqua movement was significant. The later Chautauqua involved commercialization and led to some degradation of its educational content as entertainment supplanted most of the educational programs.[33] The original program was a summer session on the shores of Lake Chautauqua, New York, begun as a Sunday School Teachers Assembly by Lewis Miller, an Ohio manufacturer, and the Reverend (later Bishop) John H. Vincent of the Methodist church. Both the content and the number of such institutes expanded rapidly. Permanent Chautauquas were founded in Ohio, Michigan, Iowa, and eventually in the Willamette Valley at Gladstone, Oregon. The original Chautauqua added a Literary and Scientific Circle, a School of Theology, and a College of Liberal Arts with authority to grant a bachelor's degree. Eminent educators, ministers, and lecturers, eventually including six presidents of the United States, contributed or sold their services. The most prominent educator and a leading figure in the Chautauqua was William Rainey Harper, later president of the University of Chicago. But the champion lecturer was surely the Reverend Russell Conwell, who delivered "Acres of Diamonds," over 5,000 times.

The self-improvement drive and the success-through-knowledge theme demonstrated again that Americans eagerly sought the available learning. This phenomenon, the free library movement, the prosperity of the book publishing industry, and the magazine boom, all indicated a thirst for knowledge and desire for culture. This search customarily led to the reaffirmation of the values rooted in experience. The benefits of private property, the beauties of competition, and the stewardship of wealth were main themes of Chautauqua lectures on social and economic subjects. But popular institutions of a society never purvey ideas contrary to accepted values. The lonely prophet, perceptive intellectual, or sensitive artist will confront a society with its failures and injustices. Culture-heroes will not.

Of course, the public was not solely interested in uplift or education. The era witnessed the rise of spectator sports, the modern circus, minstrelsy, and a "golden age" of the theater. As people moved to cities and worked in factories, organized recreation and spectator events replaced rural games and entertainments. For these spectacles, on the playing field or on the stage, the audiences were large and enthusiastic. The first mammoth three-ring circus under "three acres" of tent, and the nation's foremost opera house, the historic Metropolitan, both opened in New York City in 1883.

Three developments shaped the theater: the dominance of the "road"; the vogue for light musicals and scenic spectacles, including the scantily attired female form; and the popularity and decline of minstrelsy. A remarkable number of road stars were available. Richard Mansfield; James O'Neill, assigned to permanent stardom in the role of Edmund Dantes in Dumas's *The Count of Monte Cristo;* Edwin Booth, the supreme Shakespearian; Mary Anderson; the brilliant Italian stars, Tammaso Salvini and Adelaide Ristori; Mme. Modjeska; Joseph Jefferson in *Rip Van Winkle;* Henry Irving and Ellen Terry; the Divine Sarah herself; or, near the end of the era, Eleanora Duse. A rich and varied fare went to millions of Americans in these years. *East Lynne* played on Saturday nights, but Shakespeare and Dumas, Racine, and later G. B. Shaw and Ibsen were available. By 1893 this "golden age of the road" was drawing to a close. The development of theatrical syndicates foretold the rise of a new kind of theater that would culminate in the "star" system.[34]

The taste for lighter theatrical fare also increased, particularly in major cities. This vogue originated in the success of a melodrama called *The Black Crook,* which included a Parisian ballet sequence, the most expensive and daring show Americans had seen as of 1866. Nor could the thunderous denunciations of clergymen and angry moralists stop the trend. *The Black Crook* ran for sixteen months and broke all box-office records. It was often revived and, naturally, was followed by a number of similar shows.[35] *The Black Crook* may have set a precedent for sexual material on stage.[36]

The sprightly, melodic works of Gilbert and Sullivan were major hits after the first American production in 1878. The authors even opened the *Pirates of Penzance* in New York City. This was partly to prevent the work from being pirated by American producers.[37] This taste for *opera bouffe* helped several works by Offenbach to succeed in America in spite of the usual charge of "French indecencies"—or perhaps because of it.

Lighter theatrical fare included vaudeville, created by Tony Pastor. His Opera House in New York City became the Tony Pastor Music Hall, the "cathedral of Vaudeville." Such immortal show-business figures as the four Cohans, Weber and Fields, Harrigan and Hart, Pat Rooney, Gus Williams, Eddy Foy, and many others appeared there.[38] Pastor also founded the touring vaudeville show in 1878. The vigor and exuberance of vaudeville theater, the variety and fast pace of the acts, made vaudeville beloved to several generations.

The third major trend in show business was the rise and decline of minstrelsy. The minstrel show dated back to the between-acts numbers of black-face performers in the prewar era, especially one Thomas Rice, famed for his "Jump Jim Crow" number. The stock Negro character of the stage bore little resemblance to any actual person. The authentic minstrel company evolved to include end men, jokes, and songs, and had its heyday from 1850 to 1870. Competition to form ever bigger and more elaborate shows soon reduced the quality of performances. This and increasing expenses, and competition with vaudeville, burlesque, and musical comedy sent minstrelsy into a long decline which ended the form in the 1920's.[39]

The success of the minstrel show casts light on the public attitude toward racial minorities. The Negro was portrayed on stage, in dialect stories, and in illustrations as a comic fellow, "ludicrously inept," often putting on "airs . . . above his true station in life." But he was happy and good-natured, perhaps gifted at singing or dancing, but never a "person of consequence or dignity."[40] Racial distinctions were taken as obvious and inescapable. Those concerned about minority groups acted from paternalistic motives, not from a sense of the legitimate dignity and worth of all men.

Other racial stereotypes were equally bald. The Jew was often a shadowy and alien figure, somehow enmeshed in international finance;

or he was clannish and unassimilable. The Indian was first portrayed as a dangerous enemy, then as nature's nobleman going down to defeat bravely, and then as a romantic figure in Helen Hunt Jackson's *Ramona*. The stage Irishman was also a stock figure. The following definition appeared in the "entertainment" column of a popular monthly:

> An Irish Discussion—A contractor who was building a tunnel on a certain railroad observed one morning that the face of a member of his gang was disfigured with bruises and plasters. "Hallo, Jimmy," said he, "what have you been doin?"—"Not varey mush, sorr," answered Jimmy. "I was jist down at Bill Mulligan's last night, sorr, an' him an' me had a bit of a discooshen wid sticks." [41]

Though it was not so much P. T. Barnum as his partners who created the modern circus, "the greatest show on earth," he remains the symbol of this achievement. The growth of the circus was tied to the growth of railroads and centers of population adequate to support it. The gigantic circus was part of an age of great enterprises, from spanning a continent with iron rails to building a multimillion-dollar business empire. P. T. Barnum belonged among the empire-builders.[42]

Ballads reinforced the accepted values. The moralistic note was detectable in "Always Take Mother's Advice." The sentimental-religious theme pervaded "Flowers from an Angel Mother's Grave." [43] Respectability dominated "In the Gloaming." Sheer nostalgia filled "Down by the Old Mill Stream," or the most popular sentimental ballad of the era, "Silver Threads Among the Gold." [44]

A lusty love of life prompted many popular songs. The "greatest of all drinking songs," the "honest and earthy" "Little Brown Jug" was published in 1869.[45] The famous ballad celebrating a prostitute betrayed by her man, the classic "Franky and Johnny," came from the 1880's.[46] The celebration of individual heroics was evident in the popularity of the song "Jim Fisk." The well-known antics of this scoundrel of high finance made him a strangely sympathetic figure, and the truth was distorted to help in this ballad:

> I'll sing of a man who's now dead in his grave,
> as good man as ever was born.
> Jim Fisk he was call'd, and his money he gave,
> to the outcast, the poor and forlorn.
> We all know he lov'd both women and wine,
> but his heart it was right I am sure.
> Though he lived like a prince in his palace so fine,
> Yet he never went back on the poor.[47]

Americans were sentimental and moralistic, but could celebrate the earthier side of life.

The technology and sense of rapid change that pervaded economics, politics, and diplomacy also shaped popular culture. Newspapers and magazines revised methods and appeals. Chautauqua was commercialized and standardized. Revivalism took on business methods. Minstrelsy could not survive new competition. These changes testify to the most important development in popular tastes—the trend toward a national culture. The localism and regionalism of an earlier age could not survive the theatrical syndicate, national magazines, wire service news, or touring Chautauquas.

But in ideas the continuity of the Gilded Age and the pre–Civil War years deserved notice. Sentimentalization of human relationships was the dominant tone. The death of loved ones, the family, and romantic love were all powerful themes through the Civil War and into the postwar years. Popular works clung to older values and beliefs. The insistent celebration of these virtues of an earlier America revealed an awareness of and resistance to the forces that were transforming the nation.

But in spite of these continuities there was a characteristic quality to the Gilded Age. The period ended as the 1880's closed. The transformation of the publishing industry, the rise of theatrical syndicates, the passing of the "golden age of the road," the decline of minstrelsy, the disappearance of the cheap story-papers, all marked the change. Something would be lost, perhaps best described as the folk element, which endured into an industrial age from an earlier America. Another casualty of the more highly organized society was the uninhibited individualism, which for all its unfortunate results, lent a colorful and fascinating quality to this era. That sense of assurance and abundant optimism which, though a substantial part of the American character in all periods, was at a high point in the Gilded Age, began to decline.

These losses were bound to occur as the technology of an industrial society advanced, and mass markets for art and entertainment were both possible and necessary. Artists and entertainers, or their promoters and managers, probably should have anticipated the change. But there is legitimate nostalgia for a time when the individual seemed significant. A bold editor could display his personality in his paper. A colorful preacher could become a national figure. And every housewife could hope to be a famous writer with her latest romantic tale. And all of this they did with a firm belief in the triumph of their cause and surpassing faith in the imperviousness of their moral armor.

Contributors

GEOFFREY BLODGETT is professor of History and chairman of the history department at Oberlin College. He is author of *The Gentle Reformers: Massachusetts Democrats in the Cleveland Era* (Cambridge: Harvard University Press, 1966).

PAUL F. BOLLER, JR., is professor of History at the University of Massachusetts, Boston. He has written *George Washington and Religion* (Dallas: Southern Methodist University Press, 1965), *Quotesmanship* (Dallas: Southern Methodist University Press, 1967), and most recently, *American Thought in Transition: The Impact of Evolutionary Naturalism, 1865–1900* (New York: Rand, McNally, 1969).

ROBERT FALK is professor of English at the University of California, Los Angeles. He is a distinguished authority on late-nineteenth century American literature and culture, and author of *The Victorian Mode in American Fiction, 1865–1885* (East Lansing: Michigan State University Press, 1965).

LEWIS L. GOULD is assistant professor of History at the University of Texas at Austin. Interested in national politics from 1880 to 1920, he wrote an important case study of political development, *Wyoming: A Political History, 1868–1896* (New Haven: Yale University Press, 1968).

HERBERT G. GUTMAN is professor of History at the University of Rochester. He is an associate editor of *Labor History*, and has written many articles and reviews on organized labor.

PAUL S. HOLBO is associate professor of History at the University of Oregon, and author of numerous articles dealing with American foreign policy in the late nineteenth century.

ARI HOOGENBOOM is professor of History at Brooklyn College. He is especially interested in the development of bureaucracy, and wrote a basic monograph on the Gilded Age, *Outlawing the Spoils: A History of the Civil Service Reform Movement, 1865–1883* (Urbana: University of Illinois Press, 1961).

H. WAYNE MORGAN is professor of History at the University of Texas at Austin. He has written several books dealing with the United States in the late nineteenth century, including *William McKinley and His America* (Syracuse: Syracuse University Press, 1963), *America's Road to Empire: The War With Spain and Overseas Expansion* (New York: John Wiley and Sons, 1965), and

289

From Hayes to McKinley: National Party Politics, 1877–1896 (Syracuse: Syracuse University Press, 1969).

WALTER T. K. NUGENT is professor of History and associate dean of Liberal Arts at Indiana University. A student of populism and the currency question, his books include *The Tolerant Populists: Kansas Populism and Nativism* (Chicago: University of Chicago Press, 1963), *The Money Question During Reconstruction* (New York: W. W. Norton Co., 1967), and *Money and American Society, 1865–1900* (New York: The Free Press, 1968).

ROBERT R. ROBERTS is professor of History at California State College, San Bernardino. His special interests include late-nineteenth century religious thought and popular culture.

JOHN TIPPLE is professor of History at California State College, Los Angeles. He has written several books about American intellectual history, including most recently *Capitalist Revolution: Social Thought in America, 1890–1919*, and *Crisis of the American Dream: A History of Social Thought, 1920–1940*, both issued by Pegasus Publishers in New York.

R. HAL WILLIAMS is assistant professor of History at Yale University. He is writing an important case study of the California Democratic party in the Cleveland era.

Notes to the Chapters

2. Big Businessmen and a New Economy

1. Charles F. Adams, Jr., and Henry Adams, *Chapters of the Erie and Other Essays* (Boston: Osgood, 1871), p. 134.

2. Adolph Berle, Jr., and Gardiner Means, *The Modern Corporation and Private Property* (New York: Macmillan, 1932), pp. 10–17.

3. Cf. Frederick Jackson, *A Week in Wall Street by One Who Knows* (New York: n.p., 1841); James K. Medbery, *Men and Mysteries of Wall Street* (Boston: Fields and Osgood, 1870).

4. Adams and Adams, *Chapters of Erie,* p. 135.

5. Ray Stannard Baker, "What the United States Steel Corporation Really is and How it Works," *McClure's,* 18 (1901), 6.

6. Berle and Means, *The Modern Corporation,* pp. 2–6.

7. Charles Wallace Collins, *The Fourteenth Amendment and the States* (Boston: Little, Brown, 1912).

8. The *Nation,* Sept. 30, 1880, p. 232.

9. *Pollock vs. Farmers' Loan and Trust Co.,* 157 U.S. 429, 158 U.S., 601.

10. *Annual Report of the Secretary of the Treasury 1890* (Washington: GPO, 1890), p. xxi.

11. *Commercial and Financial Chronicle,* Dec. 18, 1886, p. 739; *U.S. Census 1910* (Washington: GPO, 1913), VIII, 32–33; Willard Long Thorp, *Business Annals* (New York, 1926), pp. 129–30.

12. Allan Nevins, *A Study in Power: John D. Rockefeller, Industrialist and Philanthropist,* 2 vols. (New York: Scribner's, 1953), II, 613.

13. James H. Bridge, *The Inside History of the Carnegie Steel Company* (New York, 1903), p. 295.

14. *Ibid.,* p. 364.

15. *The Tribune Monthly,* 4 (1892), p. 92; Sidney Ratner, ed., *New Light on the History of Great American Fortunes* (New York: Kelley, 1953), pp. xviii–xxiii; Ida M. Tarbell, *The Nationalizing of Business* (New York: Macmillan, 1936), p. 113.

16. David Graham Phillips, *The Shame of the Senate,* reprint from *Cosmopolitan,* 1906, 2, 94.

17. See John Tipple, "Who Were the Robber Barons?" (forthcoming).

18. *Commercial and Financial Chronicle,* 43 (March 27, 1886), 393.

19. James F. Hudson, *The Railways and the Republic* (New York: Harper Bros., 1886), pp. 25–66; A. B. Stickney, *The Railway Problem* (St. Paul: n.p., 1891), pp. 27–35; Frank Parsons, *The Railways, the Trusts, and the People* (Philadelphia: Taylor, 1906), pp. 25–56.

20. Henry Demarest Lloyd, *Lords of Industry* (New York: G. P. Putnam's

Sons, 1916), p. 2; Ida M. Tarbell, *The History of the Standard Oil Company,* 2 vols. (New York: Macmillan, 1904), II, 111.

21. *Report of the Special Committee on Railroads* (Albany, 1879), 49–50 (*Hepburn Report*).

22. Senate Reports, 49th Congress, 1st Session, no. 46, p. 199 (*Cullom Report*).

23. *New York Senate Report,* no. 50 (1888), 10.

24. *State of Ohio vs. Standard Oil Company,* 49 Ohio State, 137.

25. *Report of the Commissioner of Corporations on the Petroleum Industry* (Washington: GPO, 1907), I, xvi (*Smith Report*).

26. *Standard Oil Co. of New Jersey et al. vs. United States,* 221 U.S., 1.

27. Andrew Carnegie, "Wealth," *North American Review,* 168 (June, 1889), 657, 654; *The Gospel of Wealth* (New York: Century, 1900), p. 5.

28. *Cullom Report,* appendix, 213–15.

29. Ralph W. and Muriel E. Hidy, *Pioneering in Big Business 1882–1911* (New York: Harper Bros., 1955), pp. 678–79; cf. p. 43.

30. John D. Rockefeller, *Random Reminiscences of Men and Events* (New York: Doubleday, 1909), p. 112.

31. John Bates Clark, "The Society of the Future," *Independent,* 53 (July 18, 1901), 1649–51.

32. Carnegie, "Wealth," *North American Review,* 168 (June, 1889), 655.

33. John Moody, *The Truth About the Trusts* (New York: n.p., 1904), p. v.

34. See appended testimony to *Cullom Report.*

35. William Graham Sumner, "The Concentration of Wealth: Its Economic Justification," *Essays of William Graham Sumner,* 2 vols. (New Haven: Yale University Press, 1934), II, 166.

36. This view had extensive support in the business world. For a useful compendium see James H. Bridge, *The Trust: Its Book* (New York: Doubleday, 1902). See also Jonathan P. Dolliver, "Facts About Trusts: Arguments for Protection," *American Industries,* 2 (May 16, 1904); Franklin Head, ed., *Chicago Conference on Trusts* (Chicago: Civic Federation, 1900).

37. J. C. Welch and J. N. Camden, "The Standard Oil Company," *North American Review,* 136 (Feb., 1883), 181–200; Hidy and Hidy, *Pioneering in Big Business,* pp. 658, 680.

38. Rockefeller, *Reminiscences,* pp. 81–82.

39. Andrew Carnegie, "The Bugaboo of Trusts," *North American Review,* 148 (Feb., 1889), 141–42.

40. *Literary Digest,* 45 (Dec. 28, 1912), 1213.

41. Edward C. Kirkland, *Dream and Thought in the Business Community* (Ithaca: Cornell University Press, 1956), p. 27.

42. Hans B. Thorelli, *The Federal Antitrust Policy* (Baltimore: Johns Hopkins Press, 1955), p. 66.

43. *Ibid.,* pp. 500–54.

44. Henry Demarest Lloyd, *Wealth Against Commonwealth* (New York: Harper Bros., 1899), p. 496.

45. Walton Hamilton and Irene Till, *Antitrust in Action* (Washington: GPO, 1940), p. 6.

46. Thorelli, *The Federal Antitrust Policy,* p. 556.

47. Frederick Pollock, *The Genius of the Common Law* (New York: Columbia University Press, 1912), p. 95.

48. Arthur T. Hadley, *Railroad Transportation: Its History and Its Laws* (New York: Putnam's, 1885), pp. 69–70.

49. Richard Hofstadter, *Social Darwinism in American Thought, 1860–1915* (Philadelphia: University of Pennsylvania Press, 1945), p. 201.

50. John Lydenburg, "Pre-Muckraking: A Study of Attitudes Toward Politics as Revealed in American Fiction from 1870 through 1901" (unpublished Ph.D. Dissertation, Harvard University, 1946), p. 59.

51. Lloyd, *Wealth Against Commonwealth,* p. 496.

52. Senate Reports, no. 59, Jan. 10, 1900; B and D, 951.

53. Thurman W. Arnold, *The Folklore of Capitalism* (New Haven: Yale University Press, 1937), p. 211.

54. *Santa Clara Co. vs. Southern Pacific Railroad Co.,* 118 U.S., 394.

55. Arnold, *The Folklore of Capitalism,* p. 189.

56. See H. S. Commager, ed., *Documents of American History,* 2 vols. in 1 (New York: Appleton-Century-Crofts, 1949), II, 78.

57. Adams and Adams, *Chapters of Erie,* pp. 96–99.

58. Mark Van Doren, ed., *The Portable Walt Whitman* (New York: Viking, 1945), p. 400.

59. See Irvin G. Wyllie, *The Self-Made Man in America* (New Brunswick, N.J.: Rutgers University Press, 1954), p. 147.

60. Edward Everett Cassady, "The Business Man in the American Novel: 1856 to 1903" (unpublished Ph.D. Dissertation, University of California, Berkeley, 1939), p. 199.

61. Medbery, *Men and Mysteries,* p. 282; Fowler, 299.

62. Thomas W. Lawson, *Frenzied Finance* (New York: Ridgeway, Thayer, 1905), p. 174.

63. See *Report of Governor Hughes' Committee on Speculation in Securities and Commodities* (Albany, 1909), 4, 15; Alexander D. Noyes, "The Recent Economic History of the United States," *Quarterly Journal of Economics,* 19 (June, 1905), 167–209.

64. Demarest Lloyd, *Lords,* p. 341.

65. W. A. Croffutt, *The Vanderbilts and the Story of Their Fortune* (Chicago: Belford, Clarke, 1886), p. 129.

66. Francis A. Walker, "Democracy and Wealth," *Forum,* 10 (Sept., 1890), 245.

67. Joseph Dorfman, *The Economic Mind in American Civilization* (New York: Viking, 1949), III, 73.

68. Andrew Carnegie, *The Empire of Business* (New York: Doubleday, Page, 1902), p. 140.

69. Henry George, *Progress and Poverty* (New York: 1880), pp. 174–75; Lyman Abbott, "Industrial Democracy," *Review of Reviews,* 4 (June, 1890), 662.

70. Burton J. Hendrick, "The Vanderbilt Fortune," *McClure's Magazine,* 19 (Nov., 1908), 46–62.

71. New York State, *Assembly Documents,* 1867, no. 19, pp. 205–10.

72. See John Tipple, "The Anatomy of Prejudice: The Critical Foundations of the Robber Baron Legend" (unpublished Ph.D. Dissertation, Stanford University, 1958), pp. 15–17.

73. Frederick A. Cleveland and Fred W. Powell, *Railroad Promotion and Capitalization in the United States* (New York: Longmans, Green, 1909), p. 141.

74. New York State, *Assembly Documents, op. cit.*

75. See Edward Stanwood, *A History of Presidential Elections* (Boston: Houghton Mifflin, 1892), pp. 474–78.

3. The Workers' Search for Power

1. See John R. Commons *et al.,* eds., *A Documentary History of American Industrial Society* (New York: Russell and Russell, 1958), IX, pp. i–viii.

2. See Thomas C. Cochran, "The Social Sciences and the Problem of Historical Synthesis," in Fritz Stern, ed., *The Varieties of History* (New York: Meridian Books, 1956), pp. 352–56; Frank Tannenbaum, *A Philosophy of Labor* (New York: Knopf, 1951), p. 68; John Hall, "The Knights of St. Crispin in Massachusetts, 1869–1878," *Journal of Economic History,* 17 (June, 1958), 174–75.

3. The literature is voluminous, if not always accurate or comprehensive; see Harold Williamson, ed., *The Growth of the American Economy* (New York: Prentice, Hall, 1951), p. 462; Anthony Bimba, *The Molly Maguires* (New York: International Pubs., 1932); J. Walter Coleman, *The Molly Maguire Riots* (Richmond, Va.: Garrett and Massie, 1936); George McNeil, ed., *The Labor Movement* (New York, 1892), pp. 241–67; Andrew Roy, *A History of the Coal Miners of the United States* (Columbus: J. L. Trauger, 1903); John R. Commons *et al., History of Labor in the United States* (New York: Macmillan, 1918), II, pp. 179–80; McAlister Coleman, *Men and Coal* (New York: Farrar & Rinehart, 1943), pp. 42–44; Arthur Suffern, *Conciliation and Arbitration in the Coal Industry of America* (Boston: Houghton Mifflin, 1915), pp. 7–17.

4. Richard Lester, *Economics of Labor* (New York: Macmillan, 1947), p. 545; emphasis added.

5. Herbert Harris, *American Labor* (New Haven: Yale University Press, 1938), p. 75.

6. Selig Perlman, "Upheaval and Reorganization Since 1876," in Commons *et al., History of Labor,* II, 196.

7. J. A. Schumpeter, "The Problem of Classes," in Reinhard Bendix and Seymour Lipset, eds., *Class, Status and Power* (Glencoe: Free Press, 1953), p. 79.

8. *Loc. cit.*

9. Adna Weber, *The Growth of Cities in the Nineteenth Century* (New York: Macmillan, 1899), pp. 433–34.

10. *Chicago Times,* May 22, 1876.

11. *New York Times,* Nov. 20, 1876.

12. *Chicago Tribune,* July 4, 1876.

13. Samuel Lane Loomis, *Modern Cities and Their Religious Problems* (New York: Baker and Taylor, 1887), pp. 60–61, 63–66.

14. Massachusetts Bureau of Labor Statistics, *Second Annual Report 1870–1871* (Boston, 1871), p. 475.

15. See, e.g., Louis Wirth, "Urbanism as a Way of Life," in Paul Hatt and Albert Reiss, Jr., eds., *Cities and Society* (Glencoe: Free Press, 1957), pp. 36–63; Bert F. Hoselitz, "The City, the Factory, and Economic Growth," *American Economic Review,* 45 (May, 1955), 166–84.

16. "The Distribution of Wealth," *Cooper's New Monthly,* 1 (July, 1874), 7–9.

17. *Iron Molder's Journal,* Jan., 1874, 204.

18. See Ohio Bureau of Labor Statistics, *First Annual Report 1877* (Columbus, 1878), pp. 156–92.

19. A. Ross Eckler, "A Measure of the Severity of Depression, 1873–1932," *Review of Economic Statistics,* 15 (May, 1933), 75–81; O. V. Wells, "The Depression of 1873–1879," *Agricultural History,* 11 (July, 1937), 237–49; Rendigs Fels, "American Business Cycles, 1865–1879," *American Economic Review,* 41 (Sept., 1951), 325–49: Alvin Hansen, *Business Cycles and National Income* (New York: Norton, 1951), pp. 24–26, 39–41.

20. T. E. Burton, *Financial Crises and Periods of Industrial and Commercial Depression* (New York: Appleton, 1902), p. 344.

21. *Annual Report of the Secretary of the American Iron and Steel Association of the Year 1874* (Philadelphia, 1875), pp. 4–5.

22. New York Association for Improving the Condition of the Poor, *Thirty-first Annual Report* (New York, 1874), p. 28.

23. *New York Graphic,* Jan. 14, 1874.

24. *American Manufacturer,* Oct. 30, 1873.

25. *Annual Report of the Secretary of the American Iron and Steel Association for the Year 1874,* pp. 12, 81–82.

26. *Vulcan Record,* 1 (Sept., 1874), 12–14.

27. *New York Times,* Oct. 27, Nov. 2, 15, 1873.

28. *Chicago Times,* Oct. 3, Nov. 3, 1873.

29. *Iron Molder's Journal,* 1 (Dec., 1873), 161; *Iron Age,* May 26, 1874, 14.

30. *Annual Report of the Secretary of the American Iron and Steel Association for the Year 1874,* pp. 81–82.

31. See Herbert G. Gutman, "Trouble on the Railroads in 1873–1874: Prelude to the 1877 Crisis," *Labor History,* 2 (Spring, 1962), 215–35; *Cincinnati Enquirer,* Feb.–March, 1874; *Chicago Times,* Nov. 12, 1873; *Chicago Tribune,* Nov. 10–20, 1874.

32. *Workingman's Advocate,* March 28, June 27–July 4, 1874; John James, "The Miner's Strike in the Hocking Valley," *Cooper's New Monthly,* 1 (July, 1874), 4.

33. *Chicago Tribune,* April 23, 1874; *Workingman's Advocate,* July 11–18, 1874; *New York World,* July 23, 1874.

34. *Workingman's Advocate,* March 28, 1874; *Chicago Times,* Nov. 7–9, 1874; *Cincinnati Commercial,* Feb. 11, 1874; *Iron Age,* Aug. 13, 1874, 14.

35. See Herbert G. Gutman, "Two Lockouts in Pennsylvania, 1873–1874," *The Pennsylvania Magazine of History and Biography,* 83 (July, 1959), 317–18, 322–26.

36. *Iron Molder's Journal,* Dec., 1874, 138.

37. *Chicago Tribune,* Nov. 19, 1874.

38. *Workingman's Advocate,* April 14, 1874.

39. *Ibid.*

40. *Cincinnati Commercial,* Jan. 18, 1874.

41. *Workingman's Advocate,* Sept. 5–12, Nov. 7, 28, 1874.

42. *Iron Molder's Journal,* Dec., 1874, 138.

43. *Frostburg Mining Journal,* Nov. 25, 1876.

44. *Cooper's New Monthly,* 1 (Jan., 1874), 16.

45. *Iron Age,* March 5, 1874; *Cincinnati Commercial,* Jan. 29, Feb. 3, 1874.

46. *Portsmouth Times,* Feb. 7, 1874.

47. See Herbert G. Gutman, "The Braidwood Lockout of 1874," *Journal of the Illinois State Historical Society,* 53 (Spring, 1960), 5–28.

48. See Herbert G. Gutman, "An Iron Workers' Strike in Ohio Valley, 1873–1874," *Ohio Historical Quarterly,* 68 (Oct., 1959), 353–70.

49. See Herbert G. Gutman, "Reconstruction in Ohio: Negroes in the Hocking Valley Coal Mines in 1873 and 1874," *Labor History,* 3 (Fall, 1962), 243–64.

50. *Cincinnati Commercial,* May 23, June 4, 1874; Edward Wieck, *The American Miners' Association* (New York: Russell Sage Foundation, 1940), p. 141.

51. *Cincinnati Commercial,* May 23, 1874; *Hocking Sentinel,* Dec. 25, 1873, Jan. 8, 22, Feb. 12, 26, March 5, 1874.

52. *Logan Republican,* April 4, 1874.

53. *Cincinnati Commercial,* May 23, 1874; *Workingman's Advocate,* May 23, 1874.

54. *Athens Messenger,* May 7, 1874.

55. *Hocking Sentinel,* April 1, 1874; *Chicago Tribune,* June 30, 1874.

56. *Cincinnati Commercial,* June 13, 14, 15, 1874; *New Lexington Democratic Herald,* June 18, 1874.

57. *Cleveland Leader,* July 7, 1874.

58. *Cincinnati Commercial,* Oct. 3, 1874, March 22, 1875; *New Lexington Democratic Herald,* March 25, 1875; *Hocking Sentinel,* March 4, 25, 1875; *Ohio State Journal,* April 1, 1875.

59. *New York Graphic,* Nov. 10, 1873; *Chicago Tribune,* Dec. 23, 1873; New York Association for Improving the Condition of the Poor, *Thirtieth Annual Report, 1873* (New York: 1873), pp. 41ff.

60. *New York Sun,* Oct. 22, Nov. 4, Nov. 20–Dec. 20, 1873; *Chicago Times,* Dec. 1–31, 1873.

61. *New York World,* Dec. 27, 1873; see sources in note 60.

62. *New York Tribune,* Dec. 12, 1873.

63. *Ibid.*

64. *Chicago Times,* Dec. 23, 30, 1873; *Chicago Tribune,* Dec. 23–30, 1873.

65. See *Chicago Tribune,* Dec. 29, 1873; Thurlow Weed to the Editor, *New York Tribune,* Dec. 20, 1873; *Cumberland Civilian and Times* (Maryland), Feb. 12, 1874.

66. *New York Tribune,* June 22, 1874.

67. *Chicago Times,* Aug. 26, 1874.

68. *New York Herald,* Nov. 2, 1873; *New York Times,* June 3, 1874; *Cleveland Leader,* June 18, 1874; *Chicago Tribune,* April 15, 1874.

69. *Pittsburgh Post,* Nov. 21–30, 1873.

70. *Cleveland Plain Dealer,* May 7–11, 1874.

71. *New York Toiler,* Aug. 22, 1874; *New York Sun,* July 6, 1874; Board of Health of the City of New York, *Fourth Annual Report, May 1, 1873 to April 30, 1874* (New York, 1874), pp. 96–97.

72. *New York Times,* June 25–30, 1874; *New York Tribune,* June 2–14, 1874.

73. *New York Sun,* June 2, 10, 1874; *New York World,* July 23–24, 1874.

74. *Chicago Times,* May 22, 1876; *Iron Age,* April 27, 1876, 24.

75. See Gutman, "Two Lockouts in Pennsylvania, 1873–1874," and Gutman, "Trouble on the Railroads in 1873–1874: Prelude to the 1877 Crisis."

76. Louis Hartz, *The Liberal Tradition in America* (New York: Harcourt,

Brace, 1955), pp. 110–13, 189–227; Richard Hofstadter, *The American Political Tradition and the Men Who Made It* (New York: Knopf, 1948), pp. v–ix; John Higham, ed., *The Reconstruction of American History* (New York: Humanities Press, 1962), pp. 21–24, 119–56.

77. Cochran, *Railroad Leaders*, p. 181.

4. Reform Thought and the Genteel Tradition

1. A spirited and comprehensive critique of nineteenth-century liberal reform may be found in John G. Sproat, *"The Best Men": Liberal Reformers in the Gilded Age* (New York: Oxford University Press, 1968).

2. Richard Hofstadter, *Anti-intellectualism in American Life* (New York: Knopf, 1963), pp. 188, 189; undated letter by "Gail Hamilton" [Mary A. Dodge], in vol. 5, R. R. Bowker Papers, Library of Congress; J. B. Bishop to John Hay, Sept. 13, 1904, Hay Papers, Library of Congress.

3. Hofstadter, *Anti-intellectualism*, pp. 179–91.

4. Forbes to Norton [summer, 1864], Norton Papers, Harvard University; Henry Adams, *The Education of Henry Adams* (New York: Modern Library, 1931), pp. 292, 319; Schurz to T. W. Higginson, Oct. 13, 1882, Higginson Papers, Harvard University.

5. See James Q. Wilson, *The Amateur Democrat* (Chicago: University of Chicago Press, 1962), Chap. 1.

6. See Robert K. Merton's seminal essay, "Patterns of Influence: Local and Cosmopolitan Influentials," in Merton, *Social Theory and Social Structure*, revised edition (Glencoe: Free Press, 1957), pp. 387–420. Samuel P. Hays and Ernest R. May, among others, have demonstrated the relevance of Merton's suggestions to late nineteenth-century American society.

7. W. C. Ford, ed., *A Cycle of Adams Letters, 1861–1865* (Boston: Houghton Mifflin, 1920), I, 196. See George M. Fredrickson, *The Inner Civil War: Northern Intellectuals and the Crisis of the Union* (New York: Harper & Row, 1968), pp. 111–50, 183–95.

8. Bowles to Whitelaw Reid, Feb. 17, 1871, Reid Papers, Library of Congress.

9. Barbara M. Solomon, *Ancestors and Immigrants: A. Changing New England Tradition* (Cambridge: Harvard University Press, 1956), pp. 27–30.

10. Godkin to Norton, Aug. 23 [1866], and Sept. 1, 1866; Norton to Godkin, Aug. 26, 1866, Godkin Papers, Harvard University.

11. Curtis to Daniel Ricketson, Jan. 10, 1869, Curtis Papers, Harvard University.

12. Olmsted to F. N. Knapp, June 20, 1870, Olmsted Papers, Library of Congress.

13. See Paul Goodman, "Ethics and Enterprise: The Values of a Boston Elite, 1800–1860," *American Quarterly*, 18 (Fall, 1966), 437–51.

14. Olmsted to Godkin, Feb. 20 [1864?], Godkin Papers.

15. David Donald, *Lincoln Reconsidered: Essays on the Civil War Era*, second edition (New York: Vintage, 1961), Chap. XI; Stanley M. Elkins, *Slavery: A Problem in American Institutional and Intellectual Life* (Chicago: University of Chicago Press, 1959), Chaps. II and IV; Rowland Berthoff, "The American Social

Order: A Conservative Hypothesis," *American Historical Review,* 65 (April, 1960), 495–514.

16. Robert A. Dahl, *Who Governs? Democracy and Power in an American City* (New Haven: Yale University Press, 1961), pp. 11–37; Alexander B. Callow, Jr., *The Tweed Ring* (New York: Oxford University Press, 1965), pp. 5–16; Sam B. Warner, *The Private City: Philadelphia in Three Periods of its Growth* (Philadelphia: University of Pennsylvania Press, 1968), pp. 79–98; W. N. Chambers and W. D. Burnham, eds., *The American Party Systems: Stages of Political Development* (New York: Oxford University Press, 1967), pp. 11–14, 292–94.

17. Chambers and Burnham, *Party Systems,* p. 122.

18. Lea to Norton, July 4, 1866, and March 17, 1880, Norton Papers; H. A. Brown to Schurz, March 14, 1877, Schurz Papers, Library of Congress.

19. Cox to James A. Garfield, June 5, 1871, and Sept. 18, 1880, Garfield Papers, Library of Congress; William Minot to Schurz, May 8, 1885, Schurz Papers.

20. *Nation,* April 13, 1871, 252; Godkin to Norton, March 13 [1884], Norton Papers.

21. Samuel P. Hays, "The Politics of Reform in Municipal Government in the Progressive Era," *Pacific Northwest Quarterly,* 55 (1964), 157–69; Geoffrey Blodgett, *The Gentle Reformers: Massachusetts Democrats in the Cleveland Era* (Cambridge: Harvard University Press, 1966), pp. 122–27; Roy Lubove, *The Professional Altruist: The Emergence of Social Work as a Career, 1880–1930* (New York: Atheneum, 1969), pp. 1–21.

22. Godkin to Olmsted, Dec. 25 [1864], Godkin Papers; Curtis to A. D. White, Sept. 19, 1866, White Papers, Cornell University; Cox to Garfield, Jan. 1, 1866, and April 10, 1866, Garfield Papers.

23. Samuel Shapiro, *Richard Henry Dana, Jr., 1815–1882* (East Lansing: Michigan State University Press, 1961), pp. 141–53; Adams to Atkinson, Oct. 5, 1868, and Feb. 1, 1869, Atkinson Papers, Massachusetts Historical Society; Eliot to D. C. Gilman, June 18, 1883, Gilman Papers, Johns Hopkins University.

24. White to Schurz, Dec. 25, 1870, Schurz Papers; Adams to Norton, Jan. 13, 1871, Norton Papers.

25. The currency of Spencer's Social Darwinist ideology among the gentry was limited. While his formulations received respect, they rarely punctuated the private correspondence of the liberal reformers. Godkin, for one, had reservations about Spencer's view of the American scene. See "Mr. Herbert Spencer on American Civilization," *Nation,* Oct. 26, 1882, 348.

26. Joseph Dorfman, *The Economic Mind in American Civilization* (New York: Viking, 1949), III, 8–11; Wells to Atkinson, July 17, 1866, and [Jan. 15, 1867], Atkinson Papers; Wells to Garfield, Aug. 8 [1871], Garfield Papers.

27. Wells to Garfield, May 14 [1871], Garfield Papers; Atkinson to Wells [July 1883], Wells Papers, Library of Congress.

28. Bowles to Wells, June 9, 1876, Adams to Wells, Dec. 30, 1879, Wells Papers; Atkinson to Thomas F. Bayard, June 3, 1878, Bayard Papers, Library of Congress.

29. Wells *et al.* to Grover Cleveland, Jan. 26, 1885, Cleveland Papers, Library of Congress. The reformers hoped, of course, that Cleveland's election would remedy the situation. The meaning of Cleveland's popularity is skillfully explored in Robert Kelley, *The Transatlantic Persuasion: The Liberal-Democratic Mind in the Age of Gladstone* (New York: Knopf, 1969), Chap. 8.

30. Frank Luther Mott, *A History of American Magazines* (Cambridge: Har-

vard University Press, 1938), III, 337, and *passim;* Norton to Godkin, Jan. 30, 1868; James to Mrs. Godkin, May 21, 1902, Godkin Papers.

31. Burt to Godkin, Dec. 31, 1899, Godkin Papers. See Morton Keller's excellent editorial Introduction to E. L. Godkin, *Problems of Modern Democracy,* John Harvard Library edition (Cambridge: Harvard University Press, 1966), pp. vii–xli.

32. Adams to Olmsted, March 29, 1861, Godkin to Olmsted, May 9 [1863], untitled prospectus [June ?, 1863], Box 5, Olmsted Papers.

33. Atkinson to Norton, Aug. 12, 1865, Godkin to Norton, Aug. 16, 1865, and Dec. 30, 1865, Godkin Papers. See William M. Armstrong, "The Freedman's Movement and the Founding of the *Nation," Journal of American History,* 53 (March, 1967), 708–26.

34. Mott, *American Magazines,* III, 343; Curtis to Godkin, Sept. 9, 1870, Godkin Papers.

35. Eliot to Godkin, Nov. 30, 1899, Godkin Papers.

36. For Olmsted, see Albert Fein, ed., *Landscape into Cityscape: Frederick Law Olmsted's Plans for a Greater New York City* (Ithaca: Cornell University Press, 1967).

37. For the A.S.S.A., see L. L. Bernard and Jessie Bernard, *Origins of American Sociology* (New York: Crowell, 1943), pp. 527–607; Whitelaw Reid to Garfield, Dec. 15, 1868, Reid Papers; Horace White to F. B. Sanborn, Oct. 14, 1878, White Papers, Illinois State Historical Society.

38. *Brooklyn Daily Eagle,* Sept. 26, 1877.

39. G. F. Williams to Schurz, Nov. 24, 1884, W. D. Foulke to Schurz, Dec. 22, 1866, Schurz Papers.

40. Bowles to Wells, March 25, 1874, George to Wells, Dec. 9, 1880, Wells Papers; Gronlund to Schurz, Jan. 28, 1889, Schurz Papers.

41. Benjamin G. Rader, *The Academic Mind and Reform: The Influence of Richard T. Ely in American Life* (Lexington: University of Kentucky Press, 1966), pp. 28–42; Daniel M. Fox, *The Discovery of Abundance: Simon Patten and the Transformation of Social Theory* (Ithaca: Cornell University Press, 1967), pp 11, 29, 34–39; Patten to Atkinson, March 9, 1890, W. C. Ford to Wells, June 14, 1890, Wells Papers; Godkin to Gilman, Feb. 17, 1892, Gilman Papers.

42. Godkin to Norton, July 13, 1896, Norton Papers.

43. J. M. Forbes to Godkin, Feb. 27, 1891, Godkin Papers.

5. Civil Service Reform and Public Morality

1. I am grateful to the University of Illinois Press for permission to reprint portions of my book, *Outlawing the Spoils: A History of the Civil Service Reform Movement, 1865–1883* (Urbana, 1961). I am also grateful to the editor of *The Historian* for permission to reprint portions of my article: "An Analysis of Civil Service Reformers," *The Historian,* 23 (Nov., 1960), 54–78. See Charles Francis Adams, Jr., and Henry Adams, *Chapters of Erie and Other Essays* (Ithaca: Cornell University Press, 1960); Ishbel Ross, *Proud Kate* (New York: Harper Bros., 1953), pp. 246–49; W. A. Swanberg, *Jim Fisk* (New York: Scribner's, 1959); Robert Shaplen, *Free Love and Heavenly Sinners* (New York: Knopf, 1954).

2. Alexander B. Callow, Jr., *The Tweed Ring* (New York: Oxford University Press, 1966); the *Nation,* April 11, 1867, 286.

3. C. Vann Woodward, *Origins of the New South 1877–1913* (Baton Rouge: Louisiana State University Press, 1951), pp. 66–74; Albert R. Kitzhaber, "Götterdämmerung in Topeka: The Downfall of Senator Pomeroy," *Kansas Historical Quarterly,* 18 (Aug., 1950), 243–78.

4. Though no one denies that Tweed was corrupt, some historians have credited him with positive motives and accomplishments. John W. Pratt, in "Boss Tweed's Public Welfare Program," *The New-York Historical Society Quarterly,* 45 (Oct., 1961), 396–411, emphasizes Tweed's philanthropic activities, while Seymour J. Mandelbaum, in *Boss Tweed's New York* (New York: John Wiley, 1965), argues that Tweed used corruption to coordinate a fragmented city and to attack its manifold problems.

5. William L. Riordan, *Plunkitt of Tammany Hall* (New York: Knopf, 1948), pp. 3–8.

6. Rollo Ogden, ed., *Life and Letters of Edwin Lawrence Godkin,* 2 vols. (New York: Macmillan, 1907); William M. Armstrong, *E. L. Godkin and American Foreign Policy, 1865–1900* (New York: Bookman Associates, 1957).

7. See U.S. Revenue Commission, "Revenue System of the United States," *House Executive Documents,* 39th Congress, 1st session, VII, No. 34, pp. 44–51; Charles Eliot Norton, ed., *Orations and Addresses of George William Curtis* (New York: Harper Bros., 1894), II, 39; W. W. Belknap to John A. Logan, Aug. 15, 1872, Logan Papers, Library of Congress; "Senator Trumbull and the Revenue," *Harper's Weekly,* Sept. 7, 1872, 690; Curtis to Belknap, Aug. 25, 1872, and Curtis, Cattell, *et al.,* to Logan, Sept. [?], 1872, Logan Papers. For another exaggeration of statistics by reformers, see *The Congressional Globe,* 41st Congress, 3rd session, 400, 459–60, 666. In fairness to Johnson, the improvement of the Internal Revenue Service no doubt resulted more from the drastic elimination and simplification of excise taxes than from Grant.

8. Norton to Godkin, Nov. 3, 1871, Godkin Papers, Harvard University.

9. See Kermit Vanderbilt, *Charles Eliot Norton* (Cambridge: Harvard University Press, 1959); and Sara Norton and M. A. DeWolfe Howe, eds., *Letters of Charles Eliot Norton,* 2 vols. (Boston: Houghton Mifflin, 1913); Norton to Godkin, July 20, 1866, Godkin Papers.

10. Norton to Godkin, March 13, 1867, May 30, 1868, Godkin Papers; Norton to Curtis, July 24, 1868, Norton Papers, Harvard University; Norton to Curtis, Jan. 29, 1869, *ibid.;* Curtis to Norton, March 13, 1869, Curtis Papers, Harvard University; Norton to Curtis, July 22, 1869, Norton Papers.

11. See Gordon Milne, *George William Curtis & the Genteel Tradition* (Bloomington: Indiana University Press, 1956), and Hoogenboom, *Outlawing the Spoils, passim.*

12. The *Nation,* Nov. 1, 1866, 341; *ibid.,* Nov. 29, 1866, 422; Curtis to Norton, Jan. 2, 1867, Curtis Papers; "Reform of the Civil Service," *Harper's Weekly,* March 2, 1867, 130.

13. Curtis to Norton, Sept. 17, 1870, Curtis Papers.

14. The *Nation,* Feb. 20, 1873, 126–27; *ibid.,* March 20, 1873, 189.

15. Curtis to Norton, Sept. 19, 1873, Curtis Papers; "The Prospects of Civil Service Reform," *Harper's Weekly,* Oct. 25, 1873, 938.

16. Henry Adams to Charles Francis Adams, Jr., Feb. 23, and April 29, 1869,

and Henry Adams to Charles M. Gaskell, April 19 and June 20, 1869, in Worthington Chauncey Ford, ed., *Letters of Henry Adams 1858–1891* (Boston: Houghton Mifflin, 1930), pp. 152, 156–57, 161–62.

17. Henry Adams to Edward Atkinson, Feb. 1, 1869, and Henry Adams to Gaskell, Aug. 27, 1869, *ibid.*, pp. 151, 165–66.

18. Henry Brooks Adams, "Civil Service Reform," *North American Review,* 109 (Oct., 1869), 443–75; the *Nation,* Nov. 11, 1869, 415.

19. See Hoogenboom, *Outlawing the Spoils, passim.* For two recent analyses of reformers, see Geoffrey Blodgett, *The Gentle Reformers: Massachusetts Democrats in the Cleveland Era* (Cambridge: Harvard University Press, 1966), and John G. Sproat, *"The Best Men": Liberal Reformers in the Gilded Age* (New York: Oxford University Press, 1968).

20. Julius Bing, "Our Civil Service," *Putnam's Magazine,* new series, 2 (Aug., 1868), 233.

21. Joint Select Committee on Retrenchment, "Civil Service of the United States," *House Reports,* 40th Congress, 2nd session, II, No. 47, pp. 2, 7. Civil servants may actually have numbered 70,000 in 1867. Civil service statistics are frequently contradictory and must be used with caution. See Paul P. Van Riper, *History of the United States Civil Service* (Evanston: Row, Peterson, 1958), pp. 56–59.

22. Leonard D. White, *The Jacksonians* (New York: Macmillan, 1954), pp. 394–98. These generalizations on the personnel system of 1860 are applicable five years later.

23. Joint Select Committee on Retrenchment, "Civil Service of the United States," pp. 23, 40, 203.

24. *Ibid.,* p. 40.

25. "Civil Service Reform," I, 27, 31–35, 91–92, III, 558–59, Elliott Papers, Library of the U.S. Civil Service Commission, Washington, D.C.

26. See *The Congressional Record,* 47th Congress, 1st session, 79–85.

27. George F. Howe, *Chester A. Arthur* (New York: Dodd, Mead, 1934), pp. 48–49.

28. Joint Select Committee on Retrenchment, "Report," *Senate Reports,* 41st Congress, 3rd session, No. 380, pp. 1–2.

29. The *Nation,* Jan. 11, 1872, 17. See also William J. Hartman, "Politics and Patronage: The New York Customs House, 1852–1902" (unpublished Ph.D. Dissertation, Columbia University, 1952), pp. 165–72. For the report based upon the hearings, see Committee on Investigation and Retrenchment, "Report," *Senate Reports,* 42nd Congress, 2nd session, IV (in 3 parts), No. 227.

30. Richard Lowitt, *A Merchant Prince of the Nineteenth Century: William E. Dodge* (New York: Columbia University Press, 1954), pp. 275–83. See also "The Extraordinary Element in the Case of Phelps, Dodge & Co.," the *Nation,* May 1, 1873, 297–99; *ibid.,* April 24, 1873, 278; *ibid.,* Aug. 28, 1873, 138; *ibid.,* Jan. 8, 1874, 21–22.

31. See Hartman, "Politics and Patronage," 186–91; Leonard D. White, *The Republican Era* (New York: Macmillan, 1958), pp. 123–26.

32. Hayes to Merritt, Feb. 4, 1879, Hayes Papers, Rutherford B. Hayes Library, Fremont, Ohio.

33. Silas W. Burt, "A Brief History of the Civil Service Reform Movement in the United States," pp. K–L, in the Burt Writings, New York Public Library.

34. Dorman B. Eaton, "Civil Service Reform in the New York City Post Office and Custom House," *House Executive Documents,* 46th Congress, 3rd session, XXVIII, No. 94, pp. 35–37; Curtis to Burt, Aug. 18, 1879, Burt Collection, New-York Historical Society; *New York Times,* July 9, 1879.

35. Eaton, "Civil Service Reform," 39–43.

36. See Ari Hoogenboom, "The Pendleton Act and the Civil Service," *The American Historical Review,* 64 (Jan., 1959), 301–18.

6. Money, Politics, and Society: The Currency Question

1. As John Hope Franklin points out in *Reconstruction After the Civil War* (Chicago: University of Chicago Press, 1961), pp. 196ff.: "Still another widely held misconception is that the reconstruction period was of long duration."

2. The Latin Monetary Union was a significant regional exception, though short-lived, from 1865 into the seventies; see H. Parker Willis, *A History of the Latin Monetary Union* (Chicago: University of Chicago Press, 1901).

3. This outline of Civil War financial policy roughly follows the excellent discussion by Bray Hammond, "The North's Empty Purse, 1861–1862," *American Historical Review,* 57 (Oct., 1961), 1–15.

4. For an extended discussion of the beginnings of the silver question from 1865 through the Coinage Act, see W. T. K. Nugent, *Money and American Society, 1865–1880* (New York: Free Press, 1968), Chaps. 8–13.

5. The first modern analysis of the Specie Resumption Act along these lines was Irwin Unger's "Business Men and Specie Resumption," *Political Science Quarterly,* 74 (March, 1959), 46–70, and his subsequent publications, especially *The Greenback Era* (Princeton: Princeton University Press, 1962).

6. See John A. Garraty, *The New Commonwealth 1877–1890* (New York: Harper & Row, 1968), Chap. 2. For a treatment of economic and social conditions among western Populists, including a contrast between Populist and non-Populist mortgaging, see W. T. K. Nugent, "Some Parameters of Populism," *Agricultural History,* 40 (Oct., 1966), 255–70.

7. This is correctly stated in O. Gene Clanton, *Kansas Populism: Ideas and Men* (Lawrence: University Press of Kansas, 1969), pp. 31–32.

8. For a different view of Populist ideology, see Norman Pollack, *The Populist Response to Industrial America* (Cambridge: Harvard University Press, 1962).

9. Milton Friedman and Anna Jacobson Schwartz, *A Monetary History of the United States, 1867–1960* (Princeton: Princeton University Press for the National Bureau of Economic Research, 1963), p. 97.

10. Free silver was hardly a novel issue in 1896; see James A. Barnes, "Myths of the Bryan Campaign," *Mississippi Valley Historical Review,* 34 (Dec., 1947), 367–404.

11. For recent histories of the campaign and election of 1896, see Stanley L. Jones, *The Presidential Election of 1896* (Madison: University of Wisconsin Press, 1964); Paul W. Glad, *McKinley, Bryan, and the People* (Philadelphia: Lippincott, 1964); and H. Wayne Morgan, *William McKinley and His America* (Syracuse: Syracuse University Press, 1963).

7. "Dry Bones and Dead Language": The Democratic Party

1. *Atlanta Constitution,* March 5, 1885; *Washington Post,* Nov. 5, 1884. Also, *Raleigh News and Observer,* March 5, 1885.

2. James A. Barnes, *John G. Carlisle: Financial Statesman* (New York: Dodd, Mead, 1931), p. 93; the *Nation,* Jan. 14, 1886, 21.

3. *Washington Post,* March 2, 1889; Henry Watterson to Samuel J. Tilden, Nov. 29, 1878, quoted in Charles Callan Tansill, *The Congressional Career of Thomas Francis Bayard, 1869–1885* (Washington, D.C.: Georgetown University Press, 1946), pp. 221–22. Irving Katz, in *August Belmont: A Political Biography* (New York: Columbia University Press, 1968), details the efforts of the Democratic national chairman to hold the party together during these years. For the party's fragmented organization in various areas of the country, see Horace Samuel Merrill, *Bourbon Democracy of the Middle West, 1865–1896* (Baton Rouge: Louisiana State University Press, 1953), p. 57; William J. Cooper, Jr., *The Conservative Regime: South Carolina, 1877–1890* (Baltimore: Johns Hopkins Press, 1968), pp. 19–20; Geoffrey Blodgett, *The Gentle Reformers: Massachusetts Democrats in the Cleveland Era* (Cambridge: Harvard University Press, 1966), pp. 10–11.

4. See Oliver Carlson and Ernest Sutherland Bates, *Hearst, Lord of San Simeon* (New York: Viking, 1936), p. 28. The Republican party, of course, also represented a union of differing interests, but the Republicans usually managed to maintain a degree of party cohesion which eluded their opponents. A veteran Washington reporter noted of the Republican and Democratic parties, respectively: "One is an organized, well disciplined army; the other a headless undisciplined force." O. O. Stealey, *Twenty Years in the Press Gallery* (New York: Publishers Printing, 1906), p. 113.

5. The Massachusetts Democratic party's "chronic weakness for the local and the expedient," noted by Geoffrey Blodgett, characterized the party in almost every state. Blodgett, *The Gentle Reformers,* p. 69.

6. Thomas F. Bayard to Don M. Dickinson, July 11, 1891, in the Don M. Dickinson Papers, Library of Congress. See also, Horatio Seymour, "The Political Situation," *North American Review,* 136 (Feb., 1883), 153–58. Information on the Bourbon Democrats can be found in Horace Samuel Merrill, *William Freeman Vilas: Doctrinaire Democrat* (Madison: State Historical Society of Wisconsin, 1954).

7. Harold Zink, *City Bosses in the United States: A Study of Twenty Municipal Bosses* (Durham: Duke University Press, 1930), p. 71. C. Vann Woodward, in *Reunion and Reaction* (Boston: Little, Brown and Company, 1951), notes the bitter conflict between northern and southern Democrats over the question of federal appropriations. For anti-monopoly sentiment within the party, see R. Hal Williams, "Politics and Reform: The California Democrats in the Cleveland Years" (unpublished Ph.D. Dissertation, Yale University, 1968), pp. 16–73, 271–316.

8. Senator Arthur Pue Gorman of Maryland, for example, defined his tariff views in an 1883 Senate speech: "I am a protectionist to the extent of so distributing the amount of tax that is necessary to be levied for the support of the Government as will protect American interests, and no further." John R. Lambert, *Arthur Pue*

Gorman (Baton Rouge: Louisiana State University Press, 1953), p. 89. See also, Joseph Frazier Wall, *Henry Watterson: Reconstructed Rebel* (New York: Oxford University Press, 1956), pp. 87–171; James A. Barnes, "Protection, Politics, and Pennsylvania," *Pennsylvania History,* 31 (Jan., 1964), 9–18; Tansill, *Congressional Career of Thomas Francis Bayard,* p. 308; Gerald W. McFarland, "The Breakdown of Deadlock: The Cleveland Democracy in Connecticut, 1884–1894," *The Historian,* 31 (May, 1969), 385–91.

9. "The Tariff Difficulty of the Democrats," the *Nation,* Oct. 14, 1880, 267–68; Wall, *Henry Watterson,* 171; Herbert J. Clancy, *The Presidential Election of 1880* (Chicago: Loyola University Press, 1958).

10. *New York Herald,* Nov. 3, 1884; William A. Robinson, *Thomas B. Reed, Parliamentarian* (New York: Dodd, Mead, 1930), p. 155; Wall, *Henry Watterson,* p. 123.

11. William L. Wilson, *The National Democratic Party: Its History, Principles, Achievements, and Aims* (Baltimore: H. L. Harvey, 1888), p. iii. Also, Alexander Clarence Flick, *Samuel Jones Tilden: A Study in Political Sagacity* (New York: Dodd, Mead, 1939), p. 188; Carl N. Degler, "American Political Parties and the Rise of the City: An Interpretation," *Journal of American History,* 51 (June, 1964), 41; W. Dean Burnham, *Presidential Ballots, 1836–1892* (Baltimore: Johns Hopkins Press, 1955), pp. 118–58.

12. C. Vann Woodward, *Origins of the New South, 1877–1913* (Baton Rouge: Louisiana State University Press, 1951), pp. 75–106; Cooper, *The Conservative Regime,* p. 15; Dewey W. Grantham, Jr., *The Democratic South* (Athens: University of Georgia Press, 1963), pp. 25–26; Raymond H. Pulley, *Old Virginia Restored: An Interpretation of the Progressive Impulse, 1870–1930* (Charlottesville: University Press of Virginia, 1968), pp. 24–65. Republican attempts to invade the South are detailed in Stanley P. Hirshson, *Farewell to the Bloody Shirt: Northern Republicans and the Southern Negro, 1877–1893* (Bloomington: Indiana University Press, 1962).

13. Richard Joseph Jensen, "The Winning of the Midwest: A Social History of Midwestern Elections, 1888–1896" (unpublished Ph.D. Dissertation, Yale University, 1967), pp. 68–79, 207–20; Frederick C. Luebke, "German Immigrants and the Churches in Nebraska, 1889–1915," *Mid-America,* 50 (April, 1968), 121–30; William G. Carleton, "Why Was the Democratic Party in Indiana A Radical Party, 1865–1890?" *Indiana Magazine of History,* 42 (Sept., 1946), 223–28; Paul John Kleppner, "The Politics of Change in the Midwest: The 1890s in Historical and Behavioral Perspective" (unpublished Ph.D. Dissertation, University of Pittsburgh, 1967), pp. 107–108, 150–96.

14. Mark Twain and Charles Dudley Warner, *The Gilded Age: A Tale of To-Day* (Hartford: American Publishing Company, 1873), pp. 301–302. Also, Alexander B. Callow, Jr., *The Tweed Ring* (New York: Oxford University Press, 1965), pp. 60–75; Nancy Joan Weiss, *Charles Francis Murphy, 1858–1924: Respectability and Responsibility in Tammany Politics* (Northampton, Mass.: Smith College, 1968), pp. 8–18.

15. See address by Samuel J. Tilden, in Flick, *Samuel Jones Tilden,* p. 169. Blodgett, *The Gentle Reformers,* pp. 100–71; Williams, "Politics and Reform," 271–316, 361–63; Robert Kelley, "The Thought and Character of Samuel J. Tilden: The Democrat as Inheritor," *The Historian,* 26 (Feb., 1964), 176–205.

16. Festus P. Summers, *William L. Wilson and Tariff Reform* (New Brunswick:

Rutgers University Press, 1953), p. 96. For the contrasting Republican philosophy, see Thomas B. Reed, "Rules of the House of Representatives," *Century Magazine,* 15 (March, 1889), 795.

17. Cleveland to Wilson S. Bissell, November 13, 1884, in Allan Nevins, ed., *Letters of Grover Cleveland, 1850–1908* (Boston: Houghton Mifflin, 1933), p. 48; James D. Richardson, ed., *A Compilation of the Messages and Papers of the Presidents* (Washington: Bureau of National Literature, 1897), VII, 4884–88. For the circumstances of Cleveland's rapid rise, which took him from a Buffalo law office in 1881 to the presidency in 1885, see Allan Nevins, *Grover Cleveland: A Study in Courage* (New York: Dodd, Mead, 1932), pp. 37–106.

18. *New York Times,* June 8, 1888; Harry J. Sievers, *Benjamin Harrison. II. Hoosier Statesman* (New York: University Publishers, 1959), p. 279; Lane to John H. Wigmore, February 27, 1888, in Anne Wintermute Lane and Louise Herrick Wall, eds., *The Letters of Franklin K. Lane: Personal and Political* (Boston: Houghton Mifflin, 1922), pp. 18–19. Also, David Saville Muzzey, *James G. Blaine: A Political Idol of Other Days* (New York: Dodd, Mead, 1934), p. 348.

19. Cleveland to Wilson S. Bissell, April 22, 1883, in Nevins, *Letters of Grover Cleveland,* p. 21; James C. Olson, *J. Sterling Morton* (Lincoln: University of Nebraska Press, 1942), p. 329; William D. English to Stephen M. White, Dec. 24, 1886, White Papers, Stanford University Library. Tilden's advice can be found in Tilden to Daniel Manning, June 9, 1885, in John Bigelow, ed., *Letters and Literary Memorials of Samuel J. Tilden* (New York: Harper Bros., 1908), II, 687.

20. George F. Parker, *Recollections of Grover Cleveland* (New York: Century, 1909), p. 341; Henry L. Stoddard, *As I Knew Them: Presidents and Politics from Grant to Coolidge* (New York: Harper Bros., 1927), p. 150. See also, Horace Samuel Merrill, *Bourbon Leader: Grover Cleveland and the Democratic Party* (Boston: Little, Brown, 1957), p. 113; Allan Nevins, *Abram S. Hewitt, With Some Account of Peter Cooper* (New York: Harper Bros., 1935), pp. 456–59.

21. Richardson, *Messages and Papers of the Presidents,* VII, 5165–76; George Hoadly to Cleveland, Nov. 22, 1887, Cleveland Papers, Library of Congress.

22. Summers, *William L. Wilson and Tariff Reform,* pp. 49–68.

23. *Washington Post,* Dec. 7, 1887; Wilson, *The National Democratic Party,* pp. 225, 235–36; Blodgett, *The Gentle Reformers,* pp. 69–80; Wall, *Henry Watterson,* p. 198; Paolo E. Coletta, *William Jennings Bryan: I. Political Evangelist, 1860–1908* (Lincoln: University of Nebraska Press, 1964), p. 35.

24. *New York Times,* June 7, 1888; Arthur P. Gorman to Manton Marble, June 12, 1888, in Marble Papers, Library of Congress; George Tilden McJimsey, "The Life of Manton Marble" (unpublished Ph.D. Dissertation, University of Wisconsin, Madison, 1968), pp. 417–18; Henry Watterson, *"Marse Henry": An Autobiography* (New York: George H. Doran, 1919), II, 134; *Official Proceedings of the National Democratic Convention* (St. Louis: Woodward & Tiernan, 1888), pp. 94–101.

25. Cleveland to Chauncey F. Black, Sept. 14, 1888, in Nevins, *Letters of Grover Cleveland,* p. 189; Texas Democrat quoted in Summers, *William L. Wilson and Tariff Reform,* p. 89; Merrill, *Bourbon Leader,* pp. 127–31; A. T. Volwiler, "Tariff Strategy and Propaganda in the United States, 1887–1888," *American Historical Review,* 36 (Oct., 1930), 76–96; Burnham, *Presidential Ballots,* pp. 140–45, 889; Jensen, "The Winning of the Midwest," 7–12, 32–36; *Washington Post,* Nov. 7, 1888.

26. See *New Orleans Daily Picayune,* March 5, 1893; Jensen, "The Winning of the Midwest," 68–105, 183–208; Kleppner, "The Politics of Change in the Midwest," 137–282; *Chicago Times,* Nov. 6, 1890; Roger E. Wyman, "Wisconsin Ethnic Groups and the Election of 1890," *Wisconsin Magazine of History,* 51 (Summer, 1968), 269–93.

27. Cleveland to John G. Carlisle, April 7, 1890, in Nevins, *Letters of Grover Cleveland,* pp. 221–22; Blodgett, *The Gentle Reformers,* p. 99. For the "Billion Dollar Congress" and the 1890 election, see H. Wayne Morgan, *William McKinley and His America* (Syracuse: Syracuse University Press, 1963), pp. 123–51; Harry J. Sievers, *Benjamin Harrison. III. Hoosier President* (Indianapolis: Bobbs-Merrill, 1968), pp. 141–82; Jensen, "The Winning of the Midwest," 207–20; *Atlanta Constitution,* Nov. 5, 1890; *Washington Post,* Nov. 5, 1890; McFarland, "The Breakdown of Deadlock," 394–95.

28. Burnham, *Presidential Ballots,* pp. 147–55; Degler, "American Political Parties and the Rise of the City," 46–47; Merrill, *Bourbon Democracy of the Middle West,* p. 231; *Chicago Times,* Nov. 11, 1892; Donald M. Dozer, "Benjamin Harrison and the Presidential Campaign of 1892," *American Historical Review,* 54 (Oct., 1948), 49–77; George Harmon Knoles, *The Presidential Campaign and Election of 1892* (Stanford: Stanford University Press, 1942).

29. *Atlanta Constitution,* Nov. 9, 1892; *New York Times,* Nov. 10, 1892. A similar conclusion is expressed in Woodrow Wilson, "Mr. Cleveland's Cabinet," *The Review of Reviews,* 7 (April, 1893), 289.

30. Herbert J. Bass, *"I Am A Democrat": The Political Career of David Bennett Hill* (Syracuse: Syracuse University Press, 1961), pp. 201–33; Arthur Krock, ed., *The Editorials of Henry Watterson* (New York: George H. Doran, 1923), pp. 71–74; *Official Proceedings of the National Democratic Convention* (Chicago: Cameron, Amberg, 1892), pp. 76–101, 157; Cleveland to William C. Whitney, July 9, 1892, Whitney Papers, Library of Congress.

31. Cleveland to E. Ellery Anderson, Feb. 10, 1891, in Nevins, *Letters of Grover Cleveland,* pp. 245–46; *Washington Post,* Feb. 13, 1891; *Atlanta Constitution,* Feb. 13, 1891; Woodward, *Origins of the New South,* pp. 202–43; Dewey W. Grantham, Jr., *Hoke Smith and the Politics of the New South* (Baton Rouge: Louisiana State University Press, 1958), pp. 43–48.

32. Francis G. Newlands to Henry L. Wright, Jan. 16, 1895, Newlands Papers, Yale University Library.

33. See Cleveland's 1893 inaugural address, in Richardson, *Messages and Papers of the Presidents,* VIII, 5822.

34. J. Sterling Morton to Richard Olney, Aug. 18, 1893, Olney Papers, Library of Congress; John P. Irish to J. Sterling Morton, April 27, 1894, Cleveland Papers.

35. Woodward, *Origins of the New South,* pp. 270–74; Barnes, *John G. Carlisle,* p. 286; *Raleigh News and Observer,* Nov. 2, 1893; *Washington Post,* Nov. 2, 1893; *Atlanta Constitution,* March 3, 1893. For considerations of Cleveland's tactical error in giving the currency issue precedence over tariff reform, see Williams, "Politics and Reform," 237–49; Lambert, *Arthur Pue Gorman,* pp. 184–85; J. Rogers Hollingsworth, *The Whirligig of Politics: The Democracy of Cleveland and Bryan* (Chicago: University of Chicago Press, 1963), p. 19.

36. George Gray to Cleveland, March 1894, Cleveland Papers; *San Francisco Examiner,* March 30, 1894; Merrill, *Bourbon Leader,* pp. 176–85. The impact on the Democratic party of Cleveland's veto of the seigniorage bill needs further in-

vestigation. Although a minor bill, which would have added little silver to the currency, it possessed great symbolic importance to many party members in 1894, and the President's veto appears to have been a decisive event in the process of party alienation which led to William Jennings Bryan's nomination in 1896. See, for example, *Washington Post,* March 30, 1894; *Chicago Times,* March 29–30, 1894.

37. Cleveland to William L. Wilson, July 2, 1894, in Nevins, *Letters of Grover Cleveland,* pp. 354–57; *Washington Post,* July 20–24, 1894; Summers, *William L. Wilson and Tariff Reform,* pp. 174–207; Lambert, *Arthur Pue Gorman,* pp. 200–38. Careful study of newspapers, congressional debates, and the correspondence of political leaders should significantly alter the customary interpretation of the Wilson-Gorman tariff. Too often the tariff fight is treated as an isolated incident, rather than as the result of a series of events which battered the party and fostered the revival of Democratic localism. Understandably perhaps, as their national prospects deteriorated Democrats became increasingly unwilling to endanger their positions in local districts. This problem was compounded by the extremely narrow Democratic margin in the Senate which meant that a tariff bill had to satisfy nearly everyone in order to pass.

38. See the platform of the California Republican party, in *San Francisco Examiner,* June 21, 1894; Degler, "American Political Parties and the Rise of the City," 42; Blodgett, *The Gentle Reformers,* p. 194; Jensen, "The Winning of the Midwest," 260–84; Duncan MacRae, Jr., and James A. Meldrum, "Critical Elections in Illinois, 1888–1958," *American Political Science Review,* 59 (Sept., 1960), 678–81; J. Rogers Hollingsworth, "The Historian, Presidential Elections, and 1896," *Mid-America,* 45 (July, 1963), 187–88.

39. *New York Times,* Nov. 7, 1894; *Washington Post,* Nov. 7, 1894; *Atlanta Constitution,* Nov. 7, 1894.

40. John P. Irish to J. Sterling Morton, Aug. 5, 1895; Irish to Morton, Jan. 31, 1895; both in Morton Papers, Nebraska Historical Society, Lincoln, Nebraska.

41. Stephen M. White to John P. Irish, Aug. 5, 1894, White Papers.

42. See Blodgett, *The Gentle Reformers,* p. vii; Williams, "Politics and Reform," 228–70; Olson, *J. Sterling Morton,* pp. 383–85; Woodward, *Origins of the New South,* pp. 270–84; William Jennings Bryan, *The First Battle, A Story of the Campaign of 1896* (Chicago: W. B. Conkey, 1896), p. 136; Paolo E. Coletta, "Bryan, Cleveland, and the Disrupted Democracy, 1890–1896," *Nebraska History,* 41 (March, 1960), 1–27.

43. Entry for May 26, 1896, in Festus P. Summers, ed., *The Cabinet Diary of William L. Wilson, 1896–1897* (Chapel Hill: University of North Carolina Press, 1957), p. 90; *Official Proceedings of the Democratic National Convention* (Logansport, Indiana: Wilson, Humphreys, 1896), pp. 250–56, 327.

44. Coletta, *William Jennings Bryan: Political Evangelist,* 197; *San Francisco Examiner,* Nov. 11, 1896. On this point, see also Kleppner, "The Politics of Change in the Midwest," 535–44; Gilbert C. Fite, "William Jennings Bryan and the Campaign of 1896: Some Views and Problems," *Nebraska History,* 47 (Sept., 1966), 247–64.

45. Coletta, *William Jennings Bryan: Political Evangelist,* pp. 191–92; Jensen, "The Winning of the Midwest," 37–67, 358; Degler, "American Political Parties and the Rise of the City," 48–49; Gilbert C. Fite, "Republican Strategy and the Farm Vote in the Presidential Campaign of 1896," *American Historical Review,*

65 (July, 1960), 787–806; Blodgett, *Gentle Reformers,* p. 238; Stanley L. Jones, *The Presidential Election of 1896* (Madison: University of Wisconsin Press, 1964), pp. 332–50; William Diamond, "Urban and Rural Voting in 1896," *American Historical Review,* 46 (Jan., 1941), 281–305; Lee Benson, "Research Problems in American Political Historiography," in Mirra Komarovsky, ed., *Common Frontiers of the Social Sciences* (Glencoe, Ill.: Free Press, 1957), pp. 155–71.

46. Hollingsworth, *The Whirligig of Politics,* pp. 108–241, studies the course of the Democratic party after 1896. Also, John B. Wiseman, "Racism in Democratic Politics, 1904–1912," *Mid-America,* 51 (Jan., 1968), 38–58. For Democratic gains in the 1920's, see David Burner, *The Politics of Provincialism: The Democratic Party in Transition, 1918–1932* (New York: Knopf, 1967); Jerome M. Clubb and Howard W. Allen, "The Cities and the Election of 1928: Partisan Realignment?" *American Historical Review,* 74 (April, 1969), 1205–20.

47. *Chicago Herald,* quoted in *Washington Post,* Nov. 8, 1894. *San Francisco Examiner,* March 4, 1897, gives a typical Democratic post-mortem on the 1890's.

48. Degler, "American Political Parties and the Rise of the City," 49.

8. Populism and the Decline of Agriculture

1. Clarkson to Harrison, May 5, 1891, Benjamin Harrison Papers, Library of Congress.

2. See William D. Sheldon, *Populism in the Old Dominion* (Princeton: Princeton University Press, 1935), pp. 36ff; and Roy V. Scott, *The Agrarian Movement in Illinois, 1880–1896* (Urbana: University of Illinois Press, 1962), pp. 78–79.

3. Solon Justus Buck, *The Granger Movement* (Lincoln: University of Nebraska Press, 1963), pp. 288–89; John S. Spratt, *The Road to Spindletop: Economic Change in Texas, 1875–1901* (Dallas: Southern Methodist University Press, 1955), pp. 44, 70–73; Ralph Adam Smith, "A. J. Rose: Agrarian Crusader of Texas" (unpublished Ph.D. Dissertation, University of Texas, 1938), pp. 273ff.

4. C. Vann Woodward, *Origins of the New South, 1877–1913* (Baton Rouge: Louisiana State University Press, 1951), p. 50.

5. *Ibid.,* pp. 246–55; Richard Harvey Barton, "The Agrarian Revolt in Michigan, 1865–1900" (unpublished Ph.D. Dissertation, Michigan State University, 1958), pp. 51ff.

6. Compare Norman Pollack, *The Populist Response to Industrial America* (Cambridge: Harvard University Press, 1962), pp. 87–88; Walter T. K. Nugent, *The Tolerant Populists* (Chicago: University of Chicago Press, 1963), pp. 96–97; John Chamberlain, *Farewell to Reform* (New York: John Day, 1932), p. 4.

7. Stuart Noblin, *Leonidas LaFayette Polk: Agrarian Crusader* (Chapel Hill: University of North Carolina Press, 1949), pp. 79, 96, 138.

8. Sheldon, *Populism in the Old Dominion,* p. 22.

9. Barton, "Agrarian Revolt in Michigan," 29, 205.

10. Theodore Saloutous, *Farmer Movements in the South, 1865–1933* (Berkeley: University of California Press, 1960), p. 85.

11. Smith, "A. J. Rose," 126–244; Buck, *The Granger Movement,* pp. 274ff; C. W. Macune, "The Farmers' Alliance" (typescript in the Texas History Collec-

tion, University of Texas, Austin), p. 30; Martin Ridge, *Ignatius Donnelley* (Chicago: University of Chicago Press, 1962), p. 264; Chester McA. Destler, *American Radicalism, 1865–1901* (Chicago: Quadrangle Books, 1966), p. 20.

12. Noblin, *Leonidas LaFayette Polk,* p. 209.

13. John D. Hicks, *The Populist Revolt* (Minneapolis: University of Minnesota Press, 1931), p. 206.

14. *Ibid.,* p. 27.

15. James C. Olson, *A History of Nebraska* (Lincoln: University of Nebraska Press, 1955), pp. 211ff; Kenneth E. Hendrickson, "The Public Career of Richard F. Pettigrew of South Dakota, 1848–1926" (unpublished Ph.D. Dissertation, University of Oklahoma, 1967), pp. 105–106; Nugent, *The Tolerant Populists,* p. 55.

16. H. J. Fletcher, "Western Real Estate Booms, and After," *Atlantic Monthly,* 81 (May, 1898), 689–704.

17. Gene M. Gressley, *Bankers and Cattlemen* (New York: Knopf, 1966), pp. 65, 143–45.

18. Elizabeth N. Barr, "The Populist Uprising," in William E. Connelley, ed., *A Standard History of Kansas and Kansans,* 2 vols. (Chicago: Lewis, 1918), II, 1138; Gilbert C. Fite, *The Farmers' Frontier, 1865–1900* (New York: Holt, Rinehart and Winston, 1966), p. 200.

19. Allen G. Bogue, *Money at Interest: The Farm Mortgage on the Middle Border* (Ithaca: Cornell University Press, 1955), pp. 144, 146–50, 183, 272ff.

20. Barr, "The Populist Uprising," 1150.

21. Hicks, *The Populist Revolt,* pp. 55–56.

22. Charles Edward Russell, *Bare Hands and Stone Walls* (New York: Scribner's, 1933), pp. 27–28.

23. See the perceptive contemporary article by Rodney Welch, "The Farmer's Changed Condition," *The Forum,* 10 (Feb., 1891), 689–700.

24. C. Wood Davis, "Why the Farmer is Not Prosperous," *ibid.,* 9 (April, 1890), 231–41.

25. Eric Goldman, *Rendezvous With Destiny* (New York: Knopf, 1952), pp. 37–38.

26. Alex M. Arnett, *The Populist Movement in Georgia* (New York: Columbia University Press, 1922), pp. 61, 72–73; Ray Ginger, *Age of Excess* (New York: Macmillan, 1965), 68.

27. Walter T. K. Nugent, "Some Parameters of Populism," *Agricultural History,* 40 (Oct., 1966), 255–70; Nugent, *The Tolerant Populists,* pp. 94–95; and Theodore Saloutous, "The Professors and the Populists" *Agricultural History,* 40 (Oct., 1966), 235–54.

28. Roscoe C. Martin, *The People's Party in Texas* (Austin: University of Texas Press, 1934), pp. 61ff.

29. Noblin, *Leonidas LaFayette Polk,* pp. 192–93.

30. Carl Henry Chrislock, "The Politics of Protest in Minnesota, 1890–1901: From Populism to Progressivism" (unpublished Ph.D. Dissertation, University of Minnesota, 1955), pp. 24–25, 30–59. J. R. Dodge, "The Discontent of the Farmer," *Century Magazine,* 43 (Jan., 1892), 447–56, is perceptive, as is the editorial in the *Washington Post,* April 16, 1890. The letter of Dr. E. L. Sturtevant to Samuel J. Randall, Feb. 5, 1884, Randall Papers, University of Pennsylvania Library, from the Agricultural Experiment Station at Geneva, N.Y., is vey interesting on diversification.

31. Octave Thanet, "The Farmers in the North," *Scribner's Magazine,* 15 (March, 1894), 323–39; Spratt, *Road to Spindletop,* pp. 13–14; Robert S. Dykstra, "Town-Country Conflict: A Hidden Dimension in American Social History," *Agricultural History,* 38 (Oct., 1964), 195–204; Saloutous, *Farmer Movements in the South,* pp. 75–76; Woodward, *Origins of the New South,* p. 177.

32. Geoffrey Blodgett, *The Gentle Reformers* (Cambridge: Harvard University Press, 1966), p. 176; William Vincent Allen, "Western Feeling Towards the East," *North American Review,* 162 (May, 1896), 588–93; Henry Littlefield West, "Two Republics or One?" *ibid.,* 162 (April, 1896), 509–11; Francis Butler Simkins, *Pitchfork Ben Tillman* (Baton Rouge: Louisiana State University Press, 1944), p. 326; Stanley L. Jones, *The Presidential Election of 1896* (Madison: University of Wisconsin Press, 1964), p. 38.

33. Barton, "The Agrarian Revolt in Michigan," 30; Cf. Buck, *The Granger Movement,* p. 3; Stanley Parsons, "Who Were the Nebraska Populists?" *Nebraska History,* 44 (June, 1963), 83–99; David F. Trask, "A Note on the Politics of Populism," *ibid.,* 46 (June, 1965), 157–61.

34. Fred E. Haynes, *James Baird Weaver* (Iowa City: State Historical Society of Iowa, 1919), p. 255.

35. Simkins, *Pitchfork Ben Tillman,* pp. 2–3, 105, 151–54; Francis Butler Simkins, *The Tillman Movement in South Carolina* (Durham: Duke University Press, 1926), pp. 52–53.

36. Woodward, *Origins of the New South,* pp. 191, 194.

37. Russell B. Nye, *Midwestern Progressive Politics* (East Lansing: Michigan State University Press, 1951), p. 73.

38. Hicks, *The Populist Revolt,* p. 286; C. Vann Woodward, *Tom Watson: Agrarian Rebel* (New York: Macmillan, 1938), p. 178.

39. William Allen White, *Autobiography* (New York: Macmillan, 1946), pp. 228–29.

40. *Judge,* Feb. 10, 1894, 82.

41. Chamberlain, *Farewell to Reform,* p. 24.

42. Ridge, *Ignatius Donnelley,* p. 26.

43. Zornow, *Kansas,* pp. 207–208; Karel Denis Bicha, "Jerry Simpson: Populist Without Principles," *Journal of American History,* 54 (Sept., 1967), 327–38.

44. Martin, *People's Party in Texas,* pp. 99, 113–40, 141–61, 179–81, 220, 226–27, 231–35; Woodward, *Origins of the New South,* pp. 235–90; Robert F. Durden, *The Climax of Populism: The Election of 1896* (Louisville: University of Kentucky Press, 1965), pp. 1–22; Albert D. Kirwan, *Revolt of the Rednecks* (Louisville: University of Kentucky Press, 1951), pp. 85–102.

45. Martin, *People's Party in Texas,* p. 88.

46. George F. Parker, *Recollections of Grover Cleveland* (New York: Century, 1910), p. 208.

47. Robert C. Cotner, *James Stephen Hogg* (Austin: University of Texas Press, 1959), pp. 431–32.

48. *New York Sun,* July 27, 1890.

49. See Norman Pollack, ed., *The Populist Mind* (New York: Bobbs, Merrill, 1967), p. 5.

50. See Connelley, *Standard History of Kansas,* II, 1117.

51. L. L. Polk, "The Farmers' Discontent," *North American Review,* 153 (July, 1891), 5–12.

52. Hicks, *The Populist Revolt,* pp. 81–83.

53. James B. Weaver, *A Call to Action* (Des Moines: Iowa Printing, 1892), p. 5. It seems unnecessary to reproduce a chain of documentation for this conspiracy thesis, since Populist literature abounds with it.

54. *Ibid.,* p. 441.

55. Benjamin Orange Flower, *Progressive Men, Women and Movements of the Past Twenty-five Years* (Boston: New Arena, 1914), pp. 61–62.

56. Weaver, *Call to Action,* p. 6; see also, Roger V. Clements, "The Farmers' Attitude Toward British Investment in American Industry," *Journal of Economic History,* 15 (1955), 151–59. Richard Hofstadter stimulated a lengthy analysis of alleged nativism, anti-Semitism, and intolerance in Populist thought with his book *The Age of Reform: From Bryan to F. D. R.* (New York: Knopf, 1955), pp. 60–130. Norman Pollack rendered the most vigorous rebuttal, especially in "Hofstadter on Populism: A Critique of *The Age of Reform,*" *Journal of Southern History,* 26 (Nov., 1960), 478–500; and "The Myth of Populist Anti-Semitism," *American Historical Review,* 68 (Oct., 1962), 76–80. Nugent, *The Tolerant Populists,* pp. 109–15, 193–94, has a balanced and tenable view. *Agricultural History* devoted the entire issue for April, 1965, to the subject of Populism, with articles by Professors Norman Pollack, Oscar Handlin, J. Rogers Hollingsworth, and Irwin Unger.

57. Noblin, *Leonidas LaFayette Polk,* p. 19.

58. Atkinson to David A. Wells, July 6, 1882, Wells Papers, Library of Congress.

59. William Jennings Bryan, *The First Battle* (Chicago: W. B. Conkey, 1896), p. 81.

60. Hicks, *The Populist Revolt,* p. 316.

61. See Edward C. Kirkland, *Industry Comes of Age* (New York: Holt, Rinehart & Winston, 1961), p. 38.

62. Jones, *Presidential Election of 1896,* p. 33; John B. Clark, *Populism in Alabama, 1874–1896* (Auburn: Auburn Printing, 1927), p. 164, nl.

63. Francis Thurber to William A. Croffut, Dec. 5, 1885, Croffut Papers, Library of Congress.

64. Smith to Hayes, June 20, 1885, Smith Papers, Ohio Historical Society, Columbus.

65. Barker to Charles Stone, May 11, 1892, Barker Papers, Library of Congress.

66. Rutherford B. Hayes Diary, March 18, 1886, Hayes Papers, Hayes Memorial Library, Fremont, Ohio.

67. William McKinley, *Speeches and Addresses* (New York: Appleton, 1893), p. 218.

68. Cullom to Barker, June 3, 1891, Barker Papers.

69. The *Nation,* March 17, 1892, 201.

70. See Noblin, *Leonidas LaFayette Polk,* p. 293; Haynes, *Third Party Movements,* pp. 263ff; George Harmon Knoles, *The Presidential Campaign and Election of 1892* (Palo Alto: Stanford University Press, 1942), pp. 94–121, 179–202; Hicks, *The Populist Revolt,* pp. 238–73.

71. Saloutous, *Farmer Movements in the South,* p. 125; Woodward, *Origins of the New South,* p. 244; Woodward, *Tom Watson,* p. 289.

72. See Knoles, *The Presidential Campaign and Election of 1892,* pp. 179–225.

73. Hicks, *The Populist Revolt,* p. 248.

9. The Republican Search for a National Majority

1. Carl N. Degler, "The Nineteenth Century," William N. Nelson, ed., *Theory and Practice in American Politics* (Chicago: University of Chicago Press, 1964), pp. 35–36; *The Statistical History of the United States From Colonial Times to the Present* (Stamford, Conn.: Fairfield Publishers, 1965), p. 691; W. Dean Burnham, *Presidential Ballots, 1836–1892* (Baltimore: Johns Hopkins Press, 1955), pp. 118–27, 888–89.

2. Paul John Kleppner, "The Politics of Change in the Midwest: The 1890's in Historical and Behavioral Perspective" (unpublished Ph.D. Dissertation, University of Pittsburgh, 1967), pp. 107–108, 150–96; Burnham, *Presidential Ballots*, pp. 129–40. Modern treatments of the Republicans in this period either pass over the problems of the GOP or misunderstand them. George H. Mayer, *The Republican Party, 1854–1966* (New York: Oxford University Press, 1967), pp. 171–220, succumbs to the first weakness, while the shallow discussion in Milton Viorst, *Fall From Grace: The Republican Party and the Puritan Ethic* (New York: New American Library, 1968), pp. 62–96, falls prey to the second.

3. Republican "abandonment" of the Negro after Reconstruction has fascinated Gilded Age historians. The standard works are: C. Vann Woodward, *Reunion and Reaction* (Boston: Little, Brown, 1951); Vincent P. DeSantis, *Republicans Face the Southern Question: The New Departure Years* (Baltimore: Johns Hopkins Press, 1959); Stanley P. Hirshson, *Farewell to the Bloody Shirt: Northern Republicans and the Southern Negro* (Bloomington: Indiana University Press, 1962). Historians need to approach Democratic actions on the race question with the same skepticism they have applied to Republicans. In this connection, see the perceptive comments in Jerome L. Sternstein, ed., "The Sickles Memorandum: Another Look at the Hayes-Tilden Election-Night Conspiracy," *The Journal of Southern History*, 32 (1966), 351.

4. Leon Burr Richardson, *William E. Chandler: Republican* (New York: Dodd, Mead and Company, 1940), pp. 184–224, 388–436, 461–64; James G. Blaine, *Political Discussions: Legislative, Diplomatic and Popular 1856–1886* (Norwich, Conn.: Henry Bill, 1887), 278–99; John G. Sproat, *"The Best Men": Liberal Reformers in the Gilded Age* (New York: Oxford University Press, 1968), pp. 40–44.

5. Ari Hoogenboom, *Outlawing the Spoils: A History of the Civil Service Reform Movement, 1865–1883* (Urbana: University of Illinois Press, 1961).

6. Donald Barr Chidsey, *The Gentleman from New York: A Life of Roscoe Conkling* (New Haven: Yale University Press, 1935).

7. Richard Joseph Jensen, "The Winning of the Midwest: A Social History of Midwestern Elections, 1888–1896" (unpublished Ph.D. Dissertation, Yale University, 1967), pp. 119–80; Kleppner, "The Politics of Change in the Midwest," 169–96; Frederick C. Luebke, "German Immigrants and the Churches of Nebraska, 1889–1915" *Mid-America*, 50 (1968), 116–30.

8. George W. Julian, "The Death Struggle of the Republican Party," *North American Review*, 126 (1878), 292.

9. The *Nation*, 25 (Dec. 13, 1877), 360.

10. Julia B. Foraker, *I Would Live It Again* (New York: Harper Bros., 1932), p. 140.

11. George Frisbie Hoar, "Are the Republicans in to Stay?" *North American Review,* 149 (1889), 621.

12. O. O. Stealey, *Twenty Years in the Press Gallery* (New York: Publishers Printing, 1906), p. 113.

13. Robert G. Caldwell, *James A. Garfield: Party Chieftain* (New York: Dodd, Mead, 1931); Harry J. Sievers, *Benjamin Harrison. II. Hoosier Statesman: 1865–1888* (New York: University Publishers, 1959); David S. Muzzey, *James G. Blaine: A Political Idol of Other Days* (New York: Dodd, Mead, 1934); H. Wayne Morgan, *William McKinley and His America* (Syracuse: Syracuse University Press, 1963).

14. *New York Tribune,* March 22, 1877, quoted in Stanley P. Hirshson, *Farewell to the Bloody Shirt,* p. 28; George B. Sinkler, "Race: Principles and Policy of Rutherford B. Hayes," *Ohio History,* 77 (1968), 149–67.

15. Herbert J. Clancy, *The Presidential Election of 1880* (Chicago: Loyola University Press, 1958); Albert V. House, "Internal Conflict in Key States in the Democratic Convention of 1880," *Pennsylvania History,* 27 (1960), 188–216.

16. James A. Garfield to John Sherman, Sept. 25, 1880, *John Sherman's Recollections of Forty Years in the House, Senate, and Cabinet* (New York: Werner, 1895), II, 787; "The Tariff Difficulty of the Democrats," The *Nation,* 31 (Oct. 14, 1880), 267–68; William C. Hudson, *Random Recollections of an Old Political Reporter* (New York: Cupples and Leon, 1911), p. 112.

17. Samuel P. Hays, "Political Parties and the Community-Society Continuum," William Nisbet Chambers and Walter D. Burnham, eds., *The American Party Systems: Stages of Development* (New York: Oxford University Press, 1967), p. 162.

18. Blaine, *Political Discussions,* p. 452.

19. Herbert Croly, *Progressive Democracy* (New York: Macmillan, 1915), p. 87.

20. Degler, "The Nineteenth Century," 39; "What Protection Means to Virginia," *Speeches and Addresses of William McKinley* (New York: Appleton, 1893), p. 194; John A. Garraty, *The New Commonwealth, 1877–1890* (New York: Harper & Row, 1968), pp. 40–42.

21. "The Tariff of 1890," *Speeches and Addresses of McKinley,* p. 427; James A. Barnes, "Protection, Politics, and Pennsylvania," *Pennsylvania History,* 31 (Jan., 1964), 7–8.

22. Barnes, "Protection," 9; Hays, "Political Parties and the Community-Society Continuum," 161–63.

23. Blaine, *Political Discussions,* p. 449; David S. Muzzey, *James G. Blaine: A Political Idol of Other Days* (New York: Dodd, Mead, 1934), is the standard biography. The perceptive remarks in Sproat, *"The Best Man,"* 112–15 point the way toward a reappraisal of Blaine, but a full-scale, modern study remains to be done.

24. George F. Howe, *Chester A. Arthur: A Quarter Century of Machine Politics* (New York: Dodd, Mead, 1934).

25. Lee Benson, "Research Problems in American Political Historiography," Mirra Komarovsky, ed., *Common Frontiers of the Social Sciences* (Glencoe, Ill.: Free Press, 1957), pp. 123–46.

26. Horace Samuel Merrill, *Bourbon Leader: Grover Cleveland and the Democratic Party* (Boston: Little, Brown, 1957), pp. 71–134.

27. Harry J. Sievers, *Benjamin Harrison. II. Hoosier Statesman: 1865–1888*

(New York: University Publishers, 1959), does not do justice to Harrison as a politician. Jensen, "The Winning of the Midwest," pp. 7–9, has some sensible observations on the nature of Harrison's campaign; Muzzey, *Blaine,* p. 367.

28. Charles Hedges, comp., *Speeches of Benjamin Harrison* (New York: United States Book, 1892), pp. 29–187. By focusing on the inevitable banalities of campaign oratory, Garraty in *The New Commonwealth,* pp. 297–98, overlooks Harrison's adept use of protection as the theme of his canvass. Burnham, *Presidential Ballots,* pp. 140–45.

29. Herbert Adams Gibbons, *John Wanamaker* (New York: Harper Bros., 1926), pp. 257–61; A. T. Volwiler, "Tariff Strategy and Propaganda in the United States, 1887–1888," *American Historical Review,* 36 (Oct., 1930), 76–96.

30. Daniel J. Ryan, "Clubs in Politics," *North American Review,* 146 (1888), 172–77; "Permanent Republican Clubs," *North American Review,* 146 (1888), 241–65; Foraker, *I Would Live It Again,* p. 133.

31. Richard E. Welch, Jr., "The Federal Elections Bill of 1890: Postscripts and Prelude," *The Journal of American History,* 52 (Dec., 1965), 511–26; William Letwin, *Law and Economic Policy in America: The Evolution of the Sherman Antitrust Act* (New York: Random House, 1965); Morgan, *William McKinley and His America,* pp. 123–51; Nathaniel Wright Stephenson, *Nelson W. Aldrich: A Leader in American Politics* (New York: Scribner's, 1930), pp. 76–92; William A. Robinson, *Thomas B. Reed, Parliamentarian* (New York: Dodd, Mead, 1930), is the best biography of the Speaker.

32. Royal Cortissoz, *The Life of Whitelaw Reid* (New York: Scribner's, 1921), II, 176; Foraker, *I Would Live It Again,* pp. 130–34; R. Hal Williams, "Politics and Reform: The California Democrats in the Cleveland Years" (unpublished Ph.D. Dissertation, Yale University, 1968), pp. 168–73; Donald M. Dozer, "Benjamin Harrison and the Presidential Campaign of 1892," *The American Historical Review,* 44 (1948–49), 49–53.

33. Kleppner, "The Politics of Change," 137–282, and Jensen, "The Winning of the Midwest," 68–220, cover these matters in awesome detail. Dorothy Ganfield Fowler, *John Coit Spooner: Defender of Presidents* (New York: University Publishers, 1961), pp. 144–54; Horace Samuel Merrill, *William Freeman Vilas: Doctrinaire Democrat* (Madison: State Historical Society of Wisconsin, 1954), pp. 151–69.

34. Roger E. Wyman, "Wisconsin Ethnic Groups and the Election of 1890," *Wisconsin Magazine of History,* 51 (1968), 269–93; *Statistical History of the United States,* p. 691; Woodrow Wilson, "Mr. Cleveland's Cabinet," Ray Stannard Baker and William E. Dodd, eds., *The Public Papers of Woodrow Wilson* (New York: Harper Bros., 1925), I, 204; Dozer, "Benjamin Harrison and the Presidential Campaign of 1892," 49–77; George H. Knoles, *The Presidential Campaign and Election of 1892* (Stanford: Stanford University Press, 1942).

35. Degler, "The Nineteenth Century," 38; Leonard P. Curry, *Blueprint for Modern America: Nonmilitary Legislation of the First Civil War Congress* (Nashville: Vanderbilt University Press, 1968), pp. 244–52.

36. Kleppner, "The Politics of Change," 283–418; Jensen, "The Winning of the Midwest," 260–99; Degler, "The Nineteenth Century," 36–41.

37. C. S. Thomas to Grover Cleveland, April 13, 1893, Cleveland Papers, Library of Congress; Williams, "Politics and Reform," 219–70; Paolo Coletta, *William Jennings Bryan. 1. Political Evangelist* (Lincoln: University of Nebraska Press, 1964), pp. 87–89.

38. Francis E. Warren to Frank Mondell, July 8, 1894, Warren Papers, Western History Research Center, University of Wyoming; J. Rogers Hollingsworth, *The Whirligig of Politics: The Democracy of Cleveland and Bryan* (Chicago: University of Chicago Press, 1963), pp. 19–21; John R. Lambert, *Arthur Pue Gorman* (Baton Rouge: Louisiana State University Press, 1953), pp. 200–38.

39. *Statistical History of the United States,* p. 691; Degler, "The Nineteenth Century," 37; Hays, "Political Parties and the Community-Society Continuum," 159; Robinson, *Thomas B. Reed,* p. 321; Donald L. Kinzer, *An Episode in Anti-Catholicism: The American Protective Association* (Seattle: University of Washington Press, 1964), pp. 140–80.

40. Degler, "The Nineteenth Century," 41–42; Kleppner, "Politics of Change," 419–60; Jensen, "Winning of the Midwest," 260–99.

41. Morgan, *William McKinley and His America,* pp. 92–182.

42. Stanley L. Jones, *The Presidential Election of 1896* (Madison: University of Wisconsin Press, 1964), pp. 104–13, 142–44; Kleppner, "Politics of Change," 544–51.

43. Jones, *Presidential Election of 1896,* pp. 276–96; Morgan, *William McKinley and His America,* pp. 209–48.

44. Jones, *Presidential Election of 1896,* pp. 99–157; Leland L. Sage, *William Boyd Allison: A Study in Practical Politics* (Iowa City: State Historical Society of Iowa, 1956), pp. 261–64; Lewis L. Gould, *Wyoming: A Political History, 1868–1896* (New Haven: Yale University Press, 1968), pp. 231–43.

45. Jensen, "Winning of the Midwest," 171–72.

46. James A. Barnes, "Myths of the Bryan Campaign," *Mississippi Valley Historical Review,* 34 (Dec., 1947), 367–404; Gilbert C. Fite, "William Jennings Bryan and the Campaign of 1896: Some Views and Problems," *Nebraska History,* 47 (Sept., 1966), 247–64; Coletta, *Bryan,* pp. 99–160; Kleppner, "Politics of Change," 535–44.

47. Thomas Beer, *Hanna* (New York: Alfred A. Knopf, 1929), p. 153; Gilbert C. Fite, "Republican Strategy and the Farm Vote in the Presidential Campaign of 1896," *American Historical Review,* 65 (July, 1960), 787–806; Benson, "Research Problems in American Political Historiography," 155–71; Kleppner, "Politics of Change," 551–79; Degler, "The Nineteenth Century," 41–42.

48. Jensen, "Winning of the Midwest," 37–67.

10. Economics, Emotion, and Expansion: An Emerging Foreign Policy

Research for this study was supported in part by a Summer Research Award from the Office of Scientific and Scholarly Research of the University of Oregon.

1. Eugene Schuyler, *American Diplomacy and the Furtherance of Commerce* (New York: Scribner's, 1886).

2. Nelson Manfred Blake and Oscar Theodore Barck, Jr., *The United States In Its World Relations* (New York: McGraw-Hill, 1960), pp. 331–52; David M. Pletcher, *The Awkward Years: American Foreign Relations Under Garfield and Arthur* (Columbia: University of Missouri Press, 1962), is a careful study of the early 1880's, with unconvincing conclusions about the 1890's.

3. Charles A. and Mary R. Beard, *The Rise of American Civilization* (New

York: Macmillan, 1930), II, 344–82. The Beards' views resemble those of the English anti-imperialist John Hobson.

4. Beard, *The Idea of National Interest, An Analytical Study in American Foreign Policy* (New York: Macmillan, 1934); *The Open Door at Home, A Trial Philosophy of National Interest* (New York: Macmillan, 1934).

5. Joseph E. Wisan, *The Cuban Crisis as Reflected in the New York Press* (New York: Columbia University Press, 1934); Marcus M. Wilkerson, *Public Opinion and the Spanish-American War: A Study in War Propaganda* (Baton Rouge: Louisiana State University Press, 1932); Walter Millis, *The Martial Spirit* (Boston: Houghton Mifflin, 1931).

6. Julius W. Pratt, *The Expansionists of 1898* (Baltimore: Johns Hopkins Press, 1936). Pratt did resemble Beard in treating expansion as the cause of the war.

7. For a general commentary, see Richard Hofstadter, *The Progressive Historians: Turner, Beard, Parrington* (New York: Knopf, 1968).

8. Pratt himself had not stressed public opinion.

9. Walter LaFeber, *The New Empire: An Interpretation of American Expansionism, 1860–1898* (Ithaca: Cornell University Press, 1963), pp. 400–406.

10. Thomas J. McCormick, *China Market: America's Quest for Informal Empire, 1893–1901* (Chicago: Quadrangle Books, 1967); William Appleman Williams, *The Tragedy of American Diplomacy* (New York: Dell, 1962); a somewhat modified version, Ray Ginger, *Age of Excess: The United States from 1877 to 1914* (New York: Macmillan, 1965). For LaFeber's views on recent history, see *America, Russia, and the Cold War, 1945–1966* (New York: John Wiley, 1967). Critiques of the New Economic Determinists are to be found in Irwin Unger, "The 'New Left' and American History: Some Recent Trends in United States History," *The American Historical Review*, 72 (1967), 1244–49; and John Braeman, "The Wisconsin School of American Diplomatic History: A Critique," a paper read at the meeting of the Organization of American Historians, April 27, 1967.

11. There was a worldwide depression throughout much of the late nineteenth century, but there were many good years as well as bad ones.

12. Edward Chase Kirkland, *Dream and Thought in the Business Community, 1860–1900* (Chicago: Quadrangle Books, 1964), pp. 7–10.

13. Quoting Republican Henry L. Dawes, Chairman of the House Ways and Means Committee, *Congressional Record* (hereafter *CR*), 43–1, Vol. II (May 26, 1874), 4267.

14. *CR*, 45–2, Vol. VII (June 4, 1878), Appendix, 293–94.

15. *CR*, 43–1, Vol. II (May 16, 1874), 3972. Monroe had been a consul and chargé d'affaires in Brazil.

16. House Misc. Doc. No. 29, 45th Congress, 2d session, III (1879); *CR*, 43–1, Vol. II (Dec. 3, 1873), 33.

17. Pletcher, *The Awkward Years*, p. 143; *CR*, 45–2, Vol. VII (May 9, 1878), 3330.

18. Pletcher, *The Awkward Years*, pp. 325–46. J. Laurence Laughlin and H. Parker Willis, *Reciprocity* (New York: Baker and Taylor, 1903), pp. 105–25.

19. Samuel Rezneck, "Patterns of Thought and Action in an American Depression, 1882–1886," *The American Historical Review*, 61 (Jan., 1956), 284–307.

20. Laughlin and Willis, *Reciprocity*, pp. 124–27.

21. Frank L. Taussig, *The Tariff History of the United States* (London: Putnam's, 1931), pp. 253–54.

22. Allan Nevins, *Grover Cleveland: A Study in Courage* (New York: Dodd, Mead, 1932), p. 387.

23. Ida Tarbell, *The Tariff in Our Times* (New York: Macmillan, 1911), pp. 198–99.

24. Edward Stanwood, *American Tariff Controversies in the Nineteenth Century* (Boston: Houghton Mifflin, 1903), II, 275.

25. Blaine's interest in the Pan-American Conference stemmed from diverse motives, but his choice of businessmen as American delegates revealed concern with economic expansion.

26. Stanwood, *Tariff Controversies,* pp. 288–95; Tarbell, *Tariff in Our Times,* pp. 209–10; Taussig, *Tariff History,* p. 317.

27. LaFeber, *The New Empire,* pp. 160–68, 200–201.

28. For a discussion of the resulting Wilson bill, see Festus P. Summers, *William L. Wilson and Tariff Reform* (New Brunswick: Rutgers University Press, 1953), pp. 173–75.

29. *CR,* 53–2, Vol. XXVI (Dec. 4, 1893), 8–9. Compare with LaFeber, *The New Empire,* pp. 160–61.

30. LaFeber, *The New Empire,* pp. 161–68, 197–201.

31. William L. Wilson, "The Principle and Method of the New Tariff Bill," *Forum,* 16 (Jan., 1894), 544–48; emphasis added.

32. *CR,* 53–2, Vol. XXVI (Jan. 8, 9, 1894), Appendix, 193–201. Wilson's biographer does not mention foreign markets in analyzing the speech; Summers, *Wilson,* pp. 177–78.

33. Roger Q. Mills, "The Wilson Bill," *The North American Review,* 158 (Feb., 1894), 235–44; *CR,* 53–2, Vol. XXVI (April 3, 1894), 3448–52 (April 24, 1894), 4020–30.

34. *CR,* 53–2, Vol. XXVI (April 2, 1894), 3391–3400.

35. John R. Lambert, *Arthur Pue Gorman* (Baton Rouge: Louisiana State University Press, 1953), pp. 235–37; *CR,* 53–2, Vol. XXVI (July 23, 1894), 7801–7809.

36. *CR,* 55–1, Vol. XXX (July 19, 1897), 2734–43.

37. LaFeber, *The New Empire,* pp. 200–201.

38. Walter Q. Gresham to George J. Langsdale, Aug. 7, 1893; Gresham to F. P. Schmitt, Aug. 16, 1893; Gresham to Judge D. P. Baldwin, Aug. 17, 1893; Gresham to Gen. F. M. Force, Aug. 30, 1893, all in Letterbook, Gresham Papers, Library of Congress.

39. Gresham to Col. John S. Cooper, July 26, 1894, *ibid.*

40. Gresham to Judge Charles E. Dyer, May 2, 1894; Gresham to Wayne MacVeagh, May 7, 1894, both *ibid.*

41. Carl Schurz, "Manifest Destiny," *Harper's New Monthly Magazine,* 87 (Oct., 1893), 737–46. Gresham had privately kept Schurz informed of the administration's position on Hawaii, and Schurz defended it vigorously in his article. One of his major theses is that democracy cannot survive in the tropics. The reference to foreign commerce appears on p. 746 in one paragraph, which is not the summary as LaFeber says. See also Schurz to Gresham, Aug. 20, 1893; Schurz to Gresham, Sept. 24, 1893; and Gresham to Schurz, Oct. 6, 1893, Vol. 40–41, Gresham Papers.

42. LaFeber, *The New Empire,* pp. 199, 200.

43. *CR,* 56–2, Vol. XXXIV (Jan. 25, 1901), 1443–46; Walter T. Dunmore, *Ship Subsidies* (Boston: Houghton Mifflin, 1907), p. 31.

44. John H. Frederick, *The Development of American Commerce* (New York: Appleton, 1932), pp. 152–53.

45. John G. B. Hutchins, *The American Maritime Industries and Public Policy, 1789–1914* (Cambridge: Harvard University Press, 1941), pp. 316–481, 542–82; Paul M. Zeis, *American Shipping Policy* (Princeton: Princeton University Press, 1938), pp. 13–80.

46. *CR*, 56–2, Vol. XXXIV (Jan. 23, 1901), 1332–42, (Jan. 25, 1901), 1443–46.

47. Pletcher, *The Awkward Years*, pp. 120–21; John A. S. Grenville and George Berkeley Young, *Politics, Strategy, and American Diplomacy: Studies in Foreign Policy, 1873–1917* (New Haven: Yale University Press, 1966), p. 10; Robert Seager, II, "Ten Years Before Mahan: The Unofficial Case for the New Navy, 1880–1890," *Mississippi Valley Historical Review*, 40 (Dec., 1953), 491–512.

48. Samuel P. Huntington, *The Soldier and the State* (New York: Vintage Books, 1964), p. 278; Robert E. Osgood, *Ideals and Self-Interest in American Foreign Relations* (Chicago: University of Chicago Press, 1964), p. 33.

49. A. T. Mahan, *Retrospect and Prospect* (Boston: Little, Brown, 1902), pp. 24, 47–48; Grenville and Young, *Politics, Strategy, and American Diplomacy*, pp. 292–93.

50. Grenville and Young, *Politics, Strategy, and American Diplomacy*, pp. 202–38.

51. *Ibid.*, pp. 267–68.

52. See, for example, Howard K. Beale, *Theodore Roosevelt and the Rise of America to World Power* (New York: Collier Books, 1962), pp. 41–63.

53. There is a perceptive brief analysis in Frederick Merk, *Manifest Destiny and Mission in American History* (New York: Vintage, 1966), pp. 238–39; also see Ernest R. May, "American Imperialism: A Reinterpretation," *Perspectives in American History*, 1 (1967), 216.

54. Dorothea Muller, "Josiah Strong and American Nationalism: A Reevaluation," *The Journal of American History*, 53 (Dec., 1966), 487–503.

55. Edward A. Purcell, "Ideas and Interests: Businessmen and the Interstate Commerce Act," *The Journal of American History*, 54 (Dec., 1967), 574; Irwin G. Wyllie, "Social Darwinism and the Businessman," *Proceedings of the American Philosophical Society*, 103 (1959), 629–35.

56. Among the exceptions to this statement about the historians are Christopher Lasch, "The Anti-Imperialists, the Philippines, and the Inequality of Man," *Journal of Southern History*, 24 (1958), 319–31; and Ernest R. May, *American Imperialism: A Speculative Essay* (New York: Atheneum, 1968), pp. 99–101.

57. Schurz, "Manifest Destiny," 737–46.

58. *Seattle Daily Times,* Jan. 20, July 28, 1900.

59. May, *American Imperialism*, pp. 99–115, 179–81.

60. The *Nation*, Jan. 6, 1870, 5; "The St. Domingo Bargain," *ibid.*, Feb. 3, 1870, 68.

61. *Congressional Globe*, 41–2, Vol. 42 (March 28, 1870), 2238.

62. *Ibid.*, 41–3, Vol. 43 (Dec. 21, 1870), 245.

63. *Ibid.*, 244, 253.

64. *Ibid.*, 226; *ibid.*, (Jan. 10, 1871), 408.

65. George W. Baker, Jr., "Benjamin Harrison and Hawaiian Annexation: A Reinterpretation," *Pacific Historical Review*, 33 (Aug., 1964), 295–309.

66. Gresham to Thomas Bayard, Oct. 29, 1893; Gresham to Albert Willis, Feb.

5, March 14, July 22, 27, 1894, Feb. 20, 1895; Gresham to Thomas Shearman, March 5, 1895, all in Letterbook, Gresham Papers, Library of Congress.

67. *Washington Evening Star,* Nov. 15, 1893; *CR, 53–2,* Vol. XXVI (Dec. 5, 1893), 29.

68. *CR,* 53–2, Vol. XXVI (Dec. 6, 1893), 65–66, Senator Mills speaking.

69. Paul L. Vogt, *The Sugar Refining Industry in the United States* (Philadelphia: University of Pennsylvania Press, 1908), pp. 34–56, 87–89; Jacob Adler, *Claus Spreckels: The Sugar King in Hawaii* (Honolulu: University of Hawaii Press, 1966), pp. 25, 103.

70. *CR,* 55–2, Vol. XXXI (July 2, 1898), 6615.

71. *Ibid.,* 55–1, Vol. XXX (May 20, 1897), 1159, 1184–85.

72. May, *A Speculative Essay,* pp. 165–215.

73. Orestes Ferrara, *The Last Spanish War: Revelations in "Diplomacy"* (New York: Paisley Press, 1937), pp. 134–35; Fernando Soldevilla, *Historia de España* (Barcelona: Ediciones Ariel, 1957–59), VIII, 401; see also the full reports in *The Pall Mall Gazette* (London), April 1–13, 1898. Among the essential studies are Lester D. Langley, *The Cuban Policy of the United States: A Brief History* (New York: John Wiley, 1968) and H. Wayne Morgan, *America's Road to Empire: The War With Spain and Overseas Expansion* (New York: John Wiley, 1965).

74. Kenneth E. Hendrickson, Jr., "Reluctant Expansionist: Jacob Gould Schurman and the Philippine Question," *Pacific Historical Review,* 36 (November, 1967), 405–21.

75. Thomas A. Bailey, "The United States and Hawaii During the Spanish-American War," *The American Historical Review,* 36 (April, 1931), 552–60; Merze Tate, *The United States and the Hawaiian Kingdom: A Political History* (New Haven: Yale University Press, 1965), 311.

11. The Writers' Search for Reality

1. Among recent works see: Larzer Ziff, *The American 1890's: The Life and Times of a Lost Generation* (New York: Viking Press, 1966); Warner Berthoff, *The Ferment of Realism: American Literature, 1884–1919* (New York: Free Press, 1965); Jay Martin, *Harvests of Change: American Literature, 1865–1914* (New York: Prentice-Hall, 1967); Everett Carter, *Howells and the Age of Realism* (Philadelphia: J. B. Lippincott, 1954).

2. In 1922 James M. Barrie warned younger critics: "Don't forget to speak scornfully of the Victorian age. There will be a time for meekness when you seek to better it." See "Courage," *Rectorial Addresses, St. Andrews,* May 3, 1922.

3. Sinclair Lewis was amusing but unfair in saying later that criticism in the Gilded Age was "a chill and insignificant activity pursued by jealous spinsters, ex-baseball reporters, and acid professors." *Why Sinclair Lewis Got the Nobel Prize* (New York, 1930), 20.

4. Frank Luther Mott, *Golden Multitudes* (New York: Macmillan, 1947), estimates the total sale of Alger books at about 16 million copies, but figures are debatable; see also Frank Gruber, *Horatio Alger, Jr.: A Biography and Bibliography* (Los Angeles: Grover Jones, 1961); and John W. Tebbel, *From Rags to Riches: Horatio Alger, Jr. and the American Dream* (New York: Macmillan, 1963).

5. Robert Falk, *The Victorian Mode in American Fiction, 1865–1885* (East Lansing: Michigan State University Press, 1965).

6. The literature on Howells is abundant, but see especially: E. H. Cady's two-volume biography, *The Road to Realism* (Syracuse: Syracuse University Press, 1956), and *The Realist at War* (Syracuse: Syracuse University Press, 1958); H. N. Smith and W. M. Gibson, eds., *The Correspondence of Samuel L. Clemens and William Dean Howells, 1872–1901,* 2 vols. (Cambridge: Harvard University Press, 1960); George N. Bennett, *William Dean Howells: The Development of a Novelist* (Norman: University of Oklahoma Press, 1959); Clara M. Kirk, *William Dean Howells: Traveller From Altruria, 1889–1894* (New Brunswick: Rutgers University Press, 1962); Robert L. Hough, *The Quiet Rebel: William Dean Howells as Social Commentator* (Lincoln: University of Nebraska Press, 1959); and Kermit Vanderbilt, *The Achievement of William Dean Howells* (Princeton: Princeton University Press, 1968).

7. Martin, *Harvests of Change,* covers regional literature well. Jean Holloway, *Hamlin Garland: A Biography* (Austin: University of Texas Press, 1960), goes beyond its title. See also William Randel, *Edward Eggleston* (New York: Twayne, 1963); Clyde E. Henson, *Joseph Kirkland* (New York: Twayne, 1962); James F. Light, *John William De Forest* (New York: Twayne, 1965).

8. See Carter, *Howells and the Age of Realism;* and Clara Marburg Kirk, *W. D. Howells and Art in His Time* (New Brunswick: Rutgers University Press, 1965).

9. The literature on James is enormous, and the first three volumes of Leon Edel's biography of James are indispensable. F. O. Matthiessen, *Henry James: The Major Phase* (New York: Oxford University Press, 1944), and the same author's *The James Family* (New York: Knopf, 1947), are useful. Percy Lubbock, ed., *Letters of Henry James,* 2 vols. (New York: Scribner's, 1920), contains primary material.

10. Justin Kaplan, *Mr. Clemens and Mark Twain: A Biography* (New York: Simon and Schuster, 1966), is an excellent biography. Louis J. Budd, *Mark Twain: Social Philosopher* (Bloomington: Indiana University Press, 1962), analyzes Clemens' attitude toward various public issues. Gladys C. Bellamy, *Mark Twain as a Literary Artist* (Norman: University of Oklahoma Press, 1950), is an excellent book. The old authorized life by Albert Bigelow Paine, *Mark Twain: A Biography,* 3 vols. (New York: Harper, 1912), is pedestrian but has valuable raw material. The most perceptive personal account in many ways remains William Dean Howells, *My Mark Twain* (New York: Harper, 1910).

11. In 1877 he wrote Howells: "Delicacy– a sad false delicacy– robs literature of the two best things among its belongings. Family circle narrative and obscene stories." A. B. Paine, ed., *Mark Twain's Letters,* 2 vols. (New York: Harper, 1917), I, 310.

12. See Walter Blair, *Mark Twain and Huck Finn* (Berkeley and Los Angeles: University of California Press, 1950).

13. See Henry Nash Smith, *Mark Twain's Fable of Progress: Political and Economic Ideas in 'A Connecticut Yankee'* (New Brunswick: Rutgers University Press, 1964); and the same author's *Mark Twain: The Development of a Writer* (Cambridge: Harvard University Press, 1962).

14. See Lars Ahnebrink, *The Beginnings of Naturalism in American Fiction* (Cambridge: Harvard University Press, 1950), for background. Franklin Walker, *Frank Norris: A Biography* (New York: Doubleday, Doran, 1932), remains the

standard biography, but is outdated and thin. Warren French, *Frank Norris* (New York: Twayne, 1962), is a good brief account. Ernest Marchand, *Frank Norris: A Study* (Stanford: Stanford University Press, 1942), is still useful. So is Donald Pizer, *The Novels of Frank Norris* (Bloomington: Indiana University Press, 1966).

15. The newest biography is R. W. Stallman, *Stephen Crane: A Biography* (New York: Braziller, 1968). Lillian Gilkes, *Cora Crane* (Bloomington: Indiana University Press, 1960), is important. R. W. Stallman and Lillian Gilkes, eds., *Stephen Crane: Letters* (New York: New York University Press, 1960), is a basic primary source. See also: Donald B. Gibson, *The Fiction of Stephen Crane* (Carbondale: Southern Illinois University Press, 1968); Eric Salomon, *Stephen Crane: From Parody to Realism* (Cambridge: Harvard University Press, 1966).

12. The New Science and American Thought

1. Henry Adams, *The Education of Henry Adams* (New York: Houghton Mifflin, 1931), 377.

2. Sir J. J. Thomson, *Recollections and Reflections* (New York: Macmillan, 1937), 185–86.

3. J. G. Crowther, *Famous American Men of Science* (New York: W. W. Norton, 1937), 230–31.

4. Muriel Rukeyser, *Willard Gibbs* (New York: Doubleday, Doran, 1942), 266.

5. *Ibid.,* 251.

6. D. S. Jordan, ed., *American Men of Science* (New York, 1910), 351.

7. Bernard Jaffe, *Men of Science in America* (New York: Simon and Schuster, 1944), 327.

8. *Ibid.,* 329.

9. Rukeyser, *Gibbs,* 280.

10. Thomas C. Mendenhall, "Henry Augustus Rowland," *National Academy of Sciences Biographical Memoirs* (Washington, 1905), V, 131.

11. Jordan, *Men of Science,* p. 417.

12. Mendenhall, "Henry Augustus Rowland," 133.

13. Jordan, *Men of Science,* p. 420.

14. Jaffe, *Men of Science in America,* p. 375.

15. *Ibid.,* p. 361.

16. Robert A. Millikan, "Albert Abraham Michelson," *National Academy of Sciences Biographical Memoirs* (Washington, 1938), XIX, 136.

17. Isaac Asimov, *The Intelligent Man's Guide to Science,* 2 vols. (New York: Basic Books, 1960), I, 277.

18. Jaffe, *Men of Science in America,* p. 372.

19. Joel H. Metcalf, "Edward Charles Pickering," *Proceedings of the American Academy of Arts and Sciences,* 57 (Nov., 1922), 502.

20. Simon Newcomb, *The Reminiscences of an Astronomer* (Boston: Houghton Mifflin, 1903), p. 182.

21. *Ibid.,* p. 144.

22. *Ibid.,* p. 229.

23. "Einstein's Appreciation of Simon Newcomb," *Science,* 69 (March 1, 1929), 249.

24. Newcomb, *Reminiscences*, p. 213.

25. Jaffe, *Men of Science in America*, p. 337.

26. *Ibid.*, p. 340.

27. S. P. Langley, "The Flying-Machine," *McClure's Magazine*, 9 (June, 1897), 660.

28. Jaffe, *Men of Science in America*, p. 346.

29. George P. Merrill, *The First One Hundred Years of American Geology* (New Haven: Yale University Press, 1924), p. 201.

30. Jaffe, *Men of Science in America*, p. 248.

31. Jordan, *Men of Science*, p. 167.

32. *American Journal of Science*, 30, 2nd ser. (Nov., 1860), 154.

33. Louis Agassiz, "Evolution and Permanence of Type," *Atlantic Monthly*, 33 (Jan., 1874), 94, 101.

34. Jordan, *Men of Science*, p. 194.

35. Francis Darwin, ed., *The Life and Letters of Charles Darwin*, 2 vols. (New York: Appleton, 1898), II, 80.

36. *Ibid.*, p. 146.

37. Asa Gray, *Darwiniana* (New York: Appleton, 1876, 1889), p. 67.

38. Francis Darwin, ed., *More Letters of Charles Darwin*, 2 vols. (London, 1903), I, 191.

39. Leonard Huxley, *Life and Letters of Thomas Henry Huxley*, 2 vols. (London: Macmillan, 1900), II, 193.

40. Jordan, *Men of Science*, p. 250.

41. Daniel Coit Gilman, *The Life of James Dwight Dana* (New York: Harper Bros., 1899), p. 188.

42. William D. Armes, ed., *The Autobiography of Joseph LeConte* (New York: Appleton, 1903), p. 336.

43. Joseph LeConte, *Evolution* (New York: Appleton, 1888, 1897), pp. 65–66.

44. G. Frederick Wright, *Studies in Science and Religion* (Andover, Mass., 1882), p. 117.

45. Jordan, *Men of Science*, p. 451.

46. Henry Fairfield Osborn, *Impressions of Great Naturalists* (New York: Scribner's, 1928), p. 158.

47. Darwin, *Letters*, II, 100.

48. *Ibid.*, p. 417n.

49. *Ibid.*, p. 417.

50. Huxley, *Letters*, I, 463.

51. *Ibid.*, p. 495.

52. O. C. Marsh, "Thomas Henry Huxley," *American Journal of Science*, 50, 3rd ser. (1895), p. 181.

53. Charles Schuchert and Clara Mae Levine, *O. C. Marsh: Pioneer in Paleontology* (New Haven: Yale University Press, 1940), p. 232.

54. *Ibid.*, p. 240.

55. W. J. McGee, "Fifty Years of American Science," *Atlantic Monthly*, 82 (Sept., 1898), 317.

56. *Ibid.*, 308.

57. *Ibid.*, 320.

58. Henry Adams, *The Degradation of Democratic Dogma* (New York: Capricorn Books, 1958), p. 212.

59. John Fiske, *The Destiny of Man* (Boston: Houghton Mifflin, 1884, 1912), pp. 118–19.

60. Henry James, ed., *The Letters of William James,* 2 vols. (Boston: Little, Brown, 1920), II, 344.

61. William James, *Pragmatism and Four Essays From the Meaning of Truth* (New York: Meridian Books, 1955), p. 233.

62. *Ibid.,* p. 121.

63. *Ibid.,* p. 49.

64. *Ibid.,* p. 133.

65. Ralph Barton Perry, *The Thought and Character of William James,* 2 vols. (Boston: Little, Brown, 1935), I, 493.

66. Lewis Mumford, *The Golden Day* (New York: Norton, 1926), p. 95.

67. *Letters of William James, II,* 260.

68. Jordan, *Men of Science,* pp. 420–21.

69. Vernon L. Parrington, *Main Currents in American Thought,* 3 vols. (New York: Harcourt, Brace, 1927, 1930), II, 10.

13. Popular Culture and Public Taste

1. Frank L. Mott, *Golden Multitudes* (New York: Macmillan, 1947), p. 85.

2. Russell Lynes, *The Tastemakers* (New York: Harper Bros., 1947), pp. 65–66.

3. Mott, *Golden Multitudes,* p. 87.

4. Two excellent photographs of Ochre Court can be seen in Wayne Andrews, *Architecture in America, A Photographic History from the Colonial Period to the Present* (New York: Atheneum, 1960), p. 109.

5. Wayne Andrews, *Architecture, Ambition, and Americans* (New York: Harper Bros., 1947), p. 186.

6. Wayne Andrews, *Architecture in America,* p. 83.

7. Lewis Mumford, *Sticks and Stones,* 2nd revised edition (New York: Dover, 1955), p. 105.

8. Maas, *The Gingerbread Age,* pp. 63–66.

9. Morton Cronin, "Currier and Ives: A Content Analysis," *American Quarterly,* 4 (Winter 1952), 317–30.

10. Lynes, *The Tastemakers,* p. 70.

11. Mott, *Golden Multitudes,* p. 125.

12. James D. Hart, *The Popular Book* (New York: Oxford University Press, 1950), p. 97.

13. Mott, *Golden Multitudes,* p. 136.

14. *New York Ledger,* Jan. 4, 1868.

15. Hart, *The Popular Book,* pp. 99–100.

16. *Ibid.*

17. Harvey C. Minnich, *William Holmes McGuffey and His Readers* (New York: American Book, 1936), pp. 40, 89–90.

18. Harry F. Harrison as told to Karl Detzer, *Culture Under Canvas* (New York: Hastings House, 1958), p. xiii.

19. Hart, *The Popular Book,* p. 145; Harrison, *Culture Under Canvas,* p. xiv.

20. Hart, *The Popular Book,* pp. 145–46.

21. James M. Lee, *History of American Journalism* (New York, 1923), p. 352.

22. Mott, *History of American Magazines,* III, 5.

23. *Ibid.,* pp. 5–9.

24. *Ibid.,* p. 10.

25. *New York Ledger,* March 14, 1885.

26. *Frank Leslie's Popular Monthly,* 9 (June, 1880), 702; *ibid.,* 17 (June, 1884), 759.

27. Mott, *History of American Magazines,* III, 42.

28. *Scribner's Magazine,* May, 1887.

29. William G. McLoughlin, *Modern Revivalism: Charles Grandison Finney to Billy Graham* (New York: Ronald Press, 1959), p. 216.

30. Bernard A. Weisberger, *They Gathered at the River* (Boston: Little, Brown, 1958), pp. 172–73.

31. See Justin Kaplan, *Mr. Clemens and Mark Twain: A Biography* (New York: Simon and Shuster, 1966), p. 24.

32. Shaplen, *Free Love and Heavenly Sinners,* p. 5.

33. Victoria and Robert Ormond Case, *We Called It Culture* (New York: Doubleday, 1948), pp. 20–21.

34. See Lloyd Morris, *Curtain Time* (New York: Random House, 1953).

35. *Ibid.,* p. 231.

36. David Ewen, *Panorama of American Popular Music* (Englewood Cliffs, N.J.: Prentice-Hall, 1957), p. 81.

37. Morris, *Curtain Time,* p. 235.

38. Ewen, *Panorama of American Popular Music,* pp. 86–87.

39. Carl Wittke, *Tambo and Bones* (Durham, N.C.: Duke University Press, 1930), pp. 38–86.

40. Cronin, "Currier and Ives," 317–30.

41. *Frank Leslie's Popular Monthly,* 2 (Nov., 1876), 639.

42. See Irving Wallace, *The Fabulous Showman* (New York: Knopf, 1959).

43. Written, it might be noted, by a "hard-drinking" ventriloquist named Harry Kennedy. Sigmund Spaeth, *A History of Popular Music* (New York: Random House, 1948), p. 219.

44. Edward B. Marks, as told to Abbot J. Liebling, *They All Sang* (New York, 1934), pp. 43–49; Spaeth, *A History of Popular Music,* p. 196.

45. Spaeth, *A History of Popular Music,* p. 173.

46. *Ibid.,* p. 207.

47. David Ewen, ed., *Songs of America, A Cavalcade of Popular Songs* (Chicago: Ziff-Davis, 1947), p. 146.

Index